BOOTS
ON THE
GROUND

General the Lord Dannatt GCB CBE MC DL served in the Army from 1969 to 2009, during which time he led troops in Northern Ireland, Bosni~~a and K~~ ~~held the p~~ ~~ions of Commander-~~ in-Chief, Lan~~d~~ ~~of the~~ ~~l Staff. On retiring from th~~ ~~from 2009~~ to 2016. ~~orgi, 2010).~~

ALSO BY GENERAL THE LORD DANNATT

Leading from the Front: An Autobiography

BOOTS ON THE GROUND

BRITAIN AND HER ARMY
— SINCE 1945 —

RICHARD DANNATT

PROFILE BOOKS

This paperback edition published in 2017

First published in Great Britain in 2016 by
PROFILE BOOKS LTD
3 Holford Yard
Bevin Way
London WC1X 9HD
www.profilebooks.com

1 3 5 7 9 10 8 6 4 2

Printed and b   CR0 4YY

All rights re   eserved
above, no part   uced into
a retrieval sy   ectronic,
mechanical, p   r written
permission   book.

A CIP catal   Library.

ISBN: 978 1 78125 381 6
eISBN: 978 1 78283 123 5

CONTENTS

ACKNOWLEDGEMENTS

Having written my autobiography *Leading from the Front*, which was published by Transworld in September 2010, I presumed that would be the sum total of books written by myself. I was therefore a little surprised when Charlie Viney, who had been my agent for the original book, introduced me to Andrew Franklin of Profile Books, who asked whether I would consider writing a history of the British Army since the Second World War. After some considerable thought, I gave Andrew a positive, but qualified, answer – the qualification being that I wished to broaden the canvas. The book that I wished to write would be more of a commentary on Britain as a country since the Second World War, albeit seen through the perspective of the Army and allowing the account of what the Army has done since 1945 to be the handrail through the commentary. Andrew agreed to this changed prospectus and the title: *Boots on the Ground – Britain and Her Army since 1945* was agreed.

A near neighbour of mine in Norfolk is the much respected historian, Correlli Barnett. As the author of the original *Britain and Her Army* published by Allen Lane in 1970, I have been most grateful to Bill – as his friends know him – for his enthusiastic support for my project from the outset. He very kindly and most helpfully commented on the final draft. Although Bill's book covered nearly four centuries, from Henry VIII to 1970, and mine would only have about a seventy-year span from 1945 to 2016, I knew that finding the right researcher to work with me was going to be critical. I found that person in Dr Sarah Ingham whose contribution to this book has been immense. I first met Sarah when she was doing her own research for her PhD on the Military Covenant at the War Studies Department, King's College London. She duly completed her Doctorate and her thesis was published in 2014 by Ashgate under the title: *The Military Covenant: Its Impact on Civil–Military Relations in Britain*. She kindly sent me a copy which convinced me that I had found the right person to help me with *Boots on the Ground*. She has worked tirelessly on this project, researching in great detail in order to expand my original synopsis and then doing much of the initial drafting. Frankly, there would have been no book without her. That said, I take full responsibility for this book. Any errors or important omissions are mine, and any copyright inadvertently infringed is also my responsibility. Corrections will, of course, be made in any subsequent editions.

I would also like to record my enormous thanks to those who have also helped with the production of this book. In particular I would like to thank my Green Howard Regimental colleague and close friend, Brigadier John Powell, who read the final draft and made a series of detailed and wise observations. John made one comment which I had to consider most carefully. He thought that as someone who had served in the Army for forty of the seventy years covered by this book that my style was somewhat detached, given especially that I had been Chief of the General Staff at a critical time of operational pressure for the Army from 2006 to 2009. To answer that criticism, which others may share, I would point back to my 2010 autobiography. It is in that volume that you will find my personal opinions, hence my ambition for more objectivity in this volume. I reserve some final conclusions for the Epilogue.

I am also very grateful to two exceptionally busy people who have been kind enough with their time to review the text of this book – General Sir Nicholas Carter, the present Chief of the General Staff, and Lord Hennessy, eminent historian, broadcaster and colleague in the House of Lords. I would also like to record my thanks to General Sir Hugh Beach who provided invaluable advice at the start of this project. I also wish to thank the Trustees of the Imperial War

Museum for their kind permission to use materials from their collection and, in particular, to acknowledge the help of the Documents and Sound Section. My thanks also go to the Trustees of the Liddell Hart Centre for Military Archives at King's College London and to the Director and staff of the National Army Museum.

At Profile Books, in addition to Andrew Franklin, who has personally led the editorial team, I am most grateful to Penny Daniel for her patient help with the text and the illustrations and to Sally Holloway who did the detailed copy editing. Valentina Zanca is leading the publicity and marketing for this book with great energy, for which I thank her, too. My thanks also go to Louisa Dunnigan for her work on the book cover.

As ever, any project has significant domestic impact and I am much indebted to Philippa, my wife, for giving me the space to work on this book. The final stage coincided with my retirement as Constable of the Tower of London and our move from Queen's House in the Tower to our home in Norfolk. Once again, Pippa has carried the burden of this, seamlessly integrating the contents of two houses into one home, ably assisted by Colour Sergeant (retired) Steve Crighton MBE who has now worked for me for twenty-seven years. Gilly Goldsmid, my PA in the House of Lords, has managed my diary with great skill to generate enough time for this project.

My final comment, made in the Epilogue at the end of this book, is to draw attention to the Elizabeth Cross, the emblem presented to the next of kin of all those servicemen and women who have lost their lives on operations since just after the end of the Second World War. Their sacrifice and service to our country underpins this story of *Boots on the Ground – Britain and Her Army since 1945*. In all humility, I dedicate this book to their memory – and to their families, who had to come to terms with each and every loss of a loved one for our country – our England, Wales, Scotland and Northern Ireland.

INTRODUCTION

The Union flag, the khaki tents and camouflage nets were swept by chill gusts of wind and rain as Field Marshal Sir Bernard Montgomery received the delegation from the German High Command in the early evening of 4 May 1945 at his headquarters at Timeloberg on Lüneburg Heath. The five men, led by Admiral Hans Georg von Friedeburg, Commander-in-Chief of the Navy, had come to surrender all German armed forces in north-west Germany, Holland and Denmark. Montgomery, the Commander-in-Chief of the 21st Army Group, ensured they waited for him beneath the Union flag before they were taken to a tent adjacent to his command caravan. They were seated at a trestle table covered by a grey British Army blanket and required to listen to the terms of the surrender, read out to them by him. At 6.30 p.m., using an ordinary Army pen that cost tuppence, the German commanders signed the surrender document beside the single British signature of 'BL Montgomery, Field Marshal'.[1] On 7 May, at Allied headquarters in Reims, Germany agreed to an unconditional surrender which would come into effect the following day, celebrated as Victory in Europe (VE) Day. The war in Europe was over. For the British Army, this was its greatest achievement since Wellington's victory at Waterloo.

This is a book about Britain and her Army since 1945, exploring the seventy years after Montgomery's moment of triumph. In June 2015, the remaining British military units left Hohne, not far from Lüneburg Heath, another step towards the Army's final withdrawal from Germany. With the return home of soldiers and their families, a chapter on the Second World War and its long aftermath was at last coming to a close. The history of the Army in Germany illustrates much about what has happened in Britain and in the wider world during those decades. After the Normandy landings in 1944, British soldiers fought their way into Germany as the enemy, became governors of the shattered country during the military Occupation and finally, after 1955, became its allies when the Federal Republic joined the North Atlantic Treaty Organization (NATO). By then, like Germany, Europe itself was split, frozen into decades of Cold War. Montgomery's 21st Army Group had evolved into the British Army of the Rhine (BAOR). Until 1989, its soldiers were on the frontline in the event of any attack on the West by the forces of the Soviet Union and her Warsaw Pact allies. These troops had gone from being National Servicemen – most of them resigned, some of them reluctant – to volunteer regulars in an army that included an increasing number of women. Despite the ever-present threat of nuclear war and Mutually Assured Destruction, as well as the day-to-day handling of battlefield nuclear weapons, from the 1970s onwards, British bases were on the alert for attack by terrorists – fall-out from the Troubles in Northern Ireland. By then, the British military presence in West Germany had become so routine, few questioned the historical anomaly of stationing some 50,000 or so soldiers and their families on mainland Europe. Although the British Army was configured and equipped primarily to fight the Soviet's Red Army on the plain of northern Germany, the operations in which soldiers found themselves involved reflected Britain's global role and interests, as well as the shifting international scene. Looked at through the prism of Germany, something about Britain and her Army since 1945 can be seen, but the picture is far from complete.

War is the agent of change. Both of the twentieth century's world wars brought seismic social, political and economic upheaval, upending the international order. Since the end of a mid-eighteenth-century conflict, the Seven Years War, Britain's prestige and wealth had been derived from an ever-expanding empire. A global hegemon in 1900, by 1945 Britain was still one of the 'Big Three' superpowers, along with the United States and the Soviet Union. Despite millions of colonial troops making common cause with Britain during the war, events such as the 1942 fall of Singapore had shaken faith in the invincibility of the 'mother country', particularly in the Far East and Australia. In November 1942, Prime Minister Winston Churchill had told an audience at London's Mansion House: 'We mean to hold our own. I have not become the King's First Minister in order to preside over the liquidation of the British Empire.'[2] However, at a meeting of the Cabinet in April 1945, shortly before the war ended, he acknowledged the changes to Britain's status; given the Soviet domination of Europe and the United States' economic power, he questioned how Britain would be able to match the power and influence that the other two would wield in the peacetime world.[3] Just as the Republic of Ireland had established itself in the wake of the Great War, in the aftermath of the Second World War nationalist movements across the British Empire sought independence. The most determined of these was in India, where war had given further impetus to demands for self-government. The Middle East was volatile, not least in Palestine, where Zionists were demanding an end to the British Mandate for Palestine and the establishment of a Jewish state. World war was once again creating a new world order.

What follows is an account of a changing world and Britain's place in that world since 1945. Primarily, it is about an institution that has been integral to the country and its sense of self – the British Army. The history of Britain is the history of her Army and vice versa. This book is about a nation's transformation and adaptation in the decades since the Second World War. It could be an elegy to loss, focusing on the ceding of global hegemony and Great Power status, as well as the sunset of empire. Instead, in approaching these issues by considering them in the context of the Army and the Army's role since 1945, different, more positive conclusions can be reached.

The British Army remains the most renowned professional fighting force in the world. It has some 350 years of history to look back upon and from which to draw inspiration. The Army is the exemplar against which the forces of our friends – and foes – judge themselves. Like its sister services, the Royal Navy and, more recently, the Royal Air Force, it not only defends the nation but has shaped the nation. Soldiers helped forge Britain and then her Empire. For centuries, across continents, they have been respected for their grit, tenacity and courage. Instrumental in the British Empire's acquisition, they were central to the imperial end game, played out after 1945.[4] Their role was not always easy, and occasionally controversial. The missions they have undertaken have ranged from war-fighting to peacekeeping, often as part of a United Nations force, such as in Korea in the 1950s or in the Balkans four decades later. The Army's most famous counter-insurgency campaign was in Malaya; others followed, including in Kenya, Dhofar and Cyprus. The Falklands was perhaps the most unexpected expeditionary campaign in which soldiers found themselves; the Gulf War an example of a major post-Cold War coalition operation. Campaigns evolve: in Northern Ireland, where they were initially deployed to aid the civilian authorities, soldiers found themselves embroiled in an insurgency and then countering terrorism.

The world wars of the twentieth century might be fading from living memory but they are kept alive as the subject of books, films and documentaries. As a result, it is easy to forget that, in the context of the Army's long history, they are so unusual. In 1945, the Army's strength stood at 2,930,000 soldiers; in 1960, when the last intake of National Servicemen joined up, numbers had fallen to 258,000.[5] In 1992, the Cold War over, they had fallen again to 145,000.[6] By 2001, the number of regular soldiers had dropped to 110,000.[7] After 1945, the experience of British soldiers increasingly came to resemble that of their Victorian predecessors who garrisoned the Empire: members of a small regular army which sometimes found itself fighting small wars. And, just as today, the Victorian civilian public actually knew very little about the military. Thankfully, today's soldiers are held in much higher esteem than their nineteenth-century counterparts, who were regarded as 'brutal and licentious' by the public, and the scum of the earth by their most famous commander, Wellington. Rudyard Kipling captured the public's oscillating attitude towards the Empire's archetypal Red Coat in his 1892 poem 'Tommy': Tommy Atkins was spurned and shunned, unwelcome in pubs and unwanted by young women – until the band began to play, summoning him to fight for Queen and country. When today's commentators denounce yet another round of defence cuts reducing the

Army's strength, they often say that the Army is the smallest it has been since some arbitrary time in the past – perhaps the time of the Boer War or even the Napoleonic era. They forget that, tradition-ally, the British Army has always been a small force, especially when compared with the standing armies of Europe, where, until recently, conscription was the norm. Until the advent of air power, Britain relied on the 'wooden walls' of the Royal Navy for her defence, alongside voluntary militia forces such as the Yeomanry. Crucial to the defence of Empire were locally raised forces, such as Nepal's Gurkhas.

At its simplest, strategy concerns the ways and means to achieve an end. In 1940, although the situation was perilous, the challenge was clear. The grand strategic objective was the defeat of Nazi Germany. Complicating matters for Britain and her Army in the twenty-first century is that military intervention is often a matter of political choice, not of necessity. In June 1940, following the fall of France, the country's plight and mood of defiance – both against Hitler's forces and any British politicians who might have been contemplat-ing peace negotiations – was captured by David Low's cartoon of a British Tommy standing on the storm-swept coast that is about to be attacked by enemy planes: the caption declares, *'Very Well, Alone'*. Between 1939 and 1945, Germany posed an existential threat to Britain. In contrast, in the early twenty-first century, Iraq, Afghani-stan and Libya did not. Whether prompted by support for allies or by humanitarian concern, Britain's recent wars have been conflicts of choice – and the public has sometimes questioned that choice. It can withhold or withdraw its support from an unpopular mission, as was seen most recently in Iraq. The paradox today is that the men and women of the Armed Forces enjoy unprecedented public approval, even as the same public does not always support the wars they are fighting. In 1945, those soldiers commanded by Montgomery had been fighting for national survival: since then, particularly after the end of the Cold War, military intervention has often resulted from a judgement about the national interest.

Maintaining Britain's security means defending and protect-ing the nation from both internal and external threats. The military threat of enemy invasion, attack or blockade, defeated in 1945, might today seem remote, but has it disappeared for ever? The defence of the realm is the primary role of the Armed Forces, but national security depends upon international stability. Rogue states, as well as failed or failing states, can jeopardise this. The upheaval caused by civil war is never confined to national borders: most recently, conflict within Syria has led to the largest movement of refugees within Europe since the end of the Second World War. Collective security, defence cooperation and working with allies has become the norm, as this book details. Today, the uniforms of Britain's soldiers are often supplemented by the blue helmets and berets of the United Nations or the insignia of the NATO alliance. The Falklands is the only post-1945 example of a major combat operation when Britain went it alone.

In 1945, Britain was broke, beggared by war. Britain remained broke, the country's fortunes not recovering for decades. Lost, along with national wealth, was global standing, not least because of successive financial bail-outs, whether by the United States or the International Monetary Fund. Unaffordable, the Empire was to be jettisoned, economic necessity coinciding with insurgent nationalism and demands for self-government, most obviously in the case of India and, in the late 1960s, Aden. The military staging posts familiar to generations of soldiers – bases, ports, garrisons, cantonments and even tiny refuelling stations – found across the world and its oceans were wound down and shut, symbolic of Britain's changing status – and changing national priorities.

This book covers Britain's shift from warfare state to welfare state. The Armed Forces, along with the nuclear deterrent, are often described as the nation's insurance policy. With the annual bill for defence coming in at £36.43 billion in 2014/15, this seems a pretty steep price to pay. However, as a proportion of national spending, this has gone down and down – and down again. The downward spiral was briefly halted, first because of the Korean War, when the Attlee government expanded an existing Cold War defence modernisation programme, increasing spending to £4.7 billion in 1951, and secondly during the Thatcher era.[8] In 1938/9, the year before war broke out, defence spending was 25 per cent of all government spending; by 1944/5, this had risen to a staggering 83 per cent.[9] After the end of the Cold War, when just over 4 per cent of government spending was on defence, the threat to Britain's security appeared to recede, as the spectre of nuclear holocaust faded away. Cyber attack and even terrorism are less cause for national concern. Given this, it is unsurprising that cash-strapped governments have chosen to keep taking the peace dividend making further cuts to defence. In 2015, defence accounted for just 2 per cent of GDP – the minimum the government could get away with to remain credible within NATO and to justify its membership of the United Nations Security Council.

Why should the Army still matter to Britain? After all, the country is stable and secure, enjoying seven decades of peace and the sort of prosperity that would have been unimaginable to those carrying a ration book back in the 1940s. This is not just a narrative about a series of military campaigns and Army reorganisations over seventy years, it also seeks to make the case for the Army, by showing how it is still interwoven into the fabric of national life and the national psyche. Although they have huge admiration for soldiers and other forces personnel, today's public believes other areas such as the NHS should be protected from cuts in preference to defence.[10] An army only exists with the consent of the nation it serves and can only do what the nation requires of it. Soldiers, even generals, are expected to salute and do their duty: in principle and almost invariably in practice, they must leave politics to the politicians. The next time cuts are contemplated to the Army and Armed Forces, politicians should perhaps remember a 2015 poll which found that 63 per cent of the public wanted Britain to aspire to being a great power rather than accepting that it is in decline; a majority also believed that Britain has a responsibility to help maintain international security.[11] Those same politicians should reflect on the knock to national confidence after Suez in 1956 and contrast it with the boost to national self-belief after the Falklands a quarter of a century later. If the Army and the Armed Forces are diminished, so too is Britain.

In describing how the British Army has endeavoured to do its duty since 1945, this book focuses on the Regular Army. Reservists are not forgotten but are seen as an integral part of the Army. So too are women. Both the numbers of women soldiers and the roles they undertake continue to grow, particularly after the disbandment of the Women's Royal Army Corps in 1992. Furthermore, coverage of the Royal Navy and the Royal Air Force is limited by design and not by neglect. It is hoped that sailors and airmen reading this book will understand and forgive the concentration on the Army. However, as the narrative will describe, the three Armed Services have become more integrated and increasingly take part in truly joint operations, while quite properly retaining their own identities and ethos. If the history of individual campaigns or certain regiments is required, then the endnotes should point the way.

- ONE -

THE LEGACY OF WAR

*The Occupation of Germany as an Iron Curtain
Descends across Europe, the End of the Mandate
in Palestine and the Partition of India*

Almost one year after the D-Day landings in Normandy and one month after Montgomery had met representatives of the German High Command at Lüneburg Heath, Allied commanders in Berlin formalised victory. On 5 June 1945, General Dwight D. Eisenhower of the United States, Field Marshal Georgy Zhukov of the Soviet Union and Général d'Armée Jean de Lattre de Tassigny for France, together with the British Field Marshal, signed the Berlin Declaration. Kept hanging about by the Soviet delegation, Montgomery and Eisenhower had become decidedly testy.[1] It seemed to confirm Monty's misgivings about the Russians. The Declaration stated that the German armed forces on land, at sea and in the air had been completely defeated and had surrendered unconditionally. 'Germany, which bears responsibility for the war, is no longer capable of resisting the will of the victorious Powers.' Emphasising the Allies' dominance, it added: 'The Governments of the United Kingdom, the United States of America, the Union of Soviet Socialist Republics and the Provisional Government of the French Republic hereby assume supreme authority with respect to Germany, including all the powers possessed by the German Government, the High Command and any state, municipal, or local government or authority.'[2] The formal Occupation of Germany was underway. The Berlin Declaration underlined the ending of the war with Germany, but for Monty, as his *Memoirs* spell out, 'Difficulties with the Russians begin.'[3]

During the years following the Allied victory, the aftershocks of war continued. As the Four Powers sought to shape Germany, Europe and the wider world and to impose some sort of order on the chaos and devastation, peace seemed little more than the absence of formal conflict. On the home front, bankrupt and exhausted, Britain had somehow to rebuild – and to create a very different country from that of 1939. The new Labour government, elected by an unexpected landslide in July 1945, was given a mandate to introduce a welfare state. Building this new Jerusalem at home had to be balanced against the demands of empire overseas. However, the Empire was threatening to fracture, cracking under nationalist demands for independence and self-government, whether in India, Burma, Malaya, across Africa or in Palestine and the wider Middle East.

The Occupation of Germany was just one of the many missions undertaken by the British Army after June 1945. While millions of soldiers would be demobilised – the Army's strength falling from 2.9 million to 364,000 by 1950 – the introduction of peacetime National Service was approved by Parliament in 1947 to try to meet the demands for military manpower.[4] By then, the relations between the Communist East and the West were deteriorating, fulfilling the predictions of British service chiefs, including Montgomery, that the threat to Britain and her Empire would come not from a resurgent Germany but from the Soviet Union.

Against the backdrop of austerity at home, this chapter explores how Britain and her Army struggled to come to terms with the legacy of the Second World War in Germany, Palestine and India. East–West rivalries would come to be played out in Germany, leading to the formal division of both country and continent, and the frozen hostilities of the Cold War. On the frontline of this new conflict were the soldiers of the British Army of the Rhine. The development of nuclear weapons, seen with the bombing of Japan in August 1945, would add another, deadlier, dimension to any possible future war.

Britain, Her Army and the Aftermath of World War

In 1945, Britain was a global power, with global interests and global responsibilities. The last of the Allied conferences, held in Potsdam between July and August, underscored that, if no longer the world's paramount power, Britain was still one of the Big Three. As the war with Japan continued, fought by the soldiers of the so-called 'Forgotten Army', this gathering of the victors emphasised the uncertainties that accompanied peace in Europe. President Roosevelt had recently died and, part way through proceedings, Churchill was voted out of office. The British General Election of 25 July brought a Labour majority of 146. Perhaps more suited to the grinding slog of peace was the new Prime Minister Clement Attlee – 'a sheep in sheep's clothing', according to the colossus he replaced – and the less-than-flamboyant new President of the United States, Harry S. Truman. The *de facto* Soviet dominance of eastern Europe was reflected by the recognition given to the new Moscow-backed government of Poland. Germany lost 25 per cent of her land as her border was moved westwards. A few days after the conference ended, the United States signalled her supremacy – and introduced a new paradigm in strategic and military thinking – with the atomic bombing of Hiroshima and Nagasaki. Afterwards, at midnight on 15 August, Prime Minister Attlee declared, 'The last of our enemies is laid low.' The world was once again, briefly, at peace.

In the six years of conflict since 1939 when Germany invaded Poland, more than 5 million men and women had served in the British Armed Forces, 3.5 million of them in the Army. The roll call of campaigns, battles and operations in which those soldiers took part – Dunkirk, El Alamein, Normandy, Arnhem, Burma – is now etched in the British psyche. For the first time, the civilian Home Front had become one of the theatres of operation. Air Chief Marshal Sir Arthur Harris stated that Bomber Command 'had always worked on the principle that bombing anything in Germany is better than bombing nothing'.[5] Luftwaffe commanders probably thought the same about Britain. The Blitz, followed by the development and deployment of the V-1 and V-2 missiles, brought unprecedented destruction to British cities in an attempt to undermine national morale. It failed. The 'Blitz spirit' – a cheery stoicism in the face of adversity – today remains a source of national pride and inspiration. Those months in the summer of 1940 leading up to the Battle of Britain when 'The Few' of the RAF deterred a German invasion were surely the most perilous in our island's history. However, by the end of the following year, Britain was no longer standing alone; the country was now allied against the Axis forces with the United States and, more unexpectedly, the Soviet Union – the latter bearing out Lord Palmerston's observation that, 'It is a narrow policy to suppose that this country or that is to be marked out as the eternal ally or the perpetual enemy.' During the war, some 383,000 British service personnel and more than 60,000 civilians were killed.

The end of conflict had brought an end to the coalition government. Led by Churchill, it had been a successful proving ground for Labour ministers such as Ernest Bevin and Herbert Morrison. Labour's landslide election victory reflected the birth of a new Britain. This welfare state, which would have at its core a system of social security and a National Health Service, had been outlined in a White Paper written by William Beveridge. Published in late 1942, this policy document became an unlikely bestseller, with 635,000 copies bought by the public.[6] The writer toured the country, outlining his vision of a nation free from want, ignorance, disease, squalor and idleness. Labour's programme of social reform was matched by proposals for industrial change, including the nationalisation of key sectors such as energy and the railways. Unemployment, the scourge of the 1930s, had been cut to 84,000 in January 1944, down from 2 million just five years earlier; at the same time, trade union membership stood at 8 million.[7] The six years of conflict had eroded class differences; according to one, perhaps rather surprised, campaigner: 'I think one was acutely aware that, for the first time in my life anyway, everybody during the war was more or less equal.'[8] War had brought collectivism to Britain, together with the expansion of state control over most aspects of life, particularly the economy. In voting Labour, as the majority of servicemen and women did, the British people indicated that they did not want pre-war Britain reconstructed, but a very different country.

A 'financial Dunkirk' confronted Britain within weeks of the election, according to the economist John Maynard Keynes. Going from the world's creditor to debtor, the country was cleaned out by war, despite Lend-Lease from the United States partly financing the effort. The Americans had not been averse to obtaining the best possible deal when Britain sought financial help in the pursuit of victory, something that did not change with the advent of peace. The United

States economy had not done too badly: by 1945, US GDP and industrial capacity had more than doubled in five years, while Britain had
been forced to sell one-quarter of her overseas investments to pay for
imports. There was also a massive deficit in the balance of payments
with the dollar. On 21 August, President Truman abruptly terminated Lend-Lease, news of which fell on Whitehall like a V-2, without
warning.[9] Keynes was immediately dispatched to Washington to
negotiate a loan, not least to continue paying for the defence of the
Empire and other overseas commitments. But many Americans, both
policymakers and the public, had a longstanding antipathy to imperialism, exacerbated by the British policy of imperial preference and
ever-higher trade barriers erected throughout the 1930s. In exchange
for a $3.75 billion loan, which was finally paid off in 2006, the British
had to accept free trade and the convertibility of sterling. As Conservative MP L. S. Amery observed: 'The British Empire is the oyster which
this loan is to prise open.' And, while some breathing space was gained
by the loan Keynes negotiated, the money was soon running out.

   In 1945, the Empire remained at the heart of British foreign
policy and military strategy. The country's financial difficulties were
assumed to be temporary – certainly in the Foreign Office, now led
by former trade union leader Ernest Bevin. Officials warned that the
financial issue would need careful handling, 'otherwise other countries will say the lion is in his dotage and will divide up his skin'.[10] On
the other side of Horse Guards Parade, maps in the War Office showed
scores of British military bases, the garrisons of Empire, stretching
from Gibraltar, Cyprus and Malta in the Mediterranean to Palestine
and Egypt, and then beyond 'East of Suez', to India, Burma and across
Asia to Hong Kong. In Africa, there were British military outposts
scattered from Cairo to Cape Town. Singapore might have fallen in
1942 but, with victory in the East, few would have considered this to
be of lasting significance, as Britain re-established control over the
colonies that had been occupied by the Japanese. Other areas, notably
the oil-rich Middle East, were not part of the formal Empire but were
regarded as coming under Britain's sphere of influence. A commitment to the newly established United Nations did not diminish the
parallel commitment to Empire and Commonwealth. Somehow, the
demands of Empire overseas had to be balanced with radical social
reform at home.

What if Britain had cut and run from her imperial obligations? The temptation to pack up, lower the flag and ship out must have been great. Balanced against this should be a consideration of the destabilisation that could follow any premature withdrawal. In the early twenty-first century, after long-established regimes were over-thrown, the impact of a power vacuum became apparent in Iraq and Libya. Failed and failing states, including Yemen and Somalia, led to millions of refugees and the exodus of migrants. The end of war in 1945 provoked a similar humanitarian crisis in Europe, which British soldiers tried to contain. Part of the reason for this was the westward flight across the continent from the Russians, described as 'savages' by von Friedeburg at Lüneburg Heath to an unmoved Montgom-ery.[11] The Attlee government and its successors were neither oblivi-ous nor unsympathetic to nationalists' demands; however they were alive to the threat of an increasingly predatory Soviet Union, which cast a shadow over the Middle East, particularly Persia, and whose grip on eastern Europe tightened by the day. In 1946, one Moscow-based diplomat stated in a dispatch: 'Soviet security has become hard to distinguish from Soviet imperialism and it is becoming uncertain whether there is, in fact, any limit to Soviet expansion.'[12] The per-ception of such expansionist ambitions, together with the Marxist sympathies of some agitating for independence from Britain (or indeed, from France), provided the justification for resisting nation-alist demands in colonies such as Malaya. In March 1946 in Fulton, Missouri, Churchill described how an 'iron curtain' of Soviet domi-nation had fallen from Stettin to Trieste and lamented that this was not the liberated Europe that had been fought for. He added: 'Nor is it one which contains the essentials of permanent peace.'[13]

After 1945, competing demands led to a parallel process of demo-bilisation out of the Armed Forces and conscription into them. Troops were needed to garrison the Empire, to stabilise western Europe, par-ticularly in Germany and Greece, and, increasingly, for defence against any possible Soviet attack. However, post-war austerity Britain, where rationing continued, needed investment and manpower, not least to rebuild shattered housing stock and infrastructure. On Election Day in 1945, almost 5 million forces personnel were still in uniform. Demobilisation got underway, with 1.35 million servicemen and women leaving the forces between June and December 1945.[14] As they collected their demob suits, back pay and ration cards, and formally returned to civilian life, millions of others stayed on duty. Although the demob process was far better organised than in 1918, it was still somewhat sluggish. Personnel were divided into two classes: 90 per cent were classed as A; those in the B class, in jobs such as engineering and mining that were key to the reconstruction effort, could effectively jump the demob queue. The A class majority were further classified into groups according to age and length of service, with the longest serving leaving soonest, including those still overseas who would be returned home. Officers and men were to be treated equally.[15] Overseen by Bevin, the scheme was a small symbol of the more fair and socially equal Britain that the Attlee government sought to achieve. However, after V-J Day, many service personnel – but especially those stationed in Britain – chafed against being kept hanging about in uniform with little to do, losing out in the race for jobs and homes. Some men called up in 1944 would not be discharged until 1948.[16] The return to civilian life disoriented some; after the dangers, excitement and comradeship of war, the drabness of home life was anticlimactic. The divorce rate rocketed, up from 4,100 in 1935 to 60,300 in 1947.[17]

With victory and the Armed Forces' job effectively over, the nation's focus was on peace and reconstruction. Montgomery, the Empire's senior soldier in June 1946 when he became Chief of the Imperial General Staff (CIGS), was keen that the Army should not be forgotten. Political minds, however, seemed to be concentrated on the creation of the welfare state: 'The state of the world, British commitments overseas and a long term plan for the Armed Forces all seemed to have been pushed into the background'. Monty was not going to tolerate any peacetime backsliding: 'The British Army must not, as after World War I, be allowed to drift aimlessly without a policy or a doctrine.'[18] His ambitious plans required a 'New Model Army' of well-trained long-service professional regular soldiers, augmented by short-service conscripts; in times of crisis, these former conscripts, who had kept their skills up to speed in the Territorial Army, would be recalled. Unashamed about 'making a nuisance of myself in Whitehall', the CIGS relied on his celebrity rather than his political skills to fight the Army's corner.

In 1947, a single Ministry of Defence with its own minister was inaugurated. The three ministers who oversaw the three services were effectively demoted; they were no longer members of the Cabinet, although until 1964 they were members of the Cabinet Defence Committee (CDC). The service chiefs – the CIGS, the First Sea Lord and the Chief of the Air Staff – formed the Chiefs of Staff Committee. In addition, the CDC, comprising the Prime Minister, the Chancellor of the Exchequer and the Secretaries of State for the Colonies, Dominions and Foreign Affairs among others, oversaw all defence matters, including preparations for war.[19] Until 1964 each service also retained its own ministry, with the Army being run from the War Office: key to its management was the Army Council and the Executive Committee of the Army Council (later the Army Board and Executive Committee of the Army Board). Unlike in later decades, many politicians had first-hand experience of service life, including Churchill, Attlee, Eden and Macmillan. From 1946 an annual Statement on Defence was presented to Parliament: this subsequently became the Statement on Defence Estimates. Separate were the major defence reviews, less than a dozen of which were undertaken between the 1957 Sandys Review and the 2015 Strategic Defence and Security Review.

By 1947, relations with the Soviet Union were increasingly strained. For the Army's senior commanders, the possibility of conflict was never far away. The Ten Year Rule – the 1919 policy guideline which stated that Britain would not be involved in another major war for a decade – had not been reintroduced. While on a downward trend, the strength of the Armed Forces was unprecedented for peacetime: the overall number of forces personnel was 1,255,000, while the Army's strength stood at almost 775,000. This would fall to 450,000 in 1948, the maximum combined strength of all Britain's Armed Forces before the war.[20] *Future Defence Policy,* a report issued by the Chiefs of Staff in 1947, looked ahead and stated that, while the likelihood of war in the following five years was small, 'The most likely and most formidable threat to our interests comes from Russia, especially from 1956 onwards.' It gave little sense of any diminution in Britain's status: the country must fulfil its responsibilities to the United Nations, the Commonwealth and 'also to herself as a Great Power'. 'Essential' was retaining 'at a high state of readiness properly balanced Armed Forces'.[21] In 1948 the so-called Three Pillars strategy confirmed priorities: homeland defence; defence of vital sea lanes; and the defence of the Middle East, crucial for oil supplies.

In 1947, Parliament approved the introduction of peacetime conscription – National Service – for the first time in British history,
apart from in late April 1939, when the comparatively limited Military Training Act was passed. Although massive when seen in a
historic context, the existing and projected strength of the Armed
Forces was simply not enough to fulfil Britain's commitments,
which included Germany, Palestine and the wider Middle East, as
well as India, Malaya and Hong Kong, as the new Defence Minister
reminded the House of Commons.[22] The twelve-month stint was to
be introduced in January 1949, but this plan was overtaken by events:
instead National Service was extended first to eighteen months and
then to two years. The opposition of some politicians to compulsory military service was matched by senior commanders' wariness.
Field Marshal Sir Claude Auchinleck, Commander-in-Chief in India,
observed: 'The British Army by reason of its traditions, organization
and widespread duties is almost certainly the most difficult of all
modern armies to which to apply the principle of National Service.'[23]
One MP considered that the Army's optimum readiness would be
undermined 'if Forces are preoccupied with trainees and contain a
very large proportion of short-service men'.[24] The Army accounted
for the largest number of the conscripts: in 1953, out of a total intake
of 154,064 men, 113,611 entered the Army, compared with just 3,544
joining the Royal Navy.[25]

The call-up became a rite of passage for Britain's young men – to
be endured or enjoyed. For many, it was 'an education in getting on
with people'.[26] National Service was the first time many left home:

> He is straight away pitchforked into the rough and ready life of
> the Army of Private Tommy Atkins and bawling sergeant majors.
> Barrack room manners are perfunctory. There is no opportunity
> for privacy. Bad language is a ritual of soldiers' speech, and sex –
> the one outside interest common to all of them – is persistently
> and publicly discussed.[27]

Registration, a medical examination and enlistment would be followed by eight weeks of basic training. National Servicemen earned
28s. a week during their first six months' service: pay then varied
between 35s. and 84s. per week for a private and between 73s. 6d. and

126s. for a sergeant.[28] Some could expect 'a year and a half of calendar-watching and routine, unexacting work on some remote camp in Yorkshire'; others were grateful for the opportunity to broaden their horizons and see the world.[29] After their demob, the National Servicemen had to serve for another three years, either with the Territorial Army or in the Army Emergency Reserve, involving fifteen days in camp every year. Sent to Malaya or Korea in the 1950s, some National Servicemen certainly had their horizons broadened.

Just as conscription was historically atypical in Britain, so too was any military commitment in Europe. After 1945, this was also changing. The first problem that the British Army had to address after 1945 was the occupation of former enemy territory.

The Occupation of Germany

'We have now won the German war. Let us now win the peace.' Receiving this message from Montgomery in May 1945, British soldiers must have wondered where they should begin. Germany was in ruins, millions of refugees and the displaced were on the move; one diplomat likened the situation to an ant-heap that had suddenly been disturbed.[30] Agriculture and industry was smashed and at a standstill. Housing was reduced to rubble. Transport infrastructure – particularly bridges and rolling stock – was destroyed. Hunger threatened to turn to famine. Shortages of food were matched by shortages of every other commodity, from shoes and clothing to coal and steel. The defeated Germans were facing starvation and disease. At their conference at Yalta a few months earlier, the Allies agreed that Germany, like Austria, was to be divided into four semi-autonomous Zones of Occupation. A four-power Allied Control Council, based in Berlin, in the heart of the Russian Zone, would oversee matters affecting the defeated country as a whole. The British Zone covered the northwest of Germany, the industrial region that included Hamburg and the Ruhr. It was said that the Americans got the scenery, the French got the wine and the British got the ruins.[31] For both victors and vanquished, 'winning the peace' would surely have seemed impossible.

From May 1945, British soldiers embarked on a massive reconstruction and stabilisation operation. At the outset, the military was responsible for at least 20 million people, with more arriving from the east every day, either fleeing the Red Army or following their

expulsion from German enclaves such as Königsberg. It was estimated that, because of this internal migration, there were 2 million
more people to feed in the British Zone than there would have been
in 1939.[32] After the successful military intervention phase in 2003 of
Operation Telic in Iraq, some commentators unfavourably compared
the situation there with this occupation of Germany some sixty years
earlier. Long before V-E Day, the Allied Powers had considered Germany's future in the wake of her defeat, with tentative talk about a
post-conflict Germany underway in the Foreign Office as early as
February 1942.[33] However, theory in Whitehall turned out to be very
different from practice in Westphalia and Wiesbaden. Just as no campaign plan survives first contact with the enemy, soldiers actually on
the ground would find out how different Germany would be from the
country envisaged by committees and commissions. Much wartime
planning had assumed soldiers would encounter armed resistance,
but would find plentiful food stocks and a semblance of civilian government – none of which was realised. One similarity between the
occupations of Baghdad and Berlin is the disparity in the standards of
living between the new rulers and the ruled. Just as the Iraqis must
have envied the comparatively air-conditioned security of the Green
Zone in Baghdad in 2003, the Germans in 1946, who were living on
1,050 calories a day in the British Zone, would have been grateful for
the comparative riches of a soldier's ration pack. Actively assisting
those who, perhaps just days earlier, were 'the enemy' is a paradox
that many soldiers encounter.

What was wanted from Germany and what sort of Germany
was wanted in the future? The Allies were adamant that Germany
should never again threaten the peace of the world: denazification
and demilitarisation had been agreed upon, but little else. Rather
than settling matters in relation to Germany, the Potsdam Conference that began in July revealed Allied division. Throughout the
war and now in peace, the Russians demanded reparations, an issue
of little importance to the United States. Nevertheless, President
Roosevelt took a muscular view, believing that 'you have to cas-
trate the German people' to prevent them waging war again.[34] The
Morgenthau Plan, drawn up by the United States Treasury Secretary, called for the complete deindustrialisation of Germany, with,
for example, the mines being flooded. In contrast, the British sought

not retribution but rehabilitation for Germany. The Labour government stated that, ideally, the country would be 'democratic, economically self-sufficient but militarily disarmed'.[35] This vision of a united Germany living at peace with her neighbours would eventually come to be realised – but not until more than forty years later.

Germany would become the arena where the deteriorating Allied relationship was played out. The Occupation was expected to last for anything between ten and fifty years.[36] Any plans made by the Allied powers – either jointly or separately – for Germany began to unravel almost as soon as the Berlin Declaration was signed. Berlin itself – once the heart of the Reich, now divided into four separate zones – was described by the playwright Berthold Brecht as 'that pile of rubble next to Potsdam'. More widely, Europe was in a state of flux, its map being redrawn. Having suffered so grievously, it was understandable that Russia sought to create a security zone to act as a buffer against any future German expansionism. However, Stalin's forces had advanced further west than either the British or the Americans had anticipated or welcomed, entering and establishing themselves in eastern Germany, and in due course taking control of Poland, Hungary and Czechoslovakia. In addition, it looked as if Italy could well have a Communist government, while Greece remained in a state of civil war and the Balkans were uneasy.

The soldiers who ran the British Zone after Germany's surrender were to rely on the military's fabled ability to improvise. General Brian Robertson, initially Montgomery's deputy and then the Zone's first Military Governor, observed that much was left to the initiative of individuals. Like many under his command, he had neither previously visited Germany nor spoke German, admitting, 'I knew nothing about the situation at all, nothing.'[37] What confronted him must have appeared overwhelming. In Berlin, his American counterpart, General Lucius Clay, recounted: 'The transport of the sick and the dead was by hand stretcher or by cart. Dead bodies still remained in canals and lakes, and were being dug up from under bomb debris. It was a common sight to see a headstone of wood on top of a mound of debris with flowers placed at its foot.'[38] Noel (later Lord) Annan, a colonel in the political division of the Control Council Germany, describes the switch from the euphoria of victory to the realities of peace:

Having spent a happy hot summer commandeering the best
houses and stocking up the messes with wine and schnapps, the
British found themselves trying to house both refugees and the
bombed out, repair the sewers, feed the population and reconsti-
tute the German civil service and local government to perform the
tasks that the Control Commission in Berlin ordered them to do.[39]

However, those orders were, at least initially, at best patchy and were
liable to change.

Having defeated the Wehrmacht, the British Army now faced the
'Battle of the Winter', the over-riding priority of which was to avert
mass starvation. While the German civilian population appeared
cowered, the occupying authorities were ever mindful of the possibility of unrest. Major General Gerald Templer masterminded and
oversaw Operation Barleycorn, in which the tens of thousands of
German soldiers, now prisoners of war, were deployed to bring in
the harvest. Similarly, Operation Coalscuttle got men into the Ruhr
mines. Templer himself had been initially appointed as Director of
Civil Affairs and Military Government at 21st Army Group in May
1945, with orders from Montgomery to 'get on with it'.[40] While he
and the soldiers under his command did indeed get on with it, the
military administrative structure in which they worked was transformed. In August, the 21st Army Group was dissolved, becoming the
British Army of the Rhine (BAOR). Military commanders worked in
parallel with the increasing numbers of civilian administrators arriving to work for the Control Commission Germany (British Element)
(CCG/BE), while back in London civil servants puzzled over whether
the War Office or the Foreign Office should be in charge of policy –
a precursor to a similar tussle between the Pentagon and the State
Department in the US in 2002 over the future administration of
Iraq. Meanwhile, the effort in Germany was not immune from the
scratchiness that can develop between military and civilian advisors
and officials: as far as some soldiers were concerned, CCG meant
Complete Chaos Guaranteed or Charlie Chaplin's Grenadiers. Eventually, the civilian commission would take over all Military Government responsibilities. As the official historian of the administration
notes, all of this meant very little to the defeated Germans living in
the British Zone or the British sector of Berlin.[41]

The military command deserves the credit for providing the security and stability that would allow Germany not just to rebuild, but to flourish. Montgomery later said: 'I was a soldier and I had not been trained to handle anything of this nature ... something had to be done, and done quickly.' As well as successfully fighting the Battle of the Winter to provide food, fuel and shelter, the Field Marshal sought to foster a positive attitude towards the Germans, one that 'holds out hope for the future'.[42] Instead of offering the expected resistance and hostility, the overwhelming majority evinced a 'disciplined docility'.[43] Robertson observed that he had entered into 'a land of desolation and bewilderment', where government above the level of the parish council had ceased.[44] As Churchill told the House of Commons in October 1945: 'The task of holding Germany down will not be a hard one; it will be much more difficult to hold her up.'[45] Trying to bring order out of chaos, commanders realised the impracticality of many planners' directives. One of the first to be torn up was the non-fraternisation policy, which proved to be unworkable, reflected not least by the thousands of cases of venereal disease which British Army medics treated. The policy of denazification was often quietly shelved when it was realised that former Nazi party members were crucial to, for example, the successful working of the mines. This pragmatic approach to denazification can be contrasted with the policy of de-Ba'athification in Iraq in 2004. When regime change is a strategic objective there must be a plan to prevent a vacuum in governance. In Germany in 1945 such a plan existed; in Iraq in 2004 it did not, nor in Libya in 2011.

International law demands that victorious soldiers curb any impulse for vengeance. In the wake of the Siege of Badajoz in 1812, those of Wellington's troops who had survived the 'forlorn hope' of that campaign rampaged through the fortress town, killing, raping and pillaging. Arriving in Berlin, soldiers of the Red Army were as brutal. Magnanimity and restraint towards the former enemy is a key component of military discipline. The 200,000 British soldiers in Germany at the end of the war would have been tested: as one writer observed, each man overnight 'was transformed from cannon fodder to a proconsul with enormous powers'.[46] British soldiers liberating the Bergen-Belsen concentration camp, close to where Montgomery had taken the German surrender, were to find 60,000 starving inmates and 13,000 unburied dead. The subsequent Nuremberg Trials confirmed the scale of the atrocities committed during the Nazi era, not just in Germany but throughout German-occupied Europe. British soldiers must surely have asked themselves whether the German civilians they met each day were culpable and complicit in these crimes against humanity, in which millions had been murdered. Were those living near Belsen as ignorant as they claimed? According to one of the first to arrive at the camp, Trooper Fred Smith of 7th Armoured Division, the stench of death in the surrounding area was unmistakable.[47]

Many soldiers must have thought that the Germans should pay a price for the war that had killed comrades and perhaps kith and kin, while also destroying much of the fabric of Britain. In addition, the demand to rebalance the scales of justice would surely have become more pressing with the gradual realisation of the extent of the Nazi regime's barbarity. Their magnanimity must have been tested. In the summer of 1945, as he diverted imported wheat from the Allied forces to the Ruhr, Templer set out the practical arguments against a policy of retribution:

> It cannot be too often emphasized that the question is not one of sentiment but of economic facts. It may or may not be politically desirable or morally just that the Germans, or some of them, should be starved … It is also obvious that Ruhr coal will not be forthcoming if starvation in the Ruhr is allowed to proceed to a stage where disease or death is widespread.

The Ruhr was seen as central to German recovery: however, it was also regarded by many as the engine room for the country's militarism, the unwelcome resurgence of which was never far from the minds of the Allies. Consequently, the levels of output from the region's mines and factories became the cause of wrangling between the Four Powers in Berlin. Senior British commanders were mindful that the abject existence of many Germans could foment a Communist takeover of the entire country, to the advantage of the Soviet Union. General Robertson stated: 'The real menace for the future of Europe and to world peace was not Germany but Russia. The immediate objective was not to batter Germany down – she was sprawling in the dust already – but to build her up and do so wisely.'[48] One Royal Signalman was moved, not by politics but by the plight of children, to call for more clemency for the former enemy: 'The children of Germany need help now. Let the critics see the kiddies watching scraps being thrown into the bin, and when the coast is clear, rushing for those scraps and fighting for them.'

On the ground, while dealing with the responsibilities and practicalities of occupation, soldiers tried to make the best of their situation. Some did rather better than others. Colonel C. R. W. Norman, based at Bad Oeynhausen, seven miles south-west of Minden, arrived at HQ BAOR in late September 1945. He relates how his heavy kit was stuck at Tilbury because of a dock strike, but he was cheered up by a performance of *La Bohème*, performed by Sadler's Wells on tour to BAOR, which he thought was better than the production he had seen previously at Covent Garden. Norman highlights the contrast in the lives of the victors and the vanquished: 'The food here is excellent. Army rations cooked by Germans and very well cooked too. Masses of butter and sugar and meat, but hardly any coffee.' In October, he enjoyed 'some very good vintage claret in George's mess. It cost four and sixpence.' By January 1946, a new officers' club had opened, run by a Royal Army Service Corps sergeant major who had been the restaurant manager of the Savoy; there, Norman and seven chums drank seven bottles of champagne. Urging his mother to send post from England on Thursday, so that it would arrive on Saturday, he informed her: 'There's not the slightest hope of my getting you any material of any sort in this country. There are no shops at all.'[49]

In the aftermath of the war, the German economy was effectively a black market. Barter was the norm: 'Stuttgart city fathers bought liquor brewed in the surrounding countryside, shipped it to the French Zone for cigarettes, which were swapped for coal from a Ruhr mine, which was then traded for cement used for reconstruction in Württemberg. One chemical plant in the Russian Zone had the exchange rates of a range of goods including flour and coal for a 100 weight of fertiliser.'[50] Official economic policy – including the prices of all finished goods 'down to fees for dancing classes and the costs of admissions to flea circuses' – was controlled by bureaucrats from the Allied Control Council in Berlin; they exercised their power, according to an eyewitness, 'in a most cumbersome and rigid manner'.[51] The most common currency was cigarettes. With every British soldier entitled to fifty free cigarettes a week, as well as 200 at duty-free prices, the occupiers fuelled the black economy.

The Occupation drained Britain's dwindling funds still further. It was imperative that Germany became economically self-reliant. As Annan observed: 'Britain had to get the German economy going again if she herself was to survive.'[52] The winter of 1946-7 was the coldest for fifty years. In the British Zone, waterways were frozen; ice on Hamburg's Alster lagoon was thick enough to drive across. Ink froze in inkwells and one officer's cup of tea froze on his desk.[53] Across the North Sea, the new Jerusalem promised by the Labour government appeared increasingly to be a mirage – certainly during the freeze and subsequent floods, when the United Kingdom came to a standstill. Coal stocks at power stations were rapidly diminished, the railway system went into paralysis, power cuts followed and by February 2.5 million workers had become idle. The traditional dependence on imported foodstuffs, many from the dollar area, put prices up in 1947 by over a third of their 1945 benchmark. Ministerial incompetence added to the misery: 'Shiver with Shinwell and starve with Strachey' became a catchphrase. On 1 January 1947, in Germany the British and American Zones merged. The Bizone was created ostensibly to boost the German economy, but from Britain's point of view, to protect her own. However, the severe winter widened the existing trade gap between Britain's exports and imports. What remained of the US loan negotiated by Keynes that had been expected to last until 1951 was further eroded by the 'Convertibility Crisis' in July, which led to a run on sterling.

Back home in Britain, suspicion grew that some soldiers in Germany were doing a little too well for themselves. The British people were becoming browned off by austerity; by the queuing, the drabness, the rationing – and by the whalemeat, snoek and horsemeat on their dinner plates.[54] In contrast, at his farewell dinner on 26 April 1948 in 34 Mess, Brigadier H. J. D. L. McGregor of the Queen's Own Cameron Highlanders tucked into Hors d'oeuvres à la Française, followed by Potage Agnes Sorel, Poulet de Bresse poêle with Épinards aux croutons and Pommes noisettes, Pêche Melba, Fromage de Roquefort and Moka.[55] One junior officer in the HAC in 1947 remembers: 'The Army was awash with alcohol.'[56] Soldiers' comparatively large rations of food and seemingly limitless ciga-rettes fuelled growing resentment in Britain that Germany was little more than a huge holiday camp.[57] Signalman Roy Yorke, however, seemed crushed by boredom, counting down the weeks in his 1946 diary until Friday 26 April, when '8 years finished ought to be a free man!!'[58] The frequent press reports about British soldiers living the high life in the Occupation Zone were, according to him, wide of the mark:

> I do not approve of Evadne Price in the *People*, she's raising an awful atmosphere of mistrust and suspicion over everyone out here, because of a few blockheads who must be as thick as cement ... If people only knew how much the blokes resent it, 6 months ago – heroes, 3 months ago – everyone a racketeer – now we're all sex maniacs if what we read in the papers is true anyway. It's a load of hooey, I reckon a bare 5% of the blokes bother.

But a Royal Marine who was an interpreter for the Control Council spent a lot of time driving Göring's light blue Mercedes around Berlin, enjoying himself so much, 'it only served to ruin me even further for any normal civilian life'.[59]

As Germany began to rise from the ashes, the freeze in East–West relations that led to the Cold War was incremental but inexorable. Britain could do little to halt the spread of Communism through-out Europe, with Greece, France and Italy ripe for takeover. Indeed, existing British efforts to contain Communism in Greece proved unaffordable and were ceded to the United States. It was an indica-tion of how Washington rather than London would be taking the lead in post-war Europe, confounding British fears and expectations that the Americans might retreat into their customary isolationism. In September 1946, the US Secretary of State, James Byrnes, prom-ised: 'As long as there is an occupation army in Germany, American Armed Forces will be part of that occupation.' The following March, the Truman Doctrine confirmed that the United States would support 'free peoples who are resisting subjugation by armed minorities or outside pressures'. Three months later, Byrnes' successor, George C. Marshall, announced the setting-up of the European Recovery Pro-gramme to rebuild European economies, 'without which there can be

no political stability and no assured peace'.[60] Of the $13 billion of aid
provided by the Marshall Plan, $2.7 billion went to Britain: instead
of reconstruction, much of the money was spent on defence. Offered
to the whole of Europe, the plan prompted a further deterioration in
relations between the West and the Soviet Union, which ordered the
Eastern Bloc to abstain from it. The probable fissure of Europe was
indicated in early 1948 when the Foreign Secretary, Ernest Bevin,
told the House of Commons: 'We are now thinking of Western
Europe as a unit.'[61] Shortly afterwards, a coup in Czechoslovakia
brought the Communists to power. The staunchly anti-Communist
Bevin would be the architect of the Western Union, a military alli-
ance agreed in Brussels in March between Britain, France and the
Benelux countries, that was the precursor to NATO (see chapter 4).
In June, the 10-month-long blockade of Berlin by the Soviets began.
At that moment, the possibility of another war seemed real. The Cold
War was beginning.

The fissure between East and West was formalised with the
division of Germany itself and the creation of the Federal Republic
of Germany on 23 May 1949. Neither side had wanted to cede to
the other a wholly united Germany. As one analyst suggests: 'The
wealthy Ruhr looking westwards was a safer bet for the West than
a united Germany that might fall under Communist influence.'[62] In
September 1948, General Robertson had noted:

> I believe that we are committed to war with the Russians even-
> tually. We cannot be choosers in such a conflict when it comes
> to allies. The Germans, the best fighters in Europe apart from
> ourselves, are basically anti-Russian – and anti-Communist in
> consequence.[63]

In four short years, western Germany went from enemy to ally. The
divided country became the frontline of the Cold War. The British
Army of the Rhine would be stationed on that frontline for forty
years – and remain in Germany for almost three decades after that.

In mid-1946, Germany was designated a 'home station', which
meant that soldiers' wives and children could join them there. The
first contingent arrived in August, putting further pressure on the
limited supply of housing stock: their homes were to be curtained

in identical 'married families chintz'.[64] Attlee wanted the wives in particular to remember they would be looked upon as representatives of the British Empire; they should be good mannered and tactful.[65] Some senior commanders in Germany undoubtedly drew on their imperial experience, but General Robertson sounded a defensive, if high-minded, note: 'We here are Empire builders, not in the sense repeated to us maliciously by some of our critics. The Empire whose boundaries we struggle to extend is the Empire of true democracy, of peace and decency.'[66] Under Occupation, there must have been a certain irony in the colonial comparison for the Germans and Austrians. The war they had engendered had boosted nationalist movements around the world, destabilising the empires of two of the four occupying powers, France and Britain.

The defeated Germans accepted the British military presence; some 1,600 miles away in Jerusalem, it was unwelcome.

Palestine

Towards the end of the First World War, the British government issued a policy statement which would have far-reaching implications in the aftermath of the Second. The Balfour Declaration of 2 November 1917 pledged that 'His Majesty's Government views with favour the establishment in Palestine of a National Home for the Jewish people and will use their best endeavours to facilitate the achievement of this object.' This undertaking, given in a letter to the financier Lord Rothschild, represented a triumph for Zionism. The movement had gathered momentum in the last two decades of the nineteenth century in parallel with a small but steady amount of Jewish emigration from Europe to Palestine, a region then under Ottoman control. In his pamphlet *'Der Judenstaat'*, published 1896, Zionism's leader, Theodor Herzl, had called for the foundation of a Jewish state in Palestine, a vision that, at the time, appeared somewhat grandiose. In the fourth year of the Great War, the British government appeared to legitimise and endorse it.

Britain's 30-year involvement in Palestine began with the disintegration of the Ottoman Empire and ended with the fracturing of her own. In the aftermath of the Second World War, British soldiers had to confront a relentless campaign by Jewish insurgents who were determined to fulfil Herzl's vision of a Jewish state. The British underestimated the commitment of their opponents – who included Irgun and the Stern Gang, as well as members of Haganah, the official local defence force. Some of the most effective insurgents had worked for underground forces in Europe fighting the Nazis. Irgun's leader, future Israeli Prime Minister Menachem Begin, was described by terrorism analyst Bruce Hoffman as having 'an intuitive sense about the interplay between violence, politics and propaganda that ideally qualified him to lead a terrorist organization'.[67] Begin suggested that any colonial regime lives by the legend of its omnipotence and used Britain's might against itself: 'Every attack which it fails to prevent is a blow to its standing.'[68] British soldiers, expecting a respite from conflict after V-J Day, found themselves caught up in a very different sort of struggle. E. J. Rooke-Matthews, a 21-year-old Paratrooper who had served in Normandy before being shipped to Palestine, observed: 'In war as we knew it, one could identify the enemy – one knew where he was.'[69] Now their opponents could just slip back into the crowd.

In 1922, Britain had accepted the League of Nations' mandate to govern Palestine. It would become one of the burdensome items on the Colonial Office agenda: Churchill complained about the trouble caused by 'petty Palestine' compared with 'mighty India'. As mandated territory, Palestine was not a British colony: although the British ruled, it was in the expectation of creating the conditions for independent self-government. Consequently, the authorities had to work in partnership with local institutions, such as the Jewish Agency, which was to become a parallel government. The first choice of mandatory for some in Palestine was the United States: given that military service in Palestine was to become, according to one MP, 'one of the most arduous, thankless tasks that any troops have ever been asked to discharge in the whole history of the Empire', some British soldiers probably wished the mandate had indeed gone to Washington.[70]

The British military on the ground in Palestine were confronted by Arab unrest and revolt before the Second World War and Jewish insurgency after it. While undertaking to bring about a Jewish national home, the Balfour Declaration had added a proviso: '... It being clearly understood that nothing shall be done which may prejudice the civil and religious rights of existing non-Jewish communities in Palestine ...' Balfour anticipated the irreconcilable conflict between Jews and Arabs for Palestine. As Colonial Office Minister, Lord Moyne told the House of Lords in July 1942: 'The Arabs who have lived and buried their dead for 50 generations in Palestine, will not willingly surrender their land and self-government to the Jews.'[71] Conversely, Menachem Begin was told by his father: 'We Jews were to return to *Eretz Israel*: Not to "go" or "travel" or "come" – but to return.'[72] During the Mandate, Britain tried to accommodate both the Arabs and the Jews, but ended up pleasing neither side. Arab hostility intensified as the Jewish population and the number of Jewish settlements increased. At the time of the Declaration, there had been perhaps 500,000 Arabs and 65,000 Jews in Palestine: by 1939 the Arab population was just over 1.5 million, while Jews numbered almost 545,000.[73] A British White Paper restricted further Jewish immigration.

In 1945, the Middle East was crucial to Britain and the Empire. Bevin regarded it as key to the country's economic recovery and, like the Chiefs of Staff, considered it vital for Britain's security that the Soviet Union was kept out of the region.[74] It was not only the artery to India and the Far East, but was also 'the Empire's main reservoir of mineral oil'.[75] In addition, the 1936 Anglo-Egyptian Treaty, which had formally ratified a British military presence of 10,000 troops in the country, was deeply unpopular: another base was required to accommodate 'the largest concentration of British military strength outside India'.[76] In September 1945, the 6th Airborne Division had been sent to Palestine as the advanced guard of the proposed Imperial Strategic Reserve.[77] The Cabinet was reminded that 'unfortunately the future of Palestine bulks large in all Arab eyes'.[78] A change of policy in Palestine might not only lead to another Arab revolt, but also to the withdrawal of cooperation from Arab states 'on which our Imperial interests so largely depend'.[79]

When the full extent of the German genocide of 6 million Jews was revealed after the Second World War, additional moral justification was lent to demands for a Jewish state. In Palestine, bitterness against the British intensified. They had, after all, 'continued to keep the gates of the Jewish "National Home" tightly shut against the Jews'.[80] In the eyes of Begin, and many others, they had colluded in the Holocaust. The head of the Stern Gang, Friedman Yellin, told the Hungarian-British writer Arthur Koestler that his mother and three brothers had been killed 'by German sadism and the British White Paper'.[81] Despite international pressure, the change in government brought no change in policy: the Attlee government refused to rescind the 1939 White Paper. On 31 October 1945, members of Haganah, Irgun and the Stern Gang launched coordinated attacks against British installations.

The Army's top secret 'Jewish Illegal Organisations' report of May 1947 provides an insight into what confronted British soldiers. It stated that local people 'have consistently refused to cooperate' in the suppression of Irgun and the Stern Gang. The Irgun had between 2,500 and 3,000 members:

> Their storm troops are very highly-trained men, some having received specialist training in the British Army and deal with sabotage and 'Commando' type operations requiring a good deal of skill and courage ... Planning of operations is usually good and much use is made of British uniforms of which they appear to have a good supply ... The [arms] caches are very well concealed and their careful construction shows considerable ingenuity. Training in military subjects is carried out in settlements ostensibly on agricultural courses and is thought to be a full-time course consisting of map-reading, recce, field craft, night operations, sabotage and weapons training.[82]

According to Irgun's leader, Menachem Begin, 'We fight, therefore we are.' British soldiers and members of the Palestine Police Force would fight a losing battle against the terrorists in part because they were unable to win the active support of the local population.

For almost three years, British security forces found themselves embroiled in one of those 'small wars' that would have been familiar to their nineteenth-century predecessors. Attacks on British troops and installations increased. Paratrooper Rooke-Matthews found his opponents 'well-armed, they had had many opportunities to build up supplies during the War'. Synagogues were included in search operations, something that he and his comrades were unhappy about, 'but there was clear evidence that these places were being used to store arms and ammunition'. He described what soldiers had to endure as the security situation deteriorated:

We were increasingly subjected to abuse and criticism, not only from the local people but from overseas. We were 'piggy in the middle', nothing we would do was right. After losing comrades in liberating the victims of the concentration camps, we were described in terms applied to the oppressors in Germany – indeed we were now the oppressors.[83]

Previously, Palestine had been considered a pleasant posting, with a good climate, plenty of food and giving the chance for some soldiers 'to see their Sunday School pictures come alive'. Climbing poles to repair telephone lines that were continually sabotaged, Royal Signals engineers became easy targets for snipers.[84] 'A normal daily discourtesy' soldiers were spat at and they also 'had to be prepared to be attacked, ambushed or bombed at any time by anybody'.[85] As Brigadier Arthur Sisson describes, 'every camp was watched day and night. Every unit had civilian employees, both Arab and Jews and none could be trusted entirely.' Soldiers tried as best they could to enjoy themselves off duty. Trooper Roy Hammerton of the 3rd Hussars played football and rugby, while Paratrooper Rooke-Matthews went to the open-air cinema, read banned books from a clandestine pay-as-you-read library run by one of his comrades and went on trips organised by the padre to Biblical sites. 'To be able to spend Christmas 1945 and 1946 singing carols in the fields of the shepherds on Christmas Eve for me more than compensated for the aggro we had to endure.'[86] Colonel K. C. F. Chevasse of the Irish Fusiliers managed to find 'the cheapest polo in the world' at the polo club in Sarafind, where a pony could be hired for two shillings and a chukka played for sixpence.[87] These moments of light relief became less frequent as troops increasingly became confined to base.

In *Portrait of Palestine*, a short film issued by Britain's Ministry of Information in 1947, the Union flag is shown flying over Government House in Jerusalem.[88] Although it signified who held political power, the image is, in fact, misleading. By then 100,000 troops were tied down. The Irgun aimed to destroy the institutions representing British authority and undermine British morale, targeting railways, oil installations and military clubs. In one of the most notorious terrorist incidents of the twentieth century, the King David Hotel in Jerusalem was bombed in July 1946, killing ninety-one people. Housing the government secretariat and the headquarters of the British military forces in Palestine and Transjordan, it was the 'nerve centre' of British rule in Palestine.[89] After that, 'outrages have continued almost incessantly', according to one MP in a House of Commons debate on Jewish terrorism in Palestine in January 1947.[90] In October 1946, Jewish insurgents were responsible for bombing the British Embassy in Rome. Previously, in simultaneous attacks on three RAF stations in Palestine twenty aircraft were destroyed. In December 1946, a major and three sergeants were kidnapped and flogged in retaliation for the flogging of an Irgun member. The *Army Quarterly* considered this to be 'probably the greatest insult to which the British Army has ever been subjected'.[91] In January 1947, Judge Ralph Windham was abducted as he left the District Court in Tel Aviv, in response to the capture of Dov Gruner, one of Palestine's most wanted Zionist terrorists. On 17 April, Gruner and three others were hanged: in retaliation, on 4 May Irgun's assault force smashed its way into Acre's fortress prison, enabling forty-one Irgun and Stern Gang members to escape. On 31 July, hours after three Jews were hanged, Sergeants Clifford Martin and Marvin Paice were hanged from eucalyptus trees, three weeks after they had been kidnapped. Their bodies were booby-trapped and pinned to their chests were messages written in Hebrew explaining that they were guilty of 'illegal entry into our homeland'.

Laws restricting Jewish immigration to Palestine continued to be enforced at huge moral cost to Britain. The dilapidated steamer SS *President Warfield*, which had taken part in the Normandy landings, was acquired by the Haganah and renamed *Exodus*. In July 1947, as she was carrying 4,500 Holocaust survivors from France to Haifa, she was intercepted by Royal Navy destroyers just outside Palestinian waters, rammed and boarded. In the struggle that followed, two passengers were killed and dozens injured. The illegal immigrants were then deported back to Europe on three different ships, one of which sailed with a huge swastika daubed over the Union flag. Colonial Secretary Arthur Creech Jones assured the House of Commons: 'These ships will be sent to France and these passengers will be disembarked.' Anything else was 'not a matter for the British Government'.[92] Arriving in Toulon, the Jews refused to leave and the French refused to force them. The stand-off lasted twenty-four days, with some of the passengers going on hunger strike. They were then taken to Germany, where they were held in former SS camps near Lübeck. One American headline was 'Back to the Reich'. Unfortunately for Britain, the plight of the refugees on board the *Exodus* exemplified the struggle faced by hundreds of thousands of Jews across Europe. Having survived the Nazis, they were desperate to leave their Displaced Persons camps and make their way to the safety of Palestine. According to one Army report, thirty-three illegal ships carrying 33,000 Jews were intercepted between November 1945 and May 1947. 'It is considered that 99 per cent of the population are behind the Haganah in their efforts to bring immigrants to Palestine.'[93]

The Irgun deliberately targeted 'British prestige' and knew the importance of winning the propaganda war. As Begin said: 'Throughout all the years of our uprising, we hit at the British government's prestige, deliberately, tirelessly, unceasingly.'[94] Whether they were escorting illegal immigrants back on Cyprus-bound ships at Haifa or conducting searches and roadblocks, soldiers knew that the world's press could be watching. Reports about the activities of the Irgun 'covered the front pages of newspapers everywhere, particularly in the United States'.[95] The American public gave Palestine's Jews moral and financial support. Following the hanging of the sergeants, the *Daily Mail* attacked 'American women whose dollars helped to buy the rope'.[96] Mindful of the Jewish lobby, President Truman demanded that 100,000 Jews stranded in European Displaced Persons camps be allowed into Palestine.

Just as in Iraq from 2005, soldiers in Palestine in 1947 must have sensed the growing lack of support back home for their mission. At the very top, matters were not helped by disagreements between Montgomery, now Chief of the Imperial General Staff, and High Commissioner Sir Alan Cunningham, in charge of determining the authorities' approach. In a cable to Whitehall, the CIGS stated: 'The whole business of dealing with illegal armed organizations in Palestine is being tackled in a way which is completely gutless, thoroughly unsound and which will not produce any good results.'[97] The *Sunday Express* demanded: 'Govern or Get Out'. In a letter to the *New Statesman*, Arthur Koestler empathised with the terrorists, not least because 'at the very moment when the extermination of the European Jews began, the doors of Palestine were slammed in their faces'. He pointed out that Jewish labour and capital had transformed Palestine in twenty years 'from a malaria-infested stretch of swamp and desert into the most fertile country in the Middle East'.[98] A solution to the problem of Palestine seemed as far away as ever; neither side would compromise. Even Churchill had had enough:

> For 18 months we have been pouring out our wealth on this unhappy, unfortunate and discreditable business. Then there is the manpower of at least 100,000 men in Palestine, who might well be at home strengthening our depleted industry. What are they doing there? What good are we getting out of it?

The curfews, the cordons, the brief impositions of martial law were proving fruitless. As one MP said, 'terrorism is a greater power in Palestine than the British Administration itself'.[99] The British still had no clear policy. Since the start of the Mandate, successive governments had ordered inquiries and Royal Commissions and convened conferences: none had come up with a solution. In February 1947, the government declared it would be handing the problem over to the United Nations and seeking to end the Mandate.

The state of Israel was inaugurated on 14 May 1948. Today, street names in Tel Aviv include Allenby and Wingate, a reflection of the British military contribution to the country. Israel's first prime minister, David Ben-Gurion, told the United Nations Committee on Palestine that it would be to the everlasting credit of Britain that she undertook the restoration of Palestine to the Jewish people.[100] Some 230 British soldiers were killed between 1945 and 1948 during that period of transition, along with many members of the Palestinian police.

India

On 20 February 1947, three days after the statement concerning the end of the Mandate in Palestine, Prime Minister Attlee announced the transfer of power in India, 'at a date no later than June 1948'. Almost two centuries after Major General Robert Clive had led the forces of the East India Company to victory at the Battle of Plassey on 23 June 1757, the jewel was being prised from the British imperial crown. While independence had been on the horizon since the

1920s, the realisation that it was about to happen came as a shock to those serving in the Army and the Indian Civil Service. Reminiscing about the pre-war Army view, India's commander-in-chief, Field Marshal Sir Claude Auchinleck, said: 'I don't think the average subaltern thought much about British rule, and indeed, took it for granted that it would go on forever. I do remember when one of our Indian officers from the hills in the north said to me, "What is going to happen when the British leave India?" I looked at him and said, "Well, of course, the British are never going to leave India."'[101] But the British were going to leave, sooner than anyone in government in either London or Delhi anticipated, and leave behind two countries, not one. In early 1947, however, partition was far from certain.

Ever since London had taken formal control of India after the Mutiny of 1857–8, the Army had been the key institution of British authority. Towards the end of the nineteenth century when the rank and file came to be viewed more favourably by the British civilian public, the red-coated soldier-*sahib* was associated with the subcontinent, not least because of Kipling. Generations of schoolboys grew up enthralled by tales of derring-do across the Empire, but particularly on the North-West Frontier. During the Raj, the Army in India was a *yali*-like hybrid, made up of a mixture of all-British, Indian and Gurkha regiments, although all overwhelmingly officered by the British. Under their command were British troops, epitomised by Tommy Atkins, as well as indigenous *sepoys*, whether Hindu, Sikh or Muslim. As military historian Daniel Marston notes, until the First World War, senior commanders who held to 'martial race' theories were biased in favour of certain ethnic groups, but particularly towards the Sikhs. Field Marshal Lord Roberts of Kandahar, Commander in Chief, India in 1885, stated that 'Gurkhas, Dogras, Sikhs, the pick of Punjabi Muhammadans, Hindustanis of the Jat and Ranghur castes ... and certain classes of Pathans' could be relied on in the field against the Russians.[102] By 1914, 75 per cent of the Indian Army was recruited from these 'martial races', with the Sikh homeland, the Punjab, supplying more than 40 per cent of all the recruits for the combat arms of the Army by the end of the Great War.[103] 'It was not unusual for a *jawan* arriving at a regimental centre to be the fifth generation of his family to serve in the Army.'[104] It has remained a dream of many in the Sikh community in the United Kingdom today to have Sikh units in the modern British Army in the same way that Nepali citizens furnish Gurkha units.

The valour of India's soldiers in both world wars contributed to a sense of national identity, intensifying the demands for independence. Many nationalist politicians – whether Hindi or Muslim – regarded the Army as 'the sword of the Raj', the instrument not of India's defence but of continuing British rule. One analyst observed that the British had conquered and held India by the use of Indian military manpower.[105] The sluggish Indianisation of the officer corps continued to underline British dominance. While efforts were made to introduce more Indian officers, reflected by the establishment of India's Sandhurst at Dehra Din in 1932, many British officers disliked the idea of being subordinate to an Indian. Viceroy Commissioned Officers were of lower status than those who held the King's Commission and were not automatically entitled to be saluted by British soldiers.[106] In a memorandum sent out to all officers in southeast Asia, Auchinleck captured the 'us and them' attitude that had been current:

> The policy of segregation of Indian officers into separate units, the differential treatment in respect of pay and terms of service as compared with the British officer and the prejudice and lack of manners by some – by no means all – British officers and their wives, all went to produce a very deep and bitter feeling of racial discrimination in the minds of the most intelligent and progressive of the Indian officers, who are naturally Nationalists, keen to see India standing on her own two feet and not to be ruled by Whitehall forever.[107]

In 1919 and 1935 the Government of India Acts attempted to still the nationalist clamour and shore up support for the Raj. They failed. Whether from the Congress Party or the rival Muslim League, nationalist politicians including Jawaharlal Nehru and Muhammad Ali Jinnah tended to be tepid at best towards the military.

India's subordinate status was underlined by the declaration of war in 1939, fuelling further nationalist discontent. If Britain were at war, so too was India: local politicians need not be consulted. As a result, eight Congress ministers resigned from their offices in protest.

From the summer of 1942, Gandhi's Quit India movement gathered momentum. More than 2 million Indians served in the Second World War, when the country's eastern flank was open to attack by the Japanese following the crushing defeats of Burma and Malaya in 1942. The 900-mile retreat, 'the longest in British military history', was subsequently turned into advance and victory following the appointment of General ('Uncle') Bill Slim to command the 14th Army. One unwelcome consequence of the calamitous fall of Singapore in 1942 was the development of the Indian National Army, comprising about 25,000 Indian soldiers who had become prisoners of war of the Japanese and then went on to fight alongside them against the British. They won the sympathy of some nationalists who considered the men had worked for the 'freedom of India'.[108]

The advent of the Attlee government made India's independence inevitable. The question in late 1945 was not *whether* India would gain independence, but *when* and *which* India. Should India become a unitary state or be divided along communal lines, which would lead to a Hindu (and Sikh) India and a Muslim, autonomous Pakistan? If the country were to be split – an outcome British politicians wanted to avoid, hoping a federation would prevail – its armed forces would also be split.

An independent India needed an independent army; British soldiers would be, in all senses, completely redundant. In April 1946, Auchinleck had announced the creation of an Indian Army 'officered and manned throughout by Indians'.[109] By October, overall numbers in the Army had dropped to 800,000 and were expected to fall to 387,000 in the following next six months.[110] In addition, the proportion of British officers fell dramatically: in September 1945, the officer corps comprised 34,590 British officers and 8,340 Indians; by April 1947, there were 11,500 British officers to 8,400 Indians.[111] All British officers were expected to have left the Army by July 1949. It was a blow to many. Ever since the first days of the Raj, it had been said somewhat unkindly that India had given British officers without the advantage of a private income the chance to live like gentlemen. Others had fallen under the country's spell and dedicated their lives to 'a land full of gold and Gods and famine, ugly as a corpse and beautiful beyond belief'.[112] The involuntary Indianisation of the officer corps threatened to undermine military capability.

Of the non-British officers, only 500 were pre-war and Sandhurst-trained,[113] leading many to fear for the security of the North-West Frontier. Major General G. J. Hamilton, Guides Infantry noted: 'We all knew, even in the '20s, that independence for India could not long be delayed and it was our duty to see that our Indian successors, both in the Services and civil administration, were properly trained.'[114] Auchinleck told his senior commanders: 'It has been decreed and in my opinion inevitably decreed, that we – the British officers – are to go. Before we go, it is our bounden duty to do all we can to ensure the continued well-being and efficiency of our men and of the Army we have loved so well and served so long.'[115] Despite knowing they were unwanted in the new India and Pakistan, British soldiers would continue to do their duty to the Army.

As much as Britain wanted to avoid partition, it became inevitable. In April 1947 in New Delhi, the charismatic Lord Mountbatten of Burma was sworn in as the last Viceroy. To no avail, Attlee had emphasised to him the need 'to impress upon the Indian leaders the great importance of avoiding any breach in the continuity of the Indian Army, and of maintaining the organization of defence on an all-Indian basis'.[116] With the British government preparing to hand over power in June 1948, in March 1947 low-key discussions about implementing the division of the Armed Forces had begun in London. Although Auchinleck and Mountbatten opposed the strategy, Jinnah and Nehru were adamant that the forces should be split on communal lines: until then, the Army was one of the few institutions that was integrated: Sikhs, Muslims and Hindus served side by side. In May, Auchinleck noted: 'It is not merely a matter of saying Muslims to the left Hindus to the right … British, Moslem and all other classes of Indian officers are completely mixed throughout the Army without any regard to race or religion.'[117] On 4 June, the day after Mountbatten informed the Commander-in-Chief unequivocally that the Armed Forces must be divided, he dropped a bombshell: instead of June 1948, independence was to be brought forward to midnight on 15 August 1947.

At the very time the subcontinent was destabilised by the rush to independence, the Army, which should have provided aid to the civilian authorities and been a beacon of continuity, was itself turned inside out. To avoid negativity surrounding the word 'division', the term 'reconstitution' of the Armed Forces was deployed in press releases and orders.[118] Excluding the Gurkhas, the composition of the twenty-three infantry regiments of the Indian Army was roughly 9 Hindu, 7 Muslim, 4 Sikh and 3 others.[119] It was to be divided along communal rather than territorial lines: material and stores were divvied up, in theory at least, with 70 per cent going to India and 30 per cent to Pakistan. India was assigned 270,000 of the 410,000 men in the Army. Any Muslim living in Pakistan would be unable to serve in India, while any non-Muslim living in India could not join the armed forces of Pakistan. A Muslim in the 1st Punjabis wrote: 'What had taken 200 years to build was dismembered in three months.'[120] The 5th Royal Gurkhas, headquartered for a century in Abbottabad – the town where Osama bin Laden was to meet his end, had to pack up and leave within a fortnight.[121] Officers from British regiments inevitably demanded that their mess silver and other valuables be shipped home, while questions were raised about regimental funds.[122] In a Special Indian Army Order from the Commander-in-Chief, dated 14 August 1947, reference SIAO 79/S/47, R. A. Savory, the Adjutant General, stated: 'This is the last Army Order.'[123]

The possible fall-out from independence was wished away by the authorities in London, Delhi and Karachi. A warning of what could happen was given with an outbreak of four days of communal violence and slaughter in Calcutta in August 1946: the dead lay in gutters being picked over by vultures.[124] Strikes, riots and a naval mutiny reflected the subcontinent's unease, while in the Princely States some of the rulers, including the Nizim of Hyderabad, were far from happy with the new constitutional arrangements, which encroached on their power. A largely Muslim area, Kashmir, was ruled by a Hindu maharajah, Sir Hari Singh, who wanted the state to ally with India. Apart from Mountbatten, no one knew for certain where the new boundaries between India and Pakistan would lie until two days after independence, when the Radcliffe Report would be published. It had fallen to the lawyer Sir Cyril Radcliffe to decide where to draw the line: he had never visited India before and was given five weeks to complete his task.[125] His briefing for the role was 'a 30-minute session over a large-scale map with the Permanent Under-Secretary in the India Office'.[126] The uncertainty over partition added to the tension, especially in the Punjab, the region on the frontline. In the previous year's regional elections, the Muslim League had won the most seats there, but had been kept out of power by an alliance of the other parties. In March 1947, the region's rabble-rousing Sikh leader, Tara Singh, told Sikhs and Hindus: 'Our motherland is calling for blood and we shall satiate the thirst of our motherland with blood.'[127] The Governor of Punjab, Sir Evan Jenkins, repeatedly warned Delhi of impending unrest, pleading with Mountbatten to announce the boundary awards, not least because 'The Sikhs believe they will be expropriated and massacred in West Punjab and smothered by the Hindus and Congress in East Punjab.'[128] Just as India itself was to be partitioned, so too were Punjab and, in the east, Bengal.

A few weeks before independence, the Partition Council woke up to the possible danger of civil unrest in the Punjab and announced the creation of a 'special military command'. The Punjab Boundary Force (PBF) was an anachronism even as it was established on 1 August 1947. Its senior officer was not an Indian, but Major General T. W. Rees, formerly of the Rajputana Rifles, who had commanded the 19th Division that had captured Mandalay; Mountbatten described him as 'perhaps the ablest divisional commander in Burma'. A Hindustani speaker, Rees made notes in Welsh, probably in the interests of security.[129] Two brigades of 4th Indian Division, which Rees had commanded since 1946, contributed to the Boundary Force, which was to number an estimated 50,000 men. However, the force was to cover an area larger than Ireland, with a population of 14.5 million. Of its original seventeen battalions, ten were recruited from the Punjab. Rees reported to the Joint Defence Council, which included Sir Rob Lockhart and Sir Frank Messervy, still Commanders-in-Chief, India and Pakistan respectively, and Supreme Commander Auchinleck. The PBF is said to be 'the last unified force of the old Indian Army'.[130]

The violence caused by India's partition is as shocking as the genocides later in the century in Cambodia and Rwanda. No one in civilian government circles in London or the subcontinent had anticipated the mass migration that ensued: millions of Muslims left India, millions of Sikhs and Hindus left Pakistan, all in their desperation 'abandoning homes, businesses, jobs, friends, familiar places and most of their movable possessions'.[131] In the frenzy of communal violence in which many of the refugees were trapped, it is estimated that perhaps 1 million were killed. Flashpoints were the cities of Lahore and Amritsar. Sabotage disrupted the rail service; trains became killing grounds, crossing the new India–Pakistan border laden with the bodies of slain citizens from the opposing state. In the Punjab, civil society collapsed, worsening the refugee crisis. More than half of local members of the Indian Civil Service went absent and PBF personnel could not trust the impartiality of the dwindling number of police officers: a week after independence, only 700 remained on duty in East Punjab.[132] The civil authorities to whom the Boundary Force was meant to be providing aid were either obstructive – for example, either releasing prisoners or refusing to prosecute them – or rapidly becoming non-existent. Sir Evan Jenkins observed that assailants could get away with murder: 'If they were on the right side of the boundary line on 15 August, they had nothing to fear.'[133]

The overwhelmed Punjab Boundary Force had the impossible task of trying to keep order, made worse by the attitude of the civilian authorities. Delhi and Karachi closed their eyes to the civil war that was breaking out, the politicians not wanting to acknowledge any imperfection in their new states. It rankled with them that the PBF, British-led and unified, was so reflective of the Raj and the *ancien régime*. Jenkins considered the setting up of the force 'politically and constitutionally wrong'.[134] The future president of Pakistan and the future Commander in Chief of the Indian Armed Forces, who both served in the PBF, considered that the force should have been commanded by local officers, who 'would not have hesitated to order troops to open fire and who would have been implicitly obeyed'.[135] One analyst observed that in the back of British military minds could well have been the thought that, rather than being praised as impartial custodians of the peace, they could be made scapegoats and condemned as murderers.[136] The force's British soldiers knew they were unwanted by either the Indians or the Pakistanis, while the local men's neutrality was tested as they attempted to keep the peace among the various ethnic and religious groups from which they came. Major General J. C. Bruce, commander of Lahore, reminded soldiers: 'We do not take sides, we do not fight for one community against another ... You must remember that you are on the spot as the impartial instrument of justice and truth.'[137] However, realising that the political support for the force was absent, Auchinleck ordered that it be dissolved on 1 September. A few weeks later, he wrote to Attlee and the Chiefs of Staff, calling for the withdrawal of the remaining 2,800 British officers from the Indian Army: 'The conditions of massacre and bestiality of the worst kind in which many of these British officers have been working continuously for many weeks have sickened them. They have lost faith in their cloth and in their men, of whom they were so proud a short two months back.'[138] It was a melancholy end to almost two centuries in the history of the British Army.

The 1st Battalion Somerset Light Infantry was the last to leave India, departing on 28 February 1948. In India and Pakistan, the reconstituted armies continued, 'a real and lasting testament to the professionalism of the force'.[139] Since the time of the Mutiny, the Union flag had flown continuously over the ruins of the Residency at Lucknow, where the British had withstood siege for eighty-seven days. It was the only place in the Empire where, legally, the flag flew night and day. On the eve of independence, Major General Alfred 'Tiger' Curtis lowered the flag, destroyed the flagpole and cemented over the gap. He outwitted nationalists who, he correctly guessed, would want to raise the flag of the independent India on the spot that had symbolised the power of the British Raj.[140]

The flag was sent to George VI; King, but no longer Emperor.

***

Describing how an iron curtain had fallen across Europe, in his speech in Fulton, Churchill also observed: 'The United States stands at this time at the pinnacle of world power.'[141] Britain had been worn out and cleaned out by war: the country was now reliant on massive financial bail-outs from Washington. Despite this, the Attlee government was reluctant to scuttle away from Britain's overseas obligations, which towards the end of its term in office would include military operations in Malaya and Korea. With a large part of the Army permanently based in Germany and a commitment to collective security through the Western Union, Britain was going to have a sizeable force stationed in peacetime Europe, a situation that was almost unprecedented. Similarly, compulsory military service was introduced, with 174,000 young men being called up in 1949. Money that could have been invested in a new Britain was instead spent on defence.

An inquiry into the future shape and size of Britain's Armed Forces reported in February 1949. It set out the two different approaches it could have taken:

> The first consists of calculating the shape and size of the Armed Forces needed adequately to support and implement a given policy and strategy and converting this into terms of money. The second consists of calculating, in relation to the various risks, the shape and size of the force which can be provided for a given sum of money and converting it, so far as it will go, into terms of policy and strategy.

It concluded: 'We have adopted the second approach because the fixed quantity in our terms of reference is money …'[142] Unconsidered was a third approach: retrenchment and retreat. In the aftermath of a victory for which she had sacrificed so much, Britain's Army and soldiers continued to fulfil the country's defence commitments. The choice between a defence policy determined by strategic ambition or by financial constraints would resonate down the decades to the present day.

TWO

STRATEGIC SHIFTS

Malaya, Korea, Suez and the Sandys Defence Review

On 11 June 1952, Captain Nigel Bagnall of 1st Battalion Green Howards led eleven men from the machine gun platoon into the heart of the Malayan jungle. With them was a Communist terrorist, Chin Nam Fook, who had surrendered to the British security forces a few hours earlier. He was guiding the soldiers to the heart of Tampin Forest Reserve, where he had been sent from a terrorist camp to collect food by the comrades he was now betraying. Chin, Bagnall and the platoon spent hours climbing a steep and treacherous track up more than 2,000 feet. Arriving some 600 yards from the camp, they had to lie low and wait. At 1800 hours, they moved within 200 yards of the camp and waited again. At 0115 hours, as rain fell to provide cover, the patrol edged forward and divided into two, encircling the camp. Visibility was reduced to almost nil as the rain became torrential and continued until 0415 hours. A sentry's torch could occasionally be seen and, at 0530 hours, a fire was lit in the camp cookhouse, enabling the men better to get their bearings. At 0605 hours, a sentry later identified as Chin Kong moved beyond the camp perimeter to take up his post. He was immediately shot by Bagnall, a signal that general fire should be opened. In the skirmish that followed, six other terrorists were killed. Although seven terrorists had survived the attack, two were wounded. They fled into the jungle empty-handed, their weapons captured. 'The Tampin District

unit as an effective fighting force was to all intents and purposes no more.'[1]

This operation provides an insight into the British Army in the early 1950s and a glimpse into its future at the end of the Cold War. Nigel Bagnall, who was to be awarded the Military Cross and Bar during this campaign in Malaya, went on to become a field marshal and one of the Army's most visionary commanders. The raid also epitomised the counter-insurgency tactics that were being adopted by the Army. Malaya would become the exemplar against which later military campaigns in Vietnam, Iraq and Afghanistan would be compared, contrasted and measured. Insurgency has been described as a 'hybrid form of conflict which combines political subversion with guerrilla warfare and terrorism in order to implement revolution or social change'.[2] The aftermath of the Second World War saw nationalist movements gather momentum in European colonies across Africa and Asia. In parallel, Communism was advancing – and in some cases, bound up with the struggles for independence. After 1945, the ideological battle between East and West was to be fought out across the world. One of the first battlegrounds was in the British colony of Malaya, in the 1,000-mile-long peninsula that stretches down from Thailand towards Indonesia and the Equator.

From the perspective of the post-Cold War twenty-first century, a leap of imagination is needed to remember that, in the post-Second World War era, Marxist-inspired global revolution was considered possible – if not probable. While the Soviet Union tightened its grip on eastern Europe, Mao's forces were advancing in China. In 1949, closer to home, cinemagoers in Britain could see newsreel footage of police breaking up a May Day rally in Trafalgar Square, where hammer and sickle banners were torn down. The confrontation was downplayed as 'a waste of a lovely spring day'.[3] More seriously, in July almost 13,000 soldiers were mobilised under the Emergency Powers Act 1920 to keep the docks working. London was hit by a strike that some members of the Attlee government believed was engineered by members of the Communist Party as part of an international campaign 'to disrupt the economy of the Marshall Plan countries'.[4] The proclamation of the People's Republic of China on 1 October 1949 confirmed the concerns of the British Chiefs-of-Staff, who feared that 'our position' in south-east Asia would become untenable: 'The strongest possible political and associated military measures must therefore be taken immediately to halt the spread of Communism.'[5]

This chapter looks at how British troops fought to contain the Communist threat in Malaya and Korea, two of the most significant campaigns since 1945. It then examines the misadventure in Suez, a campaign that started as a demonstration of British resolve and ended highlighting the country's diminished status. Finally, it explores how the 1957 Sandys Defence Review restructured the Army, a reflection of Britain's reduced place in the world.

Malaya

The decade-long counter-insurgency operation in Malaya was one of few victories over Communist forces during the Cold War. The Malayan Emergency, which began in 1948, was primarily an anti-colonial, pro-nationalist uprising, supported mainly by Communists from within the local minority Chinese population. The insurgency had its roots in the 1930s, with the foundation of the Malayan Communist Party. In 1942, the colony, which included Singapore, fell to the Japanese. The Chinese- and Communist-dominated Malayan People's Anti-Japanese Army (MPAJA) formed the backbone of the resistance movement against the enemy occupiers. Force 136, an arm of the British Special Operations Executive (SOE), worked with them against the Japanese in the latter part of the Second World War. The Force included the legendary explorer-adventurer and jungle warrior Freddie Spencer Chapman, whose acts of sabotage were so successful that the Japanese believed at times they were under attack from 200 commandos. The future Communist Party leader Chin Peng acted as a liaison officer between the MPAJA and the British: he was awarded a Burma Star and an OBE for his contribution to the war effort. As leader of the guerrilla insurgency, he would later declare: 'Colonial exploitation, irrespective of who were the masters, Japanese or British, was morally wrong.'[6]

After 1945, the Communists gained ground in Malaya, their standing enhanced by their anti-Japanese resistance. The local population of about 6 million people comprised 49 per cent Malays, 38 per cent Chinese, 11 per cent Indians and 1 per cent aboriginals. The Chinese community was made up of comparatively recent immigrants, many of them squatters, farming land on the edge of the jungle. With few rights to land, they were impoverished as well as disenfranchised, as the British authorities attempted to exclude them from a proposed new constitution. A contemporary novelist, Han Suyin, captures the plight of Chinese youth:

> They felt no hope of career or enterprise in the Southern lands which their fathers' toil had built. Deprived by the accident of their birth and their schooling from equal opportunity, they could not become lawyers, doctors, engineers, architects or anything but at best a business merchant and at worst at waiter in a coffee shop or a manual labourer.[7]

Strikes and rioting indicated the uneasiness within civilian society: in 1948 Chin Peng remobilised guerrilla forces, who launched raids and attacks against plantations and government officials. On 16 June 1948, three European planters were murdered in northern Perak, near the Thai border; the following day, the High Commissioner declared a State of Emergency.

The insurgents' goal was to overthrow British rule and establish a Communist state. The MPAJA was reincarnated, eventually becoming the MRLA – or Malaysian Races Liberation Army. Estimated to number between 5,000 and 7,000, the MRLA was a misnomer: the force was almost exclusively Chinese. The Malays themselves were described by one Royal Green Jacket subaltern as 'overwhelmingly traditional and monarchist and respected their rulers, the Sultans ... they were also devout Muslims'.[8] A Scots Guards officer believed that the insurgents had 'no sympathy for the Malay indigenous inhabitants or for the large Indian minority. Their aim was for a complete takeover of the state.'[9] Their principal target was Malaya's economy, recovering from its wartime downturn thanks to its two main exports – rubber and tin. Plantations and mines were attacked along with symbols of colonial rule such as police stations, while railways, roads and communications were sabotaged. The jungle that covered 80 per cent of the mountainous country provided a force multiplier for the insurgents: for many British soldiers it was nothing but a 'poxy green hell'.[10] The *belukar*, or secondary jungle, 'a tangle of bushes, saplings, thorny plants, tough creepers and sturdy bamboo', created a near-impenetrable barrier requiring heavy work with a *parang* (a short-bladed sword) to force through a path.[11] For many insurgents, the jungle became hide-out and home; numerous training camps were hidden within it. Paradoxically, it provided little in the way of food. Instead, a network of sympathisers, the *Min Yuen*, supplied food, finance and information. Found in villages, plantations and mines, their clandestine network crisscrossed the country from the jungle camps. Anyone suspected of collaborating with the security forces was brutally tortured and killed, along with their families.

Between 1948 and 1950, the insurgents had the upper hand. Indeed, one of the Emergency's leading authorities, General Sir Richard Clutterbuck, suggests that by the spring of 1950 the British were undoubtedly losing the war.[12] When the Emergency was declared, six Gurkha, three British and two Australian battalions were stationed in Singapore, 'a force totally insufficient to meet the threat'.[13] The resolve of the Europeans was tested, with many feeling they had been abandoned by the Colonial Office thousands of miles away in London. One planter's wife, who kept hand grenades within reach at home, said they were given so little help that 'it was a miracle we were not all killed in the first year [of the Emergency]'.[14] In the eyes of many, it was only the hasty recruitment of 24,000 Malays into a Special Constabulary that narrowly prevented the colony's collapse into anarchy. British military reinforcements would eventually arrive, among them contingents from the Brigade of Guards, the Royal Inniskilling Fusiliers and the King's African Rifles. By 1954, there were twenty-four battalions in Malaya, including soldiers from Australia and New Zealand. However, it took years for a winning tactical doctrine to evolve.

Britain's soldiers initially fought an unconventional war, using conventional methods. Intelligence was scant and there was no integration of the military and civilian efforts. In the hunt for Communist insurgents, battalion sweeps through the jungle and 'jungle-bashing' proved fruitless. General Sir John Harding, Commander-in-Chief, Far East Land Forces, noted: 'For lack of information, an enormous amount of military effort is being necessarily absorbed on prophylactic and will of the wisp patrolling and jungle bashing and on air bombardment.'[15] According to the future General Sir Walter Walker, 'The tactics that had been learned so painfully in Burma all but seemed to have been forgotten since 1945.'[16] Walker himself, then a lieutenant colonel, established the Far Eastern Land Force Training Centre in a disused lunatic asylum in Singapore and organised the so-called Ferret Force, 'designed for travelling light and living off the land'. He believed the skills required of the jungle fighter 'are not those of the elephant, but rather of the poacher, gangster and cat-burglar'.[17] Disbanded after the Second World War, the Special Air Service (SAS) reformed in 1950 to operate deep into the jungle. Although training improved, the terrorists retained the advantage.

For British soldiers, the danger of ambush in the jungle was ever present. Despite the 'jungle orchestra' of bullfrogs, birds, crickets and cicadas, men on patrol would be on the alert for the sound of the snap of a twig.[18] For one soldier in the Queen's Own Royal West Kent Regiment who was covered in 'bumps, bites and blisters', the jungle was full of 'monkeys sounding as if they've got whooping cough and very large insects making a noise like an ARP rattle'.[19] The main problem for every platoon commander was trying not to get his men lost, as Guards officer Bill Greer describes:

> Maps were rudimentary, any stream you came across usually should not be there according to the map or should be flowing in the opposite direction and there was hardly ever a point of reference visible through the thick wall of foliage. I confess that I was often lost.[20]

Torrential rain and the accompanying humidity added to the soldiers' discomfort, along with snakes, mosquitoes, ants, midges and leeches that could insert themselves through the lace eye of a boot, round the tongue and penetrate two layers of socks before 'pumping the blood out of your boots'.[21] Little wonder, as Subaltern Burton observed, 'The regiment devoutly wished they were back on the sunny slopes of Mount Kenya, dodging rhinoceroses.'[22]

Just like their terrorist opponents, the civilian and military authorities in Malaya were to learn the lessons familiar to Mao. Official military doctrine to deal with the Emergency was confined to *Imperial Policing and Duties in Aid to the Civil Power*, updated and reprinted in 1949. Its advocacy of minimum force was hardly a new departure: the Army had always instilled in soldiers the importance of restraint; it was 'an organizational norm'.[23] There was no official counter-insurgency doctrine: senior officers were gradually to evolve one. Seeing the problem through a Maoist-like prism led to the recognition that a military-dominated campaign would never defeat the guerrillas, who were, as Mao described, 'the fish that swim in the water of the people'. The realisation dawned among military commanders and politicians that a different approach was needed in Malaya. The two men who would instigate the change were Lieutenant General Sir Harold Briggs, who had seen action in both world wars, and General Sir Gerald Templer, a former Olympic hurdler who had previously run the military government in the British Zone in Germany.

Briggs arrived in Malaya as Director of Operations in April 1950. He was determined to destroy the guerrillas by gaining the support of the local population. This would be famously characterised by Templer as 'winning hearts and minds', a phrase which has become part of the common language of counter-insurgency. Briggs described how he saw the operation:

> The problem of clearing Communist banditry from Malaya was similar to that of eradicating malaria from a country. Flit guns and mosquito nets, in the form of military and police, though giving some local security if continuously maintained, effected no permanent cure. Such a permanent cure entails the closing of all breeding areas. In this case the breeding areas of the Communists were isolated squatter areas.[24]

The Briggs Plan reoriented the security effort, an approach that would be backed by the Colonial Secretary, Oliver Lyttleton, who believed that 'the Emergency is in essence a Police rather than a military task'. More significantly, and controversially, Briggs created the 'New Villages'. These 400 areas – that by the end of 1951 would be home to 400,000 people – were islands of security protected by barbed wire and patrols against any incursions by the Communists. While the villagers were given medical care, food, clean water and education, opportunities for their lending practical support to the insurgents were curtailed. Communist sympathisers used various dodges to try to smuggle food out of the villages, including hiding it beneath layers of foul-smelling durian fruit.

The enforced relocation of Malaya's Chinese population was the blueprint for similar measures subsequently introduced in Kenya and Borneo. Along with collective punishment, it is one of the most controversial aspects of all the counter-insurgency operations undertaken by the Army since 1945. *The Times* likened the New Villages to concentration camps. Greer noted:

> In most cases, these villages were newly constructed and surrounded by barbed wire, police posts and floodlit areas, the purpose of which was both to keep the inhabitants in and the guerrillas out. People resented this at first, but in time became more content with the better living standards in the villages and, in addition, they were given money and ownership of the land they lived on.[25]

Inside villages such as Kampong Coldstream, local people were protected from the 'threat of assassination, terrorism and extortion' under which they had been living, according to John Loch, a former District Officer who became one of four officers who made up Templer's Combined Emergency Planning Staff.[26] However, uprooting unwilling families from their homes at gunpoint is, from the twenty-first-century point of view, callous and unacceptable. Controversy continues to surround the circumstances in which twenty-five villagers died at Batang Kali on 12 December 1948, where soldiers from the Scots Guards were on patrol.

The assassination of the Governor General, Sir Harry Gurney, in October 1951 appeared to represent the nadir of the British counter-insurgency effort. The years 1951–2 were the most bitterly contested of the Emergency, while the war in Korea put additional pressure on the Army. Gurney's murder caused shockwaves throughout the Commonwealth and Empire. It can, however, also be seen as the beginning of the end of the Emergency: the new counter-insurgency approach represented by the Briggs Plan was about to be boosted – as Bagnall's platoon discovered.

Arriving in Malaya in February 1952, Gerald Templer embodied civil and military authority, combining in one person the civil role of High Commissioner with complete operational command over the Armed Forces. As significantly, he had insisted that his goal be defined. Consequently, it was announced that 'The Policy of Her Majesty's

Government in Great Britain is that Malaya should in due course become a fully self-governing nation.' This immediately undermined support for the Communists: a major justification for their taking up arms had been independence and, suddenly, the colonial government was becoming the instrument to achieve this. Within weeks of arriving, he demonstrated his approach by visiting Tanjong Malim, a town that had been subject to repeated Communist attacks, which had been facilitated by Communist sympathisers. A curfew was imposed, food was rationed and local people were invited to collaborate by writing down the names and details of likely Communist supporters. The townspeople cooperated, providing valuable intelligence. For Templer, stemming the insurgency was only one part of the process of bringing Malaya to independence. To avoid the violence that had accompanied the partition of India, he realised that better racial integration had to be encouraged. He began by attempting to address the racial imbalance within the security services, including the Home Guard in which the Chinese population was under-represented.

The Psywar Section (Psychological Warfare Section), a branch of the local intelligence service, was central to the effort of winning over the minds of the Malayan population. The Malayan Races Liberation Army was rebranded the Communist Terrorist Organisation. The policy of encouraging terrorists to defect was crucial: large rewards were given to these Surrendered Enemy Personnel (SEP). Local media, including Radio Malaya and Chinese language papers, as well as millions of leaflets dropped in the jungle, carried feel-good stories about how the SEPs had gone on to prosper: the accompanying 'after' photos always showed them looking better fed than 'before'. In addition, DC-3 planes flew over the jungle, broadcasting messages to surrender: by 1955 100 per cent of those who surrendered had heard such appeals.[27] Chin Nam Fook, who accompanied Bagnall's patrol, was an example of a SEP: many soldiers were surprised by their alacrity to betray their former comrades.

The Malayan Emergency was one of the first operations involving helicopters. For Royal Signals soldier John Green, a National Serviceman, the chance of a flight into the jungle lifted his gloom. A fan of Sibelius and Dvorak, he believed that 'Regulars resent National Servicemen being in the Army ... I shudder to think what it would be like without the NS men, they are the only ones capable of thinking.'[28]

However, one regular soldier who continued to give the Emergency some thought was Walter Walker, producing *The Conduct of Anti-Terrorist Operations in Malaya*. Known as ATOM, it collated and updated intelligence. According to Templer: 'It is largely as a result of the publication of this handbook, and of its subsequent revisions, that we got militant Communism in Malaya by the throat.'[29] As always, there was no substitute for boots on the ground – and plenty of them. From 1954, there were normally twenty-four infantry battalions in Malaya, including some from the Commonwealth, together with 40,000 police personnel.[30] Such numbers allowed jungle areas to be systematically cleared of the terrorists: starting in the western coastal state of Malacca in 1953, these designated 'White Areas' began to spread across the peninsula.

The Emergency was officially declared to be over on 31 July 1960, almost three years after Malaya became independent. For those involved in other counter-insurgency operations, it is a reminder that there are no quick fixes – strategic patience has a quality of its own. One analyst, John Nagl, argues that between 1952 and 1957 the Army 'demonstrated a remarkable openness to learning', something that benefited the operation, especially when compared with what some perceive as the more rigid mindset of the US military in Vietnam a decade or so later.[31] During the Emergency, more than 500 soldiers and 1,300 police were killed, together with more than 6,000 Communists and almost 2,500 civilians. More than 3,000 guerrillas surrendered. For Signalman John Green, although Malaya was not a full-scale war, 'it does get on your nerves'. Writing from Selangor, near Kuala Lumpur, in June 1953, he tried to count his blessings:

> I might have been unlucky in my National Service but by gum, we do think we're having a cushy time when we hear the Korean news. If I had gone in the Army a month earlier, I would quite likely have been sent out to the Fusiliers, so I try to realise I'm damn lucky to be where I am.[32]

Many soldiers serving in Korea would have agreed with him.

Korea
The Korean War was the first military action to be carried out under

the auspices of the United Nations. Established in October 1945, the UN had been set up to preserve peace through international cooperation and collective security. According to its Charter, the organisation would strive 'to save succeeding generations from the scourge of war, which twice in our lifetime has brought untold sorrow to mankind'.[33] This ideal has remained an aspiration rather than an achievement. Overseeing international security matters is the 15-member Security Council, the permanent membership of which – the USA, Russia, China, France and the UK – is looking increasingly anachronistic, some commentators believe, the further away we move from the 1940s. Divisions within the Security Council have occurred regularly since its inception, most recently over Iraq, with members accused of pursuing national self-interest rather than acting in the interests of collective security. However, while flawed, the UN is – uniquely – a global forum. Its first armed peacekeeping deployment was in Egypt after the Suez Crisis. Despite failures – most catastrophically the lack of political will to halt the genocide in Rwanda and a weak mandate in Bosnia – the organisation retains its moral authority.

In 1945 the end of the War in the Pacific also brought an end to the colonisation of Korea by Japan that had begun thirty-five years earlier. The Korean peninsula borders China, but – as significantly – lies close to Russia's far eastern territories. In 1945, the country had been divided along its 38th Parallel into two zones of occupation, overseen by the Soviet Union to the north and the United States to the south, while also coming under UN trusteeship with a view to its independence. The ousting of the Japanese created a political vacuum which, in the north, local Communists began to fill. Despite the UN objective of unification, the Korean nation was formally divided in 1948. To the south, the Republic of Korea was inaugurated in August, followed a month later by the establishment of the People's Democratic Republic of Korea. The antagonistic relationship between the two Koreas peaked on 25 June 1950, when the Kim Il Sung's People's Army of North Korea crossed the 38th Parallel, invading the South. The North Korean forces swept down through the peninsula, capturing the southern capital, Seoul, on 29 June. Their overwhelmed opponents had been forced to retreat towards the southern port of Pusan. Meanwhile, the UN Security Council had recommended that 'Members of the United Nations furnish such assistance to the

Republic of Korea as may be necessary to repel the armed attack and to restore international peace and security in the area'.[34] Although the recommendation only passed because the Soviet Union boycotted the Council and therefore did not exercise its veto, the era of upholding the precepts of international law as defined in the UN Charter had begun.

The invasion presented an immediate problem for the Attlee government, despite Britain having little if any national interest in South Korea. As Number 10 considered its options, the Cabinet Secretary, Norman Brook, observed that Korea was a rather distant obligation: the Prime Minister is said to have replied: 'Distant, yes, but none the less an obligation.'[35] Permanent membership of the Security Council brings with it military responsibilities, as many of Attlee's successors were to discover: it is therefore a national imperative that adequate military means must be retained to fulfil those responsibilities. Another major consideration for the government at the time was the relationship with the United States, into whose sphere of influence Korea came, not least because of its occupation of Japan. President Truman feared that, should South Korea fall to the Communists, the rest of Asia would fall too. 'They want to control all Asia from the Kremlin.'[36] The invasion coincided with, and exacerbated, America's fear of the 'red menace', whipped up to greatest effect by Senator Joe McCarthy. Prime Minister Attlee was equally alive to the threat of Communism, 'a militant and imperialist creed held with fanaticism by its adherents' which could 'enslave the whole world'.[37] In addition, there was the element of reciprocity: in exchange for supporting the US effort in Korea, Britain would help ensure the continuation of the US military commitment in Europe (see chapter 4). On 7 July, an additional UN Resolution recommended that all members 'make such forces and other assistance available to a unified command under the United States' and 'requests that the United States to be designated the commander of such forces'.[38] In Washington, US General Omar Bradley told Britain's Marshal of the Royal Air Force Sir Arthur Tedder: 'If, repeat if, a land force contribution however small could be added it would have excellent political effect in sealing even more firmly our complete unity on this issue.'[39] However, the Armed Forces chiefs had their reservations: Britain's forces were already overstretched. Tens of thousands of troops were still stationed in Germany, not least because of treaty obligations, including to the fledgling NATO (see chapter 4), the Emergency in Malaya was continuing and, with the triumph of Mao in China, there were worries about the vulnerability of Hong Kong to Communist takeover. However, senior commanders overcame their misgivings. On 24 July, the Chief of the Imperial General Staff, General Sir William Slim, told the Cabinet Defence Committee that the chiefs believed that 'although in their view it was still militarily unsound, they recognized the strong political arguments … it would be wrong to send less than a Brigade Group.'[40] The following day, the Cabinet endorsed the Defence Committee's decision: a land force would be sent to Korea.

The British intervention in Korea was hard to justify to the public. Given that it was re-elected in February 1950 with a majority of just five, the Attlee government's existence was precarious. Rationing continued and taxes were high; another sterling crisis the previous September had prompted devaluation of the pound against the dollar by 30 per cent. Wartime drabness continued to hang around the country like the smog that often blanketed London. In a radio broadcast to the nation, the Prime Minister tacitly acknowledged public scepticism about British involvement in yet another conflict. He warned: 'The fire that has been started in distant Korea may burn down your house.'[41] The intervention put further pressure on the Armed Forces, whose combined strength had fallen to 696,000.[42] Part of the manpower problem was due to the shortfall of regular soldiers either enlisting, or wanting to continue to serve, in the Army, not least at a time of full employment in the civilian world. In September 1950, Attlee announced that the length of National Service would be extended from eighteen months to two years, which would increase Army numbers by 55,000.[43] He told the House of Commons: 'This programme will entail sacrifices from the people of Britain.' Yet more sacrifices were demanded in February 1951 when spending on an existing rearmament programme was boosted to £4.7 billion. It would cause a Cabinet split and the resignation of, among others, Aneurin Bevan. Armed Forces numbers leapt up, rising to 872,000 in 1952, with the Army's strength jumping from 364,000 to 454,000.[44]

British forces in Korea would come under the overall command of the legendary American General Douglas MacArthur. Since Japan's surrender, he had been the country's military governor. Described as the 'American Caesar', he was judged to be the commander who won the war in the Pacific and was a hero in the eyes of the public. In a characteristically flamboyant recce, he flew to Korea, telling the press on touch-down: 'To give up any portion of South Korea to the aggression of the Chinese Communists would be the greatest defeat of the free world in recent times.'[45] MacArthur decided that his forces would not land as expected at Pusan, on the south-eastern tip of the peninsula, but would approach from the west, making an amphibious landing behind enemy lines at Inchon, some twenty-five miles north of Seoul.

Among the land forces in Korea were the men of the British 27th Infantry Brigade, who began to arrive in Pusan from Hong Kong on 29 August 1950. They initially comprised a brigade headquarters and two battalions: 1st Battalion Argyll and Sutherland Highlanders and 1st Battalion Middlesex Regiment. They would be supplemented by forces from New Zealand and Australia, becoming known as the 27th British Commonwealth Brigade, later renamed as the 28th Commonwealth Brigade. Canada also sent troops, notably three battalions in succession from the Princess Patricia's Light Infantry. The Canadian contingent eventually grew to become the 25th Canadian Infantry Brigade. The 29th Infantry Brigade, arriving a few months later, included soldiers from 1st Battalion Gloucestershire Regiment (Glosters), 1st Battalion Royal Northumberland Fusiliers and 1st Battalion Royal Ulster Rifles (RUR). In July 1951 these brigades were grouped together as the 1st Commonwealth Division. In the ranks of the British units were large numbers of recalled reservists, many of whom felt they had already done their bit in the Second World War: their resentment is noted in many contemporary accounts of the conflict. Second Lieutenant Denys Whatmore observed that 'many had families and were very angry at having to leave them'.[46] A National Serviceman commissioned into the Royal Hampshire Regiment on 1 April 1950 aged nineteen, Whatmore found himself sewing the Glosters badge on to the front and back of his beret. Like many, the regiment was undermanned, leading to men being transferred into it, which could well have undermined the basis of cohesion. Whatmore was struck by the ad hoc nature of the 29th Infantry Brigade – 'a motley collection from numerous regiments' – which included many other National Servicemen. In an effort to recruit more regulars, in early 1950 their pay was increased to double that of a National Serviceman.[47] The differential was a source of irritation in the ranks, as was that between the British troops and their American and Commonwealth allies: on leave in 'dollar-inflated Tokyo, the British soldier found his pay did not go very far'.[48]

US marines landed at Inchon on 15 September 1950, beginning the fight-back for control of the Korean peninsula. They rapidly retook Seoul and fanned out across the country. As the fighting continued, Royal Ulster Rifleman Robert Maguire landed in Pusan and was transferred closer to the capital in the wake of the Communist retreat. He describes a 'wild and mountainous country ... with knife-edge winds from Siberia'. Few soldiers appeared impressed by Korea, which froze in winter and baked in summer. The Land of the Morning Sun had little to offer but mountains, paddy fields and poverty. Hundreds of thousands of refugees were on the move, fleeing the opposing forces. On a train that arrived at a station in Pusan, Private David Green of the Glosters was immediately surrounded by gangs of children who were living in derelict carriages: 'Like alley cats dressed in oversized military gear, many had the wizened faces of old men ... they were looking for anything they could scrounge or steal.'[49]

Overnight, the mission escalated. Just as the South was coming under the control of UN forces, on 7 October, the US 1st Cavalry Division breached the 38th Parallel and crossed into the North. In the weeks that followed, UN forces penetrated deeper into North Korea, each mile bringing them closer to the Yalu river and the Chinese border. Although the UN offensive initially went well, with the North Korean capital Pyong Yang falling on 19 October, six weeks later the Communists counter-attacked – aided by massive reinforcements from the Chinese People's Liberation Army. Instead of confronting North Korean soldiers, who had only the tepid backing of the Soviet Union, UN troops were under attack by the seemingly limitless manpower of China. Many blamed MacArthur, who apparently acted unilaterally without Washington's authorisation. Truman sacked him a few months later.

The provocation of China was far from welcome in London, highlighting the problems of being a junior partner in a multinational operation. Marshal of the Royal Air Force Sir John Slessor described the British role in Korea as 'to tag along behind the United

States with no previous consultation over policy and sometimes no advance notice of actions or decisions'.[50] A Foreign Office paper concurred, complaining that 'British ministers and officials were continually being faced with *faits accomplis* and expected to fall in'.[51] Following a press conference by Truman in late November, during which the President failed to rule out the use of the atomic bomb, Attlee rushed to Washington for clarification.[52] Of the twenty-one UN nations committing resources to the Korean War, sixteen fielded fighting units. In the summer of 1951, UN ground forces numbered almost 550,000, which included 248,320 Americans: excluding Korea – which was not a UN member – other nations fielded almost 33,000 personnel, of which the British contribution was about 12,000.[53] Any junior ally inevitably has less influence than the main actor over strategy and tactics: Britain had more leverage than the rest, but not enough to make much difference. For British commanders after 1945, the issues arising from being the subordinate military partner in a combat operation led by the US were first experienced in Korea. Much had changed since Montgomery's overall command of the Allied land forces in Normandy just seven years before.

With the UN forces in retreat and being pushed southwards, back towards the 38th Parallel, on 5 December Pyong Yang was retaken by the Communists. British soldiers next suffered the onslaught of the Korean winter. According to Rifleman Maguire, when the winter kit was belatedly issued, 'It was not rain or snow proof so when it got wet it was rather miserable and froze as solid as a board.'[54] Bewilderingly for his company, as they headed north, they met other UN troops, including Turks, heading south. They heard that US forces were suffering heavy losses during 'the longest retreat in American military history'.[55] Back south of the 38th Parallel, Denys Whatmore was delighted to find the NAAFI operating out of three goods trucks in a railway siding at Chochiwon.[56] It irked soldiers that higher prices for items such as soap were charged by the NAAFI in Korea than in Germany. With Hong Kong-based soldiers serving in Korea no longer entitled to the Local Overseas Allowance paid to them in Hong Kong, they actually received a pay cut. However, according to a list placed in the House of Commons Library, the Allowance was for items including white dinner-jackets, cummerbunds and golf club fees, so perhaps it was unsurprising that it was withdrawn.[57]

The ebb and flow of advance and retreat up and down the Korean peninsula saw Seoul being captured four times in a year. In 1951, the Communist forces launched a spring offensive, attempting to break through the UN line, known as Kansas, which was then about twelve miles north of the 38th Parallel. The 27th Commonwealth Brigade initially bore the brunt of the attack, holding off soldiers from the Chinese 118th division. On 22 April, to the west, in brilliant moonlight, the Communists opened a second front. Chinese forces began to attack the 29th Brigade which had taken up scattered positions in the hills around the shallow Imjin river. Commanded by Brigadier Tom Brodie, this comparatively small contingent, which included a Belgian battalion, was dispersed across a 9-mile sector of the frontline, each battalion unable to help the other. The Glosters were amassed on Hill 235 to the west; the Fusiliers to the east. To the rear were the 8th Hussars and the guns of 45 Field Regiment, Royal Artillery. Expecting to move on quickly, the British had not laid sufficient defensive mines or wires, which might have impeded the overwhelming numbers of enemy troops. Isolated and outnumbered, encircled, with the threat of being overrun, the brigade would battle for three days and three nights. Receiving little back-up and no air support, running short of ammunition, particularly grenades, many soldiers thought they had been forgotten and abandoned, surely reinforced when their wireless batteries died. Denys Whatmore observed that the enemy's tactics 'were to advance in human waves, apparently regardless of casualties, relying on sheer weight of numbers and hand-held infantry weapons to carry the day'. His company fought to 'the last round of ammunition' before retreating.[58] As the British forces withdrew, some managed to scramble on to the Hussars' Centurion tanks and ride to safety, but hundreds were taken prisoner, including the future official historian of the conflict and NATO commander, Captain Anthony Farrar-Hockley.

The Battle of Imjin River is perhaps the most legendary in the history of the British Army in the second half of the twentieth century. Goose Green in the Falklands runs it close. An American Presidential Citation, awarded to the Glosters and C Troop, Light Mortar Division Royal Artillery, states:

> Completely surrounded by tremendous numbers, these indomit-
> able, resolute and tenacious soldiers fought back with unsurpassed

fortitude and courage. As ammunition ran low and the advancing hordes moved closer and closer, these splendid soldiers fought back to prevent the enemy from overrunning the position and moving rapidly to the south. Their heroic stand provided the critically needed time to regroup other 1 Corps units and block the southern advance of the enemy. Without thought of defeat or surrender this heroic force demonstrated superb battlefield courage and discipline. Every yard of ground they surrendered was covered with enemy dead …[59]

Capturing something of the stakes involved, the Citation however overlooks the role of soldiers from other regiments in the 3,000-strong 29th Brigade, who faced down an enemy force ten times their number. Was the brigade forgotten because there was no senior British officer at Corps HQ to fight their corner and make their case to the Americans? Historian Max Hastings raises the possibility of miscommunication between the British and US militaries: 'When Tom told Corps that his position was "a bit sticky", they simply did not grasp that in British Army parlance, that meant "critical".'[60] The order to retreat came too late for seven young National Servicemen, part of a contingent of reinforcements for the Fusiliers, who found themselves in the thick of the battle hours after leaving a transit camp in Japan.[61] The British suffered 1,091 casualties – killed, wounded or captured – 622 from the Glosters.[62] More than 1,000 soldiers were taken prisoner. Overall, Korea took a heavy toll. In early January 1951, for example, the 1st Battalion Royal Ulster Rifles were caught up in action at Chaegunghyon, also known as Happy Valley. That day, 157 RUR men were captured or killed, the Hussars and the Royal Artillery lost more than forty.

The actions of the 29th Brigade at Imjin helped thwart the enemy advance on Seoul. Weeks later, the Russians and the Chinese were mooting peace talks, which finally got underway in the military no-man's-land of Panmunjom in July. By then, stalemate had been reached. Both sides regrouped, dug in and reinforced their positions. By the end of the year, the peninsula was divided by defensive lines that ran east to west for 155 miles. In a period of stalemate and holed up in their trenches and bunkers, suffering trench foot and plagued by rats, some soldiers might have had an insight into what their grandfathers had endured on the Western Front four decades earlier. Sporadic action punctuated the stalemate. In the Battle of United Hill on 4 November 1951, Private Bill Speakman of the Black Watch but attached to 1st Battalion King's Own Scottish Borderers won a most notable Victoria Cross leading numerous grenade charges against the enemy, eventually, it is alleged, throwing beer bottles when his supply of grenades ran out. His VC investiture was the first carried out by the new monarch, Queen Elizabeth II, shortly after she acceded to the throne in February 1952.

The Battle of the Hook between October 1952 and May 1953 was the last major offensive in which British forces were engaged in Korea. It involved five separate engagements. Among those taking part were 1st Battalion Black Watch and 1st Battalion Duke of Wellington's Regiment, comprising 80 per cent National Servicemen.[63] The extension of National Service to two years, along with the decision not to recall any further regular reservists, ensured that conscripts played a very full part in the campaign: by the autumn of 1952, 156 had been killed and 602 wounded.[64] As the war dragged on, it became first increasingly unpopular at home and then almost forgotten by the public. MPs urged the government to encourage the press to give it more coverage, 'otherwise there is a danger our Servicemen in Korea may become forgotten men'.[65] Like the new Churchill government, elected on 26 October 1951 with a majority of 17, the British public was more focused on a hangover from the Second World War: food rationing. With a shortage brought about in part because of continuing economic turbulence, one of its first measures was to cut the meat ration. Rationing would not end until July 1954. The war in far away Korea seemed to be on the government back burner.

For the Army, the opposite was true. More than 1,000 British servicemen were held as prisoners of war by the Communists. Many soldiers had not survived the march north, so those who reached the camps were comparatively lucky, despite the appalling conditions and subsistence diet. Their families had to write to them care of the Chinese People's Committee of Defenders of World Peace in Peking. The Communists tried to indoctrinate them, which must have at least relieved the boredom that many felt in their camps on the Yalu river on the Chinese border as the peace talks dragged on. Private John

Shaw took advantage of dance lessons, learning the quick step, along with French and how to play chess.[66] Corporal David Kaye had graduated from cribbage to rummy then whist, 'and now it's bridge night and day', with him becoming known as Grand Slam Kaye. Occasional copies of the *Daily Worker* kept him in touch with England. On 6 April 1952 he wrote: 'I was sorry to hear about the death of the King. I suppose that we are all soldiers of the Queen now.'[67] These soldiers finally began to be released following the signing of an armistice on 27 July 1953: a formal peace treaty has yet to be signed more than six decades later, to conclude a war in which 100,000 British personnel served and 1,139 died.[68] Veterans of the Korean War, many of them former National Servicemen, still recall with great pride their service on the far side of the world under the flag of the United Nations but in the uniform of the British Army.

Suez

The May 1955 General Election boosted the Conservative majority to 60. Prime Minister Anthony Eden had his own mandate, having taken over from the ailing Churchill in April. The retirement of Britain's greatest prime minister underlined that the Second World War was increasingly the stuff of memory. The threat of a possible Third World War, with the deployment of the hydrogen bomb, was, however, real (see chapter 4). The election manifestos of both the main parties had prioritised security, defence and foreign affairs. Labour warned of possible apocalypse: 'We are faced with the choice of world cooperation or world annihilation.'[69] Eden declared the age to be one of 'peril and promise'. He underlined the Conservatives' stewardship of the economy: national bankruptcy, threatened in 1951, had been staved off.[70] Both parties emphasised the Empire's transformation into the Commonwealth, which comprised a quarter of the world's people, as the Tories reminded voters: consequently, 'For us isolation is impossible.' For the colonies, the path to independence was inevitable, but not immediate. Both sides were concerned about the protection of 'minority rights' – presumably of the colonists, rather than the colonised. The Empire and now the Commonwealth were seen as bulwarks against Communism, to which less developed nations standing on their own were feared to be potential prey. The tone in both manifestos was less about Britain ruling the world than about being in partnership with it: the Tory manifesto likened Commonwealth meetings to family councils.

In the decade after 1945, Britain's status had declined. The Great Power that had rested on immense wealth before 1939 was having to adjust. The new world order was recognised by Britain's Ambassador to the UN, Sir Pierson Dixon, in 1950: 'It is difficult for us, after several centuries of leading others, to resign ourselves to the position of allowing another and greater power to lead us.'[71] However, politicians were slow to catch up, reluctant to admit to any change in Britain's circumstances – certainly not in the 1955 manifestos. The evolution from Empire was portrayed as positive: India, Burma, Pakistan and Ceylon had not been 'lost', rather they were finding their own way.

Any diminution in Britain's standing was not reflected, however, in the size of her Armed Forces. In 1955, overall strength stood at just over 800,000, although the government aimed to cut this by 20 per cent. National Service would continue despite its drawbacks. Defence Secretary Selwyn Lloyd stated: 'The Service ministers and I would do without conscription tomorrow if we could get the necessary number of Regulars.'[72] Almost half the Army's 423,000 soldiers were conscripts. In the more technical corps the proportion was higher: for example, they made up two-thirds of radio specialists in the Royal Signals Corps. Originally intended to create a pool of trained reservists, peacetime conscription had become vital to the manning of ongoing commitments. The Armed Forces were trapped in a vicious circle. Conscripts required training, which required manpower; the demands on manpower could only be fulfilled by conscription … However, there was a growing realisation among policymakers that nuclear weapons must entail a change of strategic thinking and, with it, a change in the structure of the Armed Forces. (See the Sandys Review, below.)

The reality of the post-1945 world order was confronted in Egypt in a military operation that lasted only a matter of days. In 1956, any remaining British aspirations to global leadership vanished as the country was humbled in the desert along the banks of the Suez Canal: somewhat aptly, Britain's Great Power status turned out to be something of a mirage. Suez was an avoidable crisis of Britain's own making – with more than a little help from France and Israel. It provided a fillip to Arab nationalism across the Middle East and, in bolstering the prestige of Egypt's leader, Gamal Abdel Nasser, gave the movement an inspirational figurehead. Having been denounced by the West as a 'Muslim Mussolini' and likened to Hitler, Nasser's reputation subsequently soared, while Eden's plummeted. In punishing Britain by threatening another sterling crisis, the United States demonstrated to the world the realities of global power. Some British soldiers taking part in the short-lived operation considered Washington had stabbed them in the back; others had doubted the wisdom of the intervention long before they sailed into Port Said.[73] The operation's codename, Musketeer, proved a misnomer: dash and elan – the hallmarks of a musketeer – were elusive. British troops were reduced to bystanders, marking time amid the 'smell, filth and flies of Port Said', watching the arrival of an UN Emergency Force.[74]

The Suez Canal is a 100-mile stretch of water cutting through Egypt and linking the Mediterranean with the Red Sea. Completed in 1869, it was called 'our highway to India' by the future King Edward VII.[75] A vital strategic artery for the Empire, it was run by a company that was eventually owned by the French and British governments. It became an ever-more vital shipping route, bringing an ever-more vital commodity – oil – from the Middle East to Europe. Not quite a colony, from the 1880s Egypt was, however, a protectorate under informal British control. After the Second World War, the Canal Zone became the headquarters of Middle East Land Forces, where some 80,000 troops and airmen were stationed at various bases. For Egypt's nationalists, the bases and the canal itself symbolised foreign rule. Attacks on soldiers around the Canal Zone became more frequent. In November 1951, service families were evacuated from Ismailia. The following year, a military coup overthrew Egypt's King Farouk. A leading player in the uprising, the charismatic Colonel Nasser became Egypt's president two years later. Inspiring followers across the Middle East with his Arab nationalism, he was also a fierce opponent of neighbouring Israel. In July 1954, shortly after he came to power, Britain bowed to the inevitable and agreed that her forces would be withdrawn from Egypt within two years.

On 26 July 1956, Nasser seized control of the Suez Canal for Egypt. Troops occupied the headquarters offices of the Suez Canal Company, which was then declared to be nationalised. Celebrated in Egypt – which would now benefit from the canal's tolls – the nationalisation was inevitably condemned by Britain. Reliant upon ship-borne imports of food and oil, the country's security appeared to be threatened. One MP told the House of Commons that nationalisation was 'an injury to our honour and our interests'.[76] Two-thirds of oil imports came via the waterway and British tonnage accounted for 28 per cent of the traffic through the canal. As Eden said, 'the industrial life of Western Europe literally depends upon the continuing free navigation of the Canal'.[77] Britain and France were prepared to retake the canal by force. Successful military action would lead to the downfall of the demagogic Nasser, seen in London and Paris as a force for instability across the Arab world. With the potential loss of Indo-China following the routing of French forces at Dien Bien Phu in May 1954, Paris was less than happy about Egypt's support for the nationalist movement in her colony of Algeria. Also entangled in the existing mesh of international relationships in the Middle East were Israel and the United States.

What unfolded in the months after the canal's nationalisation was, from Britain's point of view, a military success but a political disaster. On 2 August, Eden told the Commons that leaving the canal in the 'unfettered control of a single power' was unacceptable and that 'precautionary measures of a military nature' were being taken.[78] The Armed Forces' presence in the eastern Mediterranean was boosted, while members of the Army Emergency Reserve with certain specialist skills would be called up. Among the 20,000 reservists was Royal Engineer Lieutenant Pat McKeown, who returned to the military port of Marchwood on the Solent where he had trained five years earlier during National Service in port operation, construction and maintenance.[79] He joined 84 Port Regiment RE (AER). On 17 August in Dover, members of the mechanical transport (MT) platoon of 1st Battalion The Queen's Own West Kents were put on standby to move overseas. Although they received no official word, the men realised from newspapers and BBC broadcasts that some form of action against Egypt was probable. In cinemas, newsreel images of warships added to the sense of national crisis.[80] As they loaded up and set sail for Malta, they left behind a Britain which would be divided about the legality and legitimacy of military action.

The delay between drawing up military plans in mid-August 1956 and their execution in early November undermined Operation Musketeer's success. The legal case for going to war in Egypt was flimsy to the point of non-existence – shades of the doubt about the case for war in Iraq in 2003. For all the bluster against Nasser in the British press and House of Commons, the nationalisation of a company operating an international waterway was hardly a *casus belli*. In an attempt to stymie Nasser, ex-patriot Suez Canal Company pilots were ordered not to work: frustratingly for London, it transpired that their Egyptian replacements were more than up to the job. The satisfactory management of the nationalised canal – which one enterprising MP tested for himself by going north to south and back again[81] – weakened the imperative for military action. In addition, as the weeks, then months, passed, Egypt's control of the canal became entrenched and pragmatically accepted by many in the international community, who sought a diplomatic rather than a military solution to the deadlock between Cairo, London and Paris. From Washington, President Eisenhower told Eden in early September that 'American public opinion flatly rejects the thought of using force'.[82] While delay allowed for greater military readiness for an invasion, it also allowed national and international opinion to rally against it.

The repeated revisions to the operational plan and London's prevarication were manifest to soldiers in Britain and across the Mediterranean. The Chief of the Imperial General Staff, now Sir Gerald Templer, warned Eden's Egypt Committee that to retake the Canal Zone was one thing, a military occupation of Egypt after ousting Nasser another: 'Under no conditions would we agree to go to Cairo and/or Alexandria and get mixed up in complicated street fighting.'[83] Alexandria was initially chosen for the landing, but was replaced by Port Said, not least to minimise civilian casualties. 'D Day' was repeatedly delayed. The changes were apparent to those in 84 Regiment RE working and training at the military port at Marchwood: 'Owing to indecision by Eden's government, equipment was loaded, unloaded and reloaded, several times in some cases.'[84] As the weeks passed, thousands of soldiers were becoming restless as they were kept hanging about in Malta or Cyprus, where they were confined to base because of local terrorists (see chapter 3). The MT platoon of the 1st Royal West Kents on board HMS *Suvla*, in which Centurion tanks were also embarked, were similarly at a loose end. According to their commanding officer Lieutenant Colonel P.C.M. Buckle, 'the feeling was growing that we would soon become a modern *Flying Dutchman*, forever to sail the seas.'[85] To add to the pressure on the government and senior commanders, by October the 'military preparations in connection with the Suez Canal dispute' were costing the Treasury an extra £1 million a week.[86]

Operation Musketeer was mired in international collusion and conspiracy. Just as in connection with Iraq, almost half a century later, a pretext was needed to lend legitimacy to any military action which, it was anticipated, would ultimately lead to Nasser's overthrow. One was cooked up in late October 1956 at a secret meeting of British, French and Israeli diplomats at Sèvres, outside Paris. It was agreed that Israel would attack Egypt, providing the justification for an Anglo-French military intervention. A week later, on 29 October, fighting did indeed break out between Egyptian and Israeli forces, who had crossed the Sinai border into Egypt. The following day, Britain and France issued an ultimatum demanding a ceasefire and the full Cabinet authorised military action by British forces to guarantee the transit of shipping through the canal and to 'separate the belligerents'. On 31 October, the RAF and the French Air Force began bombing Egyptian airfields, while British troops finally set sail from Malta. While Eden skated over the question of possible collusion between London, Paris and Jerusalem, some of those involved in the negotiations were subsequently to be less reticent. Eden ordered his copy of the Sèvres Protocol to be destroyed, the French copies were lost, but an Israeli copy was released in 1996 on the orders of Prime Minister Shimon Peres, who forty years earlier had been one of the diplomats involved.[87] The chicanery underlines Eden's dangerous lack of judgement. Highly strung and prone to micromanagement, calling his Foreign Secretary Selwyn Lloyd thirty times over one weekend during Christmas, Eden was also in poor health as a result of a botched operation two years earlier. It is suggested that a possible addiction to Benzedrine was not much help.[88]

Musketeer was a joint operation, one of the UK's few post-1945 amphibious operations and its only battalion-size airborne assault. With military bases in Libya and Jordan out of bounds for political reasons and those in Cyprus and Malta too distant from Suez,

Musketeer was reliant on the Royal Navy's aircraft carriers, such as HMS *Eagle*, and carrier aviation. More than a hundred ships, including five aircraft carriers and eighteen troop and tank landing vessels, made up the task force sailing to Egypt.[89] For the first time, the Royal Navy had round-the-clock capability with its radar-equipped Sea Venom fighter bombers. The land order of battle involved 16th Parachute Brigade, Royal Marine Commandos and units of 3rd Infantry Division. Shortly after midnight on 5 November, members of 3rd Battalion Parachute Regiment were dropped over the desert and landed outside Port Said. Separately, French paratroopers touched down a few miles away. Despite the Seahawk and French Corsair aircraft patrolling the skies, the men would be on their own for twenty-four hours and at considerable risk in hostile territory.[90] Men of the 600-strong British force attacked the airfield at El Gamil and bridges on the outskirts of the city, as well as clearing various strongholds and emplacements. Meanwhile, allied aircraft, including the Wyverns of HMS *Eagle's* 830 squadron, bombed Egyptian positions on land, including airfields and the heavily fortified seafront. Thinking 5 November to be an apt date, Pat McKeown and his advance team of fifty Royal Engineers from 84 Port Regiment RE, aboard HM Troopship *Empire Ken*, saw smoke rising from the land in and around Alexandria.

At dawn on 6 November, the main assault force began to land. British warships launched support fire and an RAF attack strafed beaches west of the canal. Just after 0615 hours, men from 42 Commando reached the shore followed by the tanks of the 6th Royal Tank Regiment and 40 Commando. A reserve of 45 Commando, along with seven tons of stores, were then landed. It was the first battlefield deployment of helicopters. G. W. Stuchbery, a Royal Army Medical Corps (RAMC) clerk attached to the 15th Field Ambulance, reached Port Said while the fighting was still going on, finding 'a lot of naval boats, TLC [Tank Landing Craft] going to and fro, smoke and sporadic firing from the land'. The Casino Palace Hotel, 'the best billet in Port Said', was turned into a makeshift hospital. During the day there was some street fighting, with snipers attacking British positions: by nightfall, organised resistance in the port had ceased. Under the command of Brigadier M. A. H. Butler, paratroopers and a Royal Tank Regiment contingent headed south to capture Ismailia, advancing until 00.15 when they reached El Cap, twenty-four miles from the port.[91] By then, a UN-ordered ceasefire had begun. Soldiers were left bewildered and wondered what was going on. The operation looked as fruitless as anything done by the Grand Old Duke of York: they had gone a quarter of the way down the canal and it looked like they would be coming back again.

Britain was defeated in Egypt not by force of arms but by public opinion, the legal and moral force of the United Nations and the financial might of the United States. Britain might have been able to veto the UN's Security Council, but it could not silence its General Assembly. It passed seven resolutions in ten days at the beginning of November, first demanding an immediate ceasefire, then the withdrawal of all foreign troops from Egypt, and finally to establish an international force to supervise the cessation of hostilities.[92] By flouting the UN Charter, which provided a legal framework governing the use of force, Britain would be undermining the global institution she had helped to create. In addition, Commonwealth nations voiced their opposition to the military intervention. At home, the nation was split. The British government's action was unsustainable, even if the United States had not intervened. With the crisis causing a run on reserves of sterling, national bankruptcy loomed and Britain needed a loan from Washington or the International Monetary Fund. Chancellor Harold Macmillan was told that no loan would be forthcoming without an immediate ceasefire in Egypt. Eden capitulated. A quarter of a century later, former Prime Minister Harold Macmillan would advise Prime Minister Thatcher to exclude the Chancellor from the cabinet committee overseeing the Falklands campaign.[93]

Suez saw an Anglo-French military operation halted by Britain's financial weakness. It gave both countries a lesson in the realities of global power. The abrupt cancellation of another US loan – to Egypt to build a huge dam on the Nile at Aswan – had been the immediate catalyst for the nationalisation of the canal. It would eventually be financed by the Soviet Union, which in 1955 had begun selling arms to Cairo via Czechoslovakia. Nasser's skill at exploiting Cold War rivalries reflected his understanding of the changed world order. Britain had assumed that the United States would be acquiescent in her freelance military action. It was, however, a presidential election year and the Suez Crisis stirred up American suspicions of imperialism.

In 1953, Britain's overthrow of Prime Minister Mohammad Mossadegh in Iran in a *coup d'état* had ultimately boosted American oil interests at British expense. It should have served as a warning that the dynamics in the Middle East were changing.

After the ceasefire, British soldiers waited to be shipped home and tried to make sense of the operation. Some worked at clearing the canal they had been sent so far to protect: it was effectively closed by sunken block ships, following Nasser's orders to scuttle all vessels in the waterway. On 11 November soldiers from the Royal West Kents would relieve the paratroopers at El Cap. They would sit it out in the small desert town, watching crows set off their defensive perimeter trip flares, until they were ordered back to Port Said ten days later. The sappers from 84 Regiment RE, among them Pat McKeown, set out to clear the debris around the quays of Port Said: 400 of them shared a villa. RAMC clerk Stuchbery and his comrades found that their tropical kit had been stolen from their kit bags on the voyage out; they busied themselves with vaccinating 800 refugees. The human cost of the conflict was apparent in a series of mass graves in the parks and open spaces of Port Said. The Red Crescent dug up an estimated 1,000 bodies and re-buried them in Muslim burial grounds. The UN Emergency Force, which included units from India and Denmark, would arrive in Egypt on 15 November. It was the United Nations' first major peacekeeping armed deployment. Its arrival signalled that British soldiers' time in Port Said was coming to an end. McKeown observes: 'It was demoralizing to realise, as many of us had suspected from the outset, that we were not going to succeed in regaining control of the Suez Canal, and that, in effect, as a nation we had been defeated.' Despite his 'deep misgivings' about the intervention, a view which he estimates fewer than four in ten of his fellow officers shared, 'When I was called back to military service I felt, on balance, that having signed up five years previously to the Royal Army Reserve of Officers (RARO) it was my duty to go.'[94]

After Suez, the next time British public opinion would be so divided would be over Iraq almost fifty years later. As future Defence Secretary Denis Healey observed, Port Said fell to British and French troops on the same day as Budapest fell to the Red Army. He speculated that, had the Western powers not been so divided by Suez, perhaps they could have influenced the Soviets not to invade.[95] Eden resigned from office in January 1957, his cooked-up justification for military intervention having jeopardised Britain's relationship with the United States. As importantly, British interests in the Middle East were damaged by committing 'the one unforgiveable sin, combining with Israel to attack another country'.[96]

Most British forces were home by Christmas 1956. It was an anti-climactic end to months of crisis and preparation. An Eden loyalist, Templer referred to the 'Suez debacle' and, in a private paper, castigated the Cabinet for its lack of support for the Prime Minister and alluded to 'great political interference in military plans'.[97] Due to the oil shortage, Stuchbery's troopship travelled at no more than '10 m.p.h.', with its drinking water rationed, allegedly because the nationalist-leaning Prime Minister of Malta, Dom Mintoff – perhaps emboldened by Nasser's triumph – refused to let the ship be resupplied there.[98] It would arrive home where, because of the crisis, petrol was not only back on ration but subject to higher taxes, known as the 'Suez sixpence'.[99] As he left Port Said, Stuchbery saw one of the last British attempts to keep the flag flying in the Middle East: 'On the quay was a very large flagstaff, the Royal Navy lads had put a Union flag at the top with no ropes attached to it, and greased the pole to make it hard for the Egyptians to remove the flag.' Suez was the last time Britain would launch a major military operation which did not have the support of the United States. If the changing of the World Guard had not occurred before, it did so at Suez.

The Sandys Defence Review

Just as the intervention in Iraq stirred debate long after Operation Telic was over, Suez engendered recrimination and division after the troops came home. Writing to Churchill, Montgomery observed that in all his military experience he had never known anything more bungled. 'Under such conditions the captain of the ship does not go sea-bathing [a reference to Eden's Jamaican holiday immediately after the crisis], he dies on the bridge.'[100] On 10 January 1957, Harold Macmillan became prime minister. Suez had exposed the inadequacies of Britain's defence strategy, capabilities and force structure – all needed urgent review. Military historian Michael Howard noted: 'Few episodes in our history have done so much to shake the faith of our friends and the respect of our enemies as did the delay, the uncertainty and the ambiguity of that operation.' The humiliating reverses during Crimea and the Boer War campaigns had led to 'ruthless enquiry and radical reform'. He concluded: 'So one hopes it will be with Suez.'[101]

The Suez debacle called into question whether the amount of money being spent on defence was the best use of Britain's resources. In February 1957, an opposition debate called on the government to 'prepare forthwith a revised defence plan'.[102] Labour demanded a substantial cut in expenditure and an end to National Service. MP after MP complained that ever since the introduction of the £4.7 billion rearmament programme engendered by Korea at the start of the decade, money had been poured into the defence budget – to little effect. Like all NATO members, Britain had been generous to the sector: in 1955 it had received £1.57 billion, which accounted for almost 10 per cent of government spending.[103] While British industry had undoubtedly picked up after the Second World War, it was suffering relative decline, not least because of the continued focus on defence, which employed 7 per cent of the British workforce and accounted for two-thirds of all national Research and Development.[104] Labour's defence spokesman George Brown MP demanded that the government close Britain's military bases abroad and introduce a highly mobile strategic reserve based in Britain and Germany. In his view, there was little point in service personnel being scattered around the world unable to be mobilised: 'We have 18,000 in Cyprus, 10,000 in Libya, 11,000 in Hong Kong – groups here and there which would, as we have seen from Suez, have no part in any operation which we would be trying with our Armed Forces.'[105] The Conservative MP Brigadier Sir John Smyth VC observed that Cyprus had proven to be lacking: 'We could not use it as a military base because it had no deep-water port. We could not use it as an air base because we had not the transport aircraft to carry weapons heavy enough to cope with tanks.'[106] The failure to prevail against Egypt's 'third rate soldiers' particularly rankled.

Suez highlighted the issues with which many in the defence establishment had long been grappling but had yet to resolve. The development of the hydrogen bomb by the Soviet Union in 1953 had forced a change of direction in strategic thinking in Whitehall (see chapter 4). A 1956 Policy Review paper stated that the bomb had 'transformed the military situation', making conventional war with China or Russia unlikely. The biggest impact in the long term would be upon the numeric size of the individual services: 'Conventional forces, though still of great importance in some situations, have become a relatively less important factor in world affairs.'[107]

Britain's Armed Forces remained interwoven in the fabric of everyday life thanks to National Service. At the time of the Review their combined strength was 704,000, of which the Army's was 367,000: in 1956 National Servicemen had accounted for 52 per cent of other ranks, while 24 per cent were regulars signed up for only three years.[108] Under the terms of the National Service Act, the call-up was due to end in 1958 and was unlikely to continue in its current form. It was becoming ever more unpopular among voters, with 44 per cent wanting its abolition: attitudes had changed 'from qualified support to qualified opposition'.[109] Both major parties sidestepped the conscription issue in the 1955 General Election, but Templer ordered his deputy, Sir Richard Hull, to investigate the implications of returning to an all-regular Army. Hull's Committee reported in October 1956. The time had come 'to cast off the heavy burden of National Service, which both exhausts the permanent cadre of the Army and acts as a deterrent to voluntary long-term engagements'.[110] It called for a smaller force equipped with modern weapons.

The entire Army was in need of updating. The standard of accommodation was generally poor. Wood-burning stoves, identical in design to those being used during the Boer War, were still being ordered for barracks. For some reason, there was a surplus of 90,000 chairs. Troopships rather than aircraft were used as transport, with weeks set aside for voyages. The revelation that the Army was trying to get through ten years' worth of the cleaning compound Blanco, bought in 1951, underscored to many an organisation too wedded to 'bull'.[111] In the civilian world in 1955, young people suddenly became teenagers and Teddy Boys, rocking around the clock with Bill Haley. The same year ITV was launched, soon to present a less-than-flattering picture of service life in the hugely popular sitcom *The Army Game*.[112] In one episode, with the CO away, the depot is left in the charge of Sergeant-Major Bullimore until the arrival of a hapless officer, the twittish Lieutenant ffinch. The men – including actor Charles Hawtrey, complete with his knitting – are shambolic skivers, loafing about in their Nissen hut and bunking off pointless duties. Questions were raised in Parliament when the CO of a depot in Pontefract banned the programme being watched by men of the King's Own Yorkshire Light Infantry on their metered barrack room TV sets. One MP said the ban summed up many soldiers' view about the boneheadedness of the Army: 'Too many bosses, too much "bull", and too much interference in the private time of men, all of which militates against further recruitment.'[113] Slapstick rather than satire, the series was an irreverent dig at an institution known to millions thanks to the Second World War and National Service. Familiarity was breeding mockery.

The Sandys Review is seen as a turning point in the history of British defence policy. In January 1957 Churchill's son-in-law, the abrasive Duncan Sandys, became Defence Minister. He was the fifth minister to fill the post in less than thirty months, so it is unsurprising that a much-needed review of defence and security strategy had previously failed to materialise. One predecessor, Sir Walter Monckton, a lawyer who had negotiated the abdication settlement of King Edward VIII, abandoned his appointment at the ministry in the middle of the Suez Crisis: his resignation letter to Eden recognised that 'we have to start, and start now, a new chapter of urgent, anxious and burdensome work in the defence field'.[114] Tough and uncompromising, Sandys was the man for the job, but, as one commentator said, his name is not remembered with any warmth in the officers' messes of the three services.[115]

The Sandys Review overturned previous strategic thinking and boosted ministerial authority over the Armed Forces. It also began a process that over the ensuing decades reduced the power of the single services in favour of central command and control. Sandys was convinced that a major block to change was the power of the individual services, all fighting their own corners and reluctant to compromise. Sandys' immediate predecessor – who was in the job for barely three months – decided it was impossible to achieve inter-service agreement on any meaningful change. Having been a defence minister, as well as Chancellor, Prime Minister Macmillan knew what Sandys would be up against. A prime ministerial directive spelt out 'that the Minister of Defence would have authority to make decisions on all matters of policy influencing the shape, organization, size and deployment of the Armed Forces'.[116] Matters such as pay would also come within his purview. Any approach by the chiefs or a service minister to the Cabinet would in future be made through him. Sandys was behind the directive: in his unpublished biography he claimed he received Macmillan's assurances that 'the Minister must have effective overall control of the Services'.[117] For one military historian, the directive gave Sandys 'almost dictatorial powers over the three Services'.[118]

The Prime Minister's directive coincided with the appointment of new individual service ministers in the Admiralty, War Office and the Air Ministry: their comparative lack of experience made them easier to manipulate. It was a fairly low but effective tactic. Senior commanders had misgivings about Sandys: a former First Sea Lord declared him 'the worst enemy of the Navy', while the chairman of the Chiefs of Staff Committee, Marshal of the Royal Air Force Sir William Dickson, was told by Sandys in no uncertain terms that the Cabinet Defence Committee was for Cabinet members – not for service chiefs, who attended in an advisory capacity by invitation only.[119] The Army would be the service most radically affected by the Defence Review: the antipathy for Sandys felt by its chief, Templer, was 'pathological', according to Mountbatten.[120] They allegedly came to blows as they were wrangling over the White Paper. Although the Review went through thirteen different drafts, negotiation and compromise were all too often replaced by ministerial diktat.

Sandys' White Paper *Defence: Outline of Future Policy* was driven by two factors: the development of the megaton bomb and money. The two were linked throughout. Even for a minister as determined as Sandys, admitting that defence policy was based purely on financial rather than strategic considerations was unwise: MPs on both sides of the House, as well as voters outside it, would be alarmed by any hint that the government could be jeopardising the nation's security for economic reasons, especially following the invasion of Hungary by the Soviet Union in October 1956. However, change was needed: 'It is now evident that, on both military and economic grounds, it is necessary to make a fresh appreciation of defence policy and to adopt a new approach towards it.'[121]

The H-bomb was a strategic game-changer: wars must now be

prevented rather than waged. The White Paper sought to 'reflect the impact on strategic thought of the rapid progress in scientific and technological development' that had occurred since the atomic bombing of Hiroshima.[122] Consequently, 'It must be frankly recognized that there is at present no means of providing adequate protection for the whole country from the consequences of an attack by nuclear weapons.'[123] Two years earlier, the Strath Committee had concluded that one 10-megaton bomb could destroy any British city apart from London: ten such bombs would kill half the population and lead to the collapse of civil society.[124] Deterring any such attack was therefore imperative: deterrence would be achieved by threatening retaliation in kind, what would become known as Mutually Assured Destruction (MAD). From now on, 'The overriding consideration in all military planning must be to prevent war rather than to prepare for it.'[125] Acceptance of this principle would have a huge impact on the conventional capabilities for all three services.

This seismic shift in British strategic thinking meant that Britain's Armed Forces had to change. Above all, far fewer service personnel were needed, with numbers projected to halve, down to roughly 375,000 by the end of 1962. It was now 'reasonable to contemplate putting the Armed Forces on an all-Regular footing'.[126] This rather low-key signal was the first indication that National Service would come to an end, confirmed by the statement that the government would 'avoid any further call up under the National Service Acts after the end of 1960'.[127] As the service employing the majority of National Servicemen, the impact upon the Army would be profound. It would be cut to 165,000 men. To attract volunteer regulars, service life had to be made more attractive, offering better accommodation, recreational facilities and food. Many roles – including storekeeping, accounting, policing and catering – would be civilianised. Garrisons would generally be reduced. The British Army of the Rhine cut from 77,000 to 64,000, 'with further reductions thereafter'; however, 'atomic rocket artillery will be introduced which will greatly augment their firepower' (see chapter 4).[128] The majority of the reserves would still continue to be trained and equipped principally for Home Defence.

Defence: Outline of Future Policy was 'the biggest change in policy ever made in normal times'. For one analyst it was 'the key defence document of British Cold War history'.[129] It was, however, less a revolutionary and more of an evolutionary document, a collation of the trends and thinking connected to the defence sector over the previous decade. There had been scores of other reviews, reappraisals and policy papers, including the service chiefs' groundbreaking 1952 *Report on Defence Policy and Global Strategy* (see chapter 4). In general, however, British budgets, manpower levels and capabilities had remained pretty static. Suez had highlighted how Britain's forces, plagued by "ponderousness", needed to improve their speed of reaction, which demanded more helicopters, transport aircraft and assault shipping.[130] How far Sandys was able to push through his changes because of the demoralisation wrought by Suez is unquantifiable; one junior minister said that 'the stench of defeat in the defence departments really was appalling'.[131]

With its focus on nuclear forces and the NATO–Warsaw Pact standoff, the 1957 Defence Review rather overlooked counter-insurgency campaigns such as Malaya – the sort of small wars that soldiers of Britain's all-regular Army of the 1960s would soon find themselves fighting. Theory, based on nuclear preoccupation, took policy in one direction, while events on the ground, driven by the end of Empire, took practice in another. The British soldier, caught between theory and practice, just got on with the job, learning at Suez that even a well-executed campaign and military success can ultimately be rendered pointless by flawed politics. But politics and military action are irrevocably bound up one with the other. When the military theorist Carl von Clausewitz wrote words to the effect that 'war is but a continuation of politics by other means', he was describing the continuum that is the relationship between politics and military action. Matters of conflict begin with discussion in the political realm which, when incapable of peaceful resolution, invariably turn to a period of focused military action before returning once more to politics, the situation having been changed by force of arms. At Suez the political foundations were unsound and the military operations lost their purpose. In the aftermath, the Sandys Defence Review significantly changed the military instrument that politicians might have at their disposal in the future.

THREE

EMERGENCIES AND INSURGENCIES: FIGHTING SMALL COLONIAL WARS

Kenya, Cyprus, Borneo and Aden

While the divisions of Europe, Germany and Berlin all symbolised the Cold War, Britain's soldiers found themselves further afield, intervening in the emergencies and insurgencies that broke out in the post-1945 era in the country's ever-dwindling number of colonies and protectorates. Demands for independence and self-government could spark violent unrest, which called for a military response to restore law and order, as chapter 2 described in connection with Malaya. Writing in 1962, military analyst Basil Liddell Hart described insurgency as 'the only kind of war that fits the conditions of the modern age'. In identifying social discontent, racial ferment and nationalist fervour as possible triggers for revolt, he underlined that politics was at its root.[1] Consequently, although an insurgency initially demanded military action when security had broken down, resolving the social or political problems that were at its root were in the hands of civilians. Crucial, however, to the ultimate objective of peace and social stability was the British Army's approach to restoring security, summarised as 'winning hearts and minds'. The phrase first came to public attention in connection with Malaya, when General Templer declared that the answer to defeating the insurgency 'lies not in pouring more troops into the jungle, but in the hearts and minds of the people'. Different militaries in similar campaigns have adopted different tactics: the French in Algeria opted for martial law, while the Americans in Vietnam chose overwhelming military force, destroying villages in order to save them.

The British counter-insurgencies fought after 1945 have been reassessed in the twenty-first century. The campaigns in Iraq and Afghanistan have partly driven this, as the experiences of today's soldiers have been compared and contrasted with those of their predecessors. Previously, Vietnam was assessed in the context of Malaya, just as operations in Basra have been compared with Belfast.[2] Soldiers could have looked back to the Army's role in the late Victorian era, when it did little but fight irregular wars across Africa and Asia. This chapter examines four campaigns fought by British soldiers in the 1950s and 1960s – in Kenya, Borneo, Cyprus and Aden. Each was unique. The conditions in each theatre were very different: the jungle-fighting in Borneo involving British Special Forces required different tactics from operating among civilians in the cities of Cyprus. As General Sir George Erskine, Commander-in-Chief Kenya, noted, 'the Army is a versatile machine'.[3] It was also perhaps a forgetful one. Intelligence-gathering, cooperation between the various security services, as well as between the military and civilian authorities, characterise all four campaigns. None of these happened overnight. General Sir Walter Walker, who complained that much of what the Army had learned in Burma had been forgotten in Malaya, said later that lessons from Malaya were lost by soldiers in Borneo.[4]

'Winning hearts and minds' is a deceptively benign description of being at war. Military historian Hew Strachan observes that it denotes authority not appeasement.[5] When states of emergency were declared by colonial governments, some law was superseded, giving the authorities far greater leeway over matters such as detention without trial. Soldiers were deployed to regain and to reinforce government control. Their role was also to protect the civilian population from the insurgents who were terrorising them. Although the British Army's less coercive approach prioritised minimum force, armed soldiers were still setting up roadblocks in Cyprus or mounting cordon and search operations in Nairobi. Equally, those same soldiers were getting ambushed, kidnapped, shot and bombed. Coercion is perhaps simply a matter of which end of a gun barrel someone is looking at. Small wars are still wars. The campaigns have been the subject of reappraisal and controversy, with allegations of human rights abuses and torture. This will also be examined.

Kenya

In February 1952, Princess Elizabeth and her husband the Duke of Edinburgh arrived in Kenya. Although news of the death of King George VI and the Queen's accession overshadowed all other reports of the trip, newsreel footage of the first part of the tour gives no hint of any unrest. Instead, Union flag-waving crowds in their tens of thousands are shown lining the streets of Nairobi waiting for a glimpse of the royal couple in their open-topped car. Their plane had landed at the capital's Eastleigh air base, where an RAF guard of honour and leopardskin-wearing local chiefs and tribesmen greeted them. At a garden party and a reception at Government House, they met members of the local Kenya Regiment, described as 'a fine territorial organisation'.[6] Looking at the footage, no one would guess that all was far from well in the British colony or that later that year, on 21 October, Governor Sir Evelyn Baring would declare a State of Emergency, which would last until 1960. In January 1953, more than 2,000 white settlers tried to storm Government House; in May 1954, Treetops, the lodge where the Princess first learned she had become Queen, was burned down by local insurgents, the Mau Mau.

The origin of the term Mau Mau remains opaque. The Governor's Personal Staff Officer, Colonel G. A. Rimbault, puzzling over what it meant, settled on an anagram of *uma*, meaning 'get out'.[7] In Nairobi, a plaque at a memorial statue unveiled in 2015 translates Mau Mau as the Kenya Land and Freedom Army. While some Mau Mau came from the Embu and Meru tribes, most belonged to Kenya's dominant Kikuyu tribe, which in 1950 made up almost a quarter of the colony's population of 5 million people. Among them was the future President, Jomo Kenyatta. Since the 1920s he had called for land reform and African representation on the colony's Legislative Council, which was also denied to local Asians. Denounced as a Communist by his opponents, Kenyatta emerged as the chief spokesman for Kenya's disenfranchised and dispossessed. In 1947 he became leader of the pan-ethnic Kenya African Union (KAU). Although there were no formal links, the colonial authorities would regard the organisation as not only sympathetic to, but a political front for, the

Mau Mau. Nairobi became a centre for political dissent and resistance to colonial rule. In May 1950, the East African Trades Union Congress had successfully organised a general strike, which led to running battles on the capital's streets. The city was also thronged by menacing gangs, the organisational cadre of the Mau Mau.

Land hunger lay at the heart of Kenya's troubles. European settlers' appropriation of millions of the most fertile acres around the Central Highlands north of Nairobi was an open wound. The area included Happy Valley, a name that would come to mock the settlers during the Emergency. The Kikuyu's reserves comprised about 2,000 square miles of land, while Europeans – who numbered fewer than 30,000 in 1952 – enjoyed 12,000 square miles of the settled areas.[8] More than 250,000 Kikuyu lived as squatters in the Central Highlands in the late 1940s.[9] The estimated 75,000 Kenyans who had served in the British military during the Second World War felt particularly aggrieved at being kept on the economic margins.[10] Colonel Rimbault was dismissive: 'It is NOT true, however, that this land problem is the result of any land having been taken away by the White Man as Mau Mau propaganda would have the world believe.'[11] The analysis represented a certain amount of denial among the Europeans, who not only enjoyed the fruits of the land but also cheap local labour. Novelist Graham Greene described the Mau Mau uprising in terms reminiscent of a murderous *Admirable Crichton*: 'When the revolt came, it was to the English colonist like a revolt of the domestic staff … It was as though Jeeves had taken to the jungle.'[12] An additional factor was the division between the Kikuyu themselves: local chiefs and headmen were often government loyalists. One analyst observes: 'Mau Mau was a violent challenge by the "have-nots" to the privileged position of their kinsmen, as well as to that of the European settlers.'[13]

The tensions within Kenya gradually escalated, exposing the fragility of government control. A struggle for land rights could well tip into civil war. The colony was divided into districts and then divisions administered by Colonial Office district commissioners and officers, as well as local chiefs. Support for the Mau Mau was generated by clandestine rituals of mass oath-taking which was accompanied by various rites, often involving animal sacrifice. Not only was allegiance sworn during these ceremonies, but money was donated. In a superstitious society, where witch doctors were revered, the power of vowing to keep an oath on penalty of death should not be underestimated. By the end of 1949, oathing was widespread. One official stated: 'The Chiefs were forever reporting the discovering of chopped-up bodies, burnt-out huts, missing persons, slaughtered animals and other depravities.'[14] The oathing ritual became by degrees more extreme. Alluding to 'matters of a bestial nature', most official reports omitted the details: they were, however, made available under separate cover to readers of the Army's *The Kenya Picture*, a booklet issued by GHQ East Africa.[15] Those participating in taboo practices were putting themselves outside tribal society and binding themselves more strongly to the Mau Mau. As Greene wrote, Jeeves had not only taken to the jungle; he had sworn, however unwillingly, to kill Bertie Wooster 'or this oath will kill me and all my seed will die'.[16] Colonial officials in Fort Hill, who had spied on an oathing ceremony involving 900 people, described how loyalty to the government was non-existent in large areas of the district. Although the Mau Mau were banned in 1950, attacks on livestock and property continued, along with reprisals against those who refused to take the oath, among them many Christians. A colony-wide insurrection was feared. The Declaration of Emergency was prompted by 'mounting lawlessness, violence and disorder', according to the Governor. 'This state of affairs has developed as a result of the activities of the Mau Mau movement.'

At the start of the Emergency, it was estimated there were some 25,000 Mau Mau. Opposing them were territorial soldiers from the Kenya Regiment and men from the three battalions of the King's African Rifles (KAR), stationed in the colony. They would be reinforced by 4th Battalion KAR from Uganda and initially by troops from 1st Battalion Lancashire Fusiliers who arrived from the Canal Zone and later by men from, among others, 1st Battalion East Kent Regiment ('the Buffs'), and 1st Battalion Devonshire Regiment. From the civilian side were the Home Guard, the Tribal Police, the Kenya Police and the Kenya Police Reserve, into which Europeans and Asians were enrolled. As the Emergency was declared, Operation Jock Scott was launched in Nairobi: Kenyatta was among 100 local political leaders arrested and detained because of their suspected links to the Mau Mau. A gifted orator, his speeches could tip towards incitement. The day after he exhorted Kikuyu in Fort Hill district to 'Go out and water the tree of freedom with blood', the local admin-istrator described how 'the machete-hacked bodies of seven persons known not to be his followers were brought into district headquar-ters'.[17] In January 1953, administering a Mau Mau oath was made a capital offence.

Despite the surge in military numbers, security continued to deteriorate. The attack on Commander Meiklejohn and his wife in their farmhouse at Thomson's Falls in November 1952 was followed by the murder of the Ruck family just north of Nairobi in January 1953, which led to the demonstration outside Government House by Europeans denouncing the authorities' ineffectiveness; when Gover-nor Baring refused to meet them, they tried to storm the building. On the night of 26 March 1953, 120 Kikuyu who had refused to take the Mau Mau oath were massacred at Lari, where their assailants set fire to their huts and hacked them to death as they tried to escape. The same night, one company of Mau Mau attacked the police station at Naivasha, making off with rifles, sub-machine guns and ammunition from the Kenya Police Reserve armoury, while another released 137 remanded prisoners. A few days later, Colonial Secretary Oliver Lyt-tleton told the House of Commons that there was no doubt the situa-tion in Kenya 'is more like a war than an Emergency'.[18] In the middle of May, one MP referred to 'the life and death struggle in Kenya'.[19]

As thousands of British soldiers battled against Communist insurgents for control of Malaya, concurrently thousands of others were at war with the Mau Mau in Kenya. Among them was 26-year-old Captain Frank Kitson of the Rifle Brigade, who would become a global expert on counter-insurgency. He was initially sent to Kiambu, north of Nairobi, as a District Military Intelligence Officer, working alongside a handful of civilians from the Kenya Police Reserve and a Special Branch officer. His orders were vague but he worked out his objective for himself: 'To provide the security forces with the information they need to destroy Mau Mau in Kiambu and Thika Districts.'[20] Tireless, relentless, somewhat eccentric and clearly rel-ishing the pursuit of the Mau Mau gangs marauding across the dis-trict, Kitson soon had a team of 100 working for him as he built up a successful intelligence network almost from scratch.[21] Later, he set up counter-gangs. Dressing like a Mau Mau gang member and blackening his face, he would join a team hunting down the enemy in the dense forests of the Aberdares and on the slopes of Mount Kenya. As in Malaya, the British military effort was in concert with the civilian authorities: joint security committees were set up at provincial, district and divisional level to arrange matters such as population screening. Similarly, the local forces were bolstered by recruiting more Kikuyu Home Guards and establishing more guard posts, small fort-like compounds surrounded by barbed wire with moats of bamboo spikes.

The campaigns in Kenya and Malaya were similar but not identical. In June 1953, General Sir George Erskine arrived as Commander-in-Chief in Kenya. Given control over the police and auxiliaries, he had wider powers than his predecessor, although his authority fell far short of that of Templer in Malaya, who represented both military and civilian command. The division of responsibility was accepted by the General, who stated on arrival in Nairobi that 'It shouldn't take too long, in my opinion, to get the Mau Mau under control in a police and military sense.' He added, 'But of course there is much more to it than that and digging out the roots will be a much longer job. As I read it, my job is to do the former and not the latter.'[22] One of Erskine's first actions was to discourage any focus on the kill rate, as it 'tends to make the matter a cup tie and introduces an element of competition, useful in some ways but dangerous in others'.[23] Over the next few months, cordon and search operations, including Operations Buttercup, Carnation, Primrose and Bluebell, were launched in the native reserves around Fort Hall and Nyeri. In the Kandara district, Sergeant Idi Amin from the Uganda battalion of the KAR shot a Mau Mau trying to evade capture.[24] In the summer, RAF Harvards and Lincolns started bombing forests, which were designated Prohibited Areas where trespassers would be shot on sight. Royal Engineers bulldozed tracks through them: a two-day march could now be done in an hour or two by vehicle.

Separating the population from the insurgents was crucial to winning the campaign. Rural areas and the tribal reserves remained in the grip of the Mau Mau. Willing supporters or the coerced – both 'passive Mau Mau', according to Kitson – were a prime source of food, money, intelligence and ammunition for insurgents, just as the Min Yuen in Malaya supported the Communist terrorists. According to Rimbault: 'The individual Kikuyu still fears the Mau Mau far more than he does the British.'[25] District Officer W. H. Thompson describes how 'the hours of darkness were the cloak of terror'.[26] Although there were comparatively few attacks on Europeans, they were photographed dressed for dinner in their remote farmsteads with silver candelabra and guns on their dining tables. Their situation was similar to that of the settlers on the rubber plantations in Malaya. Erskine, who disliked Kenya's red dust and getting sunburnt, was as scathing about the 'white Mau Mau', who wanted the Army 'to kill all Kikuyu except for my personal servants', as he was about Baring – 'terribly wobbly and it is an uphill job keeping him up to the bit'.[27] In a process known as the Pipeline, routine screening and detention of the Kikuyu population was carried out in 100 detention camps across the colony to ascertain the strength of sympathy towards the Mau Mau.

The back of the insurgency was broken in 1954, thanks to tactics reminiscent of those in Malaya. The previous September, a surrender policy had been introduced, with rewards for those Mau Mau who turned themselves in. A programme of 'villagisation' was established in the Kikuyu tribal areas in an attempt to separate the population from the insurgents. Within a year, more than 1 million people had been relocated to 804 villages.[28] While they kept villagers safe from the Mau Mau, with their barbed wire, searchlights, watchtowers and guards, for some the villages resembled prisons in which Kikuyu women and children were held captive. Nairobi was seen by the authorities as a Mau Mau recruitment centre, bank and ammunition store. In April 1954, the fortnight-long Operation Anvil was launched, involving some 25,000 members of the security forces, including 4,000 troops. The city was cordoned and searched, with some 24,000 people detained for screening. After Anvil, the Mau Mau went to ground in the forest, including their most-wanted leaders, Dedan Kimathi and General China. Gradually large military search operations were wound down in favour of Kitson's pseudo- or counter-gangs, small patrols and tracker teams.[29] In 1955, Iain Ferguson, a junior officer in the Scots Guards, spent five weeks patrolling the slopes of Mount Kenya. The Mau Mau were so attuned to the forest that the British soldiers were told the smell of their shaving cream would be detected. Cooking had to be done with minimal smoke.

Although the patrol covered a lot of ground, and 'we were wet an awful lot of the time', no Mau Mau were to be seen.[30]

In late 1956, after a four-year war, the majority of Army units withdrew from Kenya, which became independent in 1963. The insurgency was a time of terror. The Mau Mau murdered thirty-two white settlers, but thousands of black Africans, whose plight has been too often overlooked. Although ultimately successful, the counter-insurgency campaign remains the focus of controversy and contention. At the time, there was concern about the number of detainees being held without trial: in July 1954, the government admitted that 40,000 people were being detained in various camps under Emergency Regulations and that 531 had been hanged.[31] After a lengthy legal battle, in 2013 the British government agreed to pay almost £20 million to more than 5,000 victims who had 'suffered torture and ill treatment at the hands of the Colonial administration' during the Emergency.[32] As a gesture of reconciliation, Britain funded the 2015 Nairobi statue in memory of the victims, some of whom suffered castration and rape.

One of the most notorious incidents of abuse occurred at the Hola detention camp in 1959, when eleven inmates were beaten to death by guards. These guards were employed by the colonial administration and were not serving members of the British Army. Nevertheless, on 23 June 1953, Erskine issued a warning to all officers of the army, police and security forces that 'breaches of discipline leading to unfair treatment of anybody' would not be tolerated. Frank Kitson details how they were frequently confronted by the same legal and moral difficulties as those fighting terrorist groups in the early twenty-first century: the limits of their authority to detain known terrorists or terrorist sympathisers.[33] Should they 'stand by and watch a known enemy plan some diabolical scheme and wait calmly for him to do something illegal before moving in to arrest him'? Kitson suggests that this ethical dilemma was often impossible to convey to local members of the security forces, who had a very different concept of justice and whose families were being terrorised.[34] In a statement to the High Court in connection with the 2013 compensation claim, historian Huw Bennett stated that 'without doubt the British Army was intimately involved with every aspect of the Colonial administration's policies and practices in the knowledge that detainee abuse and torture was endemic'.[35] Similarly, historian Caroline Elkins observed that following the establishment of East Africa command in May 1953, General Erskine would have 'operational control of all Colonial, Auxiliary, Police and Security Forces'.[36] With the forces in Kenya falling under Army control, some of the blame has to be shared. Separately, Bennett observed that a very large proportion of British soldiers conducted themselves honourably and that 'repeated efforts were made by GHQ to instil and maintain a disciplined fighting force'.[37] The responsible investigation of claims of wrong-doing, even many years after the events in question, remains the right course of action to follow but, in the case of some security force actions in Kenya, it has left an unwelcome footnote.

After independence in 1963, the British Army gradually established a new relationship with Kenya and the developing Kenyan Army. British infantry battalions and Royal Engineer squadrons have deployed annually to Kenya on extended exercises, carrying out both their own training and undertaking infrastructure projects, often in conjunction with the Kenyan Army. The base for these exercises has been the Nanyuki showground close to Mount Kenya – a base which has become very familiar to thousands of British soldiers. In the most intense period of the Afghanistan deployment, between 2006 and 2014, up to seven British battle groups per year conducted some of their pre-deployment training from the Nanyuki base. Mock-up villages were created and many local Kenyans were employed to populate these villages to replicate conditions in Afghanistan. If winning hearts and minds was important during the Mau Mau conflict, then continuing to win the hearts and minds of the local people around Nanyuki in recent years was just as important in order to retain consent for the British Army's vital pre-deployment training requirements. Generous wages and rental contracts were part of the equation, but so too was friendly relations between British soldiers and local civilians.

Cyprus

Bomb attacks on government buildings and security installations in Nicosia, Larnaca and Limassol on 1 April 1955 signalled the start of another insurgency, this time in the British colony of Cyprus. They were the work of EOKA (Ethniki Organosis Kyprion Agonistes, or the National Organisation of Cypriot Fighters), which sought not just independence but union (*Enosis*) with Greece. The relatively small island – 140 miles by 60 miles – had a population of about 500,000, 80 per cent of whom were Greek-Cypriot, the remainder mainly Turkish. The majority therefore looked to Athens rather than Ankara, despite Cyprus being about forty miles from the coast of Turkey and 400 miles from the mainland of Greece. Two Greek-Cypriots were central to the struggle for *Enosis*: the revered ethnarch Archbishop Makarios III, the political as well as spiritual leader of the island, where the local Orthodox Church was all-powerful, and George Grivas, a former colonel in the Greek Army. Apart from two brief periods of ceasefire, which allowed EOKA to regroup, for almost four years Cyprus suffered a reign of terror. Assassinations, bombings, sabotage and grenade attacks were all directed by Grivas, who used the *nom de guerre* Dighenis.

The British Army's campaign in Cyprus was hampered by the same obstacle it had failed to overcome in Palestine a few years earlier: a lack of cooperation from the local population. In January 1950, the Church had organised a plebiscite on *Enosis*: out of the 225,000 eligible voters, 95.7 per cent were in favour.[38] Given such a conclusive result in an era of imperial retreat, it is surprising that, far from beginning the process towards independence, four years later the Minister of State for Colonial Affairs ruled out any change. He added: 'There are certain territories in the Commonwealth, which owing to their particular circumstances, can never expect to be fully independent.'[39] He was speaking the same day that the government announced a military withdrawal from Egypt's Canal Zone, following years of anti-British unrest and the rise of Nasser. Cyprus's eastern Mediterranean location was therefore ever more vital to the defence interests of Britain, which viewed the colony as a garrison, command post and static aircraft carrier, allowing the RAF to be in range of allies such as Jordan. Its importance was strengthened, first by the transfer of the Middle East HQ from Egypt in late 1954, and then in 1955 by signing of the Baghdad Pact, a defensive alliance between Britain, Turkey, Iran, Iraq and Pakistan, that can be likened to a Middle Eastern NATO. The British government would continue to make the defence case for the status quo, despite the insurgency. In 1958, one official explained to Duncan Sandys that there had never been any question of the continuing strategic importance of Cyprus in the minds of the Chief of Staff, the Ministry of Defence and the Defence Committee. If Cyprus were lost, 'We should lose all military means of assisting to counter Soviet penetration of the Northern Middle East area and of using our influence to preserve stability in this area in which we have such important interests.'[40] Significantly, London rarely put its policy of retaining the colonial link with Cyprus in the context of defending the interests of the island's minority Turkish community.

The British military presence in Cyprus exacerbated the insurgency that soldiers would try to counter in a four-year campaign. On the day that a junior minister revealed there could be no change to the colony's sovereignty, Foreign Secretary Anthony Eden explained that British forces would be leaving Egypt because 'our defence arrangements must be based on consent and cooperation with the peoples concerned'.[41] The Army's problem was that Cyprus's Greek community was to withhold its consent and cooperation from the British. Consequently, soldiers were battling in the metaphorical dark as reliable intelligence proved elusive. EOKA's ruthless leader personified the security forces' difficulties. For more than four years Grivas was at large in Cyprus, directing the insurgency and evading capture. Despite the offer of huge rewards for information, it is claimed that he frequently walked openly in daylight through the most frequented streets of the capital, Nicosia.[42] Gallingly for his opponents, 'he was able to leave Cyprus safely, in his own time and by his chosen means after evading 25,000 British troops for 1,562 days and nights'.[43] It is said that when the British eventually removed Grivas from the island he was escorted on to his plane back to Athens by a one-armed officer, sparing the security forces the indignity of his being saluted.[44]

The Church was EOKA's most powerful ally in Cyprus. It possessed huge moral authority and unlimited wealth. For many in the security forces and colonial administration, Makarios was, if not a Rasputin-like figure, a turbulent priest. Despite reports that he had met Grivas in Athens and given his blessing – and the Church's funds – to EOKA's campaign, definite links between the Archbishop and the insurgents were initially hard to prove. One of the few intelligence breakthroughs was the discovery of the remnants of Grivas's diary in early 1956 in a farmhouse. Initially suspected to be a fake, it confirmed Makarios's complicity in the unrest. In an echo of the Mau Mau rebellion, priests administered oaths in churches, binding young people more closely to the cause. They pledged: 'I shall work with all my power for the liberation of Cyprus from the British yoke, sacrificing for this even my life.'[45] Rolls of honour of dead terrorists were read out from the pulpits, which became 'propaganda platforms'.[46] Spiritual sanctions, such as excommunication or exclusion from the sacraments, were invoked. The Troodos and Kyrenia mountains were not only natural hide-outs for Grivas and other EOKA members, but were sites of remote monasteries and churches. They formed an ecclesiastical network, providing safe havens for the terrorists, facilitating their communications, and were used as caches for arms and ammunition. The monastery at Kykkos, one of the most sacred in the Orthodox world, frequently ignored the ban on flying the Greek flag. When soldiers searched it, dynamite was found in its safe.

The separation of the population from the insurgents, central to the counter-insurgency campaigns in Malaya and Kenya, was impossible in Cyprus. Just as Greek and Turkish populations were intermingled throughout the island, so too were the insurgents and civilians. EOKA operated as a network of cells. Individual insurgents knew very little about the overall organisation and so, even when they were captured, they could not provide much in the way of useful intelligence. Support for EOKA insinuated itself into every aspect of island life among the Greek-Cypriot community. The organisation had targeted for endorsement interest groups such as the right-wing Farmers Association, with its island-wide network of clubs. Pro-EOKA sentiment was widespread among the youth, not least because of support for *Enosis* among teachers and PEON (the National Organisation for Youth), founded by Makarios. Young people who wanted actively to support EOKA were assigned small tasks such as carrying a message before graduating to more lethal acts of terrorism. EOKA's agents were everywhere: turning a blind eye in the customs service; passing on messages in barber shops; mining a drinking fountain used by soldiers after a football match; in Kyrenia Castle jail helping sixteen EOKA members escape in September 1955; infiltrating the police and the local telephone company, as well as the Governor's household staff.

Whether the Greek-Cypriots actively supported the terrorists, providing safe houses, supplies and getaways, or passively acquiesced in the campaign from fear, the security forces found it almost impossible to break through the wall of silence. A Parachute Regiment officer said: 'Postmen, telephone operators, contractors, foresters, policemen, all passed on what was required of them in the way of information. Each of them knew that it was literally as much as his life was worth to fail to do so.'[47] An officer from the 1st Battalion Oxfordshire and Buckinghamshire Light Infantry said the terrorists 'got away time and time again because they had the back-up; either the enforced or genuine sympathy of most of the Greek-Cypriots'.[48] He added: 'The majority of the people were more frightened of what EOKA would do to them than what the British military forces would do to them.'[49] This comment was very reminiscent of the attitude of many of the Kenyan people, more afraid of the Mau Mau than the British authorities.

British soldiers in Cyprus could have drawn useful parallels with the campaign in Palestine. With beaches shut off by barbed wire, sandbagged police stations, military vehicles on the roads and thousands of soldiers living in fortified camps lit by searchlights, Cypriots found their island turned into an armed camp. Although local people were less overtly hostile than they had been in Palestine, they kept their distance. One British official described how his son's Greek-Cypriot godfather refused to acknowledge him in public.[50] Grivas was an opponent almost as clear-sighted as Menachem Begin; he was determined to arouse international public opinion and undermine British legitimacy: 'The British must be continuously harried and beset until they are obliged by international diplomacy exercised through the United Nations to examine the Cypriot problem and settle it in accordance with the desires of the Cypriot people and the whole Greek nation.'[51] The British authorities knew the right-wing colonel from the days of the Greek civil war when he had raised a small private army to fight the Communists.[52] Having sensed sedition could be brewing, they refused the Athens-based Grivas a visa to visit Cyprus. In late 1954, he smuggled himself on to the island and took refuge in the densely forested mountains. A message was passed to his wife in Athens to burn all his clothes, so that the British would be unable to use them for searching for him with tracker dogs.[53]

The insurgency escalated after April 1955 with bombings, riots and acts of sabotage. Strikes spread throughout the island; those in schools were a particularly effective propaganda tactic. Radio Athens and the local press supported *Enosis*. In London, the Churchill government became alarmed that the Governor was losing control. The Chief of the Imperial General Staff, Sir John Harding, was due to retire. In September, in almost his last day in the job, he attended a Cabinet meeting where he successfully argued for the continuance of two-year National Service, which he viewed as 'essential' for the Army's effectiveness, not least because of the Malaya campaign. That afternoon he had intended to fly to Germany to say farewell to the Rhine Army, but instead was called back to Number 10 and offered the job of Governor of Cyprus.[54] Like Templer in Malaya, he combined civilian and military command. Harding arrived in late September; on 26 November he declared a State of Emergency. By then, EOKA, now an illegal organisation, had launched its 'Forward to Victory' campaign. In the six months to early March 1956, 500 attacks would be carried out; the first year of the insurgency led to 146 casualties, with 23 people killed.[55]

On his own admission, Governor Harding took a 'soldier's approach' to Cyprus. A career soldier who had seen action at Gallipoli in the First World War and commanded the 7th Armoured Division at El Alamein in the Second, the former CIGS was unimpressed by what he found on his arrival: poor command and staff work; no effective intelligence operation; a largely ineffective police force; no sense of operational urgency in government officials; soldiers' time being wasted on 'village-bashing' and washing away the blue pro-*Enosis* and pro-EOKA graffiti daubed across the island's buildings and roads. Harding saw his role as getting the main centres of population under government control and ensuring essential services were maintained. He called for an immediate increase in the number of soldiers to establish a network of listening posts and patrols across the island. Reinforcements arrived from the Royal Norfolk Regiment, the Gordon Highlanders, the Royal Leicestershire Regiment and the Middlesex Regiment. Many of them were National Servicemen. The surge in the number of patrols almost immediately paid off: a Household Cavalry roadblock near Famagusta stopped a car carrying four men, arms and ammunition.[56] The Royal Navy's Cyprus Patrol was established to halt the infiltration of weapons and personnel on to the island, while on land Harding set up district security committees similar to those in Kenya and Malaya.

For two years Britain's former top soldier battled against one of the colonial era's most determined insurgents. Harding said Grivas was 'not only a skilful guerrilla leader but an extremely ruthless one who exercised total authority over his subordinates ... Anything was acceptable or admissible if it helped advance the cause of *Enosis*.'[57] Grivas's major problem was the lack of military experience in EOKA: out of an estimated 200 or so active terrorists, he was one of the organisation's few trained soldiers. The quality of their arms and ammunition also frequently let them down. As Harding observed: 'They weren't all that expert, all that efficient, which was lucky for us.'[58] The Governor was extremely lucky when one of his household staff planted a bomb under his bed. The detonator – from a batch distributed to resistance movements by the British during the Second World War – was wrongly set, timed to go off in twenty-four rather than twelve hours. Discovered, it was carried out of Government House on a shovel and placed in a weapons pit. It exploded, blowing out all the windows. Harding dismissed the incident as 'an occupational hazard'.[59] However, Grivas continued to win the intelligence war, vital to any successful counter-insurgency. The Governor conceded EOKA had excellent information and plenty of informers: 'They knew a good deal about my movements wherever I went.'[60]

British forces struggled to win the propaganda war as much as the intelligence war. EOKA made much of the flogging of local youths and the collective fines imposed on towns and villages. Cordons and curfews had a negative cumulative effect on local people: a taunt by Grivas that they were 'tanks to catch mice' began to ring true – and the mice generally managed to evade capture anyway.[61] Searches were incessant, whether of buses, lorries laden with oranges or donkeys' panniers. Soldiers stripped out houses and knocked down walls to find terrorists' hiding places. Sometimes this paid off: searching a farmhouse in Paphos, members of 3 Para moved the family away from a fireplace, doused the flames and found EOKA members hiding in a dug-out beneath the hearth stones. During Harding's tenure, considerable military progress was made against EOKA. Operations such as Pepperpot and Sparrowhawk in the mountains captured arms and ammunition. However, the terrorism continued. Ledra Street in Nicosia was known as 'Murder Mile' and the Governor as 'Hangman Harding'. The death penalty could be imposed not just for carrying weapons, but for 'consorting or being in company with' a person carrying a weapon, outraging civil libertarians internationally. The measure opened the possibility of people being hanged for engaging in a casual conversation at a bus stop with a stranger who possessed a weapon. Echoing the campaign in Palestine, EOKA executed Lance Corporal Gordon Hill of the 1st Battalion Lancashire Regiment and Private Ronnie Shilton of the Royal Leicestershire Regiment after one of their men was hanged. By early 1957, sixty men were facing capital charges, Grivas's principal lieutenant Grigoris Afxentiou had been killed and the organisation's morale was undermined to the extent that Grivas suspended the insurgency.

Central to the British failure to win over local support was Makarios. In March 1956, Harding exiled the cleric along with three priests, arguing that the only course of action was to get him off the island: 'Inflicting defeat and the suppression of EOKA could not be achieved with the Archbishop active in Cyprus.' Although he was a threat to the colony's security, it was impossible to detain the Archbishop without trial. To minimise any propaganda damage, the British authorities ensured Makarios was given a rather cushy billet in the Seychelles. Despite this, the measure backfired. A colonial official argued that, while the Archbishop's 'deep personal complicity' in EOKA justified the measure, his exile was politically inexpedient: 'This more than any other single factor turned the Greek-Cypriot people against the British administration.'[62] Makarios would return to Cyprus in March 1959 to a tumultuous welcome.

Throughout the Cyprus Emergency, the British authorities underestimated the support for EOKA and *Enosis*. As the violence was renewed, soldiers were not only being shot in the back of the head in hit-and-run attacks, but were being goaded into over-reaction, providing EOKA with a propaganda gift. A booklet reminded them that, although they were involved in a shooting war, many tasks they would undertake in Cyprus were 'police tasks, calling for patience, good humour and tact'.[63] Many of them were National Servicemen, including future broadcaster Martin Bell. Attached to the Suffolks as an acting corporal, he seemed to spend much of his time dozing or, because he was due to go up to university, doing paperwork for his comrades.[64] Another conscript with the Royal Green Jackets said that many were baffled by the politics behind the insurgency: 'We wondered what the hell we were doing out there and why; nothing was ever explained to us ...'[65] A reporter sent out to spend time with 1st Battalion Welch Regiment at their camp in Cyprus's north, wrote that a soldier's life could be 'a monotonously lonely one', with little to do off duty in a place with few cinemas, bars or dance halls. In a hot and dusty camp of prefab huts, where men slept eight to a tent and the food was 'grim', one evening only three soldiers out of 400 bothered to sign themselves out.[66] On 17 June 1956, twenty-one soldiers were killed in a forest fire: among the casualties were thirteen men from the Gordon Highlanders and five soldiers from the Royal Norfolk Regiment.

Occasional chinks were made in the EOKA wall. A local reporter was always first on the spot in the wake of any bombings: the penny dropped that he was the perpetrator of the attacks. If an insurgent broke ranks, all the local men would be rounded up in a dawn raid, put in a large outdoor cage near the local police station and then paraded past a Land Rover: inside, the insurgent would identify any comrades.[67] This was unusual, but effective. The same tactic was to be used on the streets of Belfast twenty years later. However, one MP complained: 'The fact remains that we must stamp out the terrorists before we can win the cooperation of the people.'[68] But the contrary fact remained that the cooperation of the people was needed to stamp out the terrorists, and, given that the civilian population knew that if they passed on information they 'would probably be murdered the following day', their reluctance to help was unsurprising.

A counter-insurgency operation aims to create enough security for a political solution to work. Having taken a soldier's approach, Harding knew the solution had to be found 'on the political plain'. However, in Cyprus the British military presence was exacerbating rather than solving the security crisis, as it would in southern Iraq after 2003. In October 1958, a Royal Artillery sergeant's wife, Catherine Cutcliffe, was shot and killed while shopping in Famagusta; her companion was injured. An estimated 150 soldiers rounded up all the local men in the vicinity; one judge later described their level of force as 'entirely unjustified'.[69] In addition, the Greek government,

Makarios and the Human Rights Committee of the Nicosia Bar Association accused soldiers and police of torturing detainees, and the authorities of human rights abuses. In the first ever action between two states, Greece began an action against Britain in the European Court over alleged breaches of the European Convention on Human Rights. Military historian David French suggests that the Cyprus Emergency brought the first deployment of 'lawfare' – legal action against Britain's Armed Forces 'that threatened to paralyse their actions'.[70] While the accusations of abuse were not entirely baseless, 'many of the allegations made against the security forces were propaganda fabrications'.[71]

Strategic developments beyond Cyprus forced London to rethink its policy towards the colony. In early 1958, the Sandys Defence Review cut the size of the Army. In October, the Director of Operations, Major General Kenneth Darling, warned that, given EOKA's mass support, Britain would need to deploy a similar level of force to Cyprus as the Soviet Union had against Hungary. Along with diverting thousands of troops to Egypt, the Suez Crisis had raised questions about Cyprus's effectiveness as a base. Jordan's unilateral abrogation of the Anglo-Jordanian Treaty meant that the country could no longer be used as a staging post by Britain in support of Baghdad Pact allies: Cyprus was suddenly redundant for anything other than airborne operations. In any talks with Makarios, Harding had always insisted 'not now, but not never'; political change would happen at some unspecified time in the future and according to Britain's strategic needs. Suddenly, it was 'now'.

Any political change would affect the island's Turkish community. In the event of *Enosis* with Greece, it demanded *Taksim*, or partition. Cyril Radcliffe, who had drawn up the border between India and Pakistan, arrived on Cyprus to investigate dividing the island, a proposal which was indeed 'a bombshell' and 'greeted with horror and indignation on the Greek side'.[72] Inter-communal fighting broke out. With *Enosis* perhaps leading to the island's division, the Greeks had to be careful what they wished for. In early 1959, in London and Zurich, a compromise agreement was reached between Macmillan's government, Makarios, Athens and Ankara on Cyprus's future: independence, not *Enosis*; no partition but safeguards for the Turkish-Cypriot minority; and, for the British, two Sovereign Base

Areas at Akrotiri and Dhekelia. Soon to be the first president of an independent Cyprus, Makarios made his message to Grivas clear: 'EOKA is not a political body, and therefore it will accept any solution approved by the political leadership.'[73] EOKA's triumphalism at inflicting a defeat on the British was misplaced: the result was, at best, a score draw. Although Cyprus was going to be independent, *Enosis* had eluded them.

The British presence on Cyprus continues to this day. The antipathy between Greek and Turkish Cypriots reached a climax in 1974 when Turkish forces invaded northern Cyprus. Then, as now, British forces remain as part of a UN peacekeeping force maintaining a buffer zone between the two communities who seem eternally resistant to finding an accommodation with each other. Elsewhere on the island Britain has retained its Sovereign Base Areas which include Episkopi Cantonment and an airfield at RAF Akrotiri. Between 2003 and 2014, aircraft on detachment from the United Kingdom to the static aircraft carrier at RAF Akrotiri have contributed to air operations over Iraq, Libya and Syria. Troops based on Cyprus were deployed as reinforcements to Iraq and Afghanistan, often at short notice. The island has become a staging post for many others, a base to acclimatise to hot weather before a mission or to decompress after one.

Borneo and the Indonesian Confrontation

After the British Army's successful counter-insurgency operation in Malaya paved the way to independence, Anglo-Malayan cooperation continued. Britain remained heavily involved in the 11-state federation, not least because of a 1957 defence agreement and the base at Singapore, headquarters of Far East Land Forces and 'the linch-pin of British defence policy in South East Asia'.[74] In May 1961, Malaya's Tunku Abdul Rahman endorsed a longstanding British proposal that the federation should incorporate Sarawak, North Borneo (later Sabah) and Brunei. The three territories were to be found some 500 miles from Malaya, across the South China Sea in the north of the world's third largest island, Borneo. This proposal would amalgamate Britain's collection of protectorates, colonies and former colonies in the region and take them off London's pay-roll, while maintaining British influence, thanks largely to Singapore. Swiftly, the plan was beset by trouble, not least because of an attempted *coup d'état* in

Brunei, and more importantly by the vehement opposition of Indonesia, which threatened a 'confrontation' if the plan went ahead. Not only was the southern half of Borneo – Kalimantan – Indonesian territory, but Malaya and Indonesia were longstanding rivals and past enemies.

The former Dutch colony of Indonesia became independent in 1949. The republic's first president was the left-of-centre nationalist leader Sukarno. His task was to forge a nation out of an equatorial archipelago of an estimated 17,500 islands that stretched across three time zones. Its population of 100 million, which included more than 300 ethnic groups, was predominantly Muslim. In the 1950s and early 1960s, millions of its citizens were members of the PKI (Partai Komunis Indonesia), the largest Communist party outside the Soviet Union and China. The republic's early years were politically chaotic. One institution that provided continuity and contributed to the country's stability was the powerful army. In 1963, it had an estimated strength of 300,000 soldiers.[75]

The post-1945 nationalist movements which had toppled empires across the globe continued into the 1960s. In his seminal 'Winds of Change' speech of February 1960, Prime Minister Harold Macmillan obliquely attacked racial apartheid and spoke of the awakening of national consciousness across the African continent. The address in Cape Town, which included an aside about 'two staggering wars which have bled our economy white', warned of a battle between East and West for the allegiance of the millions in Asia and Africa: 'The struggle is joined and it is a struggle for the minds of men.'[76] While Macmillan was signalling the winding-up of the British Empire in Africa, he also anticipated decades of bloody conflict in the post-imperial world, as pro-Western and pro-Communist forces battled it out in many former colonies. With the United States' involvement in Vietnam and a British intervention in Borneo, from 1961 the allies would be committed to two protracted military operations in the jungles and swamps of south-east Asia, thousands of miles from home. Paradoxically, although the Vietnam campaign is frequently compared with the counter-insurgency in Malaya, it is rarely analysed in the context of Borneo, which was a concurrent conflict involving some 30,000 British and Commonwealth troops. With the last National Servicemen leaving the Army in May 1963, the Borneo

Confrontation was Britain's first post-1945 operation involving only regular soldiers. Central to the military effort were Special Forces.

The first salvo of the Confrontation was in Brunei. Attempting to stymie the creation of the new Federation of Malaysia, Jakarta was behind an attempted coup in the oil-rich enclave. Thanks to a swift military response by Britain, it was over almost before it had begun. On the night of 7/8 December 1962, an estimated 3,000 rebels sought to overthrow the autocratic Sultan, who was earning a suitably princely £12 million a year from the Brunei Shell Petroleum Company. While some of the rebels were members of the People's Party that had long demanded political change, others claimed membership of the pro-Indonesian, anti-British North Kalimantan National Army, an organisation which was opposed to any federation with Malaya. Macmillan believed Jakarta was complicit in the insurrection, observing in his diary: 'No doubt this is fermented from Indonesia by Sukarno.'[77] Within hours of the uprising, British forces, including Royal Marines, the Queen's Royal Irish Hussars and the Queen's Own Highlanders, were on their way from Singapore. A Malaya veteran, the jungle warfare expert Sir Walter Walker, Major General of the Brigade of Gurkhas, was appointed Director of Operations. In Brunei, a Communist takeover was feared. Within a week, however, most of the rebels had surrendered: some 700 were taken prisoner and about sixty killed. One young Royal Green Jackets lieutenant, sixth-generation Army officer Robin Evelegh, remembers creeping through a pepper plantation before attacking the enemy: 'This was where one's training ended ... Rather like a lot of football hooligans we surged forward.' Later, he rested his rifle between the ears of a garden gnome to take aim against a rebel.[78] For London, the coup attempt indicated Indonesia's capacity to destabilise the region.

The Confrontation with Indonesia was fought out for three years in Borneo. The new Federation of Malaysia, which included Singapore, Sarawak and Sabah, was inaugurated in September 1963. Immediately, the British Embassy in Indonesia's capital, Jakarta, was burned down. The Sukarno regime considered the new Malaysia merely a British puppet, Foreign Minister Subandrio describing the Malays as 'henchmen of neo-colonialists and neo-imperialists'.[79] Jakarta had legitimate grounds to perceive the Federation as a threat: Indonesian islands such as Sumatra, where the standard of living was far lower, might be tempted to join it.[80] In line with its primary foreign policy of containing Communism, the Kennedy government in Washington welcomed the Malaysian Federation as an anti-Communist bulwark. However, the US was also giving economic aid and military assistance to the non-aligned Indonesia: it wanted to avoid rupturing relations with Sukarno. If alienated, he would turn to the Soviet Union; if ousted, local Communists could replace him. However, as the Confrontation intensified, Washington gradually began to take sides – and a harder line against Indonesian intransigence. The US feared that, should the Confrontation escalate, it would have to become involved, in part because of obligations laid down in existing defence treaties in the region. Given its deepening involvement in Vietnam, with US troop numbers rising from 16,300 in 1963 to 385,000 in 1966, this would have been a commitment too far.

In April 1963, seventy-five raiders crossed the Kalimantan border and attacked a police station in Sarawak. This was judged to be 'the start of the Indonesian insurgency campaign against Malaya', according to the Joint Intelligence Committee Far East. Indonesia introduced an external dimension to this small war in Borneo, threatening to turn it into a major conflict. British and Commonwealth soldiers would confront not only local insurgents, but foreign troops. The job of the British and their allies was to protect the almost 1,000-mile long Borneo–Kalimantan border, preventing incursions into Malaysian territory, either by regular Indonesian forces or by Indonesian-backed local insurgents. Throughout the three-year Confrontation, the British governments of Alec Douglas-Home and Harold Wilson sought to contain and play down Indonesian belligerence. It was indeed 'the undeclared war', as Walter Walker described it.[81]

Previous counter-insurgency experience and tactics were replayed during the Confrontation. Just as in the Malayan Emergency, the loyalty or otherwise of the Chinese population in Borneo had to be taken into account. The authorities believed that Chinese youth movements were the principal forces behind what was identified as the 'Clandestine Communist Organisation' (CCO).[82] In mid-1963, about 1,000 CCO members crossed into Kalimantan and enrolled in guerrilla training camps. According to the 1960 census in Sarawak, the Chinese population stood at 250,000, about a third of the total.[83] However, land ownership in Borneo was almost closed to them, which was a longstanding source of grievance, contributing to communal tension. Villagisation echoed counter-insurgency practice in Malaya and Kenya. In mid-1965, thousands of Chinese living around the capital Kuching were rounded up during Operation Hammer and resettled.

For any soldier who had fought in the jungles of Malaya, Borneo would have felt familiar – only hotter and rainier. Its dense rainforest is one of the planet's most biodiverse areas, home to orangutans, pygmy elephants, rhinoceros and leopards. Mangrove swamps fringe the coastline. The indigenous peoples, the Dayaks, were made up of dozens of different tribes, all with different languages and customs: many lived in longhouses that could be likened to sheltered hamlets. Headhunting was not unusual, having become resurgent during the Japanese occupation of the island. Tribesmen, particularly the Iban, were used by the Army as trackers. Even in the early 1960s, very little of Borneo had been charted: the maps that existed proved to be inaccurate. Helicopters were vital to the operation: it was estimated that one hour in the air was equal to five days on foot.[84] In December 1964, the BBC broadcast *Jungle Green,* a black-and-white documentary about a three-day patrol through the jungle undertaken by Royal Marines. The men were shown making camp, purifying water and cooking limited tinned rations of rice, stew and beans. Cigarette breaks were a chance to burn off leeches. The chief gripe concerned their boots; far from waterproof, they were like walking in puddles of water.[85] The forthright Walter Walker complained about the quality of soldiers' kit, calling for the introduction of the Armalite rifle and lighter ration packs. The infantry in Borneo was judged to be worse equipped than their predecessors when they had started to fight the Japanese twenty years earlier.[86]

By 1965, a string of forward bases had been constructed along the Borneo–Kalimantan frontier. The jungle had been cleared around each base, replaced by barbed wire, trenches, grenade bays and machine-gun posts. Ron Cassidy of 2nd Battalion Royal Green Jackets was one of the men living in the bunkers; without electricity, there were 'pretty long nights with nothing to do'. All stores and food were dropped by air: often the parachutes failed and their loads, including cigarettes and rolls of camera film, would be scattered across the jungle. For the men, 'It was Christmas every time they came in off patrol.' In Cassidy's view, soldiers were 'fighting the Indonesians and carrying out a hearts and minds exercise with the locals'. Soldiers' wives had sent out dresses and cardigans that were handed out at a Christmas party: 'They were totally out of place, but it made for a smashing day.' At another party, Father Christmas arrived by helicopter.[87] Jungle patrols could last for fourteen days, with the troops 'ambushing and being ambushed'.[88] David Henderson of the 1st Battalion Royal Hampshires said every regiment which went to Borneo lost someone; his best mate was killed. 'The Indonesian Army had commando troops who could put up a fair fight. We knew where a camp was, we could hear them night training.' Every Sunday, he would go river fishing on an assault craft loaded with beer.[89]

The Confrontation was a misnomer: British forces might have been engaged, but the government publicly minimised any conflict with Indonesia. Conversely, Jakarta ratcheted up the tension. In 1964 it launched raids on the Malaysian mainland, landing paratroopers in Johor in September to coincide with the anniversary of the Federation. Jakarta's grandstanding over the rights of Royal Naval vessels – in particular the aircraft carrier HMS *Victorious* – to sail through the Sunda Strait between Java and Sumatra was played down by London.[90] Full-scale war had to be avoided: not only would Britain's increasingly overstretched Armed Forces be facing a massive Indonesian army, but international support was far from guaranteed. Alert to the danger that Sukarno could make political capital out of any misstep by Britain, especially among the newly independent nations that saw him as a champion of decolonisation and self-determination, Whitehall generally sought the face-saving compromises. As one commentator suggested, Jakarta could portray Britain 'as a bullying colonial power' that was transgressing the sovereignty of a third world underdog.[91] The perception that Sukarno was standing up to Britain played well domestically and in the United Nations, where Egypt in particular was keen to stir up anti-British sentiment. However, Sukarno's brinkmanship was beginning to alienate the United States. Having identified 1965 as 'The Year of Living Dangerously', he would find the phrase prophetic. Relations between his government and his army began to deteriorate. Following an unsuccessful military coup in September, a clique within the army led by

General Suharto continued to plot against the government. The PKI was banned, its leaders jailed and members of the Suharto faction began to establish themselves in key positions of power. Across Indonesia, an anti-Communist purge ensued, with up to 500,000 people killed. In March 1966, Sukarno ceded authority to Suharto, who within months ended the Confrontation.

The Borneo campaign underscored the value of Commonwealth forces. Soldiers from Australia, New Zealand and Malaysia worked alongside British soldiers and the Gurkhas. As their operational commander, Walter Walker had fought to save their numbers from being cut. His lobbying of both the King of Nepal and the American Ambassador in Kathmandu was regarded as an incursion too far into politics, earning the wrath of the powerful General Bill Slim. Walker, however, argued that 'only Asian troops are acceptable in an Asian country': as long as Britain maintained a presence East of Suez, the Gurkhas were vital, not least because they were the one major fighting formation outside Europe that was maintained in readiness for war.[92] Also central to the effort in Borneo were Special Forces. With their experience in Malaya, the Special Air Service (SAS) was ideally suited for the campaign. Expert at jungle warfare, their four-man missions could sometimes last for months. With some soldiers able to speak Malay or local dialects and others having medical skills, they could also win the trust of local people and glean valuable intelligence against the enemy. In a rather breathless article in the *Daily Telegraph*, they were described as the 007s of the Borneo jungle, 'eyes straining into the tangled vines and creepers are as keen and perceptive as any that seduced a curvaceous enemy agent across a vodka martini'.[93] More usefully, members of the SAS and the Gurkhas took part in the top-secret 'Claret' operations, sanctioned by Defence Secretary Denis Healey. *Jungle Green* stated: 'We only work on our side of the border.' However, soldiers began crossing into Indonesian territory, first for up to 3,000 yards and then 10,000 yards. The deniability surrounding these raids meant that the full circumstances which led to the award of the Victoria Cross to Lance Corporal Rambahadur Limbu of the 2nd/10th Gurkha Rifles were not released until three years later.[94]

The little-known campaign in Borneo was both a military and a political success. Denis Healey compared the Confrontation with

Vietnam, arguing that the campaign was a textbook demonstration of how to apply economy of force, under political guidance, for political ends: 'At a time when the United States was plastering Vietnam with bombs, napalm and defoliant, no British aircraft ever dropped a bomb on Borneo.'[95] A former major in the Royal Engineers, Healey remains the longest serving post-war Defence Secretary. He and the Armed Forces got on well, but he never forgot to remind senior commanders who was in charge: 'A feature of campaigns East of Suez was the need for close and continuous control of military operations in the light of their political implications.'[96]

Aden, almost the last of Britain's small colonial wars, reflects the perils of getting the politics wrong.

Aden and Radfan

Found in present-day Yemen, the port city of Aden stands guard on the eastern approach to the Red Sea. A British colony since 1937, the free port had been a key refuelling point on the voyage to India since the early Victorian era when the British first established a presence there. From the late 1950s, Aden began to assume greater significance for Britain's Armed Forces, who had become increasingly unwelcome guests across the Middle East. In the light of their ejection from Egypt's Canal Zone, their tenure of the Sovereign Base Areas in Cyprus, independent in 1960, seemed far from guaranteed. With another base needed, the existing facility at Aden would be expanded. Air-conditioned huts for 400 administrative staff, 241 married quarters and accommodation for an infantry battalion were installed in early 1960 as a large construction programme got underway. One of the world's deepest ports, Aden was to become a key British overseas base, second only to Singapore. In 1960, it replaced Cyprus as Headquarters of British Forces Middle East; by 1964, it was home to 8,000 service personnel and their families. A BBC documentary of the time describes Aden as a place of 'camels and Cadillacs', and shows packets of Omo washing powder on sale in its bazaars and soldiers drinking Double Diamond beer.[97] Some 6,000 ships were at anchor every year, while RAF Khormakhsar was the busiest RAF base outside Britain, station to fleets of Victors and Shackletons, Lightnings and Hunters. Temperatures in Aden often exceeded 38 degrees. For many, Aden was synonymous with heat, dust, flies – and from, late 1963, with insurgency.

The Colony of Aden was surrounded by tribal statelets known as the Aden Protectorates. Covering an area about the size of England, they comprised more than twenty feudal fiefdoms, including Radfan. Thanks to decades of regular bribes and various treaties, the Protectorates' emirs, sultans, sheikhs, sharifs and imams were generally friendly to Britain. Security was provided by the Aden Protectorate Levies, a force of local men under the command of British officers and NCOs. In 1959, a process of federation got underway, with the different Protectorates incrementally coming together to form the Federation of South Arabia (FSA). Aden would join the 14-member federation in January 1963. However, many in the colony were uninterested in federation: they wanted independence. For Britain's critics in Cairo and the UN, federation was seen as another piece of chicanery to ward off independence and protect the country's defence interests by creating a buffer state around the Aden base. As High Commissioner Kennedy Trevaskis observed, federation without independence was like a song without the music: 'In South Arabia, it was the music that counted far more than any number of immaculate stanzas.'[98]

The expanding British military base in Aden symbolised British rule and dominance. A series of facilities – some up to twenty-five miles apart – it was scattered over a quarter of the colony's total area. An Intelligence Corps officer who arrived in Aden in 1960 said that, with the millions being invested, 'it looked as though we were going to stay for fifty years'.[99] However, many doubted the wisdom of developing the base. Reporting to the Cabinet's Defence and Overseas Policy Committee in December 1964, a senior civil servant warned that the base was 'very vulnerable' and 'dependent on the goodwill of the bulk of the local population', with its water coming by pipeline from outside the colony. The base could not survive 'if the adjoining States of the Protectorate were in hostile hands'.[100] The base became the prism through which the governments of Macmillan, Douglas-Home and Wilson viewed the future of Aden.

Strategically well placed – providing Britain with a tiny foothold on the oil-rich Arabian Peninsula – Aden was politically far from perfect. Members of organisations such as the Aden Trades Union Congress and the People's Socialist Party were Arab nationalists, opposed to continuing British rule and demanding an extension to the existing limited franchise. The rise of Egypt's President Nasser and the Suez debacle had boosted anti-British sentiment. Britain's record in Aden was undistinguished: in the week of the triumphant visit by Soviet leader Nikita Khrushchev to Egypt for the opening of the Moscow-financed Aswan Dam, the House of Commons was told that only an estimated eleven miles of tarmac roads had been built in Aden in 130 years. The cosmopolitan, bustling colony was very different from the sparsely-populated hinterland of the Protectorates. Politically and socially conservative, they welcomed British rule, putting them at odds with the people of Aden itself who were demanding independence.

Civil war across the border in Yemen compounded deteriorating security in Aden. In September 1962, Imam Muhammad al-Badr was overthrown in a military coup. Republican forces were backed by Egypt, which sent upwards of 25,000 troops into the new Yemen Arab Republic, while Saudi Arabia supplied royalist militias with arms and money. In addition, the Saudis funded covert action by British mercenaries. Although deniable, the operation allegedly received tacit backing from the so-called Aden Group of MPs, which included Duncan Sandys and Defence Secretary Peter Thorneycroft, for whom the humiliation of Suez still rankled.[101] The conflict in Yemen would continue for most of the decade, with the destabilising forces of civil war and revolutionary nationalism crossing into the wider Aden Protectorates zone and the colony of Aden. In March 1964, the RAF bombed a mud fort in Harib in Yemen. The British action was a comparatively minor response to Egyptian air strikes on the Protectorate of Beihan, in which napalm was used. However, the Arab League, the United States and the United Nations condemned the British action.

In December 1963, members of Aden's National Liberation Front (NLF) attempted to assassinate Trevaskis and his entourage in a grenade attack at the airport. One woman was killed and fifty people injured. An insurgency had begun: a State of Emergency was declared. Within months, rebellion broke out in Radfan, a mountainous region sixty miles north of Aden, in territory bordering Yemen. These internal and external threats to the security of Aden and the wider Protectorates jeopardised the base. British soldiers would be in action on three fronts: lending military assistance to the Protectorates to deal with the external threat from Yemen, trying to quell an internal insurgency in Aden and putting down the Radfan rebellion.

In Radfan, local tribesmen had long collected tolls from the Sacred Road, an ancient 1,000-mile long caravan route linking Aden with Mecca, part of which cut through the region. When the new federal government ordered this practice to stop, the Radfani attempted to close the road. Tensions escalated between the tribesmen and the authorities, who drafted in the Federal Regular Army, the successor to the Protectorate Levies. With the backing of members of the NLF and weaponry arriving from across the Yemeni border, the Radfanis fought back successfully, mining the road. Radfan quickly became a no-go area. To restore order, in April 1964 the brigade-size Radforce was sent in, which initially comprised members of 3rd Battalion Parachute Regiment, 45 Commando Royal Marines and 1st Battalion East Anglian Regiment.

For soldiers who have fought in Helmand, Radfan would not seem too unfamiliar. At 6,000 feet above sea level, the area is rocky and desolate, with mountains honeycombed by caves. Temperatures can reach 40 degrees. The warlike local tribesmen knew every inch of their territory. The boulder-strewn roads and tracks snaking through the mountain passes took a heavy toll of vehicles, including Ferret scout cars, truck-towed Wombats and the new all-terrain Stalwarts. Eventually, after land was cleared – sometimes by hand until a Royal Engineers bulldozer was flown forward in pieces and reassembled – and rough landing strips constructed, many stores would come in by air.[102] Food, including ready meals of chicken supreme, which the soldiers had to eat every day for a week, and water in one-ton containers, allowing each man two gallons a day, arrived either by parachute, a Beverley transporter or helicopter – perhaps a Wessex from 815 Naval Air Squadron doing the 'grocery run'. Mail and newspapers would be dropped from passing planes. As in Helmand, soldiers would go out on daily patrol from forward camps, encountering snipers and landmines. They would spend three to four weeks in the province, before returning to Aden.[103] Back in London, politicians made clear who was behind the uprising. Prime Minister Douglas-Home told the House of Commons: 'There is no doubt that violent subversion in the Radfan area had been encouraged and sustained from the Yemen.'[104] Shortly afterwards, the Defence Secretary stated:

'What we are meeting here are tribesmen who are armed, equipped and trained – armed with light automatic weapons, equipped with radio and mortars, and trained over the frontier.'[105]

In contrast with the clandestine operation against Indonesia during the Confrontation, the counter-insurgency in Radfan was conducted very publically. As one analyst has observed, the 1960s was the beginning of the era of photojournalism.[106] In addition, documentaries such as *Soldiers in the Sun*, made by the Panorama team for the BBC, were prominent in the television schedules. The High Commissioner was uneasy about the attention being given to Radfan by the media, which was being 'deliberately courted' by senior commanders, with reporters offered 'aircraft, helicopters and motor transport to see things for themselves'. He believed that the insurgents and their cause were boosted by the oxygen of publicity. What was little more than local skirmishing had been 'quickly blown up into precisely what the Cairo propagandists wanted to present to New York and London: a nationalist rebellion with British troops embattled in defence of their federal puppets'.[107] While the operation was declared a success by July 1964, troops would have to garrison the area for thirty more months.[108] Royal Engineers upgraded roads and dug wells, described by one brigadier as 'political work'.[109] British forces also deployed 'proscription bombing' in Radfan and other pockets of insurgency in the Federation of South Arabia. Local people were warned about an impending strike, to allow them to clear the area. Although the bombing was militarily effective, it played badly internationally, with Britain painted as the vindictive imperialist bully, bombing impoverished tribes-folk and their livestock. An Amnesty International report chronicling the alleged torture of prisoners at Fort Morbut and Al Mansoura prison would subsequently compound Britain's image problem.

In Aden, the insurgency intensified. So-called Cairo Grenadiers attacked bars and cinemas frequented by service personnel and their families. They were warned not to buy a certain brand of Thermos flask which was easily booby-trapped. Armed British soldiers patrolled the narrow streets either on foot or in armoured cars. Roadblocks were established, stops and searches conducted and curfews imposed. The graffiti that was a backdrop to these operations was a reminder of the nationalist cause. Based in the Arab area of Crater, the NLF relentlessly targeted and killed any suspected informers; consequently, intelligence was minimal. Rewards were offered in exchange for information or weapons being handed in, but little was achieved. In addition, the NLF had unofficial political authority and could order strikes, demonstrations and go-slows, bringing the colony to a standstill. To keep out infiltrators, the 'Scrubber Line' of miles of barbed wire encircled parts of the port city.[110] Despite all the precautionary measures, terrorism escalated with the emergence of another militant nationalist faction, the Egyptian-backed Front for the Liberation of South Yemen (FLOSY). The grenade attacks, shootings and bombings worsened, the number of incidents reflecting the breakdown in security: 64 in 1964, 279 in 1965 and 480 in 1966. In the first two months of 1967, there were 265 attacks, in which 44 people were killed and 239 injured.[111]

It is the soldier's job to deal with the security aspect of any insurgency, but the politicians' challenge to take the lead in finding solutions to its political causes. In the case of Aden and the wider Federation of South Arabia, the politicians could not find a workable political formula. The absence of a clear political strategy from London was complicated by the change of government from Conservative to Labour in October 1964. Throughout, British officials on the ground recognised that an injection of trade and developmental aid was needed to turn around the dire state of the local economy, along with improvements in education and the institutions of democratic government.[112] In late 1963, the Middle East Commander-in-Chief General Sir Charles Harrington, told *Life* magazine: 'We're here to stay. Aden is essential for the defence of our vital oil and strategic interests in the area.' [113] In July 1964, a conference in London convened by Duncan Sandys set a new direction of political travel: independence by 1968 but a mutual defence agreement by which Britain would retain the military base in Aden. Britain's about-turn dismayed some of the Protectorate chiefs, British supporters who felt betrayed. One told Trevaskis he wished he had listened to Nasser. Two years later, Labour's 1966 Defence Review, prompted not least by the state of the British economy, tore up the existing defence arrangements: the base would be abandoned in 1968. A British administrator observed that the government's policy kept on changing at a dizzying speed. 'Everything we had been doing and were trying to achieve was now going to be overturned … It was a difficult period to represent Britain in Aden.'[114]

The end of the counter-insurgency campaign in Aden was decided by the clock and economic instability in London not by conditions on the ground. In this, it resembled in part the British departures from Iraq in 2009 and Afghanistan in 2014. Announcing a departure date is rarely an effective military tactic: knowing they are about to be abandoned, local people have little incentive to help the security forces and intelligence can dry up. Whether Taliban, EOKA or Adeni dissidents, insurgents want to give the impression that their opponents are being driven out so that they can claim victory. Ideally, the campaign in Aden should have ended like Malaya: the Army and security forces had stamped out an insurgency, establishing peace and security, while the colonial authorities had developed robust local political institutions, allowing them to cede power to a stable successor government. None of this happened in the Federation of South Arabia. The announcement that the British were leaving intensified the existing unrest, not least because of a power struggle between the rival factions of the NLF and the Nasser-backed FLOSY. In addition, up country in the Protectorate states, British soldiers came under attack from dissidents within the Federal Regular Army, with whom they were working to counter Yemeni attack. A grenade was thrown during a film being shown in the camp at Beihan one Sunday night as soldiers sat in the sand; another was thrown into a canteen a month later at Wadi Ein.[115] In Aden Colony, John Jago, adjutant of the Royal Horse Artillery, had the melancholy but ever more frequent duty of ensuring that the gun carriage to transport dead soldiers' coffins to the Silent Valley cemetery was in order.[116] As service personnel, their families or as tourists from cruise ships walked near centres such as Steamer Point, grenades would be thrown from the narrow alleyways. Eventually the decision was taken that the service families were to be evacuated: worries about their safety had undermined the morale of forces' personnel. In an atmosphere of lawlessness and violence, the British gave the impression they were cutting and running.

The British lost control of Aden city for two weeks in June 1967. On the night of 19/20 June, members of the Aden police mutinied, broke into an armoury and stole guns. Men of the Royal Northumberland Fusiliers were watching the film *The Battle of the Bulge* when gunfire was first heard. Next, the mutineers attacked a truck killing eight members of the Royal Corps of Transport and then later killed twelve British soldiers in the Crater area. More soldiers came under fire when they attempted to retrieve the bodies. For two weeks, nationalist flags flew over Crater: with a British battalion handover due and the local security forces unable to be trusted, there was no alternative for the British but to sit it out. On 3 July, Lieutenant Colonel Colin 'Mad Mitch' Mitchell of the 1st Battalion Argyll and Sutherland Highlanders led a force back into Crater, accompanied by a bagpiper who sounded the regimental charge, 'Monymusk'. Mitchell said: 'It is the most thrilling sound in the world to go into action with the pipes playing. It stirs the blood and reminds one of the heritage of Scotland and the Regiment. Best of all it frightens the enemy to death.'[117] Although Crater was retaken, in London the government lost its will to continue the fight in Aden and brought the date of departure forward to November – a reflection both of events on the ground and of the continuing economic crisis at home, described later in Chapter 4.

After almost 130 years, on 29 November 1967 the British left Aden. Pathé News covered the departure: with warships in the bay and a flypast of jets and helicopters, somewhat ironically, an impressive display of force was mustered. Photographs show a portrait of the Queen being carried unceremoniously by a departing British soldier, while on the front of an NLF vehicle is a photograph of Nasser.

Decades of instability and war followed the departure of the British from Aden. The former colony and the wider Federation of South Arabia became the People's Democratic Republic of Yemen. In 1990, it merged with its northern neighbour and became Yemen. A fragile if not failing state, Yemen has been a destabilising force in the Arabian Peninsula and across the Red Sea into the Horn of Africa. At times, it has been a safe haven and training ground for the terrorists of al-Qaeda and ISIS (also known as the self-styled Islamic State), while in 2015 civil war broke out once again.

The 1950s and 1960s can been seen as time of transition from Empire to Commonwealth and the start of the era when Britain became a multicultural society. Any assessment today of the British Army's role in the process of decolonisation can be influenced by opposition to the very idea of Empire. The counter-insurgency campaigns involving tens of thousands of British soldiers are perceived by some to be a continuation of the racism, repression and exploitation that, for its critics, typified the imperial era. This is to be ungenerous and deliberately forgetful of the sound administration and valuable development brought by British governance to most of its colonies and dependent territories. In general, the settled policy of successive post-war governments in London was independence and self-government for Britain's colonies, but strategic and defence priorities could block or delay the process, as in Cyprus and Aden. Malaya was an example of a successful handover; Aden was not. What happened to Aden after independence stands as a warning to all politicians not to run out of strategic patience during a military campaign. The creation of the Commonwealth, however, refutes a negative audit of Britain's imperial past. The Emergencies and insurgencies were the last post of the British Empire, pragmatic attempts at ensuring an orderly transition to self-government during a time of international uncertainty between East and West, and against a background of debilitating financial pressure. Where the transition went well and good relations remained, the foundations of the Commonwealth were laid successfully, resulting in a unique international institution whose influence and membership increases as memories of Empire recede.

The counter-insurgency campaigns were not without cost: 200 British soldiers and members of the security forces were killed in Kenya; 371 servicemen and women lost their lives in Cyprus; 114 in the Borneo Confrontation; and 68 in Aden. However, while some British soldiers were fighting small wars in colonies far from home, more than 60,000 others were in Germany preparing for possible global war.

FOUR

CONVENTIONAL SWORD AND NUCLEAR SHIELD

*NATO and BAOR, Withdrawal from East of
Suez, Northern Ireland and Dhofar*

While Emergencies and insurgencies had resulted in real combat and casualties in the last years of the colonial era, the decades between 1950 and 1980 consolidated the role of collective security and alliance deterrence. This was underlined in a Ministry of Defence recruitment film from the early 1970s, which stated that the British Army's 'first priority is support for NATO'.[1] The frontline of British defence was no longer the white cliffs of Dover, but across the North Sea in Germany, where the 55,000 soldiers of the British Army of the Rhine (BAOR) were based. Their job, in the event of nuclear deterrence failing, was to put a brake on any possible advance by the conventional forces of the Soviet Union and the Warsaw Pact. The development of tactical battlefield nuclear weapons that became part of the Rhine Army's arsenal, along with larger strategic nuclear weapons, was a reflection of what one analyst describes as the 'nuclear bias' that entrenched itself within the NATO alliance.[2]

Britain's smaller, all-volunteer Army mirrored the country's evolving relationship with the wider world. The nuclear focus allowed successive governments to make dramatic cuts, realised after the Sandys' Defence Review of 1957 and the Healey Review of 1966. The Army's strength more than halved in fifteen years, down from 398,000 soldiers in 1956 to 200,000 in 1961 and 173,000 in 1971.[3] In an echo of action taken by the post-war Attlee government, after 1966 the Wilson administration dramatically scaled back military commitments due to prolonged economic trouble and a sterling crisis. One casualty was Aden, as chapter 3 has detailed. In 1968, Britain's East of Suez strategy was abandoned, leading to the loss of the base at Singapore. Five years later, Britain finally joined the European Economic Community. This shift towards Europe further distanced the country not just from its imperial and colonial past, but from previous global leadership. This chapter examines how, although Britain and the United States were allies, the nuclear issue in particular underscored the reality of Britain's subordinate status. However, while Australia sent soldiers to Vietnam – 'All the way with LBJ,' declared Prime Minister Harold Holt – Britain's Prime Minister Harold Wilson resisted President Johnson's request for support.

Set against the backdrop of the continuing Cold War between East and West, this chapter details how Britain's defence became dependent upon the nuclear shield as well as on the conventional military sword. While much of the Army could be found in Germany, some soldiers were battling in the Dhofar region of Oman. The success of their unsung mission was crucial to the West. In August 1969, the first troops were sent to Northern Ireland, beginning a campaign that would grind on into the twenty-first century.

NATO, BAOR and the Nuclear Deterrent

According to its first Secretary General, Churchill's former Chief of Staff Lord Ismay, NATO's purpose was 'to keep the Americans in, the Russians out and the Germans down'. Inaugurated in the Washington Treaty of April 1949, the Organisation joined ten European nations with the United States and Canada in a defensive alliance. The demands of collective security were spelt out in Article 5 of the North Atlantic Treaty: the Allies agreed that 'an armed attack against one or more of them … shall be considered an attack against them all'; following such an attack, each ally would take 'such action as it deems necessary, including the use of armed force'. Although the Article was not to be invoked for the first time until after the 9/11 attacks on the United States (see chapter 8), its existence has always been the cornerstone of the Alliance. In NATO's very early days, Foreign Secretary Ernest Bevin reminded the House of Commons that this was the first time in the history of the United States that she had entered into a peacetime commitment for the joint defence of Europe. One MP had doubts about the Treaty, describing it as 'a return to the type of military alliance which we had before 1914, and can only divide the world into two hostile blocks and make a contribution not to peace but to war'.[4] With the formation of the Communist Warsaw Pact in 1955, Europe was indeed divided militarily; however, the peace – or at least the absence of major war – was kept for decades.

The threat from the Soviet Union and the advance of Communism gave the initial impetus for the necessity of collective security to defend western Europe. Peacetime defensive alliances – the 1947 Anglo-French Treaty of Dunkirk, the 1948 Treaty of Brussels, the 1954 Western European Union, and NATO – along with compulsory conscription and the military commitment provided by the British Army of the Rhine reflected the seriousness of the situation. As the military historian David French notes: 'A degree of military readiness that would have been unthinkable in the past now seemed essential.'[5] However, the countries of western Europe were reluctant to commit themselves to prioritising defence at Britain's behest. According to Montgomery, the Continental nations were 'deeply suspicious of Britain's intentions', not least the apparent desire to turn western Europe into a buffer zone to protect the homeland in the event of any Soviet advance.[6] To them, Britain was more concerned about her interests in the Middle East: even if British forces were committed to Europe there was no guarantee that, in the event of war, there would not be another Dunkirk and retreat back across the Channel. In the early days of the Cold War, just as Britain wanted the Americans 'in', the western Europeans wanted Britain 'in'.

In 1949, with the detonation of a Soviet atomic bomb, the inauguration of the People's Republic of China and the signing of the Sino-Soviet Pact, Communism was relentlessly gaining ground. A US document, NSC-68, which set out the United States' response, became one of the most important policy papers of the Cold War. It painted an apocalyptic picture of a Soviet Union 'animated by a new fanatical faith' and bent on 'world domination'. Devastation caused by Moscow's existing atomic stockpile would include 'laying waste to the British Isles'.[7] NSC-68 demanded any further Soviet expansion be blocked. This containment strategy would lead to a massive

increase in American military spending, as traditional peacetime isolationism was rejected – much to British relief. As far as NSC-68 was
concerned, the Americans were 'in'.

NATO evolved over several years after the Washington Treaty
was signed. Although being fought on the other side of the world,
the Korean War underscored the Soviet threat, which demanded
better military cooperation in western Europe. The Organisation
consolidated its command structures, headed by the Supreme Allied
Commander Europe (SACEUR), and established a permanent headquarters near Versailles (SHAPE). Montgomery, Deputy to the first
SACEUR, General 'Ike' Eisenhower, described the international
dimension of day-to-day planning: 'It is possible to find a Turkish
Air Force officer working on a problem concerning the lines of communication between England and Scandinavia for the support of the
Norwegian Army.'[8] Later, however, he criticised the next SACEUR,
General Matthew Ridgway, for shutting out non-Americans: 'We got
the feeling that there was too much "United States Eyes Only" in the
Headquarters.'[9]

In 1952, NATO expanded to include Greece and Turkey, but
proposals to admit West Germany were controversial. With Korea
making heavy demands on British and American manpower, Washington in particular was determined that Bonn should contribute to
collective Western defence. However, as future Defence Secretary
Denis Healey noted: 'Our activists were overwhelmingly against
German rearmament on any terms.'[10] Equally hostile was France,
whose proposals to include a militarily hamstrung Germany in a
European defence community came to nothing. In late 1954, at the
London Conference, a solution was found: Germany would be admitted to NATO, but various conditions were attached. Among them
was an undertaking by Britain to retain forces in West Germany
for the next forty years, with four armoured divisions and a tactical
air force initially stationed there. The presence of the Rhine Army
was tangible proof to western Europe of the British commitment to
collective defence. West Germany's accession to NATO in 1955 also
brought a formal end to the Occupation.

NATO membership provoked little of the national soul-search-
ing and division that followed Britain's joining of the EEC/Euro-
pean Union in the 1970s. Given Britain's wariness towards European

institutions – Pandora's boxes full of Trojan horses, to paraphrase Bevin – it is surprising that it was France rather than the United Kingdom which turned out to be NATO's awkward squad. After his election in 1958, President Charles de Gaulle appeared interested in promoting only the French national interest rather than European collective security. One diplomat observed that the President 'just does not like NATO ... he seems on the face of it to have nothing but contempt and a certain veiled hostility'.[11] Wrangles over the French Mediterranean Fleet, tripartite global strategic planning, the military command structure and integration of forces, as well as nuclear deployment, irritated the other members. In March 1966, France pulled out of NATO's integrated command structure, staying out for forty years. The Organisation's HQ was ordered off French soil and relocated to Belgium. In the NATO context, it is the British who have proven to be good Europeans. Today, Britain hardly gives the Alliance a second thought. Politicians of all colours rapidly 'took NATO for granted as the natural framework for defence policy'. In addition, Britain has been a 'model ally', contributing a high level of professional competence to the Organisation.[12] Long after the fall of the Berlin Wall that symbolised the end of the Cold War, the 28-member NATO remains at the heart of the West's defence. To many, the Organisation has defied history by remaining in being after the threat that spawned it had evaporated.

BAOR evolved from an army of conquest and occupation. Housed in many former Wehrmacht and SS barracks throughout north-west Germany, it became a major presence in towns and villages in the region. With families joining the soldiers, a cocoon of Britishness was created in Germany, centred on the Army's headquarters at Rheindahlen. With their own schools, hospitals, sports facilities and the NAAFI, along with the British Forces Broadcasting Service on the radio, the communities were self-contained. The little German that most soldiers spoke was usually limited to '*Ein Bier, bitte*'; '*noch another zwei for my two friends*' or, for the more linguistically ambitious, '*Er bezahlt*' ('He's paying').[13] Like NATO, the Rhine Army swiftly came to be taken for granted: by the early 1960s all regular soldiers expected to spend at least part of their career in Germany. Few considered the historical anomaly of stationing a large part of the British Army in a foreign country for which Britain had no political responsibility. Helping to normalise the military presence in West Germany was the musical request programme *Two-Way Family Favourites*, linking the forces with their families back home in Britain, which millions listened to on the BBC Light Programme every Sunday lunchtime.

Although the threat of Soviet invasion never quite went away, BAOR and its soldiers learned to live with it. Back in London, the cost troubled successive governments. Valuable sterling had to be exchanged to pay roughly 50,000 local civilian employees in addition to forces' personnel who, even if they shopped tax free in the NAAFI using sterling, still needed Deutschmarks to go to the *bier-keller*. Another cost was training exercises, guaranteed to fill local pockets, especially when heavy-duty property-damaging tanks were involved. The damage compensation budget was always generous to ensure the landowner's continuing goodwill and consent. Unsurprisingly, local people generally welcomed BAOR, even if young German men were sometimes not quite so friendly. Fighting between them and British soldiers, usually over the prettier girls, was not unknown. In July 1962, Parliament debated a curfew which had been imposed on unmarried private soldiers in Germany by the Secretary of State for War, John Profumo, whose own conduct with call-girl Christine Keeler was soon to be the subject of inquiry. The curfew followed a series of widely publicised courts martial earlier in the year involving the Cameronians (Scottish Rifles) among others. One MP alleged that there was 'a press campaign against BAOR', with the Army portrayed as 'a collection of drunkards'.[14] Another stated that the state of the barracks in Minden for unmarried soldiers was so deplorable, it was unsurprising that they took the quickest road out through the gate and into town: the Commons heard that there was little for them to do after 4.30 p.m. except buy spirits at 3d a shot. With the Army appearing to 'divide its time between maiming the local population with beer bottles and rescuing them from flood disasters', another MP pleaded for consideration to be given to its role. He wanted the House to debate 'what the Rhine Army does between Mondays and Fridays, rather than what some of those in the Rhine Army happen to do on a Saturday night'.[15] It was a good point.

In late 1952, BAOR came under the formal command of NATO. As part of the Northern Army Group (NORTHAG), it formed part of what became known as the 'Central Region'. NATO's Forward Defence Strategy determined how far east western Europe should be defended. In the event, how long British forces would have been able to hold off a Warsaw Pact advance was never tested. Given the discrepancy in numbers, this was just as well. In the late 1970s, the West mustered 975,000 armed forces personnel in Europe, including 228,000 Americans and 67,000 from the United Kingdom, while the Warsaw Pact forces were estimated to number 1.1 million, including 535,000 from the Soviet Union.[16] Throughout the Cold War, BAOR underwent changes in its force composition, with its numbers settling at around 50,000 troops from the mid-1960s, down from 77,000 a decade earlier.[17] The Rhine Army, officially considered a home posting, provided a reserve of troops who were sent to other theatres, whether to Cyprus, Aden or Indonesia, just as the United States took men from the Europe-based 7th Army to send to Vietnam. One commentator likened BAOR to a 'sort of military refrigerator'.[18]

The nuclear deterrent was the core component of Britain's security strategy from the early 1950s. With the atomic bombing of Hiroshima ending the Second World War, the global security landscape changed for ever. 'The modern conception of war to which in my lifetime we have become accustomed is completely out of date.' Prime Minister Attlee was not alone in sensing that, with the development and successful deployment of an atomic bomb, a revolution in military affairs had occurred. As American nuclear strategist Bernard Brodie declared in 1946: 'Thus far the chief purpose of a military establishment has been to win wars. From now on its chief purpose must be to avert them.'[19] Defence thinking was being turned upside down and inside out. Were conventional, manpower-intensive armies still required in the nuclear age?

The United States' monopoly in atomic weapons did not last long: the Soviet Union exploded its own bomb in 1949, years earlier than expected. For Britain, this was 'a shattering moment of truth', according to Margaret Gowing, the official historian of the British nuclear energy programme. The Soviet's A-bomb was countered by the United States' development of the ultimate weapon, tested in November 1952 – the hydrogen bomb. President Eisenhower's 'new look' for defence underscored that the response to any Soviet attack would be 'massive retaliation' by the United States and her

allies. With the H-bomb, that retaliation would indeed be massive
– as would that from the Soviet Union, which successfully tested its
own H-bomb in August 1953, shortly after the death of Stalin. The
deterrent effect of Mutually Assured Destruction promised by the
H-bomb meant that neither Washington nor Moscow was willing to
push the nuclear button: East and West were to become locked into
decades of military stalemate.

In the Cold War nuclear arms race, Britain would come a distant
third to the United States and the Soviet Union as they battled for
supremacy. An early British technological lead in the early part of
the Second World War was conceded voluntarily to the Americans
as the scientists who had been the original atomic pioneers crossed
the Atlantic to take part in the Manhattan Project. The pooling of
their knowledge would not, however, be reciprocated. The United
States was determined to retain its atomic monopoly, formalised
by the 1946 McMahon Act. It put nuclear weapons under civilian
rather than military control and banned foreign access to technical
information, thereby reneging on the wartime undertakings made by
Roosevelt to Churchill. This end to nuclear collaboration was, according to Gowing, 'a disaster for the British'.[20] With access to US nuclear
know-how shut off, the Attlee government and the Chiefs of Staff
decided that there was a paramount need for a British bomb, not least
because it was the only counter to the overwhelming superiority of
Russia's conventional forces. Few were aware of this seismic policy
shift. Attlee restricted atomic decision-making to a tiny circle, who
were members of various ad hoc committees. Finances for the bomb
were hidden in plain sight in Ministry of Supply figures, while the
matter was never debated in Parliament or received much attention
in the press: 'Extreme secrecy shrouded the project.'[21] In October
1952, an atomic bomb, 'Hurricane', was tested at the Monte Bello
islands, a haven for pearl fishermen off the Australian coast. Seven
years after Hiroshima, and three years after the Russians detonated
their own atomic device, the British finally had, as former Foreign
Secretary Ernest Bevin demanded in 1946, 'a bomb with a bloody
great Union Jack on top of it'.

From the early 1950s, Britain's strategy was reoriented towards
nuclear weapons and deterrence at the expense of conventional forces.
Re-elected in 1951, Churchill sought a reappraisal of defence policy,

not least because the cost of the Attlee government's rearmament programme was unsustainable. After a conference in Greenwich in April 1952, the service chiefs published their *Report on Defence Policy and Global Strategy*, also known as the Global Strategy Paper. As significant a milestone in the development of British strategy as NSC-68 had been to the United States, this paper has been described as leading Britain to 'become the first nation to base its national security strategy planning almost entirely on a declaratory policy of nuclear deterrence'.[22] As Montgomery said, 'It was a big change to go over to basing our defence organization on nuclear weapons.'[23] The shift would allow Britain eventually to cut its conventional forces, particularly the number of soldiers, seen most dramatically in the 1957 Sandys Defence Review and the end of National Service.

Bound up with a determination to demonstrate Britain's continuing global significance, the development of an independent nuclear deterrent actually emphasised the post-war reality of decline. As Gowing observes, the inescapable facts of the change in the world balance of power were dramatically emphasised by the atomic bomb.[24] How far Britain's independent nuclear deterrent has been – to quote Harold Wilson – 'British, independent or a deterrent' has often been at the heart of the debates surrounding the country's nuclear capability since the 1950s. Blue Danube, the first atomic weapon, was delivered to the RAF and its V-Bomber force at RAF Wittering in November 1953; five years later, Britain had an estimated arsenal of 150 warheads.[25] Compared with the stockpiles of weapons that the two superpowers would eventually amass, the British nuclear punch was somewhat puny: in 1968, when the Non-Proliferation Treaty was signed, the UK had just 280 weapons out of a global stockpile of 38,000, almost 29,000 of which belonged to the United States.[26] In 1986, there were an estimated 65,000 weapons, but between 1975 and 1981 only 350 of these were British. The exact number of weapons is contested, but it is unsurprising that many people, including Denis Healey, feared that a nuclear war might break out 'through accident or miscalculation'.[27] Given the overall numbers, senior civil servant Michael Quinlan's description of Britain's nuclear arsenal as 'a modest optional extra' appears apt.[28]

The nuclear strategy sheds light on Britain's post-war relationship with the United States and says much about the two nations' relative standing. In the 1950s some of the British Army's senior commanders, concerned about the opportunity costs, questioned the rationale of developing an independent deterrent, rather than relying on the security shelter that was being provided by the Pentagon, in particular the powerful US Strategic Air Command. Conversely, others, still mindful of the abrupt ending of Lend-Lease, had reservations about the reliability of the United States. Britain – which still had the visible scars from the Blitz – was geographically vulnerable to Soviet attack. Would the United States really go to war on behalf of the housewife in Canterbury or Cologne, jeopardising the safety of the housewife in Kansas? In 1949, the physicist and former government scientific adviser Lord Cherwell warned that without an independent nuclear capability, 'We shall sink to the rank of a second-class nation, only permitted to supply auxiliary troops, like the native levies who were allowed small arms but not artillery.' A British bomb guaranteed the country's continuing place at the global top table and also freed Britain from dependence upon the United States for the nation's security. It, however, relegated the Army in the services' pecking order: the RAF's fleet of V-Bombers – Valiants, Victors and Vulcans – would deliver Britain's strategic nuclear strike capability until 1969. However, concerns about the aircrafts' vulnerability led to the development of Blue Streak, a ground-launched ballistic missile.

The nuclear cooperation between Britain and the United States which continues into the twenty-first century was renewed in the late 1950s. After the launch of the Soviet Sputnik in October 1957, Washington reviewed the nuclear relationship with Britain. The realisation that Moscow could now bomb the American continent provoked a security crisis. In 1958, the McMahon Act was repealed and the two governments signed a Mutual Defence Agreement, 'the cornerstone of UK–US cooperation on nuclear defence issues'.[29] Oiling the diplomatic wheels was the cordiality between Prime Minister Macmillan and President Eisenhower, not least because of their shared wartime experience in North Africa. Macmillan believed that in future the two nations' security strategy would be more strongly interwoven, with the British role complementary rather than subordinate. He declared: 'I am an unrepentant believer in interdependence.'[30]

For all his optimism, even the Prime Minister came to be concerned that the relationship was too one-sided. Keen to access Britain's stockpile of uranium and to station its Thor missiles on British soil and its submarines at Holy Loch in Scotland, Washington was prepared to share its nuclear technology – at a price. Macmillan complained about the salesmanship deployed by the US in connection with the Sergeant short-range ballistic missile, likening the terms to those 'most commonly arranged for vacuum cleaners or washing machines'.[31] In June 1962, he noted that the NATO allies were 'angry with the American proposal that we should buy rockets to the tune of umpteen millions of dollars, the warheads under American control'. He concluded: 'This is not a European rocket. It's a racket of American industry.' When the homegrown Blue Streak was cancelled, the American air-launched Skybolt missile was to have been a substitute for it. The Kennedy administration abandoned the missile's development without warning in November 1962, leaving London high and dry. It brought home how Britain was at the mercy of defence development programmes across the Atlantic. Macmillan was rueful: 'The concept of interdependence with the United States seemed to be becoming a somewhat one-sided traffic.'[32] The reality was, argued one analyst, 'British dependence and American control'.[33]

The Nassau Agreement of December 1962 led, literally, to a sea change in connection with Britain's nuclear deterrent. At a summit in Nassau, held shortly after the observation by US Secretary of State Dean Acheson that Britain had lost an empire but had yet to find a role, Macmillan acquired Polaris missiles, a submarine-launched system. This would remove responsibility for Britain's nuclear deterrent from the RAF and give it instead to the Royal Navy. The missiles would be used for the purposes of international defence of the Western Alliance 'except where Her Majesty's government may decide that supreme national interests are at stake'.[34] With that proviso, Macmillan believed he had protected British sovereignty over the weapons system. Many remained sceptical about the independence of Britain's deterrent, arguing that it was entirely dependent on the goodwill of the United States for the supply of increasingly complex delivery systems. However, 'It has permitted a medium-sized state with an overextended foreign and defence policy to maintain a great-power-by-proxy status on the cheap.'[35]

In 1954, NATO approved the deployment of tactical nuclear weapons within Europe. It was a year after 'Atomic Annie', a 280 mm atomic cannon, was fired in the Nevada desert.[36] Subsequently, BAOR 'revised its doctrine for corps-level tactical battle' and by 1964 'had a full range of integrated tactical nuclear weapons all with American warheads under dual-key control'.[37] As General Sir Hugh Beach noted, fortunately there has never been such a thing as a nuclear battlefield, but BAOR 'spent much time and effort trying to imagine what such a battlefield might look like and in preparing to cope with it'.[38] Beach was sceptical about the utility of battlefield nuclear force, suggesting that in most tactical settings, friendly forward troops would be within the danger radius for blast.[39] The merit of training exercises was also questionable: 'Simulating a nuclear strike meant detailing a party of Sappers from the Control Staffs to light some oily rags in an empty 40-gallon drum, let off a loud bang and then, because neither of these had been noticed by anybody, sending umpires round to tell the troops in the notionally affected area that they were either fried, shot-blasted or radioactive, and probably all three.' In the 1970s, NATO's tactical nuclear arsenal stood at 5,500 weapons. Given that one-third of them were for use by US forces and the rest were under dual-key control, how much discretion a British commander – or any non-American NATO commander – would have had in their deployment was a moot point.[40]

Throughout the decades of the Cold War, East–West tensions fluctuated. Periodically, the conflict threatened to turn hot, particularly in the late 1950s and early 1960s. The construction of the Berlin Wall in 1961 was followed by the Cuban Missile Crisis in October 1962, when the world seemed on the brink of nuclear annihilation. After that, tensions eased: massive retaliation and Mutually Assured Destruction gave way to non-proliferation, détente, the Washington–Moscow hotline and the doctrine of 'flexible response'. In the event of conflict, this offered escalating military responses short of a full nuclear exchange. After more than a quarter of a century of post-Cold War peace in Europe, it is a major mental effort – especially to anyone born after 1989 – to understand that both East and West believed their adversary's threat to deploy the weapons was credible and that the sirens sounding the four-minute warning of Soviet attack might indeed ring out. However, at the time British nuclear strategists were well aware of the potential might of their opponent. The Soviet Union was described as a state which had previously demonstrated great national resilience and resolve: 'Its history, outlook, political doctrines, and planning all suggest that its view of how much destruction would constitute intolerable disaster might differ widely from that of most NATO countries.'[41] From almost the start of the Cold War, the nuclear deterrent was a cost-effective way of cutting conventional forces, which in any event would be outnumbered by those of the Soviet Union.

The strategy of nuclear deterrence continues to be controversial. Until the mid-1950s, the majority of people in Britain supported the development of an independent nuclear capability; subsequently, opposition grew more organised and vociferous.[42] The Campaign for Nuclear Disarmament (CND) was founded shortly after the successful test of a British H-bomb in November 1957. The nuclear cause – civil and military – was not helped by a fire in a reactor at Sellafield, which sent radioactive material across the Lake District. Weeks earlier, the issue of unilateral nuclear disarmament provoked division at the Labour Party conference, which saw the champion of the welfare state, Aneurin Bevan, speaking up for the nuclear warfare state: 'Bevan became Bevin.' In 1958, *The Times* produced *The Nuclear Dilemma*, a booklet of letters to its editor that explored the moral and strategic issues surrounding the development of nuclear weapons. For Canon L. John Collins, Chairman of CND's Executive Committee, the weapons were 'totally evil. To contemplate their use, even in defence of the highest values, is wicked.'[43] Lord Halifax wanted to know, 'Why is a block-buster bomb morally tolerable and a nuclear bomb intolerable?'[44] For some civilians, whether CND members marching on Aldermaston in the early 1960s or the women camped at Greenham Common in the 1980s protesting about cruise missiles, all nuclear weapons should be banned. Prime Minister Margaret Thatcher wisely observed that nuclear war is a terrible threat, but conventional war is a terrible reality.[45] During the Cold War, however, there is no denying that the British deterrent provided the West with an all-important second centre of nuclear decision-making, thereby giving Moscow pause for thought.

After 1945 and throughout the Cold War, the British Army and its NATO allies were involved in various conflicts, including Korea and Vietnam, but all sides refrained from deploying their nuclear weapons. During Suez, RAF Valiants dropped conventional bombs. Was it a further irony that Britain's Resolution class submarines began to patrol carrying Polaris nuclear missiles while US forces tried to counter the Tet Offensive with tube artillery and machine guns? Conventional conflict on such a scale inevitably raises questions about the utility of nuclear force. The nuclear deterrent may well have prevented catastrophic war for nations but it did not deter conventional war – or the small wars that continued to need British boots on the ground. One such small war, fought at the height of the Cold War, was in Oman. However, the Wilson government refrained from any military intervention in the former colony of Rhodesia, which broke with Britain in November 1965, announcing a unilateral declaration of independence.

Withdrawal from East of Suez

In April 1964, a small but hugely symbolic change occurred: the head of the Army was no longer to be known as Chief of the *Imperial* General Staff but more simply as the Chief of the General Staff. The new CGS would no longer preside over the War Office. Like the Air Ministry and the Admiralty, it was to be abolished as part of far-reaching changes set in train after the Sandys Defence Review. All three separate service ministries were subsumed into the new Ministry of Defence (MoD), where the Permanent Under Secretary would have oversight of the defence budget. In future, each service would be run by its own board, and those boards would be subordinate to the new Defence Council. Historian Michael Howard described this as 'an administrative revolution'.[46] The new regime was seen as a triumph for the Chief of the Defence Staff, Lord Mountbatten, whose role had been expanded at the service Chiefs' expense; they were politically demoted. Mountbatten's ultimate goal of combining all the services into a 'joint' force, was however seen off.

In October 1964, Harold Wilson's new government inherited the Confrontation with Indonesia, along with unrest in Aden and surrounding South Arabia. As Defence Secretary in the restructured MoD, Denis Healey was responsible for a department overseeing 458,000 servicemen and women, 406,000 civil servants, as well as perhaps 1,000,000 defence contractors.[47] A review of defence policy got underway, the first results of which would be announced in February 1966. The defence budget was 7.1 per cent of the country's GDP: given Britain's continuing financial difficulties, this had to change. As a percentage of national spending, Britain was not only investing more in defence than any NATO ally, with the exception of the United States, but also spending more on warfare than welfare. In power for the first time in thirteen years, some Labour MPs wanted a greater commitment to education, not least to raising the school leaving age to sixteen. The projected defence budget was capped at 1964 levels. Despite rival claims on the country's finances, like many senior members of his Cabinet, Wilson defended Britain's global role. He told Parliament: 'We cannot afford to relinquish our world role, our role which for shorthand purposes is sometimes called our 'East of Suez' role.'[48] In 1965, 55,000 military personnel were still stationed east of Suez accounting for some 15 per cent of the defence budget.[49] While the base at Aden provided a focus for insurgency abroad, Simonstown in South Africa was opposed by anti-Apartheid campaigners at home.

Although the government was committed to the continuation of Britain's overseas military role, which symbolised the country's global status, the country's finances could not support it. Ever since the Second World War and the financial Dunkirk that followed, Britain had essentially been living from hand to mouth, lurching from financial woes to financial troubles to financial crisis. The convertibility crisis of 1947 had been followed by devaluation of the pound from $4 to $2.80 two years later. The 1950 rearmament programme engendered by Korea, no sooner announced than cut back, was followed by 'economic haemorrhage' during Suez.[50] While the economy undoubtedly picked up in the 1950s with the ending of austerity and the rise of consumerism, reflected by Macmillan's declaration that 'you never had it so good', Britain suffered relative economic decline, not least in the share of world trade. The years 1964–7 have been described as 'one continuous crisis', with the pound having to be repeatedly rescued, with the help from the United States.[51]

The Wilson era coincided with the beginning of the United States' most divisive military engagement in the country's history since the Civil War – Vietnam. In 1965, Operation Rolling Thunder saw the bombing of North Vietnam and the arrival of 200,000 US ground troops. The conflict would escalate. Despite a longstanding antipathy to British colonialism, Washington began to see the advantages of a stabilising British presence overseas. The US foreign policy tune changed, as the Johnson administration sought the continuation of the East of Suez policy as well as support for, and British troops' involvement in, Vietnam. With Britain's economic troubles worsening, some officials in Washington began to link the financial and the military. The 'Hessian Option' would put British soldiers into Vietnam in exchange for backing the pound. In July, the National Security Advisor McGeorge Bundy told President Johnson that a 'British Brigade would be worth a billion dollars at the moment of truth for Sterling'.[52] With British soldiers engaged in Borneo, Wilson, however, had a legitimate excuse to avoid sending even a symbolic British contingent to Vietnam. Castigated by some colleagues for not condemning the US intervention, he told them, 'We can't kick our creditors in the balls.'[53] In a memo to the President ahead of the Prime Minister's visit in July 1966, the section 'What We Want from Wilson' is 'support instead of trouble on Vietnam. Avoidance of anything that will look like a pull-out from East of Suez'.[54]

Attempting to shape the Armed Forces for the 1970s, the Defence Review of February 1966 was drastic but not as radical as what would come later. The defence budget would be cut to 6 per cent of GDP, the planned CVA-01 aircraft carrier would be scrapped along with the Anglo-French replacement for the Canberra strike aircraft. The Aden base, already under insurgent pressure, would be closed in 1968. The Defence Secretary emphasised that alliance warfare was central to British strategy: 'In future, Britain will not accept commitments overseas which might require her to undertake major operations of war without the co-operation of allies.'[55] Resigning, not least because of the carrier decision, Healey's Parliamentary Under Secretary for the Royal Navy, Christopher Mayhew, said that Britain was becoming the auxiliary rather than the ally of the United States. Healey described the review as 'essentially an exercise in political and military realism'.[56] In what could have been a portent of financial trouble, he warned that Britain would only be able to keep forces in Germany at their current strength if foreign exchange costs were fully met. The following month, the government was re-elected, with an almost 100-seat majority.

Events often render defence policy obsolete almost as soon as it is drafted. Just as the armed forces were assimilating the White Paper, within a matter of months, the government was knocked off course by another financial crisis, narrowly staving off a devaluation of sterling: the Review immediately had to be reviewed and additional cuts made. Meanwhile, international developments such as the official end of the Confrontation and the Arab-Israeli Six Day War of June 1967 called into question the utility of a permanent overseas British military presence: perhaps all those bases and installations were just 'crumbling sandcastles' as strategist Basil Liddell Hart had described them.[57] In July 1967, a supplement to the White Paper confirmed that the British military presence overseas would be reduced: the base facilities in Singapore and Malaysia would be shut sometime in the mid 1970s and the number of military personnel, including Gurkhas, halved. Just a few months later, these plans had to be torn up following the shock devaluation of sterling in November: the pound fell from $2.80 to $2.40. The government was humiliated. Although Wilson claimed that the 'pound in your pocket' was worth the same, the cost of imported goods or overseas spending immediately rose. With an estimated £50 million added to defence costs, something had to give. The British military presence east of Suez was to be axed.

The decision to withdraw from east of Suez was as significant for Britain as the Suez Crisis a little more than a decade earlier. It marked a turning point in defence and foreign policy. On 'Black Tuesday', 16 January 1968, the Cabinet, influenced by Chancellor Roy Jenkins, determined that with the exception of Hong Kong, British forces would leave all remaining bases throughout the Middle East and across Asia by the end of 1971. The base at Aden had already closed prematurely. For one minister, Tony Benn, it was a chance to replace imperial Britain with industrial Britain and to 'cut Queen Victoria's umbilical cord'.[58] Although it can be argued that in applying to join the Common Market for the second time in July 1966, like the emphasis on the commitment to NATO, Britain was already orienting towards Europe, there was widespread dismay about the relinquishing of global responsibilities and what appeared to be the abdication of existing defence treaty obligations. Both Canberra and Washington feared destabilisation. Singapore was particularly shocked about the abrupt closure of the base, which employed one fifth of the nation's workforce and accounted for 20 per cent of annual earnings. Described as 'the barbicans of world power', Britain's network of military outposts, fuelling stations and air bases across the Indian Ocean were 'the most extensive overseas military network the world had ever seen'.[59] With the retreat of Britain's armed forces from East of Suez, the country ceded its global role.

The term 'East of Suez' had been coined by Kipling in his poem 'Mandalay', about a soldier nostalgic for his time in Burma. After more than two centuries, soldiers like him had finally gone, 'home to the blasted English drizzle and the gritty pavin' stones'.[60] As if to underscore the loss of Britain's global status the Army's attention shortly came to be focused on part of the United Kingdom. There is nothing like 'trouble at home' to bring a sense of reality.

Northern Ireland

In August 1969, centuries of sectarianism and bitter folk memory, together with decades of political neglect and discrimination, coalesced in Northern Ireland: the province appeared to be on the brink of civil war. In the so-called Battle of the Bogside, three days of violence broke out on the streets of its second city, known as Londonderry to its Protestant population and Derry to Catholics. In Belfast, seventy miles away, the 'Orange–Green Line' between the Protestant Shankill Road and the Catholic Falls Road was a war zone. Tear gas and rubber bullets were met with petrol bombs, nail bombs and missiles of broken paving slabs; barricades made up of trees, telegraph poles, scaffolding and sixty Corporation buses had been set up; whole streets were on fire, with Bombay Street being burned nearly to the ground. Six people were shot dead. More than 5,000 people lost their homes in the three-day battle and one local dairy estimated that 43,000 of its milk bottles had been used to make the petrol bombs.[61] Whole tranches of the cities became 'no go' areas, beyond the control of the local forces of law and order, which were primarily the paramilitary Royal Ulster Constabulary (RUC). As security deteriorated, Northern Ireland's government, Stormont, decided it had no alternative but to ask the government in London to send in troops. A few hours later, soldiers from the 2nd Battalion Queen's Regiment and the Royal Regiment of Wales were mobilised; they were filmed arriving on the streets in full battle gear.[62] It was the start of Operation

Banner, the longest continuous operation in the history of the British Army, which would last thirty-eight years.

The roots of the Northern Irish 'Troubles' were centuries old, long embedded in the colonisation of Ireland, but also entangled in the protracted battle for Irish independence. The Irish Free State, established in 1922, divided the south of Ireland from the north. As in many future partitions – India, Palestine, Cyprus, Bosnia, Kosovo – the seeds of trouble were sown. The partition of a burdensome colony might have allowed London a hasty exit strategy, but it often left a legacy of chaos. As the writer Christopher Hitchens noted: 'As a general rule it can be stated that all partitions except that of Germany have led to war or another partition or both. Or that they threaten to do so.'[63] The population of the six counties of Northern Ireland was divided. By the late 1960s it comprised 1 million Protestants who wanted to retain the union with Britain and 500,000 Catholics, some of whose first loyalty was to the Irish Republic. The province had a large degree of political autonomy, with its own government based at Stormont. Anti-Catholic discrimination was rife. Protestant loyalists controlled both national and local government, as well as the other instruments of state, such as the judiciary and the police.[64] In addition, Ulster's largest employers had few, if any, Catholics among their workforce: the shipbuilders Harland and Wolff, which built the *Titanic*, employed 10,000 Protestants and 400 Catholics. With religious sectarianism seeping into every aspect of life, from schools to sport, few could remain neutral.

Although Northern Ireland is just twenty-five miles across the sea from the British mainland, for successive generations of MPs at Westminster it appeared remote. In 1922, the Speaker of the House of Commons ruled that questions concerning Northern Ireland could not be raised. Consequently, although Ulster sent MPs to the House of Commons, from partition until the outbreak of the Troubles, discussion about the province's affairs averaged fewer than two hours a year.[65] Given subsequent protestations that Northern Ireland was as British as anywhere on mainland Britain, this neglect is curious, especially as British protectorates and colonies around the world were all regularly subject to parliamentary scrutiny. The hands-off, out-of-sight, out-of-mind approach by London led to Northern Ireland being a world apart, despite its red post and telephone boxes and the presence of household chains such as Boots on its major shopping streets. A small military garrison was retained, headquartered at Lisburn, south-west of Belfast: it was seen by some as an agreeable eve-of-retirement posting for its General Officer Commanding (GOC), with plenty of shooting and fishing.

With civil rights movements gaining global traction throughout the 1960s – whether to end racial discrimination in the United States or apartheid in South Africa – the endemic anti-Catholic discrimination in Ulster would not go unchallenged. In February 1967, the Northern Ireland Civil Rights Association (NICRA) was set up, demanding not least equal access to social housing. In August 1968, during a banned march in Londonderry, civil rights supporters clashed with Unionists and police; among the injured was local MP Gerry Fitt. Images of police violence were captured on camera and drew international attention. A year later, as the Bogside and Belfast burned and the troops went in, the international media once again focused on social inequality. One US news anchor likened the Unionist Orange Order to the Ku Klux Klan, reporting that the plight of Catholics in Ulster was not dissimilar from that of minorities in the United States: 'And like Blacks they've revolted; and like Blacks they've burned down the very ghettoes that were built to contain them; and like Blacks they've been shot down.'[66] Global condemnation, along with the loss of control of Ulster's streets, finally awakened Westminster to the problems in the province.

In Britain, the Rule of the Major Generals under Cromwell in the 1650s has cast a long shadow. A cornerstone of the 1689 Bill of Rights following the Glorious Revolution of 1688 was the reassertion of parliamentary control over the Army. Even today, this is regularly renewed in the Armed Forces Act. As recently as 2005, the Defence Committee warned that the government's proposed Armed Forces Bill 'would diminish Parliament's right to exercise control over the Armed Forces, which is central to our constitution'.[67] Before the advent of the metropolitan and county police forces in the 1830s, the Army regularly gave peacetime support to civilian authorities to maintain public order and quell disturbance. However, civilian primacy was always underscored by the presence of a magistrate who would read the Riot Act, which licensed regular soldiers or local militia members to act. In 1908 War Secretary Richard Haldane stated:

1. Field Marshal Sir Bernard Montgomery takes the surrender of all German Armed Forces in North-West Germany, Holland and Denmark at his headquarters on Lüneburg Heath on 4 May 1945.

2. One of the initial tasks of the British military occupation of Germany was the disarming of members of the defeated Wehrmacht.

3. After the Red Army captured Berlin, the city was divided into four sectors. Armoured cars of the 11th Hussars, part of 7th Armoured Division – the 'Desert Rats' – enter the city on 4 July 1945 as part of the garrison of the British Sector.

4. Complete with 'Demob' hat, coat and suit, a British soldier bids a farewell to arms under the watchful eye of the Royal Military Police.

5. Soldiers and members of the Palestine Police work to rescue victims from the ruins of the King David Hotel, Jerusalem, Headquarters of the British military forces in Palestine, July 1946. Britain gave up the Mandate for Palestine on 14 May 1948 when the State of Israel was formed.

6. Following the Partition of India on 15 August 1947, the last British unit to leave India was 1st Battalion Somerset Light Infantry who left Bombay, now Mumbai, on 28 February 1948.

7. The Malayan Emergency lasted from 1948 to 1960. A convoy of vehicles of the Malayan Armoured Corps, escorted by a pair of Daimler scout cars, move along a road through the jungle in 1951.

8. The fighting in the Korean War lasted from 25 June 1950 to the signing of the Armistice Agreement on 27 July 1953. Men of the Argyll and Sutherland Highlanders occupy a hasty defensive position near Chonju on 16 November 1950.

9. Brigadier MAH Butler DSO MC, Commander 16th (Independent) Parachute Brigade and his staff in flight in a Hastings aircraft to seize El Gamil airfield during the ill-judged Suez operation in 1956.

10. Soldiers questioning civilians in Nairobi during the Mau Mau Emergency in Kenya which lasted from 1952 to 1960. Kenya was granted independence in 1963.

11. British soldiers quelling a street riot by Greek Cypriot EOKA supporters in Nicosia, Cyprus, in 1956. The EOKA campaign to gain independence from Britain and union with Greece lasted from 1 April 1955 to 31 March 1959.

12. A briefing in a jungle base in Borneo during the Indonesian Confrontation which was conducted as a low key campaign from 20 January 1963 to 11 August 1966.

13. A street riot in Aden in 1967. The closure of the base was brought forward to 1968 as domestic financial pressures accelerated the withdrawal from bases East of Suez.

14. In 1969 the British Army was deployed on to the streets of Northern Ireland on Operation Banner, which lasted thirty-eight years.

15. Countering improvised explosive devices became a major characteristic of the Northern Ireland campaign. A remote 'wheelbarrow' neutralises an IED.

16. The Dhofar War, which ended in 1976, secured the future of Oman and a close relationship with the United Kingdom. British Special Forces played a key role in the campaign.

'We want the Army to be a popular institution and not a menace to civil liberty.' Consequently, in the context of public order, the Army came to be seen as an instrument of last resort. For Stormont to call on Westminster to authorise the Army's intervention gave rise to an additional complication: soldiers were coming to the 'aid of a civil power', but which civil power? The Home Secretary or the Northern Ireland Prime Minister? As one analyst notes, the point was pretty immaterial in mid-August 1969: 'Whatever the legal theory, the soldiers were no longer acting in aid of the civil power, but in certain areas acting in place of that civil power.'[68]

The soldiers arriving in the besieged Catholic areas were given a hero's welcome, despite the traditional wariness felt towards the British military by some within the nationalist community. Troops flying in from the mainland to Belfast's Aldergrove airport were so unprepared they had to buy maps of the city at a filling station.[69] Major Ken Draycott of the Royal Regiment of Wales was sent to the Falls Road: 'The first night was like Bonfire Night with explosions, flames and gunfire lighting up everywhere.' He had to collect flak jackets for his men that the British Army had not used since Korea.[70] Major Mick Sullivan of the Prince of Wales' Own Regiment of Yorkshire said that both the loyalists and the nationalists welcomed the troops and brought out cups of tea as they stood on the street: 'The loyalists saw us as on their side and the Catholics saw us as an unbiased organisation coming in to separate the two communities and keep the peace.'[71] Jim Parker of the Light Infantry remembers driving into Belfast in an open four-ton lorry: 'We drove through streets littered with debris. Cheering people behind improvised barriers greeted us. Some threw cigarettes at us.'[72] As so often before, many expected the soldiers to be home by Christmas, including the troops themselves. Into 1970, they were seen as saviours and protectors, able to socialise with local people from either side of the divide and live a fairly normal life, down to dating local girls from both the Falls Road and the Shankill, and being able to use the corner shops and dry cleaners. Many Army marriages of the next ten to twenty years came out of those early social encounters.

The Army took over a policing operation but became engulfed in a counter-insurgency and then a counter-terrorism campaign that lasted more than a quarter of a century. In August 1969, Home

Secretary James Callaghan instructed Northern Ireland's GOC, Lieutenant General Sir Ian Freeland, 'to take all necessary steps, acting impartially between citizen and citizen, to restore law and order'.[73] The operation's evolution from peacekeeping into counter-insurgency has been the subject of much inquiry, with questions raised whether the escalation might have been avoided if politicians, the police and in particular the military had acted differently. Arriving in Northern Ireland in those early days, soldiers stood between two warring factions, ultimately pleasing neither side – a situation that would have been familiar to their predecessors in the Palestine of 1946. Claims that troops' 'ill-considered actions' and 'clumsiness' compromised long-term goals assume that some sort of checklist of long-term goals existed.[74] The Army's initial role was to provide 'military reassurance for the minority Catholic community'.[75] Freeland saw this as 'holding the ring' until Westminster and Stormont came up with some political solutions. However, soldiers were operating in a puzzling environment of political intransigence and timidity, which led to a policy vacuum: Catholics demanded wholesale change, the loyalists were resistant to any change, while the British government was hesitant to get involved at all. In addition, the Army was the servant of two masters – Westminster and Stormont. Not only did this complicate command and control, but also raised constitutional questions, particularly after 28 August 1969, when the GOC was given overall responsibility for security operations, including the deployment of the RUC.[76] Like the controversial auxiliary force, the Ulster Special Constabulary or B Specials, the RUC was overwhelmingly Protestant. Given the complicated constitutional arrangements, Army commanders had to report to the Home Office in London as well as the MoD. Stormont had sought oversight of the Army, but 'Westminster was not prepared to deploy forces without retaining operational control of security'.[77] Freeland came to describe the Army as 'a whipping boy if ever there was one'.[78]

All major British military operations since 1945 involving boots on the ground had an overarching political goal. The Army's presence as peacekeepers on the streets of the United Kingdom should have alerted policymakers that something in that society needed to be put right. The Wilson government was, however, at best semi-detached: it feared re-entering the historic quagmire that was

Anglo-Irish relations and challenging what was, after all, the demo-
cratically elected government at Stormont, even if that government
had diminishing, if any, legitimacy in the eyes of one-third of the
province's population. Indeed, almost half a century after the Government of Ireland Act, there were some Ulster Republicans who
still looked to Dublin and refused to acknowledge the authority of
Stormont. At this time, the Republic's constitution asserted the goal
of reunifying the whole of the island of Ireland, a prospect that filled
the Unionists with trepidation. Their paranoia was fuelled by the
Irish Taoiseach, Jack Lynch, who had established field hospitals on
the Irish border during the Battle of the Bogside and called for negotiation with London 'to review the constitutional position of the Six
Counties of Northern Ireland'.[79] Such statements did little to defuse
the fear and loathing between its rival communities.

The first decisive policy introduced by the Wilson government
in connection with Northern Ireland resulted in a gun battle between
Unionists and the Army. Caught out in August 1969, policymakers
in London subsequently tried to catch up and get to grips with the
complexities of political life in the province.[80] In September, a report
by the Cameron Commission – set up by Stormont in the wake of the
civil rights violence the previous summer – was required, if uncomfortable, reading. It underscored how little progress had been made
on the key issue of Catholic civil rights. In October, a second report,
from a hastily convened committee chaired by the Everest leader,
(Lord) John Hunt, recommended the abolition of the B Specials
and the disarming of the RUC. It also suggested that a new locally
recruited part-time force under the control of the Army should be set
up: the Ulster Defence Regiment (UDR) would become operational
in April 1970. London accepted Hunt's recommendations, inflam-
ing Protestant sensibilities. The resulting eight-hour 'Battle of the
Shankill' resulted in the deaths of one RUC officer and two civilians,
as well as scores of military personnel and civilians being injured.
BBC reporter Martin Bell thought he was 'in the middle of World
War Three'.[81]

As it tried to rush through measures such as the introduction of
an anti-discrimination clause in government contracts, Westminster
only underlined its previous neglect of Northern Ireland, where religious bigotry was exacerbated by poverty and high unemployment.

One MP questioned whether Northern Ireland's problem was, in fact, sectarianism: 'Is it not really a problem of no votes, no homes, no jobs and no hope?'[82] Bernadette Devlin, the 21-year-old radical independent MP, told the House that 97 per cent of the houses in the Protestant Shankill area had no hot water and only 5 per cent had a bath, basin or indoor lavatory.[83] For her, deprivation and poverty, not sectarianism, lay behind 'the near-revolution in Northern Ireland'.[84] If the problems of the province had been seen more rapidly through a politico-economic prism, a political strategy could have been decided upon, to which military action was the adjunct.

At this point, the Irish Republican Army (IRA) was an almost dormant historical relic with little credibility among Ulster's Catholic community. It had done nothing to protect the nationalists as they were burned out of house and home in August 1969; indeed, IRA was said to stand for I Ran Away. This was to change. Later that year, the organisation regrouped, dividing into the Official IRA and the Provisional IRA. While both factions were committed to a united Ireland, the Provisionals – or Provos – were prepared to go to war to end British rule in Northern Ireland. For them, the Army symbolised British authority and soldiers were legitimate targets. As opponents, the IRA was far from tactically obtuse and was said to have studied the EOKA campaign in Cyprus. To gain popular support among the Catholic community, it became more active in its protection. It sought to decouple, and then to exploit, both the Army's presence in Northern Ireland and the struggle for civil rights. The IRA went into action on 27 June 1970, in what was described as 'the Provisionals' first battle' during a gun battle with loyalists in the Catholic Short Strand enclave in east Belfast. Five Protestants were shot dead.[85] Suddenly the Army's role changed from policing to 'countering a formidable urban guerrilla movement'.[86]

As in Palestine, in Northern Ireland British soldiers had to endure the abuse of the civilian population they were meant to be protecting and became the target of terrorists. The days of being given cups of tea in nationalist areas were over. On 6 February 1971, an IRA sniper shot and killed Gunner Robert Curtis of the Royal Artillery; by the end of that year, forty-three soldiers had been killed.[87] In the most shocking incident, three soldiers of the Royal Highland Fusiliers – John McCaig aged 17, his 18-year-old brother Joseph and their cousin

Dougald McCaughey, aged 23 – were lured into a car to go to a party and executed on the side of a country road. Soldiers on patrol became used to being spat at and sworn at, attacked by nail bombs and petrol bombs. Sergeant Roy Davies of the Royal Regiment of Wales related how TVs, bricks, sofas and chairs rained down on soldiers from the upper storeys of flats during a riot in Belfast's Divis Street.[88] On 25 May 1971, Sergeant Michael Willetts of 3rd Battalion Parachute Regiment died protecting civilians, including children, from a bomb that had been delivered to Belfast's Springfield Road police station. He was awarded a posthumous George Cross.

As it became clear that the operation was far from short term, everyday issues such as soldiers' accommodation had to be addressed. This was, in many cases, 'appalling', according to Defence Secretary Denis Healey. Extra allowances were introduced in August 1970 for service in Northern Ireland: 7s. 6d. a day for lieutenant colonels and above, 6s. a day for other officers, 5s. a day for warrant officers and senior NCOs, and 3s. 6d. a day for corporals and below.[89] Ordinary soldiers were none too impressed by the equivalent of an extra 18p a day; Palestine had at least offered a duty-free NAAFI. In Northern Ireland, in the temporary bases occupied by the Army, the 'char wallah' made a reappearance – and a profit – often at the expense of the NAAFI. These char wallahs – a name corrupted from the Hindi 'chai'/tea – were invariably from the same extended families that had served the British Army around the world for decades. Some produced tattered letters of commendation from unit commanders in far-flung corners of the Empire from times gone by. Nevertheless their work ethic had not changed – a cup of tea and a bacon sandwich at three in the morning was readily available if required. At the end of a battalion's tour of duty, an agreed proportion of the char wallah's profit was donated back to the unit's welfare fund.

The alienation of the Catholic community from the Army was incremental. On 18 June 1970, the General Election saw the return of a Conservative government led by Edward Heath, who demanded a tougher approach to Northern Ireland. The following month, when the number of troops in the province had reached 11,500, a report of imminent IRA action was received. It prompted a 36-hour curfew in Belfast's Lower Falls area, which involved a massive house-to-house search of more than 2,000 properties: according to local reports, soldiers allegedly wrecked homes, causing damage to holy statues and family portraits but, nevertheless, uncovered caches of arms and ammunition. With three people killed, the movement of an estimated 10,000 local people restricted and their food supplies affected, the Falls Road Curfew was a turning point in the Army's relations with Catholics, who perceived it as losing its impartiality. From being the saviours of Catholics in Bogside and the Falls area, soldiers came to be seen as the 'forces of occupation' and upholders of the reviled Stormont status quo.

A major political misstep was the introduction of internment. Superficially, it was an attractive option: violence was bringing normal life in parts of the province to a standstill and crippling the local economy. The temporary removal of those suspected of being key perpetrators of the unrest seemed logical. On 9 August 1971 Operation Demetrius was launched, in which almost 350 Catholics were rounded up and taken to a makeshift centre at Long Kesh, later known as the Maze. The majority were released without charge. Most of the leading IRA commanders had been tipped off about their imminent arrest and had fled to the Irish Republic. Significantly, not one Protestant was arrested. Internment sparked massive unrest, including rioting at the Ballymurphy estate, where eleven people died in three days. Ardoyne in north Belfast was barricaded for three days before being stormed by soldiers from 1st Battalion Green Howards and 1st Battalion Parachute Regiment. In the five months leading up to internment, there had been 382 bombings and ten soldiers killed; in the five months after internment the figures were 1,022 and thirty-three respectively.[90] This author began his commissioned service on 14 August 1971, taking over a platoon of twenty-seven soldiers. Three weeks later that platoon could muster only nineteen unscathed soldiers. Between August and December 1971, his battalion had five soldiers killed and forty-one seriously injured. Internment would continue until December 1975: in all, almost 2,000 people were detained, just over 100 of whom were Protestants.[91]

Internment crystallised the perception among nationalists that, far from being neutral, the Army was on the Unionists' side. A vicious circle was established: the greater the alienation of the Catholic population, the bigger the increase in no-go areas, and the larger the no-go areas from which the Army was excluded, the greater the opportunity for the IRA to 'organize, recruit, train, intimidate, and carry out its racketeering operations without hindrance', as one officer described it.[92] The IRA was certainly ahead in the propaganda war: a week after the introduction of internment, as the Army held a press conference to explain the effectiveness of the policy and claiming that the IRA had been fatally undermined, the IRA's senior commander, Joe Cahill, was concurrently giving his views at a rival event, mocking the Army's claims.[93] The controversy surrounding internment was compounded by revelations that 'interrogation in depth' was being deployed (see chapter 5). Many senior commanders had misgivings about internment, not least because the RUC-generated intelligence on which detention was based was often inadequate. Veteran campaigner and counter-insurgency expert Frank Kitson, now a brigadier, arrived in the province in September 1970 in command of 39th Infantry Brigade. Having relied on the RUC for intelligence, the Army set up 'a more effective network of intelligence gathering'.[94]

With nationalists' trust in the Army being eroded, the IRA had gained ground in the crucial battle for hearts and minds. The infamous Bloody Sunday would destroy any remaining trust. On 30 January 1972, soldiers opened fired during a banned civil rights march: thirteen people were killed outright. The controversy surrounding events that afternoon would set back the cause of peace for many years.

Dhofar, Oman

While the financial pressures of the late 1960s were driving the decision to withdraw the British Armed Forces from East of Suez and the chaos on the streets of Belfast and Londonderry was driving an increasing deployment of the British Army to Northern Ireland, events elsewhere took another turn which demanded a military response from Westminster. If Communist insurgents had succeeded in taking over Dhofar in the early 1970s, the West's oil supplies would have been jeopardised. Given that the stakes were so high, few at the time had heard of the campaign in this southern province of Oman. Indeed, few had heard of Oman, many confusing it with Amman in Jordan. Until 1970, it was one of the world's least developed nations, with few roads and little electricity or advanced medicine. The gates of its capital, Muscat, were locked every night. Located in the south-east quarter of the Arabian Peninsula, Oman lies on the Persian Gulf, giving it a maritime border with Iran and Pakistan. A northern enclave, the Musandam peninsula, juts into the Middle East's most strategically significant waterway, the Strait of Hormuz.

The discovery of oil in the 1960s should have transformed Oman's economic fortunes, prosperity bringing with it much-needed development. The autocratic and isolationist ruler, Said Bin Taimur, was however determined, Canute-like, to hold back progress, fearing that modernisation would undermine the core of his society – Islam. In July 1970, in a bloodless coup in which British military personnel were involved, he was overthrown by his son and flown to London, where he lived out his final days quietly in the Dorchester Hotel. Oman's new ruler, Sultan Qaboos bin Said al Said, had been a cadet at the Royal Military Academy Sandhurst, an officer with the Cameronians (Scottish Rifles) and had also served in Germany with BAOR.

About the size of Wales, Dhofar lies some 600 miles south of Muscat. A narrow strip of coastal plain, where the provincial capital Salalah is found, gives way to steep mountains, or *jebel*, which run parallel with the coastline for about 150 miles. Although not particularly high, the mountains rise up in places almost vertically to a wide plateau. The rugged and vertiginous terrain is crisscrossed by gorge-like *wadis*: what might be three miles as the crow flies could involve a day of climbing down 3,000 feet and then clambering back up again.[95] In addition, the *wadis* were filled with thick bush and spiky frankincense trees. As one SAS commander noted: 'Suddenly the long range open warfare of the plateau would change to the tactics of the jungle, where visibility is down to a few yards and the first man to shoot usually wins.'[96] Uniquely for the Arabian Peninsula, from June to September parts of Dhofar are touched by the south-west monsoon or *khareef*. While replenishing deep aquifers and ideal for grass, livestock and crops, 'the continual rain and mist and swarms of mosquitoes make living wretched. The red soil turns into mud and movement up or down hill becomes difficult at best and in many places impossibly dangerous.'[97] The *khareef* shrouds the region in fog for a quarter of the year, making flying hazardous and adding to the logistical problems. Given that, in 1970, there were almost no roads in Dhofar, and the few that existed were mined or controlled by insurgents, all supplies arrived by helicopter or Skyvan. On Dhofar's western border was the People's Democratic Republic of Yemen (later also known as South Yemen). Emerging from the chaos of British withdrawal from Aden in 1967 and the short-lived Federation of South Arabia, this rogue new Marxist state exported instability.

When Sultan Qaboos took over Oman, Dhofar was in danger of being lost to a Marxist insurgency. The chronic lack of investment in infrastructure, education and healthcare throughout the country had fuelled a previous uprising in the late 1950s – on the Jebel Akhdar – which had been quelled with the help of British forces. Rebellion broke out for the second time in 1965 as the separatist Dhofar Liberation Front sought to break away from the eccentric autocracy of Sultan Said, whose bugbears included trousers, sunglasses and radios. If Oman as a whole was underdeveloped, Dhofar was more so. Future Chief of the Defence Staff Air Marshal Sir Jock Stirrup described the Salalah he visited when on secondment to the Sultan's armed forces as a 'small and impoverished fishing village'.[98] There was a cultural divide and little love lost between the tough, multi-tribal, highland Dhofaris, who were ethnically akin to Ethiopians and whose language had its roots in Aramaic, and other Omanis, whether living around Muscat or on the gravel plains of the interior.

With the destabilisation of neighbouring Yemen, the rebellion in Dhofar intensified, evolving into a Marxist-driven insurgency. Supporters of the Dhofar Liberation Front were joined by the Aden-based People's Front for the Liberation of the Occupied Arabian Gulf (PFLOAG). Backed by the Soviet Union and China with money, arms and training, the campaign had a base in the Yemeni coastal town of Hauf, a few miles from the Dhofari border. The future General Sir John Akehurst, Commander of the Dhofar Brigade in 1974, observed that the insurgents not only had a secure base, with the terrain providing them with good natural cover, but also – and more importantly – plenty of support from the civilian population.[99] In 1969, the town of Rakhyut fell and its *wali* (governor) was publicly executed; by the end of the year, the only parts of the province under government control were Salalah, Mirbat and Taqa. Marxist insurgents controlled the *jebel* and, with it, most of Dhofar, as well as the only road between the province and the rest of the sultanate. Deploying Russian Katyusha rockets, they were able to mortar the RAF base at Salalah.[100] Given the situation in Yemen, the West could ill afford another Communist success in strategically crucial Oman, leading to possible Marxist control of the Strait of Hormuz. The continuing insurgency in Dhofar meant the sultanate itself, as well as the wider region, was at risk of destabilisation. The domino theory, used to justify US military involvement in south-east Asia, could well have applied to the Middle East.

Links between Britain and Oman date back to a 1798 treaty with the East India Company. Oman had never been a client state, colony or formal protectorate, although the country came under the British security umbrella, with two RAF bases at Salalah and al Mussannah. Since the late 1950s, British Armed Forces personnel had been attached to the Sultan's Armed Forces (SAF), whether serving officers on secondment or former officers 'on contract'. Although creaking, under Sultan Said the SAF had been one of the few almost functioning instruments of state; by 1970, however, it was clear that it was looking at defeat in Dhofar. The *adoo* (enemy) or insurgents were thought to number about 2,000, with a hard core that had been trained in Yemen – or further afield in Libya, Cuba, Russia or China – and equipped with the revolutionary's favourite weapon, the AK-47 Kalashnikov. In contrast, SAF personnel for the most part were making do with .303 bolt action Lee Enfield rifles.[101] In addition, the SAF's local knowledge was sketchy; they had few, if any, Dhofari personnel and the maps that existed were of such a small scale that they were not much help. According to one British officer who tried to decipher them, 'There were very few place names and most of those there were had the words "Position Approximate" or simply a question mark in brackets beside them.'[102]

With his military background and modernising agenda, the 29-year-old Qaboos was clearly the right ruler in the right place at the right time for Oman. The extent of outside involvement in the coup remains deliberately hazy, but change at the top was vital for the implementation of any sort of effective counter-insurgency operation. The Sultan was not only head of state but also commander-in-chief, which simplified lines of authority. Reporting to him was the CSAF or Commander Sultan's Armed Forces, who during the counter-insurgency were Major Generals Tim Creasey and Ken Perkins. They were among the scores of British officers attached to the SAF, which was to triple in size between 1970 and 1972.[103]

For some in 1970, filled with boredom at the prospect of sitting out the Cold War in Germany, Dhofar represented adventure, derring-do and the sort of proper soldiering they had signed up for.[104] The rank and file were either Omani, Indian or men from Baluchistan, with which Oman had longstanding ties. This international dimension to the counter-insurgency would be later augmented by teams from Jordan and Iran, whose shah could foresee trouble if the Communists took hold twenty-one miles across the Strait of Hormuz. Officially, Britain would only supply military support but not regular combat personnel. It was realised then that a conspicuous presence of British, non-Muslim boots on the ground would have led to accusations of neo-imperialism both at home and by the insurgents in Dhofar, who would have portrayed Oman as a puppet state. Moreover, Vietnam, on which global media attention was focused, was showing that heavy-handed foreign military intervention had little utility in a nationalist revolutionary conflict. However, fortuitously for Oman in the 1970s, sound strategic and tactical judgements were reached.

Central to the counter-insurgency operation in Dhofar were the men of 22nd Special Air Services. Arriving in late 1970, they were divided into small groups – British Army Training Teams (BATTs) and even smaller Civil Action Teams (CATs) of perhaps four men – and dispersed throughout the province. They were focused initially on a hearts and minds operation. The five fronts identified by their commander, Lieutenant Colonel John Watts, included medical and veterinary aid, as well as intelligence-gathering and 'when possible, the raising of Dhofari soldiers to fight for the Sultan'.[105] Although Qaboos was half Dhofari on his mother's side, his capricious father had considered that the inclusion of any Dhofaris in the SAF would risk security: this ultimately rebounded on the counter-insurgency operation, which was hampered by a lack of local intelligence. In the early days of the campaign in Dhofar, the SAS teams generally tried to make themselves useful to the local people, doing everything from sinking wells to organising a postal service and clinics, as well as setting up noticeboards to disseminate local news, as part of the effort to counter enemy propaganda pouring out of Radio Aden.[106]

A key aspect of the counter-insurgency operation was the creation of the *firqat*, irregular forces comprising Dhofaris from rival tribes. Used to fighting each other over grazing rights and water, they became the unlikely protégés of the SAS. Many had joined the insurgents but, given that almost all were devout Ibadhi Muslims, their allegiance to hardcore Marxists who had forbidden praying was considered friable. Senior commanders identified the conflict between Islam and Communism as a possible wedge to separate the tribes people from the more fanatical and committed insurgents. As in Malaya, those who changed sides were identified as Surrendered Enemy Personnel who might be persuaded to join a *firqat*. The rag-tag bands – Firqat Salahadin, Firqat Al Nasr, Firqat Umr al Kitaab, etc. – were trained by different BATTs and frequently exasperated the British officers who had dealings with them, especially with their demands of *ureed* – 'I want'. Unwanted by them was the new FN rifle that one SAS commander tried to give them:

'Is it fully automatic?' asked one.

'No.'

'It is too heavy,' said another.

'Can we not have Kalashnikovs?' asked a third.[107] Some refused to operate during Ramadan. Akehurst observes that the *firqat* were best used in small groups attached to SAF companies: 'They were much too independent, excitable, argumentative and undisciplined to be gathered together in a single fighting group.'[108] Another officer said that dealing with them was like herding cats, but that their presence made the SAF look less like an army of occupation. 'For all their limitations, I do not believe we could have won the war without the Firqat.'[109]

One of the most legendary episodes in SAS history was the Battle of Mirbat on 19 July 1972. A nine-man BATT had been living in the small coastal town for three months. Alongside them that morning were some twenty members of the Omani gendarmerie and a handful of *firqat*. As the counter-insurgency had gained traction, reflected not least by the growing number of defections, the *adoo* needed to regain the initiative. Controlling Mirbat would be a huge propaganda boost.

Just after dawn during the *khareef*, a force of about 300 men supported by rocket-propelled grenades, machine guns and mortars began to attack the garrison in its mud and stone fort. The *adoo* were courageous and determined, having to cross hundreds of yards of open ground on the coastal plain in order to close with their enemy.

As the attack intensified, the BATT commander, Captain Mike Kealy, called for air support and reinforcements. He and his team tried to fend off the attack; meanwhile, 400 yards away, in a gun pit at the main fort, Fijian Sergeant Talaiasi Labalaba of the SAS was single-handedly and most gallantly manning a 25-pounder gun, a task which normally required a team of six. As the *adoo*'s anti-tank weapons were reducing the mud and stone buildings to rubble, he was fatally wounded.

Low cloud cover limited the air support but three Strikemasters arrived overhead from RAF Salalah and attacked the enemy forces on the ground. In a lull in the fighting, Kealy called for a helicopter to evacuate the wounded. It arrived, only to have to abort its mission empty-handed, riddled with bullet holes. As Trooper Tom Tobin attempted to reach the gun pit to help Sergeant Labalaba, he was shot in the jaw and later died of his wounds. With the garrison pinned down, it seemed a matter of time before the *adoo* overwhelmed Mirbat.

Napoleon once wondered whether a soldier was lucky. Kealy and the rest were lucky that day. SAS comrades from G Squadron due to take over the following day had gathered in Salalah and were on the firing range to test their weapons, including four M79 grenade launchers, machine guns and semi-automatic rifles, as news of the battle arrived.[110] Jumping into helicopters, the 23-man force landed on the southern edge of Mirbat and began a counter-attack. By shortly after mid-day the battle was over – three members of the security forces had been killed and in excess of eighty *adoo*. According to one analyst, the coincidence that a second SAS squadron was in Dhofar, along with the skill and courage of the Sultan of Oman's Air Force pilots, undoubtedly saved Mirbat[111] – a battle that was to be a turning point in the campaign. In the next few months the number of SEPs went up, reflecting growing confidence in the counter-insurgency operation. Successful military action against overwhelming odds was proving to be a powerful physical and psychological weapon in the battle for the hearts and minds of the local population. Consistent with the British government's determination to keep a low profile in this campaign, gallantry awards were not made to the key combatants of Mirbat until three years after the battle.

'To secure Dhofar for Civil Development.' Arriving in August 1974 as Commander Dhofar Brigade, Brigadier John Akehurst hit upon these words as his mission statement. For the next eighteen months, until he could announce to the Sultan that the objective had been achieved and the war was over, the brigade had to be flexible enough to work with trigger-happy allies, hold an existing line while reinforcing others, capture the Shershitti Caves where the insurgents had cached their stores, seize the town of Rakyuk – the insurgents' proclaimed capital – and relocate hundreds of head of cattle owned by local tribesmen. The province was gradually brought under government control, from roughly east to west: once an area was deemed safe, a well would be drilled, a track bulldozed for vehicles and a shop, school and clinic built, along with a mosque. As one observer noted: 'A salient feature of these projects was the speed with which they were initiated. Major efforts were made to demonstrate to the population the real tangible benefits that were theirs when the *adoo* moved out and the Sultan's forces moved in.'[112]

The insurgents' supply and communication lines were disrupted by a series of defensive picquets crossing the province: the Hornbeam Line, which started on the coast at Mughsayl, ran for thirty miles into the mountains, studded by eight company positions, where soldiers lived in protective stone sangars. Further west, Iranian forces began work on the Damavand Line in late 1974. While appreciative of the political impact of the Iranian presence in Dhofar, British observers were less than impressed by their counter-insurgency expertise. One said: 'Those boys use ammunition like confetti … It's like the Normandy landings up there at night.'[113]

The Dhofar campaign has been described as one of the 'best counter-insurgency campaigns ever fought'.[114] It is also one of the least well known: neither the new Omani government of Sultan Qaboos nor the London government sought publicity for it. The war was a striking example of what a multinational force could achieve. On 17 December 1975, a House of Commons motion, 'Arab Victory over Communism', stated:

> … that this House is greatly encouraged by the successful conclusion to the ten-year war in Oman, congratulates the Sultan's troops on achieving one of the very few victories over Communist-inspired rebels since the Second World War, records with pride the contribution made by hundreds of present and former members

of the British Armed Forces and pays special tribute to the work of the Special Air Service.[115]

Writing in the context of the Iraq intervention, one academic notes that Dhofar was 'a clear example of how to effectively support an ally's counter-insurgency efforts with a minimal commitment of men and material'.[116] For Field Marshal Lord Carver, Dhofar was one of the 'little wars' in which British servicemen had been engaged for centuries, most of them on the shores of the Indian Ocean. 'It was a model of its kind.'[117]

1968 – A Moment in Time

In the history of the Army in the twentieth century, 1968 is unique: no British soldiers were killed in combat. It was also the height of the Vietnam War in which more than 500,000 American troops were involved. A year earlier, the Six Day War between Israel and the forces of Egypt, Jordan and Syria had reinforced how inter-state conflict was far from obsolete. Despite the continuation of the Cold War, underlining the deterrent effect of strategic nuclear weapons, British boots had continued to be needed on the ground throughout the 1960s, whether in Aden, Borneo or Oman. The military presence provided by BAOR might have been primarily a political gesture, as some have argued, 'signifying Britain's commitment to the common cause of the defence of Western Europe', but it also represented how Britain's focus was shifting from Empire to the Continent, emphasised by the UK's continuing attempts to join the European Community.[118] Throughout the 1970s and 1980s, British soldiers would continue to fight the Cold War in Germany and a counter-insurgency in Northern Ireland.

Few would have predicted they would be heading to the South Atlantic; even fewer knew where the Falkland Islands, let alone South Georgia, were. In one syndicate discussion room at the Army Staff College in Camberley, on hearing that the Argentines had invaded the Falklands, a member was dispatched to the library to get an atlas.

– FIVE –

AN ARMY FOR ALL SEASONS

A Changing Britain, Northern Ireland 1972–9,
the Falklands War, the Bagnall Reforms

An Army recruitment film from the mid-1970s shows that there is nothing new about drones. With their frequent deployment by the United States in the campaign in Afghanistan from 2001, civilian qualms about the use of UAVs (unmanned aerial vehicles) have intensified. Reconnaissance drones – like the film itself – provide useful perspectives. Emphasising that the Army's 'first priority is support for NATO', the film concentrates most of its eight minutes on soldiers battling across the North German Plain. Chieftain tanks roar forward, Rapier missiles are launched, helicopters land and a brick building is destroyed. The use of a computer is highlighted, but a communications centre is shown with dial-up telephones and is 'manned' by women. The film states that the Army seeks to recruit 'intelligent men from all walks of life' and claims that 'when good men come forward' they will be well paid. Shots of skiing, sailing, boxing and games of cricket and rugby are followed by the promise of adventure training expeditions in India, Canada, the Andes and the Arctic. With pictures of youths throwing stones and petrol bombs, the film concedes that security in Northern Ireland represents a 'massive task'. There are pictures of the Royal Military Academy Sandhurst but no glimpses of what soldiers' day-to-day life was like in terms of accommodation, food, welfare or discipline. Any viewer would conclude that, at the time, the Army was Germany, Northern Ireland, sporty, white and over-whelmingly male.[1]

Against a background of seismic shifts in the attitudes of the civilian population and almost continuous economic turbulence, this chapter examines the role of the Army in an era between two General Elections which returned two Conservative prime ministers: that of 16 June 1970, when Edward Heath came to power, and 9 June 1983, when Margaret Thatcher was re-elected for a second term in a landslide which gave her a majority of 144. Throughout those thir-teen years, the Army focused on its NATO role in Germany and on Operation Banner in Northern Ireland. This chapter examines the Army's continuing campaign in the province and then looks at the most significant operation undertaken since 1945 – the Falk-lands War. It concludes with a brief account of how Britain's forces in Germany were revolutionised by one of the Army's most visionary leaders, Field Marshal Sir Nigel Bagnall, that young officer who twice won the Military Cross in Malaya.

The Army in a Changing Britain

The late 1960s and 1970s can be considered the start of an era when the Army became out of step with civilian society. With the end of National Service, the close connection between Army and nation had been severed. By the mid-1970s, what had once been consid-ered counter-cultural was becoming mainstream. One officer noted in a 1975 edition of the *British Army Review* – the house journal of the Army – 'There are a number of trends in contemporary society which, apparently, do not favour military institutions.'[2] The ques-tioning of authority, reflected by the growth of protest movements and pressure groups, growing materialism, rising crime and hooli-ganism, more relaxed teaching methods in schools, declining church attendance and 'individual happiness being preferred overwhelm-ingly to national greatness' were all cited as evidence of the way in which society was changing. 'Young people today tend to be resentful of arbitrary authority, egalitarian in their outlook and non-conform-ist in their behaviour.'[3] In 1969, one-third of all soldiers leaving the Army said service discipline was the reason for their decision to quit. As an institution embodying traditional values, the Army was not readily at ease with long hair and flower power, let alone peace and love, tuning in and dropping out. It did not embrace feminism, officially rejected homosexuality and, like many in Britain, had much to learn about racial equality. As the recruitment film showed, it was in the vanguard of new technology, routinely using computers on the battlefield while most civilian companies were using typewriters well into the 1980s.

Just as civilian and military life were diverging in the 1970s, traditional values were being challenged by new social attitudes. Britain was ill at ease. Colour television was becoming the norm, but the national mood seemed dark. According to one analyst, the years 1970–77 were 'exceptionally violent', in terms of terrorism, strikes and demonstrations, while 'our economic performance was dismal', with fear taking hold that the economy was 'galloping towards collapse' – which belied the optimism that had sprung from Britain's belated entry to the Common Market in 1973.[4] The industrial unrest that had dogged Harold Wilson's government continued under Edward Heath, most famously with the miners' overtime ban and strike of 1973/4, which led to the country shutting down and shivering by candlelight during a three-day week. The Six Day War of 1967, which had brought a decisive victory for Israel, was followed by less certain success against Egypt and Syria in October 1973 – the so-called Yom Kippur War. The resulting oil embargo by OPEC (Organisation of the Petroleum Exporting Countries) led to the first 'oil shock', with prices going from $3 a barrel to $12. The petrol shortages led to long queues at filling stations and a cut in the speed limit to 55 m.p.h. More seriously, global recession followed and the word 'inflation', which peaked at 25 per cent, became part of everyday language. The new decimalised currency, introduced in February 1971, seemed to be worth less and less.

The country's dire financial plight had an impact on BAOR, where the amount of money available for training, new equipment and maintenance was 'continually decreasing'.[5] The price of replacing tanks parts had increased five-fold in a single year, while the cost of 7.62 mm rounds of ammunition rose 18 per cent between 1973 and 1974.[6] The arrival of the 'floating' pound in August 1971 further complicated Army finances. Denis Healey, Chancellor in the Wilson and Callaghan Labour governments of 1974–9, estimated that the added burden to Britain's defence budget in foreign exchange costs amounted to £1 billion a year.[7] The economic situation lurched from bad to worse in the summer of 1976, due to a massive balance of payments deficit and a sterling crisis, prompted not least by industrial unrest at the car firms British Leyland and Ford. Interest rates rose to 15 per cent. National pride took a hit, with the embarrassing arrival of the 'gnomes of Zurich' from the International Monetary Fund, who insisted on examining the national balance sheets ahead of agreeing a loan.

The 1970s was an era when the Cold War seemed aptly named. The division of Europe appeared to be deep frozen, with neither the East nor the West doing anything to break the deadlock. Indeed, militaries, along with their attendant bureaucracies and institutions such as NATO, rarely questioned if or when or how the Cold War would end. Paradoxically, the possibility of a nuclear war with the Soviet Union seemed remote: in the 1970s, movements such as the Campaign for Nuclear Disarmament (CND) were more or less dormant. The struggle against Britain's Warsaw Pact adversaries was seen as being covert rather than overt: this was the era for espionage, real or imagined. Films, television series and books reflected the public's continuing fascination with spies, whether James Bond, Harry Palmer or George Smiley. Linked to conflict in the Middle East was a wave of terrorism, either by radical Arab groups like the Lebanese Amal or their sympathisers such as Germany's Baader-Meinhof Gang. Terrorist attacks included the massacre of eleven Israeli athletes during the 1972 Munich Olympics and the 1978 kidnapping of Italian Prime Minister Aldo Moro. From 1972 the IRA brought terror to the British mainland.

The 1974 Defence Review was undertaken in the context of a warning by Chancellor Denis Healey to the Cabinet that 'the country is confronted by an economic situation which might well be the worst which has ever been faced in peacetime'.[8] Defence Secretary Roy Mason argued that Britain was still 'acting as a world policeman' and remained East of Suez to a far greater extent than was generally realised.[9] Keen to fight the Armed Forces' corner against the left-wingers in the Labour Party who were demanding £1 billion of defence cuts, and mindful of the continuing Soviet threat reflected by the crushing of the Prague Spring in 1968, Mason ensured his Review retained the major acquisition programmes such as the Chevaline upgrade to Polaris – then the heart of the UK's nuclear deterrent.

On land in Europe, the Warsaw Pact forces outnumbered and outgunned the NATO Alliance's forces by 2.5 to 1 in tanks and 2 to 1 in aircraft and artillery and had up to 40 per cent more soldiers.[10] The Defence Review – 'the most extensive and thorough ever undertaken in peacetime' – aimed to cut defence as a proportion of GNP from 5.5 to 4.5 per cent over ten years, producing savings of £4.7 billion. Service manpower overall would be reduced by 35,000, with the Army's strength falling from 180,000 in 1973 to 159,000 a decade later.[11] The Defence Secretary told the Commons that, with priority being given to Britain's contribution to NATO, cuts would be achieved by 'a contraction in our commitments outside the Alliance'.[12] The Gurkhas would be withdrawn from Brunei; the Simonstown Agreement with South Africa would be terminated; the facilities at Diego Garcia would be expanded by the United States; Malta would be given up in 1979; the presence in Cyprus and Hong Kong reduced; the forces seconded to the Southeast Asia Treaty Organisation (SEATO) in the Far East cut.

The future of Britain's Armed Forces appeared to lie closer to home.

Northern Ireland 1972–9

On 31 July 1972, the British Army undertook one of its biggest deployments since the Second World War – Operation Motorman. Although American forces had begun to draw down in Vietnam and the Cold War was going through a period of détente, Northern Ireland was one of the world's trouble spots which seemed impervious to any sort of progress towards a better peace. The year 1972 was the peak of the Troubles, witnessing 1,853 bombings and more than 10,000 shootings.[13] It was the worst year for military fatalities since Korea; 102 soldiers would lose their lives in the province. Reprisal would follow reprisal; the divide between the Catholic Republicans – the nationalists – and the Protestant Unionists – the loyalists – deepened and became more entrenched. As Prime Minister Edward Heath described, there existed 'the bitter, tribal loathing between the hardline elements in the two communities, springing from an atavism which most of Europe discarded long ago'.[14] For almost three years since they had been sent to the province, soldiers had attempted to hold the line between the two communities; in doing so, they had been drawn into the conflict, ending up being perceived as part of the problem – a precursor to the situation some three decades later in Iraq and Afghanistan.

The existing disaffection within the Catholic community had hardened with two missteps: internment and Bloody Sunday and its aftermath. Catholics had made up 95 per cent of those being held without charge in detention centres such as the Maze. After the introduction of internment, GOC Northern Ireland, Lieutenant General Sir Harry Tuzo, estimated that half of the province's Catholics sympathised with the IRA and one-quarter – 120,000 people – were ready to give the organisation active support.[15] Following Bloody Sunday, the Widgery Report swiftly exonerated the military personnel involved. Not only would this reprieve prove temporary, but the 'Widgery Whitewash' would further undermine Catholics' dwindling trust in the Army. Prime Minister Heath observed with hindsight that Bloody Sunday 'provided the IRA's propagandists with an opportunity to publicise what they claimed had been a barbaric and premeditated act of cold-blooded murder by the Army'.[16]

Soldiers on the ground, once hailed as saviours, observed how previous gratitude had soured irrevocably. Arriving in Belfast for his second tour of duty, Major Mick Sullivan of the Prince of Wales' Own Regiment of Yorkshire found that, following Bloody Sunday: 'There were no cups of tea this time. Soldiers were burned by petrol bombs, hurt in riots and shot at by snipers. There would be riots every night, and you had bricks and bottles raining down on you.'[17] Three weeks after Bloody Sunday, the IRA bombed the Parachute Regiment's mess in Aldershot, killing a padre and six civilian staff. In addition, a second front had opened with an escalation in violence from loyalist paramilitaries such as the Ulster Volunteer Force (UVF) and the Ulster Defence Association (UDA). In December 1971, fifteen people died when the UVF bombed McGurk's Bar in a Catholic area of Belfast, the worst atrocity of its kind since the Troubles began. The number of soldiers on operational tours of duty in Northern Ireland reflected the security crisis: up from 3,000 in 1969 to 14,218 in January 1972 to 15,702 in 1974.[18]

The introduction of Direct Rule in March 1972 was a decisive reordering of the governance of Northern Ireland. For more than half a century, the province had seemed a faraway country of which

Westminster knew very little. However, with civil war threatened, the Heath government had to act. It literally took Northern Irish matters into its own hands. To Unionist outrage and Catholic approval, it suspended Stormont. Instead, power was vested in the Northern Ireland Office, headed by the newly created Secretary of State for Northern Ireland, Willie Whitelaw, who would reside in the suitably viceregal Hillsborough Castle. The transfer of power was to provide a fresh start 'to promote feelings of tolerance, understanding, fairness and impartiality', according to the ever-optimistic Whitelaw.[19] The constitutionally complicated issue of control over the Armed Forces was a background factor to Direct Rule. The hastily passed Northern Ireland (Temporary Provisions) Act made clear that all senior commanders were to take their orders from the Westminster government, demoting local politicians in matters to do with security, as well as law and order. Politically, the suspension of Stormont reflected that London was prepared to address local concerns, including discrimination. It offered the prospect of a political solution to the Troubles, not least when Secretary of State Whitelaw began secret, if unsuccessful, talks with the IRA.

Operation Motorman saw the Army moving into IRA strongholds and loyalist enclaves of Derry city and Belfast, taking back control. It was triggered by 'Bloody Friday' ten days earlier, on 21 July, when, during sixty-five terrifying minutes, a series of nineteen IRA bombs exploded around Belfast city centre, killing nine people and injuring more than a hundred. Press reports described how people were fleeing from the site of one explosion into the path of another. So much for tolerance and understanding. One local woman said that Whitelaw 'should take off his coat and mop up the blood'.[20] On the morning Motorman began, 'Catholics and Protestants alike woke up to find the Army all round them, occupying schools, football grounds, halls and blocks of flats'.[21] More than 30,000 security forces personnel took part, including 22,000 regular soldiers and 5,300 members of the Ulster Defence Regiment.[22] Riot gear, including extra helmets and shields, had been flown from Hong Kong.[23] Some analysts see Motorman as a strategic turning point, identifying it as the moment at which violence in the province began to decline. For civilians and soldiers on the ground this is moot: the level of death and destruction remained unacceptably high for decades.

The cornerstone of the Army's tactics in Northern Ireland was the patrol – as in many campaigns since 1945. Whether in vehicles or, more valuably in urban areas, on foot, the physical presence of soldiers is visible evidence of domination of the ground. A static overt presence was also established in numerous observation posts (OPs). Covert, close observation was carried out by teams who could make themselves invisible for weeks at a time.[24] The military presence would be underscored by searches, roadblocks, vehicle check points, observation helicopters clattering overhead and mobile patrols by an assortment of vehicles, including the venerable Humber 1-ton 'Pigs' armoured personnel carriers and the lightly armoured 'snatch' Land Rovers. Soldiers went out on to the streets in four-man teams, known as 'bricks', led by a corporal or lance corporal. Three, four or five teams made up a 'multiple' commanded by a subaltern officer or a sergeant. They were warned never to establish patterns or use regular routes, because lookouts – 'dicks' – were constantly watching. Local women would bang dustbin lids on the ground or blow whistles to warn of troops' approach. In their first three weeks on the streets of the Upper Falls, one battalion was fired at by 2,500 rounds and had a man hit each day.[25] A soldier from 1st Battalion Gloucestershire Regiment says: 'It was a battleground. I don't care what anybody says, we were at war and against an enemy that was good. The snipers were always out there, waiting for us ... You could feel the hatred.'[26] An 18-year-old from the Royal Regiment of Wales, on his first patrol in Belfast city centre, saw a teenage 'picture of beauty' walking towards him; when he smiled and said hello, she looked at him horror-struck, replying, 'Away to fuck, ye British bastard.'[27] Soldiers from the Cheshires doctored 'Cheshire Bastards Out' graffiti to 'Cheshires are Outstanding'. Some soldiers from the Glosters unofficially stencilled their regimental back badge and a scoreboard on the tall chimney of the Albert Street Mill in the heart of Lower Falls, an IRA enclave. The scoreboard would be updated: for example, Glosters 2, IRA 0.[28] These moments of black comedy were few. One senior commander described how one of his young officers was lying in the street, dying, with local people spitting on him.[29]

Intelligence was crucial in trying to counter the enemy. Every patrol was an opportunity to glean snippets of information, about a house move perhaps, which could be added to the existing picture.

Undercover intelligence-gathering was carried out by units such as 14th Intelligence Company and the Mobile Reconnaissance Force (MRF), established by Brigadier Frank Kitson during his tenure as commander of the 39th Infantry Brigade. In Belfast, a company called Four Square was set up – a bogus laundry service, its van was 'a little observation post going round on wheels'.[30] Laundry would be collected from IRA suspects and examined for traces of explosives. A massage parlour was bugged. In March 1973, intelligence enabled the Irish Navy to interdict the Cyprus-registered *Claudia* off the coast of Country Waterford, laden with Libyan-supplied weapons, including 250 rifles. In an echo of Kitson's counter-gangs, IRA members were turned and became informers; many of these 'Freds' were subsequently hidden away in armoured cars and driven around Republican areas, identifying IRA personnel. It is alleged that the Army's Information Policy Unit was also not above planting disinformation, such as exaggerating the amount of money stolen by the IRA in bank robberies, to spread mistrust within its ranks. But the Army did not have it all its own way: in 1974, the IRA allegedly bugged its HQ at Lisburn.[31]

A campaign on British soil had been unforeseen by the British Army. Although Operation Banner is often analysed in the context of the Army's other post-1945 counter-insurgency campaigns, Northern Ireland was the last place official guidance expected the Army to be. Ironically, the first part of *Land Operations Volume III – Counter-Revolutionary Operations* was released in August 1969, days ahead of soldiers being sent to the province.[32] Issued in three booklets, which looked at counter-insurgency and internal security operations, as well as their general principles, it expected soldiers to be deployed to British overseas dependencies, Commonwealth countries or in support of the United Nations. Described by one writer as 'the bible for Army operations in Ulster', the pamphlets feature pictures of Palestine and other unidentified locations that appear to be East of Suez.[33] Among guidance such as how to set up roadblocks, crowd dispersal and the wraparound method for disconnecting overhead telephone lines, *Internal Security* focuses on the legal aspect of operations and the use of minimum force: 'Force must never be used with punitive intent nor as a reprisal.'[34] In 1972 in Northern Ireland – and later in Bosnia – soldiers would be issued with the Yellow Card guide to the rules of engagement, which underscored that they could only react rather than act, and open fire solely in self-defence. Some soldiers taped the guidance on to their rifles.[35]

Human rights were becoming a weapon of war, with proven transgressions a propaganda gift to the enemy. Measures such as internment, the juryless 'Diplock' courts and the 1974 Prevention of Terrorism Act troubled civil libertarians. Edward Heath observed: 'As so often in our dealings with Northern Ireland, we found ourselves forced to introduce draconian measures which we would never have contemplated in any normal situation.'[36] GOC Tuzo reported to Whitelaw that at least sixty-four former internees released by the Secretary of State had returned to active service with the IRA.[37] As in Kenya, accusations of torture and brutality were made against the security forces. In March 1972, the government-commissioned report by the Parker Committee into five techniques of interrogation – sleep deprivation, wall-standing, subjection to noise, hooding, deprivation of food and drink – considered them to be illegal under UK law. The MP for Republican-leaning Fermanagh and South Tyrone, Frank McManus, condemned 'barbaric practices', while a political opponent quoted Parker's conclusion that the techniques 'have saved innocent lives'.[38] Complaints lodged against the Army jumped from four in January 1971 to 366 a year later.[39] As one commentator observed: 'The correlation between military success and false allegations seemed solid.'[40] Nevertheless, in early 1972, HQ Northern Ireland set up an office to process claims against the Army and the MoD which ended up making 410 out-of-court settlements, 'payments for military misdeeds, a *de facto* admission of guilt, if not one in law'.[41] In 1978, the European Court of Human Rights ruled that the five interrogation techniques did not amount to torture, but by then the Callaghan government had banned them. The issue would resurface in connection with Iraq (see chapter 8). In addition, lurid allegations about extra-judicial killings carried out by various branches of the security services appeared in the press, particularly after the SAS was sent to the province in early 1976, in a deployment that was well publicised by the government for political ends. The MRF was perceived as an 'undercover hit squad with a licence to kill'.[42] In a liberal democracy based on the rule of law, such actions would never have been sanctioned.

British and international public opinion was another weapon

in the campaign. Lieutenant Colonel Paddy Palmer of 1st Battalion Argyll and Sutherland Highlanders concluded that 'the enemy can only be fought by methods which public opinion at home, and indeed fair-minded opinion abroad, finds acceptable'.[43] As in Vietnam, television cameras recorded Operation Banner. As in Palestine, the British Army had to contend with public opinion in the United States, where IRA sympathisers raised funds, supplied 200 Armalites and in 1976 stole machine guns from a National Guard armoury.[44] The Army's critics routinely suggested that it preferred far-flung operations where soldiers could escape the media and legal spotlight. The inference seemed to be that the Army was itching to impose martial law and a regime of curfews, torture and Guantanamo-style detention in Northern Ireland. The Army knew better than anyone that this is counter-productive. One of the principles of the use of force is the maintenance of public confidence: 'Every effort must be made to win and foster public confidence and support, as by doing so this will depress the morale of dissidents.'[45]

The Army's role in Northern Ireland was to give aid to the civil powers, until a political solution could be found to the Troubles. The Sunningdale Agreement of December 1973 ended Direct Rule. It was replaced by the power-sharing Northern Ireland Executive, supplemented by the cross-border Council of Ireland. For some Unionists, happy to conform to their 'bigots in bowlers' stereotype, Sunningdale was 'the supreme sell-out, the supreme betrayal'.[46] Power-sharing seemed a step along the road to rule by the reviled Dublin. The Agreement was badly wounded in the February 1974 General Election, when Unionist hardliners were almost unanimously elected, only to be finally killed off by a fortnight-long general strike in May convened by the Ulster Workers Council. It brought the province almost to a standstill. On 17 May 1974, one of the bloodiest days of the Troubles, the UVF exploded three car bombs in Dublin and Monaghan: thirty-three people were killed.[47] On 28 May, Harold Wilson's minority government re-established Direct Rule. A failure of political will on both sides of the sectarian divide blighted any chance of peace in Northern Ireland for many years.

By the mid-1970s, the IRA was contained if not defeated. Essentially, it was failing, unable to force a British withdrawal from Northern Ireland. The level of violence had declined: the number of bombings fell from 1,853 in 1972 to 535 in 1977, while the number of shootings dropped from 10,564 to 1,081.[48] However, by then the IRA campaign included the mainland. In February 1974, the M62 bombing in West Yorkshire saw an explosion on a coach carrying service families: eleven were killed. Off-duty soldiers were targeted in the Guildford pub bombing in October, when five died. The bombing of two crowded pubs in Birmingham city centre in November killed twenty-one and injured 189. One man caught up in the blast said, 'It filled everything. It filled you. The room. I remember being picked up and doing a half somersault and hitting the wall.' A fireman at the scene gave up counting casualties once he had reached 150 or 160.[49] The wave of terror continued into 1975 with the capital's shops, bars and restaurants under attack. One commentator observed: 'London was on the verge of panic.'[50] Among the victims was *Guinness Book of Records* co-editor and broadcaster Ross McWhirter, who was shot dead after he offered a reward for information about the bombings. The four IRA men responsible – the so-called Balcombe Street Gang – were finally captured after a five-day siege in central London in December 1975. The London bombings reflected changes within the IRA: it was reorganised into a cellular structure of multiple active service units (ASU) and, like many terrorist organisations, it had grasped the importance of the 'propaganda of the deed'. Terror is a two-fold process: the act and the aftermath of the act, including media coverage. This idea was summed up by one analyst who argued that the Provisionals had two basic aims: 'To hit the security forces; and to hit the headlines.'[51]

In 1976, in a process of 'Ulsterisation', the government introduced a policy of police primacy. In future, the RUC was to be the lead service for security, reflecting increasing stability within the province. As in Malaya, the province was divided into areas classified Black, Grey and White, according to the level of terrorist activity. White indicated an area in which a military presence was judged unnecessary and where normal policing could be resumed.[52] By then, some IRA members thought the campaign should be called off. 'Things weren't going well and it was getting very rough. We were short of money, short of arms and men were getting arrested. Things were getting a bit critical.'[53] Although the Army was winning the war across Northern Ireland, an area that remained a Black zone was the so-called 'bandit country' of South Armagh, centring on the border town of Crossmaglen, where 'to stay alive a soldier had to be good, and alert. People had forgotten the days when policemen last walked the streets alone.'[54] A concrete sangar, used as an observation post, which dominated the square was named the Baruki Sangar after a Paratrooper who had been killed nearby. Terrorists knew that once they had crossed the border into the Republic, which soldiers were officially forbidden to enter, they should be safe. More than once, soldiers made 'map-reading errors'. The adjustment to police primacy was far from easy. The RUC was overwhelmingly Protestant, stoking up Catholic fears. The new Northern Ireland Secretary, Roy Mason, appointed by Prime Minister James Callaghan, noted there was too much rivalry between the RUC and the Army: 'Each side [is] just a little too zealous about guarding its own patch of turf. It's a common enough problem when dealing with terrorism but one which had to be solved.'[55] RUC competence in intelligence-gathering was called into question by the Army, which was often reluctant to share its sources.

Despite the Army's lower profile and the IRA being on the defensive, the Troubles were far from over. From 1977, the Provisionals began talking about the 'Long War'. Acknowledging the war weariness in the province even among its own supporters, it sought to undermine public will on the mainland.[56] Political targets were chosen for assassination, such as the British ambassador to Dublin. In addition, off-duty members of the RUC and UDR began to be targeted. Meanwhile, as well as combating terrorism, Secretary of State Mason considered economic revival urgent. In 1978, unemployment in Northern Ireland was double the UK average, while in West Belfast more than 35 per cent of all adult men were without a job and youth unemployment stood at 50 per cent. Mason recorded: 'Here was the pool of misery on which the IRA could draw. Here was where it found its recruits, its safe houses and its political support.'[57] Although internment had ended, Mason authorised pre-dawn raids to pick up and hold batches of suspected terrorists in RUC-run detention centres such as Castlereagh. In all, more than 3,400 people were interrogated. He swept aside criticism by Amnesty International: 'We were arresting and charging and convicting people who were putting bombs in shops and killing innocent civilians, innocent children.'[58] Underscoring his point was the bombing of the La Mon hotel in February 1978, which was engulfed in a fireball of such intensity that those who died were almost unidentifiable. Such incidents inevitably made some in the Army question the wisdom of police primacy.

A secret report, *Future Terrorist Trends* (1978), written by Army intelligence chief Brigadier James Glover, suggested that the IRA would be far more focused in future, concentrating on 'a few spectacular attacks to indicate that their normal lower posture stems from restraint rather than weakness'.[59] On 27 August 1979, a bomb exploded on a fishing boat just off the coast of County Sligo. It killed the last Viceroy of India, Lord Mountbatten, and three others, including his grandson. A few hours later, at Warrenpoint, South Down, a bomb hidden under some hay on a flat-bed lorry exploded. Six soldiers of 2nd Battalion Parachute Regiment, travelling in a three-vehicle convoy, were killed. Some twenty minutes later, a second bomb was detonated nearby, killing many of the survivors of the first device. In all, eighteen soldiers died that day: two from the Queen's Own Highlanders, including their commanding officer, and sixteen from the Parachute Regiment, its largest loss of life in a single day since Arnhem in the Second World War.

Almost ten years to the day after soldiers had first been sent to Northern Ireland, peace remained elusive.

The Falklands War

Immediately after entering 10 Downing Street, Britain's first woman prime minister wasted no time. Defence had been run down under the Callaghan government and service personnel were demoralised. Cutbacks to equipment throughout the 1970s led to 'a significant level of equipment obsolescence and an Army with the reputation for being one of the worst equipped in Germany'.[60] As Leader of the Opposition, Margaret Thatcher promised much for the Armed Forces. In January 1976, she stated defence should be strengthened, a commitment repeated in the Conservative Election Manifesto of 1979: 'While we shall seek value for money in defence expenditure as elsewhere, we will not hesitate to spend what is necessary on our Armed Forces even while we are cutting expenditure on other things.'[61] Immediately after the election, forces' pay was increased and a rise of 3 per cent per year for the next seven years was implemented. The Iron Lady was as apparently uncompromising in her attitude towards the Soviet Union as she was to everything else, finding an ideological soul mate in new American President, Ronald Reagan. Relations between East and West worsened, not least because of the threat to Europe from Soviet SS20 missiles and the Russian invasion of Afghanistan in December 1979. However, in the spring of 1982 the world's attention was focused not on Europe or the Hindu Kush, but the South Atlantic.

On 3 April 1982, the House of Commons sat for the first time on a Saturday since November 1956 when it had met to discuss the Suez Crisis.[62] The Prime Minister explained: 'British sovereign territory has been invaded by a foreign power.'[63] The previous day, Argentine forces had landed on the Falkland Islands and entered the capital, Port Stanley. The few dozen Royal Marines who made up the tiny garrison there were overwhelmed. Within hours, they were bundled on to a plane to Uruguay, along with the Governor, Rex Hunt, as thousands more Argentinian soldiers were flown in. The flags of Argentina might now be flying over the Falklands but, as the Prime Minister said, the 1,850 islanders were 'British in stock and tradition and they wish to remain British in allegiance'. She was unequivocal: 'It is the Government's objective to see that the islands are freed from occupation and are returned to British administration at the earliest possible moment.'[64] A Royal Navy task force would sail as soon as all preparations were complete: 'HMS *Invincible* will be in the lead and will leave port on Monday.' Two days later, the aircraft carrier was heading for the South Atlantic.

The Falklands War was the catalyst for revolutionary change in Britain: the post-1945 political consensus would end and the country would be set on the path it would follow into the twenty-first century. In early April 1982, however, the conflict seemed surreal: no one had anticipated the Argentine invasion, while the bellicose British response to it was expected to peter out somewhere in the middle of the ocean into a fudge of a diplomatic compromise. In the seemingly unlikely event of actual combat, the British were thought likely to come off worse, not least because they would be heavily outnumbered and fighting in what was effectively Argentina's back yard. The Falklands were 400 miles from Argentina, 8,000 miles from Britain.

The logistics appeared impossible. Margaret Thatcher's instinctive response seemed a nineteenth-century reaction to a nineteenth-century problem – the defence of an empire, or rather a tiny outpost of a former empire, one of the 'dots on the map' that former Prime Minister James Callaghan rightly believed had the capacity for causing a disproportionate amount of foreign policy trouble.[65] Max Hastings notes that when he first heard that the Prime Minister was thinking of sending a task force, 'I thought she had gone mad'.[66]

The Falklands – sparsely populated, rocky and gale-swept – were of little, if any, strategic value to the United Kingdom. Some of the few remaining colonial outposts – Hong Kong, Gibraltar and Bermuda – clearly earned their keep: if invaded, any British insistence on their being retaken would have been more understandable. Were these tiny islands in the stormy South Atlantic really worth going to war over? Anthony Parsons, British Ambassador to the UN, says that it seemed so improbable that he had a difficult time convincing his fellow diplomats that Britain meant business.[67] The potential loss of blood and treasure seemed even more bizarre given that, leading up to the invasion, successive British governments had been rather tepid towards the Falklands, unwilling, for example, to make any meaningful investment in the local economy. Consequently, the population was diminishing: those who remained were dependent upon Argentina for many services, including the provision of fuel, many everyday goods and specialist medical care. In addition, under the terms of the 1981 British Nationality Act, the islanders were granted only restricted British citizenship. For many in Buenos Aires, it must have seemed just a matter of time before the islanders bowed to the inevitable and formally acknowledged that their day-to-day links with Argentina superseded any historic ties to Britain.

In late 1980, Foreign Office minister Nicholas Ridley had mooted a possible leaseback arrangement, by which British sovereignty over the Falklands would be ceded to Argentina. He quickly had to back down in the face of the islanders' dismay and MPs' opposition. However, the MP who observed that 'for 20 years we have been trying to withdraw from this outpost of empire, if we could decently cede sovereignty' was far from wrong.[68] The Falklands was number 242 in a list of priorities for the Foreign Office.[69] Ridley had told islanders to compromise with Buenos Aires, allegedly warning them at a meeting in Stanley town hall in 1980: 'This isn't the Victorian era. We're not going to send a gunboat down to save you if you get yourselves into trouble.'[70]

As much as the Falkland islanders clung to Britain, Argentines were as convinced that Las Islas Malvinas rightfully belonged to them. In their eyes, Britain had no claim to the islands which, they asserted, had been illegally occupied since 1833. There had been half-hearted talks about their future between London and Buenos Aires on and off throughout the 1970s but, with both sides intransigent, nothing had been achieved. However, the 150th anniversary of British occupation loomed large in Argentina, a country that, for all its rackety charm, seemed permanently on the brink of chaos, having in 1976 lurched from runaway inflation to financial default to oppressive military dictatorship. Led from December 1981 by General Leopoldo Galtieri, the *junta* had been fighting *la guerra sucia* ('dirty war') with dissidents: torture and kidnapping were commonplace. The Disappeared – many assumed to have been thrown from planes over the Atlantic – are estimated to number 30,000. Despite this grim human rights record – justifying the islanders' fears about being handed over to Buenos Aires – Argentina had a crucial ally in the United States, which saw the dictatorship as a bulwark against the Communism it feared might engulf Latin America. Future Minister for Defence Procurement Alan Clark MP described Argentina as 'a bankrupt, totalitarian country with an inflation rate of 130 per cent and in an exceedingly precarious social condition'.[71] The invasion of the Falklands was a masterstroke by Galtieri, turning a reviled government into local heroes, with hundreds of thousands of ecstatic Argentines turning out to cheer it on in Buenos Aires' main square.

With British Armed Forces personnel going into action so imminently, any censure of the government on that historic Saturday was inevitably muted. A few questioned the obvious failure of diplomacy and intelligence, with claims that ample warning had been given of the *junta*'s intent.[72] An Argentine landing a few weeks earlier on South Georgia now assumed far more sinister significance. Discovered by Captain Cook in 1775 and the burial ground of Antarctic explorer Ernest Shackleton, the island is a dependency of the Falklands some 900 miles away – and feels even more desolate and remote. On 19

March, some Argentines landed to remove scrap metal from a former whaling station. The commander of the British Antarctic Survey base at Grytviken reported that they had set up camp and hoisted the Argentine flag. Uncertain what the trespassers were really up to, or how to dislodge them, the British government had sent the ice patrol vessel HMS *Endurance* to undertake a reconnaissance, leaving behind twenty-two Royal Marines as a precaution. The matter was successfully played down to the extent that US Secretary of State Alexander Haig considered it involved nothing more than a mix-up over paperwork.[73] However, at dawn local time on 3 April – about the time the Prime Minister was addressing the Commons – some 100 Argentine marines and ten members of Special Forces landed. The British marines surrendered but not without a fight, shooting down a helicopter and damaging an enemy frigate.

Margaret Thatcher's political fortunes were bound up with the Falklands. She was completely wrong-footed by the invasion, learning on 31 March that it was imminent – 'the worst moment of my life', she later admitted.[74] However, senior commanders in the Royal Navy had been concerned for some months that trouble might be brewing. The Commander-in-Chief Fleet, Admiral Sir John Fieldhouse, ordered contingency plans to be drawn up after Captain Nick Barker of HMS *Endurance*, on what was assumed to be the ship's last tour, reported a tangible shift in attitude during a goodwill visit to Buenos Aires. An article in the Argentine press indicated that the military was going to retake the Falklands by force. Mrs Thatcher also noted to civil servants in early March, 'We must have contingency plans.'[75] However, as she stated, 'I never, never believed they would invade.' She explained:

It was such a stupid thing to do, as events happened, such a stupid thing even to contemplate doing. They were doing well – if I may put it that way – doing too well in pursuing their case with the United Nations. They had seen what happened to other countries which were using plain straightforward invasion tactics. They had seen how the whole of the non-aligned movement turned against the Soviet Union to which they had previously been friendly on Afghanistan.[76]

Fortunately for the Prime Minister, as soon as he got word of the imminent Argentine attack, the First Sea Lord Admiral Sir Henry Leach – in her words, 'quiet, calm and confident' – had gatecrashed a meeting in her Commons' office on 31 March. He assured her that a task force could be put together within forty-eight hours and 'such a force could retake the Islands'.[77] Such a claim appears astonishing, but it was a lifeline for the Prime Minister, whose future was at stake. As one of her backbenchers stated, despite being the third greatest naval power in the world and the second in NATO, Britain had suffered a humiliating defeat.[78] Foreign Secretary Peter Carrington also spoke in terms of national humiliation when he resigned. It can be assumed that Margaret Thatcher did not want to be reminded of Suez – and the ignominious place in history it had consigned one of her predecessors, Anthony Eden. However, it was not just the Prime Minister for whom the head of the 'Senior Service' had offered the chance of a reprieve – it was the Navy itself.

Under the proposals drawn up for the 1981 Defence Review, the Royal Navy was set to be badly wounded. The most significant decision was the replacement of the Polaris nuclear deterrent by the Trident system. As with many previous and subsequent reviews, John Nott, the Defence Secretary, tried to pass off financial expediency as deeply considered national strategy. With the economy still mired in difficulty, cuts were to be made. With a 'continental' strategy preferred over a 'maritime' strategy, the Army came off reasonably well. Although BAOR was to be cut, it was to be re-equipped; the Territorial Army was to be expanded, up from 70,000 to 86,000.[79] The most dramatic impact was on the Royal Navy, which took 57 per cent of the cuts to the defence budget.[80] It was scheduled to lose a quarter of its manpower and 20 per cent of its destroyers and frigates. Two carriers were to be sold off: HMS *Invincible* to Australia and HMS *Hermes* to India. The loss of amphibious ships *Fearless* and *Intrepid* undermined expeditionary capability and underlined that 'out of area' operations could soon be the stuff of history. The axing of the Royal Marines had been considered. Dockyards – including Chatham, Gibraltar and Portsmouth – were scheduled to close. Nott summarised the Review: 'The RAF better off, the Army about the same and the Navy considerably worse off.'[81] Unsurprisingly, the Navy's reaction was 'negative, totally negative', recalled the Falklands commander, Rear

Admiral Sandy Woodward. It considered the Review nothing more than a short-sighted financial stitch-up, driving long-term military strategy in completely the wrong direction. As he stated, 'Subsequent events proved us completely correct.'[82]

When the Defence Review was published in June 1981, the fate of HMS *Endurance* might well have been regarded as a footnote. The news that this ice patrol vessel was to be withdrawn from the South Atlantic was fairly small beer compared with the introduction of Trident and the loss of the carriers. In the context of the Falklands, however, it was crucial, reinforcing a message about Britain's lack of commitment to the islands. In a Commons debate on the nuclear deterrent just days before the Argentine invasion, it was pointed out that somehow £8 billion could be found to introduce Trident but the country was unable to muster the £3 million a year it would cost to save *Endurance*.[83] Unknown to MPs, hours later down in the South Atlantic, the vessel would be tracking the movements of ships from the Argentine navy as they approached South Georgia and the Falklands. Given that the core task force ships – *Hermes, Invincible, Fearless* and *Intrepid* – had been sentenced to be axed in the Defence White Paper, it is unsurprising that Sir Lawrence Freedman, the official historian of the conflict, observes that the Falklands 'was precisely the war for which Britain was planning least'.[84]

Along with the Inchon landings in Korea and the invasion of Suez, the Falklands was one of the few amphibious operations undertaken since Normandy. Such operations are completely different from, for example, the Gulf War, when it could be assumed that overseas infrastructure facilities such as ports and hospitals within manageable distance of the theatre of operations would be made available by friendly powers to aid the military effort. With no country in Latin America willing publicly to side with Britain against Argentina, we would be very much on our own, in the South Atlantic, some 2,000 miles further away from Britain than Tokyo.[85] The Defence Secretary doubted the wisdom of the enterprise: 'My own initial reaction was that this was just not a viable logistical operation.'[86] Operation Corporate, as it was codenamed, would be the sort of amphibious operation in which the Royal Marines specialise; consequently, when it came to deciding who to send to the Falklands, 3rd Commando Brigade was the inevitable choice. Royal Marines Major General

Jeremy Moore, who was later to be appointed Commander British Land Forces, observed that Corporate was what the Royal Marines had long been training for: 'The only difference was that this time instead of sailing from Plymouth and turning right to Norway, the force was turning left, and they had a heck of a lot further to go.'[87] The Royal Navy was to be the 'lead' service. Keeping up the Army's end in the first wave of deployment would be the 2nd and 3rd Battalions of the Parachute Regiment and small detachments from the Army's combat support corps, as well as the SAS. Brigadier Julian Thompson of 3rd Commando Brigade was a mite sceptical about the Paras, given that 'they'd never seen landing craft or assault ships'.[88] A few weeks after the task force sailed, hastily gathered reinforcements from 5th Infantry Brigade followed it south, but whether they were intended to be part of the assault force or subsequent garrison troops was not entirely clear.

The Falklands are made up of the two main islands, West and East – where the capital Stanley is located – and about a hundred smaller outcrops. Soldiers and marines discovered that the land was generally either rock or peat bog, where the water table was a few inches under the surface; most vehicles literally got bogged down, while walking was wet, cold, hard-going and thoroughly miserable. Fresh water uncontaminated by liver fluke from sheep droppings was in short supply. Settlements were few and very far between; roads stopped a few miles outside Stanley. Royal Marine Major Ewen Southby-Tailyour, who knew the Falklands and, crucially for the operation, had charted much of its coastline, said: 'People had to realise that once we landed, every mouthful of food would have to be brought in by us.'[89] This self-sufficiency extended to ammunition, fuel, medical supplies, water purification, spare helicopter engines, tents ... In fact, everything needed to keep a fighting force at maximum strength and fighting ability.

An armada of ships was needed to transport the men and *matériel* to the South Atlantic. Although the cuts to the Royal Navy were yet to bite – and indeed, because of the demands of the operation, many of the planned cuts, including the sale of the carriers, were immediately shelved – merchant ships were requisitioned for the campaign, with Her Majesty the Queen signing the necessary orders on 4 April. The forty-five 'ships taken up from trade' (STUFT) would carry 9,000 personnel and 100,000 tons of freight as well as additional helicopters.[90] Although described rather dismissively by one MP as 'rent-a-fleet', the process was part of a centuries-long tradition of merchant vessels coming to the aid of the nation at a time of conflict.[91] The *QE2* and SS *Canberra* were modified from luxury cruise liners to troop ships in a matter of days after their paying passengers had disembarked. Each was to carry more than 3,000 personnel. Ballroom floors and swimming pools were boarded over and helicopter pads were added to their decks. SS *Uganda* was refitted as a hospital ship. After the annual 'Springtrain' naval exercise near Madeira, warships, including HMSs *Antrim*, *Sheffield* and *Coventry*, and the nuclear-powered submarine *Spartan*, had gathered at Gibraltar when the call came to head for the South Atlantic. Resources and personnel were swapped around the fleet as the ships staying behind offloaded all their stores and ammunition on to those due to sail. HMS *Glamorgan* was the only ship to have the right charts. Not only was she painted grey on the voyage but, because its splinters can cause serious injuries, all Formica was removed from her interior. More than 110 ships were finally deployed, including forty-four warships and twenty-two from the Royal Fleet Auxiliary.[92]

As the task force carriers left Britain to link up with those ships already on the voyage south, crowds gathered on the Solent to give them a huge send-off. Many aboard thought that a settlement would be reached long before they crossed the Equator. Both marines and soldiers spent the voyage keeping fit by running around promenade decks carrying their kit and practising medical procedures in case of battlefield injury. Major Philip Neame, D Company commander of 2 Para, who was aboard MV *Norland*, said everyone had mixed feelings: 'we'd sail to the Equator, top up our sun tans, then come home; but on the other hand, we were Parachute Regiment; it would be nice to put the training to the test at some stage before we finished our careers.'[93] Inter-service relations took a blow when soldiers from 2 Para shot an albatross, upsetting Royal Navy personnel on board. Sergeant Major Peter Richens explained: 'It was a tempting target.'[94]

More than 4,000 miles from Britain, Ascension Island was a vital stepping stone in the journey to the Falklands for both ships and planes. The tiny island had been leased to the United States, which allowed British forces full access to use it as a forward operating base

(FOB). Soon the air corridor between Britain and Ascension was known as the 'Motorway', as cargo planes dropped supplies. It was 'the most intensive air transport effort since the Berlin airlift'.[95] The island was central to the logistical effort, with 5,500 personnel and 6,300 tons of equipment being moved through it.[96] The break in the voyage also allowed ships to sort out and repack their stores; in the rush to weigh anchor, they had been loaded haphazardly. One unit discovered that its radio batteries were on either the *Nordic Ferry* or the *Baltic Ferry*, while the battery chargers were on the QE2.[97] Ships' corridors were crammed with boxes of tinned food, while holds were full of mysterious, unmarked boxes that could contain anything from breakfast cereal to empty jerrycans. It was vital to keep track of the hundreds of tons of goods, but in the days long before bar codes, scanners and GPS tracking, it was a hard job, made harder because the ships had to anchor in offshore swells of up to ten feet. Helicopters flew between the shore and the ships, transporting thousands of tons of goods and personnel, including Lieutenant Colonel H. Jones, who flew into Ascension and met up with his 2 Para on the *Norland*.

While the task force headed to the South Atlantic, diplomatic efforts continued to try to find a solution to the impasse. Although the Falkland Islands' future had been considered sporadically for many years by the United Nations, the crisis 'hit the Security Council like a bolt from the blue'.[98] Britain secured a swift diplomatic advantage with the passing of Resolution 502, which condemned the invasion and demanded an Argentine withdrawal. The vote was conclusive – ten in favour, Panama against and four abstentions (China, the Soviet Union, Poland, Spain). In the weeks that followed, both Ambassador Parsons and the Prime Minister managed to sidestep the contentious issue of colonialism, to which member states of the non-aligned movement were sensitive, and instead continued to focus on the illegality and illegitimacy of the invasion. Britain argued successfully in terms of the Falkland islanders' right to self-determination: should Argentina go unchallenged, a dangerous precedent would be set, potentially affecting some fifty nations with disputed border regions. Although Argentina managed to get the backing of the Organisation of American States, Britain had the support of much of western Europe and the Commonwealth, which imposed sanctions on Argentina. In addition, Chile would lend covert assistance: the debt owed to its controversial leader General Pinochet would be underscored by Margaret Thatcher, who gave him very public support in the late 1990s when he was under house arrest in Britain. Underpinned by Resolution 502, 'the sheet anchor of the British case throughout the world', Article 51 – the right of self-defence – was invoked to justify military action. The government's scrupulous adherence to international law in the early days of the crisis would serve it well when military action began.

The diplomatic efforts to avert military action could well have succeeded inadvertently. With the southern hemisphere winter fast approaching, the window for an attempt to repossess the islands would shortly be closing: any action had to be concluded by the end of June. Margaret Thatcher was convinced the Argentines were playing for time. However, to ensure the continuing support of the international community, Britain had to be seen to participate in the diplomatic process with sincerity and good faith. The protracted attempts to reach a compromise – particularly by US Secretary of State Alexander Haig, who shuttled between London, Washington and Buenos Aires – had one advantage: it gave the media something to report during the weeks that the task force took to make the long journey south. After Haig threw in the diplomatic towel, the UN Secretary General and the president of Peru also tried to find a solution. In May, a clearly exasperated Prime Minister reminded MPs that she had been involved in seven rounds of negotiations and believed that Argentina was deliberately time-wasting: 'We are bound to conclude that its objective is procrastination and continuing occupation, leading to sovereignty.'[99] Although possession might not be nine-tenths of international law, the danger existed that the world would reconcile itself to Argentina's *de facto* government of the islands. The Prime Minister wanted a decisive battle, but knew she could well have to face down international pressure for a ceasefire. Even when the fighting was underway, she was alert to the danger of diplomatic defeat being snatched from the jaws of military victory.[100]

The waning of public support at home was another danger for all those involved in Operation Corporate. The nation was clearly behind the government at the outset, with trade, industry, haulage firms, the railways and the unions pulling together that first weekend to ensure the task force sailed. Thanks to the Defence Review, some of those working at Portsmouth had received their notices of redundancy. The government had the backing of the Opposition led by Michael Foot, but a few Labour backbenchers were unhappy with the rapid resort to force. However, pictures of Argentine soldiers lording it over captive Royal Marines spread-eagled on the ground and reports that the islanders were being forced to drive on the 'wrong' side of the road, encouraged public backing for military action. Former Prime Minister James Callaghan described the mood as 'quite hysterical', with the 'tabloid press practically handing out white feathers to all those who dare express their reservations'.[101] If the BBC's attempts at impartial reporting made it appear lukewarm, the *Sun* was unashamedly on the side of 'our boys': its jingoistic fervour – 'Gotcha' after the *Belgrano* was sunk – was lampooned by *Private Eye* as 'kill an Argie and win a Metro'. The national mood might swiftly change, should momentum be lost or a ship go down. At naval headquarters in Northwood, Middlesex, Admiral Sir John Fieldhouse recognised that, while the Prime Minister 'has held out resolutely for victory not ceasefire', what could undermine her position and turn public opinion would be 'a catastrophe at sea with large loss of life'.[102] Journalists sailed with the task force but, once it had left the Solent, there was initially little to report. The British public was 'gasping for information', according to ITN correspondent Michael Nicholson, 'but we had nothing to give them for six weeks'.[103] The process of filing copy or pooled ITN/BBC camera footage via the ships' communications system was far from simple: media reports were competing for time with operational traffic.[104] Film was sometimes seen days after it was recorded. Television reporters often had to act as if they were working for radio, painting pictures for the audience. Inevitably, some reporters made nuisances of themselves by trying to glean any information about helicopter pilot Prince Andrew, irritating naval commanders even more than usual. For Captain Jeremy Black, the five reporters aboard the *Invincible* took up as much of his time as 'the Argentinians and my thousand sailors'.[105]

The Falklands campaign involved all three services but, at the time, the concept of joint operations was at the earliest stages of development. Indeed, the operation would provide a huge impetus to improve 'jointery'. Today, the British Armed Forces' Permanent Joint Headquarters (PJHQ) is at Northwood, but in 1982 it was purely a Royal Navy establishment and the nominated headquarters for Operation Corporate. On paper the chain of command was clear enough, but, certainly at the outset, it was complicated for those actually on the ground in the islands. Admiral Fieldhouse was in overall command and responsible for planning Operation Corporate; Rear Admiral Sandy Woodward was the task force's senior officer; Commodore Michael Clapp commanded the Amphibious Task Group; while Brigadier Julian Thompson of the Royal Marines commanded the landing force and the tactical operation on land. According to one senior naval commander: 'We needed a three-star vice admiral sitting over all three of us in theatre. Instead, all three reported back up to Northwood, who had to draw together the threads of a battle taking place 8,000 miles away.'[106] The lines of authority were further complicated by the belated appointment as commander of the land forces of Major General Jeremy Moore of the Royal Marines, who was then *incommunicado* and effectively out of the picture for about a week as he travelled on the *QE2* from Ascension with the 5th Infantry Brigade, while plans for the landings were being finalised and executed.

The Argentine forces were concentrated around Stanley – or Puerto Argentino, as it was now called. Soldiers were also dug in around the Goose Green settlement – where more than a hundred islanders were being held captive in the community centre – in neighbouring Darwin and on West Falkland. With numbers estimated at 10,000, they would be no walkover. The Argentine air force – to which British ships were vulnerable – included Skyhawks, Mirage 3s and Super Etendards, strike fighters which carried deadly sea-skimming Exocet missiles. If a British carrier had been lost to them, the campaign undoubtedly would have been halted and the retreat sounded. It is unsurprising that Woodward sought to protect his carriers – and the aircraft on them – but personnel on the ground sometimes considered it was at their expense. Air superiority is normally a precondition for amphibious operations to minimise the risk to the forces coming ashore: as Thompson observed, the British had learned this lesson through bitter experience in Crete and Norway.

With the bombing of the Argentine mainland ruled out – and therefore the bombing of the country's air force and navy bases, where some 200 aircraft were secured – huge risks were going to have to be taken. Britain's combat aircraft – including the Fleet Air Arm's twenty-eight Sea Harriers and the RAF's fourteen Harrier GR3s – were heavily outnumbered.[107] Although publicly neutral until 30 April, the United States – in particular Defense Secretary Caspar Weinberger – gave the UK enormous moral and practical help behind the scenes; for example, supplying Sidewinder missiles for the Harriers and getting a million gallons of aviation fuel to Ascension, where fuel supply lines had to be laid within days.[108] Given the enormity of the undertaking and the distances involved, much could go wrong. A fault with the gearbox that developed on HMS *Invincible* within hours of leaving port showed how the 'friction' identified by the military philosopher von Clausewitz can develop in any operation, no matter how well planned. Friction almost within sight of the British coastline was a very different prospect from friction thousands of miles away in the stormy South Atlantic.

Retaking South Georgia was to provide a useful fillip. A comparative sideshow, it would boost the campaign's momentum and enable the Prime Minister to give the public and media some good news. However, Operation Paraquet almost ended in disaster before it began. Having landed on the island from the destroyer HMS *Antrim*, a contingent of SAS troops had to be pulled off a glacier because of appalling weather: blizzards, temperatures of minus 20 and winds at 70 knots. The first, and then the second, helicopter sent to rescue them crashed. It was 'a terrible and disturbing start to the campaign' for Margaret Thatcher.[109] Finally, at the seventh attempt of flying, the expedition's last remaining helicopter, a 21-year-old Wessex, managed to pull them out. On 25 April, the Argentine submarine *Santa Fe* was discovered leaving Cumberland Bay; it was disabled by air-to-surface missiles and depth charges from Wasp helicopters. As the *Santa Fe* limped back to Grytviken, HMS *Antrim* and HMS *Plymouth* began to bombard the settlement, and an improvised force of marines and Special Forces landed on the island. The garrison at Grytviken and the crew of the *Santa Fe* surrendered within fifteen minutes. Shortly afterwards the task group commander, Captain Brian Young, signalled: 'Be pleased to inform Her Majesty that the White Ensign flies alongside the Union Flag in Grytviken South Georgia. God save the Queen.'[110] The Prime Minister told the country to 'rejoice'.

In early May, as the lead ships in the task force approached the

Falklands, came two demonstrations of British resolve. After London's declaration of a total exclusion zone around the islands, the longest bombing mission ever yet attempted was undertaken with the attack on Stanley's airfield by a Vulcan bomber on 1 May. The damage to the runway itself might not have been extensive – Hercules transporters could continue to land – but the shock in Argentina was intense, with the realisation that the country itself was now in range of British bombers. With the Vulcans designed to carry the nuclear deterrent and fight the Cold War in Europe, the attack on Port Stanley – codenamed Operation Black Buck – was only achievable thanks to engineers from both industry and the RAF working around the clock to extend the aircrafts' range with the introduction of an air-to-air refuelling system. During that first mission, flown out of Ascension, Vulcan XM607 spent 15 hours and 50 minutes in the air and was refuelled eighteen times.[111]

On 2 May, with the Argentine aircraft carrier *25 de Mayo* coming in from the north and the cruiser *Belgrano* approaching from the south, the task force was vulnerable to attack. The operations officer aboard HMS *Broadsword* said it was obvious that the Argentine navy was trying to execute a pincer movement: 'Even a curious stoker, coming into the Ops Room to find out what was happening, could see it.'[112] As the commander of the frigate HMS *Glamorgan* observed: 'There was 14 hours of darkness and *Belgrano* was within ten hours' steaming of the carriers. It wasn't out there for a sunshine cruise, and was a specific threat to us.'[113] The submarine HMS *Conqueror* torpedoed and sank the *Belgrano*, with the loss of 323 lives. A few days later came the Argentine retaliation, with an Exocet from a Super Etendard aircraft blasting into HMS *Sheffield* on its starboard side, killing twenty sailors. It was the first such attack on a Royal Navy vessel since the Second World War. The sinking of the ships was the point of no return, bringing home to all those involved that this was war – and one that could be lost. However, following the loss of the *Belgrano*, the Argentine navy, including its aircraft carrier, returned to port and would be no further threat to the task force. For Mrs Thatcher, the attack on the Argentine cruiser 'turned out to be one of the most decisive military actions of the war'.[114]

British forces began to land on East Falkland on 21 May. Falkland Sound, the site of the first wave of landings, quickly became known as Bomb Alley. The sheltered stretch of water between the two main islands, some fifty miles across East Falkland from Stanley and fifteen miles from Goose Green, had been judged the optimum site to ensure the defence of ships and personnel during the perilous process of disembarkation at four beaches in San Carlos Bay. The risks were high, not least because of the absence of air superiority. Thompson pointed out to Woodward: 'If, for example, Canberra is sunk, any landing is out of the question.'[115] Woodward scarcely needed reminding: he was keeping his carriers as far out of harm's way as possible, even at the expense of reducing air cover. As Lawrence Freedman observed, before the landings 'no single event was more likely to scupper the whole operation than the loss of Hermes or Invincible'.[116] At a meeting of the War Cabinet on 19 May with the Chiefs of Staff, when final authorisation was given to land, it was spelt out that up to half a dozen destroyers or frigates might be lost.[117]

The disembarkation and the days immediately after it were among the most perilous of the campaign. On the morning of the landing, the men of 2 Para on board the Norland were woken to the sound of their regimental march, 'The Ride of the Valkyries', and a church service.[118] They spent two hours in an open boat going through the Sound before wading ashore and moving immediately to high ground. On Mount Sussex they had a grandstand view of the water below, cloud and rain permitting. Over the next few days, as thousands of soldiers and marines came ashore along with tons of stores, British warships and merchant vessels were massed close together and vulnerable to attack. According to Major Philip Neame: 'We realised that the main Argentine effort was not going to be directed against us on the hills, but the ships below.' The determination – and recklessness – of the Argentine air force had been underestimated. Despite four lines of defence, their bombers got through. Although fifteen Argentine aircraft were destroyed on 21 May, the frigate HMS Ardent went down with the loss of twenty-two sailors; two days later, HMS Antelope was hit. The merchant ships were ordered to sail away from the anchorage; Canberra left, taking with her 94,000 24-hour rations packs and a designated medical dressing station, which instead had to be set up ashore.

The men needed to break out from the beachhead, but supplies had to be unloaded first. Many were frustrated by the wait. Neame observes: 'We were in limbo for the next four or five days.' One sergeant major said that for the first ten days ashore, 'We didn't dry out from getting wet making the landing ... Our Army issue boots let in water very badly': fourteen out of ninety-four men got trench foot.[119] However, Brigadier Thompson held firm, arguing that no one should 'swan out of a beachhead with a packet of sandwiches in one pocket and five rounds of ammunition in the other'. On 25 May, on their national day, the Argentine pilots hit hard twice. First, they struck the Type 42 destroyer HMS *Coventry* – whose captain had considered her a 'sitting duck' – killing nineteen sailors; then, further out, the *Atlantic Conveyor* was hit. The huge cargo ship had become known as Britain's third aircraft carrier after transporting nineteen Harriers from Ascension. On hearing the early reports of the attack on the ship loaded with vital supplies, the Prime Minister thought that the operation might be fatally wounded. She could only wait for further news, also knowing that 'somewhere east of the Falklands, was the *QE2*, carrying 3,000 troops. For me, this was one of the worst nights of the war.'[120] Fortunately, the Harriers had been flown off and joined *Hermes* and *Invincible*, but 4,500 winter tents were lost, along with three Chinook and six Wessex helicopters. To reach Port Stanley, the men would have to walk.

The days of inactivity as the beachhead was established were undoubtedly irksome for Lieutenant Colonel H. Jones. David Cooper, chaplain to 2 Para, said that the Colonel wanted to test the enemy: 'He believed that one serious, effective fight with us winning would lead to an Argentine collapse.'[121] CGS General Sir Edwin Bramall, 8,000 miles away, was recalling Gallipoli and Anzio, two successful landings that subsequently floundered; he also wanted a break-out of the beachhead and the military initiative seized.[122] As Freedman suggests, 'Over time all the attritional factors of weather, wear and tear, equipment losses and extended supply chains would conspire to work against the British cause.'[123] In short, the longer the British lingered, the more likely they were to lose. Jones planned a full-scale attack on the Argentine position at Darwin and Goose Green. Any element of surprise vanished as the enemy forces were tipped off by a BBC report of a speech in Parliament by the Defence Secretary, who implied an attack was likely. Jones drew up a six-phase battle plan, during which his four rifle companies would secure a series of positions – including Camilla Creek House and the airstrip – on a 14-mile attack down a narrow isthmus to the Goose Green settlement itself. It was first time since Korea that a British commanding officer had led his battalion into a high intensity battle.

The battle for Goose Green began at 2 a.m. on 28 May as the men from 2 Para advanced towards Darwin. The night was very windy, wet and cold, with some snow. The frigate HMS *Arrow* shelled enemy positions. The terrain was hard going; for hours, ravines and streams, trenches and minefields had to be negotiated, the pitch dark broken by the light of tracer. The Paras came under fire from shells, mortars, machine guns and phosphorus; their fightback included grenades and bayonets. Progress was slow, far slower than Jones liked, and the plan was falling behind schedule. As it grew light, the troops realised how vulnerable they were: they were in open territory with little if any cover. They could see for miles – and be seen. They could come under fire from snipers over 1,000 yards away and from Skyhawk aircraft or Pucaras, which carried napalm. The back-up – whether from Harriers or from naval gunfire support from ships – was failing to materialise. With ammunition running short, it seemed as if the Argentines had the advantage, particularly on Darwin Hill, lying between the British and their objective. British casualties were mounting. Journalist Robert Fox, accompanying the Paras, thought that things were going very badly wrong, not least because of the absence of British air strikes. 'An earlier Harrier attack would have saved a great deal of fighting.'[124] Later, Brigadier Thompson regretted not mounting a two-battalion attack, acknowledging the 'daunting task' 2 Para had undertaken 'virtually on their own'.[125] D Company commander Philip Neame halted his men and told them to make a brew: 'There was nothing else rational we could do, and they needed the energy to fight until evening.' Suddenly, on the battalion radio net, the call came: 'Sunray is down.'[126] Jones had been shot in an attempt on an Argentine machine-gun position, an action which would win him a posthumous Victoria Cross. Far from morale collapsing, the soldiers' determination was renewed. Major Chris Keeble took over command and the advance continued.

As daybreak approached, three Harriers appeared, two dropping cluster bombs. Argentine resolve began to weaken and flags of surrender were reported being seen at the airfield. However, some of the bitterest memories of the conflict concern an incident when British soldiers were shot by enemy troops holding white flags – a shocking violation of international norms, if indeed it was deliberate. With the British now advancing towards Goose Green, Keeble deployed two newly captured Argentine prisoners of war as go-betweens to urge an Argentine surrender. Hemmed in by British forces, and with no room to manoeuvre, the Argentine commander formally capitulated on the morning of 29 May. More than 1,000 Argentine personnel surrendered to a force almost half their number. At 12.50 p.m. on 29 May, the Union Jack was flying over Goose Green and the islanders freed. Their bluff called, it was a devastating defeat for the Argentines, who lost forty-seven men, with scores wounded. The British lost seventeen. The fighting spirit shown by 2 Para during the battle for Goose Green created the moral and psychological ascendancy over the Argentines that H. Jones had intended.

Victory at Goose Green counterbalanced the losses at sea, but the war was far from over. Although sixty-two enemy aircraft had been destroyed, including eleven in a night raid by the SAS on Pebble Island, British forces remained vulnerable. On 1 June, as Major General Moore arrived to take up overall command, the 5th Infantry Brigade began to land. Commanded by Brigadier Tony Wilson, these vital reinforcements comprised 1st/7th Battalion Gurkha Rifles, 1st Battalion Welsh Guards, 2nd Battalion Scots Guards, as well as support units including 97 Battery, 4 Field Regiment Royal Artillery and 36 Engineer Regiment, Royal Engineers. On landing, the Gurkhas were transferred by Chinook to relieve 2 Para at Goose Green.[127] Overall, however, the brigade 'was carrying insufficient logistical support' and 'had brought with them almost no additional means of moving men, material and equipment'.[128] Units began to advance towards Stanley. After a gruelling trek across East Falkland – 45 Commando 'yomping' and 3 Para 'tabbing' – they would secure the Douglas settlement and Teal Inlet, while 42 Commando would advance on Mount Kent and Mount Challenger, the western approaches to the capital.[129] In the best tradition of his regiment, new 2 Para CO Lieutenant Colonel David Chaundler arrived in San Carlos after parachuting into the Atlantic in force 8 winds.

A second front opened in the battle for Stanley. To the south-west, forward bases were being set up around Bluff Cove and Fitzroy settlements, where 2 Para were now digging themselves in. Thousands of soldiers, along with ammunition, fuel and stores, would have to be transferred from San Carlos, necessitating a sail around East Falkland. On 5/6 June the Scots Guards and a few of the Welsh Guards were the first to land. They sailed on the assault ship HMS *Intrepid*, transferring to four unarmed, unarmoured open landing craft, low in the water because of stores and equipment, including a few Land Rovers. The voyage to Bluff Cove took seven hours and several soldiers suffered exposure. Worse could have happened: no warning had come through to HMS *Cardiff* or HMS *Yarmouth* that British forces were on the move; a blue-on-blue attack was narrowly averted. The remaining Welsh Guards on HMS *Fearless* should have landed but were thwarted, in part, because of bad weather: arriving back in San Carlos they were directed on to the RFA vessel *Sir Galahad*. The ship arrived in Bluff Cove on 8 June, when for once the weather was clear and sunny. As the men waited to disembark, the ship and her sister vessel, *Sir Tristram*, were hit by an air strike from four Argentine Skyhawks. The bombs hit *Sir Galahad* aft and fire engulfed her, igniting fuel tanks and ammunition. The ship was burned out and forty-eight men died, thirty-two from the Welsh Guards; another forty suffered serious burns, including Guardsman Simon Weston. The number of fatalities would have been higher but for the courage of helicopter pilots who flew into the smoke to winch survivors to safety, hovering just feet above the burning ship. Controversially, air cover from HMS *Hermes* was reduced because the carrier had relocated 100 miles further east to have her boilers cleaned.

The final assault on Port Stanley began on 11/12 June, with 3 Commando Brigade mounting a three-battalion night attack. By then, marines and soldiers were weakened by the physical effort of trying to survive in such a hostile climate, where temperatures were just above freezing during the day and the ground was waterlogged. The mountains that form a ring to the west around Stanley were stormed: in a 10-hour assault, 3 Para secured Mount Longdon, with Sergeant Ian McKay earning a posthumous Victoria Cross; 45 Commando captured the Two Sisters; and 42 Commando took Mount Harriet. That night, HMS *Glamorgan*, which had been bombarding positions around Stanley, was hit by an Exocet: thirteen men died but the ship survived. The following night, 13/14 June, 2 Para captured Wireless Ridge; after heavy fighting the Scots Guards secured Mount Tumbledown, while the Gurkhas – their bloodthirsty reputation provoking mass surrender – had a comparatively easy time taking Mount William.

On the morning of 14 June, with the British forces encircling the outskirts of Stanley, the battle for the Falkland Islands was over. The Prime Minister noted that 'the speed with which the end came took us all by surprise'.[130] Less surprisingly, the senior Royal Marines commanders wanted marines to lead the way into Stanley, but Company Sergeant Major Peter Richens of 2 Para was having none of it: 'Well, it was a red rag to a bull; we were the first ashore, the first into action and the first into Stanley, so that was the end of it.'[131] Just before 9 p.m., the Argentine commander, General Mario Menéndez, formally signed the instrument of surrender. Moore agreed that the word 'unconditional' could be struck out; how much comfort that brought to the 11,848 exhausted, defeated Argentines can only be guessed at. It was alleged that the young Argentine lieutenant colonel who was General Menéndez's Military Assistant and who had once been a student at the Army Staff College at Camberley was heard to remark on capture: 'I wish I had paid more attention to the General War lectures during my year.'

The campaign to retake the Falklands was, to echo Wellington, the nearest run thing you ever saw in your life. It could have turned out very differently if, for example, the bombs hitting thirteen British ships had not failed to detonate.[132] With supply lines stretching halfway around the world, the unsung heroes of the campaign were the logisticians, ensuring every 'bean, bullet, gun and gallon of fuel' reached the men on the ground.[133] Known as 'humping and dumping', logistics is usually overlooked but essential to any successful campaign: faulty supply lines would ultimately scupper Napoleon in Russia. Not enough credit in the campaign has gone to the Commando Logistic Regiment and the other support units, particularly those providing medical care, including the 'Red and Green Life Machine' in Ajax Bay. Without them, British casualty figures would have been far higher. As it was, 225 were killed and 770 wounded. For Brigadier Tony Wilson, commander of 5th Infantry Brigade, the Argentines were far from callow conscripts: 'The enemy was not inept and frightened. Nor was he badly equipped and starving. His use of air was audacious. His defensive positions well sited and well constructed. He fought with skill and bravery. Some units resisted to the last man.'[134] Some 900 of them lost their lives.

The Falklands demonstrated the courage, toughness and professionalism of Britain's Armed Forces. Having prepared for war in Europe and been patrolling the streets of Northern Ireland, soldiers had to adapt to very different terrain in the South Atlantic. The campaign necessitated inter-service cooperation long before joint operations became part of the forces' day-to-day experience. In addition, it reflected the importance of a positive relationship between the Chiefs and the Prime Minister. Bramall said that Margaret Thatcher was an ideal war leader: 'robust, quick, thoroughly informed and decisive'.[135] Deliberately excluding the Chancellor of the Exchequer from the War Cabinet meant that she was not distracted by being forced to consider the mounting financial cost of the campaign.

Bagnall and BAOR

The Falklands did wonders for the morale of the country and the Armed Forces. Both had been rather in the doldrums throughout the 1970s. Paradoxically, for some soldiers Northern Ireland had been a welcome change from BAOR, where training was described as sometimes lacking in reality, being 'all too often hampered by restrictions on mileage, ammunition and money for repayment of damage'.[136] Operation Banner forced junior officers in particular to get to grips with a complex political landscape, follow new rules of engagement and, above all, understand that 'now, for the first time, the enemy is a real one'.[137] When he arrived at the MoD, Defence Secretary John Nott was shocked to learn that BAOR only had about one week's worth of ammunition stocks. 'So assuming that the Russians did attack, we could only have fought a conventional war for a few days before we had no choice but to go nuclear.'[138]

The outstanding performance of soldiers at the tactical level on the ground during Operation Corporate coincided with some rethinking within the Army about the higher levels of war-fighting in major conventional operations, which might be required against the Warsaw Pact forces in Germany. At the vanguard of what would be a shift towards a greater emphasis on the operational level of war – that campaign level which sits between the strategic and the tactical – and towards an approach to warfare that sought success through manoeuvre on the battlefield not just bloody attrition was future Chief of the General Staff, Sir Nigel Bagnall. Commander of 1 British Corps between November 1980 and April 1983 and NATO's Commander-in-Chief Northern Army Group from July 1983 to June 1985, he was the Green Howard captain who had won the Military Cross twice in Malaya before he transferred to 4th/7th Dragoon Guards in Germany. For military historian Gary Sheffield, Bagnall was 'one of the most significant reformers in the 300-year history of the British Army'.[139]

The mission of 1 (BR) Corps was to defend a 40-mile-wide sector to the west of Hanover. For years, in the event of a Soviet attack, NATO forces would defend the North German Plain in accordance with principles laid down in the *Concept of Forward Defence*. Chief of the General Staff 1997–2000, General Sir Roger Wheeler, suggested: 'It's said he asked for the [BAOR] General Defence Plan and the reasons behind it and was told, "Well, that's how it's always been." He said that's not a good reason and set about developing a completely different doctrine.'[140] Bagnall relocated his forces and restructured the Corps. He changed its make-up from four armoured divisions of two brigades to three armoured divisions of three brigades, with a fourth infantry division to be kept in reserve in the UK. New equipment was introduced, including the Challenger tank, which gave the forces greater mobility. Not only did Bagnall demand more flexibility but he expected the Army to fight back more effectively to buy time. He instilled an offensive spirit reminiscent of the Falklands campaign. His three-brigade divisions meant that one armoured brigade of the two forward divisions, having fought a short delaying action, would then be able to withdraw, refurbish and be available to conduct counter-offensive moves, as was the complete third armoured division. The practical effect of the Bagnall initiatives on the officers and soldiers of BAOR was to reinvigorate a belief that the Warsaw Pact could be confronted successfully on the conventional battlefield: withdrawal and defeat were not inevitable. Just as morale soared after the Falklands, both morale and effectiveness soared in BAOR.

Over the next decade Sir Nigel Bagnall embedded his transformation of the Army's thinking by ordering that its enduring operational principles should be formalised. Eventually published in 1989, *Design for Military Operations: The British Military Doctrine* was the first official doctrine publication in the Army's history which focused on the operational level of its role. Moreover, he set up in 1988 the Higher Command and Staff Course (HCSC) at the Army Staff College in Camberley to educate the brightest of the colonels and young brigadiers each year in a full understanding of the operational level of war and the value of manoeuvre, rather than attrition, on the battlefield. When the three Service Staff Colleges merged in the mid-1990s, Bagnall's HCSC became a fully joint course incorporating equal numbers of officers from the Royal Navy and the Royal Air Force. His legacy has been profound.

At the end of the Falklands campaign the Prime Minister stated: 'We have ceased to be a nation in retreat … Britain found herself again in the South Atlantic and will not look back from the victory she has won.'[141] The short conflict had captured the world's imagination. The cover of *Newsweek* featured a task force carrier at sea and the headline 'The Empire Strikes Back'. Having previously suffered record disapproval ratings, Margaret Thatcher swept back to power the following year, with a mandate to implement a radically different economic programme. The 'sick man of Europe' would be restored to health.

Those learning lessons from the Falklands were not just Britain's Armed Forces but their adversaries, too. The Soviet Union was shocked by British resolve. Fighting spirit allied with the changes implemented by the Bagnall reforms underscored that, should the Cold War turn hot, British forces in Germany would stand firm, just as British forces in the Falklands had prevailed, against the odds.

SIX

FROM COLD WAR TO NEW WORLD ORDER

The Berlin Wall Falls, Options for Change, the
Gulf War of 1990–91, Northern Ireland

The fall of the Berlin Wall in 1989 surprised the world. No one was expecting it, including the 3,000 British personnel of the Berlin Infantry Brigade. Among their tasks was manning the city's border checkpoints in the British sector of the city and carrying out 'Flag Tours' – visiting the Soviet sector every day. Like BRIXMIS – the British Commanders'-in-Chief Mission to the Soviet Forces in Germany – the right of access to the Russian occupied area of Germany was a legacy of the Four Power Agreement, some elements of which had been drawn up in the aftermath of the Allied victory in 1945, before the Cold War had begun. Suddenly, the conflict was coming to an end. One by one, the nations of the Eastern Bloc freed themselves from their Communist governments and control by the Soviet Union. The Iron Curtain, dividing Europe for four decades, was torn down and the Warsaw Pact dissolved. Soldiers in the Berlin Infantry Brigade, on the western side of the Brandenburg Gate, were in the front row as history was being made. However, with the Cold War at an end, for them and for soldiers of the British Army of the Rhine, the future was uncertain. Probably none anticipated that, within a year, they would be preparing for war in the Gulf.

The end of the Cold War transformed the global strategic landscape. The British Army – which had been on the frontline in Europe – could take satisfaction in a major victory, achieved without firing a shot. In the aftermath, Britain's Armed Forces had to go through a process of re-examination. No longer Cold Warriors, what exactly was their new role? How far was the Army under threat from politicians anxious to take a peace dividend? The White Paper *Options for Change*, setting out a vision for Britain's post-Cold War defence policy, is examined in this chapter. It then looks at the Gulf War that followed the Iraqi invasion of Kuwait. Finally, it assesses how Operation Banner in Northern Ireland was evolving.

The End and a New Beginning

Descriptions of the end of the Cold War and the fall of Communism in eastern Europe are numerous. For Margaret Thatcher, 'the world turned right side up'. By 1989, 'The cracks in the eastern European Communist system were widening into crevices and soon, wing by wing, the whole edifice fell away.'[1] The United States' Central Intelligence Agency noted that, for a brief span of time, the extraordinary became an almost daily event.[2] Although at the forefront, if covertly, of the fight-back against the advance of Communism, even the CIA had been taken by surprise at how quickly the end came. Analysts, politicians, the public and the armed forces who were actually conducting the Cold War were all confounded by the revolution that occurred – 200 years after a far bloodier revolution had finished the absolutist rule of the monarchy in France. Like the French Revolution, 1989 will be seen as a key moment in history, even if it did not actually turn out to be the end of history.[3]

The military stalemate of the Cold War had appeared endless. One historian observed that an entire generation had grown up regarding a divided Berlin in a divided Germany in a divided Europe as unremarkable.[4] In the 1980s, three leaders – Margaret Thatcher, Ronald Reagan and the Soviet Union's Mikhail Gorbachev – questioned the existing assumptions about the international security system and, in doing so, contributed to overturning them. Reagan sought not only to neutralise the Soviet defence effort, but, for the first time since almost the start of the Cold War, was a leader who actively called for the rolling back of Communism. Elected in 1980, like Mrs Thatcher he had little truck with the prevailing détente between East and West – or with the crisis of confidence that seemed to have afflicted the post-Vietnam United States of the 1970s: 'Too

often in recent times we have just drifted along with events respond-
ing as if we thought of ourselves as a nation in decline.'[5] Given that
the Prime Minister had expressed similar sentiments about Britain,
it is unsurprising that she welcomed his presidency. According to
her, Reagan's strategy was 'to win the Cold War, which the West
had been slowly but surely losing'.[6] In 1982, in a forthright speech
to the British Parliament, he predicted that Communism would be
consigned to the 'ash heap of history'.

In the early 1980s, defence spending rose across the NATO alliance as a deliberate policy in most member countries. In the United
States, it increased 42 per cent in real terms in the first five years of
the Reagan presidency.[7] The introduction of Pershing II and nuclear-
armed cruise missiles in Europe underlined Washington's harder
line. In 1982, the British government's willingness to site the warheads at Greenham Common and RAF Molesworth, along with the
upgrade to Trident, led to the resurgence of the anti-nuclear movement, which had been almost dormant for twenty years. CND was
back on the streets, while the Greenham women camped outside the
base near Newbury. They became the focus of growing unilateral-
ism, which was adopted by the Labour Party – to disastrous effect
in the 1983 General Election. Reagan's Strategic Defense Initiative,
announced in March 1983, was a multi-billion dollar programme to
develop a space-based shield to deflect incoming missiles. Known as
Star Wars after the film, to many critics it was pie in the sky, but it
reinforced the message about a changing defence posture from the
United States. Relations between East and West worsened. Presidential rhetoric, such as the condemnation of the Soviet's 'evil empire',
contributed to growing international tension.

Changes within the Soviet Union were a crucial step along the
path to the 1989 revolution. Key was the elevation of Mikhail Gorbachev to the country's leadership in March 1985. Mrs Thatcher
famously described him as a man one could do business with. Like
her, rather than accepting the status quo, he demanded radical social
change. Two decades younger than the hawkish Leonid Brezhnev,
who had been in power from 1964 until 1982, as well as his immediate predecessors, Gorbachev personified the move away from his
country's social and economic sclerosis. He called for 'new thinking', *glasnost* (openness) and *perestroika* (restructuring). The state's

control over every aspect of Soviet life began to loosen. The relaxation of censorship led to unprecedented criticism by the media of Soviet institutions, including the military. One analyst observed: 'Military *glasnost* has allowed some light to penetrate the veil of secrecy that has hidden military affairs from public gaze.'[8]

Until then, at least in public, the armed forces had commanded respect verging on reverence: they were the link to the Great Patriotic War, one of the Soviet Union's foundation myths. From the exhibitions of military hardware in the May Day parades to brides placing their wedding bouquets at memorials to the fallen, they remained visible in the fabric of Soviet life. Away from civilian gaze, all was far from well: morale was threatened by corruption and nepotism; alcoholism was rife; and recruits had to endure brutal initiation rituals, *dedoveschina*. However, the armed forces were the defenders of the ideological flame. Promotion was dependent upon membership of the Communist Party, with promotions to high command scrutinised by the Party's Politburo. Gorbachev's Defence Secretary, General Dmitry Yazov, would explain that Lenin had recognised the need for the revolution resolutely to defend itself.[9] It was a measure of how far and how fast the new thinking had progressed that Yazov expressed these views in an article for the journal of the Royal United Services Institute, the Whitehall think-tank founded by the Duke of Wellington.

Throughout the years of the Cold War, NATO and Warsaw Pact troops watched one another through binoculars from watchtowers and behind the barbed wire that separated West from East in Germany. The threat became routine. Indeed, the IRA were to prove more lethal, targeting bases in West Germany with, for example, a car bomb attack on the officers' mess at Rheindahlen in March 1987. Conversely, after four decades of stasis, by the latter half of the 1980s many NATO soldiers doubted whether the Warsaw Pact would attack at all. Despite this, field-training exercises continued in northern Germany, which in 1984 included squadrons of NATO jets practising landing on an autobahn as part of Exercise Lionheart. (Readers may wish to ponder, when next driving through today's western Germany, whether a straight section of autobahn with a 'Rastplatz' at either end was indeed constructed as a stretch of road or as a Cold War emergency airfield.) It brought together 130,000 personnel, the largest massing of force since the Second World War, but some soldiers noticed that their training was sometimes skimped for the sake of economy. While some tanks might travel 400 miles during the three-week exercise, others might cover just four miles in ten days because of stipulations about track mileage and a shortage of spares.

In Berlin, it was perhaps just as well the Cold War never turned hot. There, British soldiers were in a precarious position over sixty miles behind the Iron Curtain. Trapped in its Four Power time warp, while some parts of the city had been rebuilt in an impressive way, much of it – especially in the east – was shabby if atmospheric: many buildings were still pockmarked by bullets from 1945. With their overland travel by vehicle through East Germany restricted to one very pot-holed autobahn, British soldiers often arrived in Berlin by the daily British Military Train, overseen by 62 Transport and Movement Squadron, Royal Corps of Transport. The journey from Brunswick in West Germany to Charlottenburg station in Berlin took four hours, with stops to change engines and check documents in the Russian sector at Magdeburg. Personnel from BRIXMIS, based in Berlin, had far more licence to travel. Officially, their job was to liaise with their Soviet counterparts, providing a channel of communication about matters such as prisoner exchange; unofficially, they were spies, tearing across the East German countryside in souped-up Opel cars, trying to amass information about Soviet strength and weaponry while avoiding being rammed by military vehicles keen to restrict their movement.[10]

On the other side of the Iron Curtain, from 1985 the Soviet Union's armed forces began to come under attack from their own civilian leadership, also worried about rising costs. One of the most formidable militaries in history, the ground forces comprised more than 200 divisions grouped in five main theatres of operation. They possessed more than 54,000 main battle tanks and 4,500 helicopters; more than 5 million personnel were on active service, with reserve forces estimated to number 55 million.[11] The recently introduced SS20 medium-range missile, posed 'a new and heightened threat to NATO security'.[12] In his day, Brezhnev had been determined that the Soviet Union would remain 'a military superpower at any cost' and inevitably defence spending rose.[13] By the mid-1980s, it was estimated to account for 15–17 per cent of GNP, up from an estimated 12–14 per cent in 1970.[14] Given the comparatively poor standard of living of most Soviet citizens, Gorbachev was right to question whether this was money well spent. Radically, he sought to cut defence spending by introducing an overarching policy of deterrence. In future, forces should be of 'reasonable sufficiency' to deter attack, with the Soviet Union no longer letting itself be dragged 'ever deeper into the quagmire of an arms race',[15] which the US Strategic Defense Initiative was deliberately encouraging. Change in the international system was imperative. Writing about a 'common European home' and the 'archaic nature of the Iron Curtain', he stated: 'Today's generation inherited Soviet-American confrontation from the past. But are we doomed to carry the enmity on?'[16] The explosion at the Ukrainian nuclear power plant at Chernobyl in 1986 underlined to Gorbachev the potentially catastrophic nature of even a conventional war in Europe; he suggested that if Europe's 200 reactor units and major chemical works were destroyed, the whole continent would be made 'uninhabitable'.[17]

Glasnost forced into the open an issue that the Soviet High Command wanted to keep shrouded – Afghanistan. On Christmas Day 1979, the Soviet Union's 40th Army crossed the border to prop up the Communist government in Kabul that was under attack from a growing insurgency. One analyst suggests that the Soviets' goals were modest: 'they aimed to secure the main towns and roads, stabilise the government, train up the Afghan Army and Police, and withdraw within six months or a year'.[18] As many militaries have discovered in the past, and doubtless more will in the future, the Soviets learned to their cost that, with Afghanistan, plans tend to go awry. On learning of the invasion in 1979, Gorbachev had predicted privately that the Afghan campaign was 'a fatal error that would cost our country dearly'.[19] By 1986, more than 600,000 troops had passed through the country and the conflict had cost 60 billion roubles. A newly appointed Soviet Chief of the General Staff observed that in the previous seven years, 'Soviet soldiers have had their boots on the ground in every square kilometre of the country': as soon as they left, the enemy returned and restored everything to the way it was before. 'We have lost this war. The majority of the Afghan people support the counter-revolution.'[20]

The Soviet invasion stirred up the forces of Islamic

fundamentalism and their troops faced the greatest resistance from the mujahideen. These holy warriors, financed chiefly by Washington, would give the world a lesson in unintended consequences: evolving into the Taliban government, in the late 1990s they would give a safe haven to Osama bin Laden and al-Qaeda (see chapter 8). Meanwhile, the Soviet campaign was surrounded by secrecy. Almost 90 per cent of Soviet troops who served in Afghanistan fell sick or were wounded.[21] 'Afgantsy' (veterans) were barred from Moscow during the 1980 Olympics and the coffins of the fallen arrived home without ceremony in the dead of night in huge transport planes which became known as Black Tulips. Their families were given the minimum of information and were allowed no war memorials. Soldiers' mothers began their own vocal battle with the authorities, 'one of the first effective civil rights movements to be organised in the Soviet Union'.[22] Many Afgantsy, shunned by the civilian population because of rumours of war crimes, and disillusioned by their battles with bureaucracy for pensions and benefits, joined the chorus demanding change.

The Soviet armed forces were squeezed between Gorbachev's push for internal social and economic reform allied with a transformed approach to foreign policy. As the General Secretary himself said: 'There was a growing awareness that things could not go on like this much longer.'[23] His misgivings about the armed forces were confirmed in a surreal episode when on 28 May 1987 an amateur pilot from Germany, Mathias Rust, landed his light plane in Red Square – somehow managing to avoid Soviet air defences during his flight from Helsinki. More significantly, Moscow–Washington relations thawed in a series of summits – at Geneva, Reykjavik and Washington – when Gorbachev wooed the world. Soviet High Command was shaken up and the old guard purged; meanwhile, the Intermediate-Range Nuclear Forces Treaty of 1987 reduced the number of nuclear weapons in the world and in 1988, in an address to the United Nations, Gorbachev announced massive unilateral cuts in forces' personnel, reducing their numbers by 500,000. Not only would all the troops be withdrawn from Afghanistan by early 1989, but the 40th Army – 'one of the most powerful in Soviet history' – was disbanded.[24] In Britain, the Army had long tried to keep abreast of developments within the Warsaw Pact, principally through the much-respected Soviet Studies Research Centre at Sandhurst. In its inaugural year of 1988, the new Bagnall-inspired Higher Command and Staff Course devoted two full weeks to studying Soviet operational art. This sound use of time, however, came late in the Cold War as, within a year, the Warsaw Pact itself had begun to unravel.

The end of the Cold War was a civilian, not a military, victory. The break-up of the Soviet empire came as much from within, as from without. The implosion which began in Hungary and Poland spread outwards throughout the Warsaw Pact countries. A fissure in the Eastern Bloc monolith appeared in May 1989, with the general elections in Poland, when opposition parties won 99 out of 100 seats. Opposition to the Communist regime had first surfaced in 1980 with the creation of the Solidarity trade union, led by Lech Walesa: throughout the decade it had been sustained by the moral support of the Polish-born Pope, John Paul II. In June, hundreds of thousands turned out in Budapest for the formal reinterment of Imry Nagy, the former Hungarian Prime Minister, executed by the Soviets for his part in the 1956 uprising. In August, Hungary opened its borders, which gave East Germans a means of escape to the West. As thousands continued to drive their spluttering two-stroke Trabants towards freedom, Gorbachev visited East Berlin for the fortieth anniversary celebrations of the German Democratic Republic. He warned: 'Those who do not learn the lessons of history will be left behind in life.' The GDR President Erich Honecker had predicted that the Berlin Wall – the very symbol of the Cold War – could be standing for a hundred years. On 9 November, the frontier separating East and West Berlin was opened and Germans on both side of the Berlin Wall began to use chisels, pickaxes and sledgehammers to tear it down, ahead of the bulldozers moving in. As thousands of East Germans streamed into West Berlin, British soldiers set up refreshment stands, brewing up gallons of tea and coffee and handing out soup and sandwiches. Some were met by a regimental band and Billy the Goat, the immaculately groomed mascot of 1st Battalion Royal Welch Fusiliers.[25]

The upheaval across the Warsaw Pact and within the Soviet Union itself raised questions about the future not only of the West's armed forces but also about NATO. One civilian official working in NATO headquarters admits that, while he and his colleagues were watching events across the Eastern Bloc unfold on their television screens, they were also updating their CVs and scouring the situations vacant columns.[26] Meanwhile, Europe faced instability. More than 225,000 East Germans had headed west between the fall of the Berlin Wall in November 1989 and the end of January 1990. West German Chancellor Helmut Kohl's plans for the reunification of Germany in late November were initially opposed by France's President François Mitterrand, Gorbachev and Mrs Thatcher, who, like their predecessors in 1945, were wary about a resurgent Germany with the capability of dominating Europe. Conversely, US President George H. W. Bush supported a united German state which would retain NATO membership, underlining Washington's continued commitment to collective security in Europe. Although welcome, this was something of a paradox. With the formal demise of the Warsaw Pact on 31 March 1991, NATO was surely to lose much of its *raison d'être*; however, it was to defy history by remaining as a defensive alliance expanding its membership to include former adversaries. With Europe experiencing the aftershocks of revolution, the alliance proved to be an anchor of institutional stability, providing a vital international forum for defence and security.

Another institution that would profit out of continental turmoil was the European Community. For Chancellor Kohl, the prize of German reunification, attained on 3 October 1990, was worth concessions over national sovereignty, including the eventual abolition of the mighty Deutschmark. For Margaret Thatcher, there was 'a rush to Euro-federalism as a way of tying down Gulliver'. There was only one answer to this, as she told the House of Commons: 'No. No. No.'[27] The Conference on Security and Co-operation in Europe (CSCE) in Paris in November 1990 brought leaders together formally to mark the end of the Cold War. Just like the Potsdam Conference which marked the end of the Second World War, Paris was a similar reminder of the transitory nature of political power. Churchill and Roosevelt had left the stage in July 1945; forty-five years later, Reagan had gone, Thatcher was just days away from going and Gorbachev would be the victim of an attempted coup in August the following year.

The British military presence in Berlin was gradually drawn down after reunification. The brigade headquarters and signal squadron were disbanded in January 1991, the military train stopped in February and the military hospital closed in May. The Queen's Birthday Parade was scaled down and the final British Berlin Military Tattoo held in October 1992.[28] The last elements of the British Army finally left Berlin in 1994. It was the end of a very unusual era – with British soldiers, and their families, stationed sixty miles behind the potential frontline. Meanwhile, as the Soviet empire fragmented, in East Germany almost 500,000 Soviet soldiers and their dependants marked time until they could return home: those that did witnessed 'poverty-stricken chaos'.[29] When the West German Bundeswehr took over East German bases they found rows of trucks 'with perhaps 100 km on the clock, fuelled and full of ammunition, ready to go', a reminder that the Cold War might not have ended so peacefully.[30]

Meanwhile, British soldiers who had been trained to fight a Soviet enemy in Germany were preparing to go into action in the Iraqi desert.

The Gulf War

On 2 August 1990, Iraqi forces invaded Kuwait. More than 100,000 troops backed by 700 tanks crossed the border into the oil-rich state in the early hours of the morning. Christopher Fathers, a British businessman staying in the capital's main hotel, was awakened at 5 a.m. by his windows reverberating and the rattle of machine-gun fire; outside, armoured vehicles were amassing on the main ring road.[31] Kuwaiti troops were overwhelmed and the ruling Emir fled to neighbouring Saudi Arabia. Throughout the day, communications with the outside world were progressively cut off. Like thousands of foreign workers who made up the majority of Kuwait City's population, Christopher Fathers would be trapped. Like the rest of the world, he was taken by surprise. Although there had been some sabre-rattling by Baghdad in the previous weeks, he had received 'business-as-usual telexes' from the British Embassy in Kuwait before his planned four-day trip. Along with hundreds of others, Fathers would become part of a human shield, taken prisoner by the invading forces and held hostage for months in Iraq at strategically important sites, such as the Haditha Dam.

Iraq's invasion was condemned by the international community. By coincidence, Margaret Thatcher was in the United States and was able immediately to confer with President Bush. At their joint press conference in Aspen, she was characteristically clear: 'What has happened is a total violation of international law. You cannot have a situation where one country marches in and takes over another country which is a member of the United Nations.'[32] On 6 August, the Security Council passed Resolution 661, which demanded an Iraqi withdrawal from Kuwait and imposed an international embargo on trade with Iraq. Fearing that the Iraqi forces might use Kuwait as a staging post into Saudi Arabia – and perhaps not unmindful of the military coup of 1958 in which Iraq's King Faisal was overthrown and publically executed – the country's leader, King Fahd, called on the United States and NATO for protection. On 8 August, President Bush announced that US forces personnel would be sent to the kingdom to deter any Iraqi aggression. Operation Desert Shield was underway. It would bring together an unlikely coalition, including troops from across the Middle East. British forces would make up the second largest contingent.

The world's fourth largest military, the Iraqi armed forces were battle-hardened. They had spent eight years – 1980–88 – inconclusively fighting Iran, a conflict which prompted former US Secretary of State Henry Kissinger to observe, 'It's a pity they both can't lose.' In a war of attrition, medieval in its barbarism, the conflict claimed an estimated 400,000 lives and another 750,000 wounded. Bodies were still being found years later. The cost to both sides is estimated to have been more than $400 billion each in damage and loss of oil revenues. Determined to show their devotion to Islam and the theocratic regime of the Ayatollahs, Iranian troops – some of them children – attacked the Iraqis in 'human waves', volunteering to run through minefields and clear the ground for other soldiers. In turn, Iraq deployed chemical weapons, in contravention of the Geneva Convention. In the most notorious incident, in March 1988 thousands were killed in the Iranian-occupied Kurdish town of Halabja, some 150 miles north of Baghdad. Mustard gas and the nerve agents tabun and sarin were dropped, along with cyanide, from Iraqi MiG and Mirage aircraft. Consequently, anti-nuclear, biological and chemical attack training (NBC) was made integral to the preparation of troops deploying in Operation Desert Shield.

Against the background of the global thirst for oil, the complexities of Middle East politics, with their ever-shifting alliances, were brought into focus by the invasion of Kuwait. The sheikhdom is surrounded by large and comparatively powerful neighbours: Iraq to the north and west, Saudi Arabia to the south and Iran across the waters of the Persian Gulf. Although tiny, in 1990 Kuwait produced some 10 per cent of the world's oil: if the Iraqis pressed on into Saudi, which accounted for 30 per cent of the total global supply, close to half the world's oil would be under their control. Kuwait and Saudi – along with the United States and Britain – had backed Iraq in its war against Iran. It had also received almost $16 billion of arms from the Soviet Union and Eastern Bloc countries between 1985 and 1989.[33] Although under-performing, Iraq was itself an oil producer with significant oil reserves, although its oil industry was very inefficient. Notwithstanding all its difficulties, in the first seven months of 1990, Iraq's oil represented about 9 per cent of US oil imports for the year.[34] However, after eight years of conflict, it owed billions of dollars – in a time when oil prices were falling, not least because of Kuwait's refusal to limit supply. In addition, the frontier between the two states was a source of periodic dispute between them, particularly concerning the ownership of islands in the Gulf. Before 1918, both the areas that would become Iraq and Kuwait were part of the Ottoman Empire, with Kuwait part of the Basra administrative district. Twice before, Iraq had come close to annexing Kuwait, in 1938 and in 1961 – the latter averted by the dispatch of British and Arab League troops in a much-forgotten episode.

Iraq's leader, Saddam Hussein, was a source of international instability and would remain so until his execution in 2006. With the invasion of Kuwait, 'the West finally awoke to the true nature of the monster it had nurtured'.[35] Formally taking over as president in June 1979, he evolved into a dictator as feared as Stalin, his regime similarly characterised by purges, terror and totalitarian control of the state. However, he was not an entirely unsympathetic figure to some in the wider Middle East because of his anti-imperialist and anti-Zionist rhetoric, which 'generally found an echo in the streets and refugee camps of Jordan, the West Bank and Gaza as well as among a surprising number of Arab intellectuals'.[36] In addition, the West readily backed him against Iran, which, if victorious, would have set up a second Islamic state in Iraq. Although he dressed in military uniforms and styled himself a field marshal, Saddam was not a soldier. General Sir Peter de la Billière, the joint commander of British Forces in the Gulf, and other senior officers who analysed the Iran–Iraq conflict concluded that, for all his posturing, Saddam was 'useless as a strategist and tactician'.[37]

Operation Granby – the codename for the British campaign for the liberation of Kuwait – initially involved the RAF and the Royal Navy. In the days immediately after the invasion, a squadron of RAF Tornados was sent to Saudi Arabia and extra ships sailed to boost the Armilla patrol, the Navy's permanent presence in the Gulf. Throughout August, rumours circulated in the British Army of the Rhine that 7th Armoured Brigade would also be deployed. Descendants of the famous Desert Rats who had fought with such distinction in the North Africa campaign, including at El Alamein, the brigade was based at Soltau, Hohne and Bad Fallingbostel, near the Army's largest training facility in Europe. Commanded by Brigadier Patrick Cordingley, the brigade comprised two main battle tank regiments – the Queen's Royal Irish Hussars and the Royal Scots Dragoon Guards; one armoured infantry battalion – 1st Battalion Staffordshire Regiment; a gunner regiment – 40th Field Regiment, Royal Artillery; an engineer squadron and numerous supporting units.[38] The brigade was part of 1st Armoured Division, which in turn was one of the four divisions that made up 1st British Corps, Britain's principal land contribution to NATO. On 12 September the corps commander, Lieutenant General (future Field Marshal) Sir Charles Guthrie, advised Cordingley that the brigade and its 117 Challenger tanks were indeed going to Saudi, where they would be under the command of the US Marine Corps. Three days later this was publicly confirmed by the Defence Secretary, Tom King. On the insistence of the Prime Minister, overruling a reluctant Secretary of State, de la Billière was appointed Commander British Forces. He had come to Mrs Thatcher's attention as the overall commander of the SAS during the successful Iranian embassy siege of 1980. An Arabic speaker, who understood the politics and culture of the region, having served in the Canal Zone, Aden and Oman, he was an ideal fit for the job.

Overnight, Britain's Armed Forces had to prepare for a different war. As Cordingley observed, 7th Armoured Brigade had been assuming that any operation in which it was involved would be in Europe.[39] Having planned for decades for a confrontation on the North German

Plain, they would be going instead to the desert – an eventuality that the Policy Director in the MoD had categorically and publicly ruled out as an option only a few years before. However, to produce one fully operational armoured brigade, the Army was turned inside out, with personnel and equipment taken from many other units. During the Cold War, everything had been in the shop window with little stock put behind in the store room, now real war-fighting sustainability was required. The Staffords, who had been training for months for a tour of Northern Ireland, were re-tasked and supplemented by a company from the Grenadier Guards. According to de la Billière: 'Some of our armoured vehicles were old and plain worn out; others were run down and not properly maintained or else not used, due to the lack of spares, money and training.'[40] Tanks were cannibalised and all the petrol Land Rovers had to be swapped for diesel. Weeks of intense training focused on 'firing, fitness, first aid and f–ing NBC warfare'.[41] Soldiers had to get used to wearing double-thickness charcoal-impregnated boilersuits and putting on respirators within nine seconds. Meanwhile, horse-trading had ensued between senior commanders and their civilian masters. With forces being deployed to Saudi more to 'prevent a war rather than to provoke one', Whitehall initially was determined to keep troop numbers down to about 6,000. The Army made a bid for 10,000 but, according to de la Billière, was prepared to settle for 7,500.[42] The first wave began to arrive in the Gulf in October.

Saudi Arabia would prove to be a diplomatic minefield. Like every minefield, it had to be negotiated with the utmost caution. Home to the two most sacred sites in Islam, the kingdom was, and remains, intensely conservative. Although secular authority is vested in the absolute monarch who is a member of the al Saud family, the country's legal framework is provided by Sharia law derived from a conservative understanding of the Koran. Consequently, the religious authorities are in effect partners in power. These fundamentalist religious leaders, who could destabilise the monarchy, were decidedly uneasy about a vast influx of infidel foreign troops arriving in the kingdom. Under a memorandum of understanding, soldiers were given immunity from Sharia law, but were warned to conduct themselves with the utmost respect for Islam. Alcohol was banned, although a few inevitably tried to smuggle it in in shampoo bottles.

With Saudi women barred from driving, the issue of the deployment of female personnel in combat zones took on a new immediacy. The Saudis were less than happy with reports of an all-women American football match that was filmed by CNN. Padres were asked not to wear dog collars and religious services were conducted well away from public gaze. Christmas celebrations were to be kept deliberately low-key. HRH Prince Khalid bin Sultan, a nephew of King Fahd and Chief of the Saudi Air Defence Forces, acted as a liaison officer between the Saudi ruling family and the foreign forces. Like the Sultan in neighbouring Oman and King Hussein of Jordan, he had been trained at Sandhurst.

The change of environment from Europe to the Gulf reflects how fast soldiers are expected to adapt. Armoured vehicles had to be repainted and modified to deal with driving through fine sand. Vehicles and supplies were shipped to Al Jubayl, a port on Saudi's east coast, where personnel were quartered in transit accommodation comprising two giant hangars each holding up to 5,000 soldiers. Metal-walled and concrete-floored, they had no air conditioning. The area came to be known as Camp Blackadder after the TV series. The question most frequently asked of Cordingley 'did not concern military planning but "How long do we have to put up with this crap food?", with a quickly remembered "Sir" being tagged on as an afterthought'.[43] Another issue was water, being consumed by British personnel at a rate of over 200,000 gallons a day by the end of November. The desalination plant at the port supplied the capital Riyadh and was considered a priority target for Iraqi attacks. Whitehall penny-pinching led to hesitation over approval for the charter of two water ships: these turned out to be vital at the end of the conflict following sabotage of the desalination plants in Kuwait.[44] There was also a shortage of desert combat uniforms, stocks of which were rumoured to have been sold to Iraq. Soldiers arrived in jungle combats of uncomfortable rash-inducing manmade fibre. When the new kit finally arrived, the Defence Secretary, Tom King, was keen that it was photographed being worn, perhaps more for political than military motives.[45]

In the Gulf War, the Army had to adapt to being part of a multinational coalition. It would be very different from the Falklands campaign, when Britain went it alone. Operation Desert Shield was American-led, with British personnel under the tactical command of General Norman Schwarzkopf. The Commander-in-Chief of the Coalition Forces was an impressive six foot three and seventeen stone. With coalition campaigning, senior commanders have to be far more mindful of the political dimension. Describing him as a 'true professional soldier, a brilliant strategist and tactician', de la Billière acknowledges Schwarzkopf's grasp of the practicalities of commanding a coalition: 'He was always prepared to compromise on the military front if faced by a political imperative.'[46] Influence over the conduct of an operation is determined by the level of force that a nation deploys. As the weeks passed and Iraqi forces showed no sign of leaving Kuwait voluntarily, an offensive campaign to expel them appeared more likely. If the British were to have any input into this, troop numbers would have to be increased from a brigade to a division.

In mid-November 1990 the operational concept began to shift from the defensive Operation Desert Shield to the offensive Operation Desert Storm. The conflict would be the chance for the United States to exorcise the humiliation of Vietnam. The experience and fall-out from the campaign in Indo-China was 'indelibly etched in the minds of America's senior officers', according to General David Petraeus, who would command US forces in Iraq some fifteen years later.[47] Vietnam had called into question civilian strategic patience and tolerance for casualties. After a period of radical reform within the US military in the 1970s – including the purging of racism, criminality and drugs – senior officers rethought the conduct of warfare. The Powell Doctrine, set out by the Chairman of the Joint Chiefs, Colin Powell, had built on the foundations of the Weinberger Doctrine laid down by former Defense Secretary Caspar Weinberger. It called for overwhelming military force. In drawing up his battle plans, General Schwarzkopf sought a fast, conclusive victory that minimised coalition casualties. To achieve that end, the campaign would be divided into two: the air war and the ground war. In addition, existing forces would be supplemented. The US VII Corps would be deployed from Germany, as well as much of the remainder of Britain's 1st Armoured Division, which included units from 4th Armoured Brigade, to join its sister brigade, 7th Armoured Brigade.

For soldiers preparing for war, Prime Minister Thatcher's abrupt departure from office on 28 November 1990 was an unwelcome distraction. Described by the British commander as being 'firm as a rock in her determination to see off Saddam Hussein', she had once again grasped the imperative of decisive military action. As strategy was being discussed out in the Gulf, Mrs Thatcher was facing her own battle with her Parliamentary Party and Cabinet – which she would ultimately lose. The result of the first round of the Conservative leadership contest was announced while she was in Paris for the CSCE summit. Her departure provoked consternation and dismay among the coalition's senior commanders, including General Schwarzkopf. The Commander US 9th Air Force, Chuck Horner, joked: 'The bad news is that Margaret Thatcher has been forced to resign. The good news is that she's joined 7th Armoured Brigade.'[48] Soldiers, who could soon be putting their lives on the line, were unimpressed by the coup against the Prime Minister. One of her last acts in her final Cabinet meeting was to give approval for the deployment of 4th Armoured Brigade, taking the total number of British service personnel to 45,000. However, the message about reinforcements seemed not to have percolated through Whitehall, which was still quibbling over numbers and imposing limits, which senior officers called 'rate-capping'. Troops were flown out to Dhahran on Saudi Arabia's east coast but, because approval for them had yet to be given by Whitehall, some were told to reboard the aircraft and were flown straight home.[49] One of the military principles of war – the identification and maintenance of the aim – was not widely understood by some of those who went to work in suits.

The deployment of 1st Armoured Division led to the provisional battle plans being revised once again. Boosting the British numbers to a division enhanced 'the chances of fighting the war we wanted to fight, and in the way we wanted to fight it', not least because the British would be able to install British staff officers in the American corps headquarters. This would allow greater influence over the planning and direction of the battle.[50] The 7th Armoured Brigade had originally been ordered to join the US Marine Corps (USMC), which was going to head due north into Kuwait. Instead, it was going to be one of the main formations joining the sixty British units that would make up the 1st (United Kingdom) Armoured Division. The much-respected Major General Rupert Smith had just taken over command of the division shortly before he and his headquarters arrived in the Gulf on 12 December. According to the revised battle plan, British forces would advance from the north-west of Saudi and briefly enter Iraq before heading back east into Kuwait, towards the capital itself where the Iraqi strategic reserve had been positioned. The US Army VII Corps would make up the bulk of the forces for this so-called 'left hook' against the Iraqis, with the British division as an integral part of the US Corps. De la Billière told a less-than-enthusiastic Cordingley: 'Politically and militarily we have to be where the action is. If VII Corps is there, we want a part of it with them.'[51] The 7th Armoured Brigade and the USMC had built up a good relationship, not least because the marines were unofficially swapping American camp beds for British field Compo rations; their own MREs (Meals Ready to Eat) being known unofficially as Meals Rejected by Ethiopians.[52]

Planning and training took on a new urgency after 30 November 1990, when the UN Security Council passed Resolution 678. This stipulated that 15 January 1991 was the final date for Iraq to withdraw from Kuwait and approved 'all necessary means to compel them to go'. Just as in the Falklands, when military operations needed to be concluded before the onset of winter, the timing of any campaign was crucial. Ramadan was due to begin on 15 March: if action were delayed until after it was over, the heat would make any operation involving armoured vehicles and NBC suits 'exceedingly unpleasant if not physically impossible'.[53] During Ramadan, the combat effectiveness of Muslim forces from Egypt, for example, would be compromised. Just like the Argentines, Saddam Hussein seemed to be playing for time, presumably hoping that delaying tactics would undermine international resolve. In addition, according to General de la Billière, over in Washington General Colin Powell was giving the impression that he was prepared to wait for up to two years for the Iraqi forces to withdraw from Kuwait. Such a delay would have strained, if not broken, the 39-nation military coalition. It could also have been jeopardised if Saddam had ordered a partial retreat.[54]

Soldiers left the transit quarters in Al Jubayl and dispersed with their units over hundreds of miles of the Saudi desert. In an effort to retain a sense of cohesion and common purpose, a newsletter called the *Sandy Times* was launched with a print run of 10,000 every fortnight. A radio station was set up, not least to counter the propaganda efforts of Baghdad Betty, who was broadcasting from Kuwait. To boost morale in the days before email, soldiers were allowed a single-sheet airmail letter which could be posted for free. With its limited space, the 'bluey' could be filled up quickly but was considered 'a war winner'.[55] Similarly, free phone booths, provided by the telecoms company Mercury, which allowed soldiers to call home for a few minutes a week, proved vital. For the troops themselves, especially those in the more far-flung areas, one danger was isolation. They were 'living on the side of the wagon', as one soldier described it, 'sat in the middle of the desert with nothing else for miles around'.[56] The arrival of tons of parcels and cards, from well-wishers back in Britain including from the Kray twins, brought some Christmas cheer. 'Everywhere people had strung up their cards and tried to make a little corner like home, even if it was only in the back of an M109 gun.'[57] One soldier who confided to a journalist that he felt a bit isolated started receiving more than a dozen sacks of mail a day from people back home.[58] The Christmas spirit did not extend to Bahrain, where troops who had spent months roughing it out in the desert of Saudi Arabia, without receiving a penny in extra allowances, confronted RAF personnel who had been living in air-conditioned comfort in five star hotels.[59] While many expected intense heat, few anticipated the cold and wet. Soldiers from the 14th/20th King's Hussars were kitted out with waterproof ponchos and parkas, thanks to a regimental history read by their commanding officer on the eve of departure. It described a landing in Basra in 1917 when the rain caused the *wadis* to flood and the soldiers' horses to drown, as well as a deployment to Iraq in the Second World War when temperatures had reached minus four.[60]

While plans were being drawn up to retake Kuwait, training continued. On their arrival in Saudi, 7th Armoured Brigade had been given Al Fadili in which to train, a 400 square mile area which was prime camel-grazing land. It allowed the armoured vehicles to be tested. The Challenger initially proved to be disappointing; its six-ton power pack – combined gears and engine – was frequently a problem. With money, for once, no object, technicians and vehicle mechanics from the Royal Electrical and Mechanical Engineers (REME) worked alongside staff from civilian firms such as Vickers, General Electric and Land Rover to iron out the problems and ensure the vehicles' optimum performance. Fitted with a thermal imaging system (TOGS) and a revolutionary satellite navigation system – judged to be 'battle winners' – Challenger tanks and new MLRS rocket launchers proved invaluable.[61] Sat-nav, so taken for granted just a decade later, would prove decisive in an attack by the Staffords on an Iraqi position codenamed Platinum.[62] Furthermore, a helpful insight into enemy tactics was gained from the Egyptians, who, like the Iraqis, had been Russian-trained.

While the British trained, the United States was amassing 425,000 troops, backed by a huge arsenal and one of the largest air forces in history. Convoys some forty miles long left Al Jubayl port every day. There was a sticky moment for senior British officers who had to own up to General Schwarzkopf that a laptop belonging to a middle-ranking RAF staff officer with the entire British battle plan on it had been stolen from a car on its way to Joint Headquarters in High Wycombe.

The principles of Operation Desert Storm were finalised in December. President Bush and the new British Prime Minister, John Major, were given a presentation on the battle plan, which included the British contribution, codenamed Desert Sabre. General Schwarzkopf sought to prepare the way for a ground war with a massive four-stage air campaign against Iraq and Iraqi forces. There were an estimated 400,000 Iraqi troops in or around Kuwait, including the praetorian Republican Guard. There might have been more, but with Turkey boosting its military presence along its 150-mile frontier with Iraq, an estimated eight enemy divisions were tied down, which might otherwise have been deployed to the south.[63] In all, the coalition comprised 670,000 troops from twenty-eight countries. John Major noted: 'Overall it was the most intensive and complex campaign mounted since War War II.'[64] Major clearly felt responsibility for the human cost of war and the possible impact on the 45,000 British personnel who were in the Gulf. He reflected that they were not fighting for home and hearth as in the two great wars of the twentieth century, and nor were they fighting for the recovery of a British possession like the Falklands. 'They were fighting to prevent a dictator extending his power. They were fighting for something less tangible: the maintenance of international law.'[65] An able negotiator, during his visit to the Gulf the Prime

Minister secured an undertaking from the Saudis that they would meet many of the financial costs of the conflict.

The campaign to liberate Kuwait began at 0001 hours on 17 January 1991. The air war would take just over five weeks. More than 6,100 sorties would be flown by the RAF, with Tornados flying by night and Jaguars by day. It would be the largest effort of any nation other than the United States, and, as the RAF observed, 'more than two and a half times that flown by our French friends'.[66] First the enemy's air force and its air defence installations were attacked, then its chemical and nuclear facilities, followed by logistics routes to disrupt supplies, then the troops themselves, with the aim of reducing combat effectiveness by 50 per cent. The operation woke the world up to the advanced technology that was routinely used by the world's first-rank militaries. Smart bombs, including laser-guided Hellfire and Tomahawk Cruise missiles, radar-evading Stealth bombers, anti-Scud Patriot missiles that cost £800,000 each, as well as the use of GPS, which would soon become standard in civilian life, allowed an unprecedented level of precision. The fog of war seemed to be lifted. When the air war began, President Bush promised his nation: 'This will not be another Vietnam.'[67] In less than a week, air superiority had been achieved over the Iraqis.

Almost as soon as it was launched, Operation Desert Storm was under threat not from the Iraqis but from the possible intervention of Israel. On 17/18 January, Iraq attacked Tel Aviv and Haifa with Scud missiles. Israel's F-16 fighter bombers immediately took to the skies. If Israel had retaliated, the coalition would have broken. Israeli participation in the coalition would have been a contribution too far for its Arab members. On 22 January another Scud exploded in Tel Aviv, injuring seventy people. Members of British Special Forces were sent into Iraq's western desert to track down the mobile Scud launchers. Working in an area of several thousand square miles, which became known as Scud Alley, they went to work 'in typically vigorous and effective fashion', according to de la Billière.[68] Not only did they knock out Scuds with their own Milan anti-tank missiles, but they destroyed communications bunkers and relay towers, engaged with the enemy, captured an Iraqi artillery officer who was carrying battle maps and caused general mayhem. One thing they had underestimated was the weather. The desert was exceptionally cold, with sleet, snow, hail and frost: fires had to be lit under Land Rovers to stop the diesel from freezing. Four men were killed behind enemy lines. The SAS's exploits – described in a series of bestsellers by Andy McNab, Chris Ryan and others – captured the British public's imagination and further embedded the mystique of Special Forces.

The ground campaign began at 0400 hours on 24 February. After five months in the scorching heat and the surprising chill of the desert, what Saddam Hussein described as 'the mother of all battles' was about to begin. The 4th and 7th Armoured Brigades had been moved to the west of Saudi. Cordingley said the area was so desolate 'it was as if someone had rubbed out the landscape'.[69] The logistic centre, Log Base Alpha, which served 1st Armoured Division and the US VII Corps, was huge, storing sixty days' worth of supplies, spares and ammunition, as well as plastic water bottles covering acres of land. G-Day saw the 1st and 2nd US Marine Divisions head north and break through into Kuwait. Simultaneously, to the west, units from the American XVIII Corps, with French reinforcements, arced across the desert towards Iraq's Highway 8, which runs between Baghdad and Basra, for an assault on Saddam's Republican Guard. On G+1, British forces joined the land battle, with the Queen's Royal Irish Hussars, under the command of Lieutenant Colonel Arthur Denaro, spearheading 7th Armoured Brigade into minefields previously cleared by the armoured bulldozers of the US 1st Mechanized Infantry Division. The Royal Scots Dragoon Guards battlegroup, under the command of Lieutenant Colonel John Sharples, and the 1st Staffords battlegroup, under Lieutenant Colonel Charlie Rogers, followed. A series of enemy positions – codenamed Copper, Brass, Steel, Zinc, Platinum, Lead and Tungsten – were the markers on the way through the desert of south-east Iraq into Kuwait. On G+2, the British suffered a blue-on-blue in which nine soldiers from 3rd Royal Regiment of Fusiliers were killed by an American A-10 tank buster aircraft. The following day, G+3, 1st Armoured Division had crossed the border into Kuwait, which Cordingley's team celebrated with a cup of tea.[70] As British forces reached Objective Cobalt on the Basra road, offensive operations were suspended. The vivid images of the destruction of the Iraqi Army broadcast worldwide risked the loss of international support. The war had lasted for just 100 hours. The Iraqis were routed: some 60,000 were prisoners of war, among them a whole battalion that had surrendered to the Staffords. After weeks of bombing, they were demoralised, starving and exhausted.

Kuwait City was shrouded in a black cloud of smoke from burning oil wells and burning slicks in the waters of the Gulf. The country had been liberated and the war aims met. In all, forty-seven British personnel were killed in action and in non-combat accidents, while 383 US personnel died. In the light of Iraq's future non-compliance with international norms, the question is often raised about why the coalition did not take the opportunity to press on to Baghdad and effect regime change. John Major was adamant that halting the campaign at Kuwait was correct: no Arab nation would have wanted regime change and no similar coalition could have been formed in the future. In his view, exceeding the UN's mandate would have engendered a lack of trust in the Arab world and wider international community, encouraging canards about Western imperialism. 'We would have won the war but lost the peace.' [71] Although the war had been authorised by international law, it was concluded by moral and practical common sense – this was a text book endeavour, in sharp contrast to what was to come a decade later.

The Impact of the Gulf War and Options for Change

A major conflict such as the Gulf War forces one of those periodic stock-takes of defence policy. The Armed Forces assess what military lessons are to be learned, while Westminster and Whitehall consider existing priorities and assumptions. The Gulf War can be said to have been an old-fashioned state-on-state conflict that was caught between two technological eras. It was very different from the post-Cold War campaigns in which British soldiers were to be involved later in the decade, when the world's leading armed forces became, according to some analysts, 'post-modern'. In the Gulf, soldiers wrote their blueys and relied upon the British Forces Post Office to deliver letters with news of friends and family. Meanwhile, high technology helped deliver smart bombs able to go down the lift shafts of 10-storey buildings.

One innovation that all future commanders would have to consider was 24-hour news media. Almost 1,400 journalists were officially accredited to the Gulf campaign. In the Falklands, the press had been kept largely under control because they were reliant upon the military to get them to the theatre, look after them while they were there and to get their copy or footage back to Britain. During Operation Desert Storm, the public was given – or believed it was given – a ringside view of the action almost as good as that enjoyed by the senior commanders in the Central Command Headquarters in Riyadh. The advent of Cable News Network (CNN), the 24-hour news channel, enabled events to be viewed with unprecedented immediacy. Footage from the nose-cameras of smart bombs allowed the civilian public to see images relayed live from the battlefront. This capability would become a double-edged sword both for the military leaders conducting the war and the politicians who had ordered them to war. As much as the public might feel sympathy for the plight of RAF pilot John Peters and his navigator John Nichol, shot down and then paraded on Iraqi TV, the public was also angered by mistakes such as the killing of an estimated 400 Iraqi civilians in the bombing of a shelter at Amiriyah, which Saddam Hussein was quick to exploit. The coalition might have taken care to avoid damaging sites such as the Shi'ite shrines of Karbala and Najaf, but any moral advantage was eroded by footage of civilian casualties. The air war also became the battle of the airwaves. Some over-colourful remarks by Patrick Cordingley to British defence correspondents led to lurid headlines such as the Evening Standard's 'Bloodbath in the Gulf'. As General de la Billière said: 'Television is something a modern commander cannot ignore.'[72] Although some commentators likened the media coverage to an action film or video game, one poll established that only 5 per cent of the public considered the conflict in those terms.[73] However, for the French philosopher Jean Baudrillard, the imagery of the war became more important than the war itself, consequently, in his view, 'the Gulf War did not take place'.[74]

In July 1990, just before the invasion of Kuwait, Parliament's Defence Select Committee published a report on the transformation in Europe since 1989. With the ending of the Cold War, substantial reductions in Soviet and American military personnel were predicted, along with the destruction of large quantities of weapons. According to the report, there would be 'profound and far-reaching implications for United Kingdom defence policy'.[75] The same day, Defence Secretary Tom King announced some provisional results of the defence policy review to be known as Options for Change that had been underway since February. Although the process had yet to be finalised, some early conclusions had been reached. Inevitably, cuts would be made. 'The aim is smaller forces, better equipped, properly trained and housed, and well-motivated. They will need to be flexible and mobile and able to contribute both in NATO and, if necessary, elsewhere.'[76] To many soldiers, 'smaller and better' meant just one thing – smaller. The retention of four Trident submarines and three aircraft carriers was among the main proposals. Significant from the Army's point of view, manpower was to be reduced by 18 per cent over five years to 120,000; the strength in Germany would be halved, with the Army's overall order of battle reducing from four divisions to two. The reserves would also be restructured. One MP observed that the public expected a more substantial peace dividend than what was being offered: 'We are left, as before, with the best defended cardboard cities and dole queues in Europe.'[77] However, King declared: 'It is a time for opportunity and hope for change … Our aim is an orderly and planned transition to the new world now unfolding.'[78] But this new world that was unfolding was not destined to be at peace: a week later Iraq invaded Kuwait.

Operation Granby highlighted the difference between the theory of defence reviews and the actual practice of conflict and combat. The Falklands campaign had confounded many of the assumptions and predictions set out in the Nott Review. Operation Granby offered the Armed Forces the opportunity to learn many lessons, not least about their equipment, their training, logistics and the reserve forces. It had also highlighted the possibility that defence capability was on the threshold of entering a new technological era, which would create what analysts described as another Revolution in Military Affairs (RMA). However, for historian Jeremy Black, the 1991 campaign against Iraq, as well as that of 2003, was a reflection less of a revolution than simply 'what happens when a weak and poorly commanded force is attacked by a stronger and better-led one'.[79] Above all, however, Kuwait reinforced the paramount significance of the human factor – something that defence reviews generally neglected. Army doctrine would subsequently identify this as the moral component of fighting power: the ability to fight and win. This is fostered not least by unit cohesion derived from service in corps and regiments with long and proud histories. Ahead of his visit to the

Gulf in early January 1991, John Major asked what he should talk about to service personnel. General de la Billière sent back a message that all the regiments were desperately anxious about *Options for Change* and concerned that 'when they arrived home after the war, they would find that their regiment had disappeared, amalgamated with others'.[80]

Many Armed Forces personnel considered *Options for Change* as nothing more than options for cuts – an inevitable consequence of the end of the Cold War, despite Operation Granby. Former Chief of the Defence Staff Field Marshal Lord Bramall noted: 'There seemed to have been no clear ministerial view of the way ahead or of what the government wanted to do – hence the title.'[81] This view was echoed by Alan Clark MP, who in July 1989 had been appointed Minister for Defence Procurement: 'There shouldn't be any f****** options. It should be, "It's like this. Now get on with it." We're just heamorrhaging away on needless expenditure and morale is plummeting with the uncertainty.'[82]

Clark grasped earlier than many that the Cold War was indeed over: one priority, he correctly predicted, should be the defence of the Bahrain causeway in the northern Gulf. His call in late July 1989 for the Armilla patrol to be stepped up was rejected by the Royal Navy: 'They don't like the Armilla because it "strains resources". What are resources for?' In mid-October 1989, he observed: 'The career structure of the British Army for the last 40 years has been anchored in the "Rhine Army". They simply cannot come to terms with the change that has occurred.' He wished he could do 'what Stalin did to Tukhachevsky' – purge three-quarters of all senior officers of field rank or above and put them in front of a firing squad.[83] Towards the end of the year, the maverick MP had secured Mrs Thatcher's cautious consent to his reappraising the procurement programme. Clark seized this as his chance to present an alternative defence review. He noted on New Year's Day 1990: 'We are at one of those critical moments in defence policy that occurs once every 50 years.'[84] However, once Operation Granby was underway, Clark had little to do and was sidelined – probably to the relief of senior officers, as well as the Defence Secretary whose job he wanted.

Together with personnel numbers, the changes affecting each service in any defence review are conveyed in the context of ships for the Royal Navy, aeroplanes for the RAF and, for the Army, in the disbandment or amalgamation of regiments. Any regimental changes are usually unwelcome and politically fraught, not least because of a regiment's historic ties to a local area. As previously described, Walter Walker lobbied the King of Nepal in his battle to fight off cuts to the Brigade of Gurkhas. After Aden, Colonel 'Mad Mitch' Mitchell was at the forefront of a campaign to save the Argyll and Sutherland Highlanders from disbandment, an issue in Scotland which transcended any party political loyalty. A former commanding officer described how the 'gnomes of Whitehall' wanted mercenaries rather than soldiers, 'with no allegiance anywhere'.[85] In 1991, Keep Our Scottish Battalions, a campaign to prevent the amalgamation of four Scottish regiments into two, gained 800,000 signatures and finally persuaded the government to reverse the proposed union of the King's Own Scottish Borderers with the Royal Scots.

Soldiers invariably consider themselves to belong first to a regiment or corps *but also* to the Army. At a gathering of regimental colonels in November 1956, Her Majesty the Queen said: 'There is no first among the regiments and corps of my Army and there is no last: all are bound in the same spirit of brotherhood and proud service to sovereign and country and each regards itself – with every reason – as second to none.'[86] Unlike the Royal Navy and the Royal Air Force, there is no 'Royal' British Army. It is sometimes said that the British Army is a grouping of fiercely independent fighting tribes who come together by common accord to fight the Queen's enemies when required and to fight each other otherwise. However, for more than 350 years, regiments have been the bedrock of the British Army. *Esprit de corps* may be a French expression but it has a particularly British meaning. To boost recruitment during the American War of Independence, most line regiments were given county titles. In a letter to *The Times* in 1854, an anonymous cavalry officer described the regimental system as 'the keystone of the military arch'.[87] Prompted not least by the professionalism and success of Prussia's army, the system was reshaped in the 1870s and 1880s, under two reforming Secretaries of State for War, Edward Cardwell and Hugh Childers. Among the more significant measures was the abolition of purchase – when an officer bought his commission or stepped up his rank. In addition, local ties were strengthened, as were the links between regulars and local auxiliary forces. There were also general improvements to pay and conditions, including the abolition of flogging. Throughout the twentieth century, the regimental system was periodically reshaped to suit evolving defence needs.

The regimental system has its critics. For them, loyalty to a particular cap badge encourages an unhealthy tribalism. During defence reviews such as *Options for Change* or at a time of cuts to the defence budgets, regiments can fight for themselves rather than for the greater good of the Army. At the time of the Gulf War, roughly one-third of soldiers were attached to a regiment ('the teeth'); the rest belonged to technical corps such as the Royal Electrical and Mechanical Engineers ('the tail'). *Options for Change* gave momentum to a long-mooted reorganisation of the tail, introducing the Adjutant General's Corps and the Royal Logistic Corps. According to military historian Hew Strachan, the teeth arm regiments have 'the near monopoly of power and prestige in the Army and so come to dominate its upper ranks'.[88] At times, certain regiments appeared consistently to provide the Army's leaders, with the Royal Green Jackets known as the 'black mafia' and the Green Howards producing within two decades two Chiefs of the Defence Staff and two Chiefs of the General Staff, one of whom was Field Marshal Bagnall. Regimental rivalries are most apparent at times of defence cuts, when regiments are fighting for their survival. In the aftermath of *Options for Change*, 'The Army turned in on itself, regiments jockeying for position in order to establish who would survive.'[89]

The British Army is not alone in this. During the Gulf War, General de la Billière suspected that the 'exceptionally gung-ho' US Marine Corps were 'mustard keen' to be the main thrust of the attack against the Iraqis: 'We knew that the Marine Corps were nervous about their own future – as were all the US Armed Forces – and they imagined the best way of avoiding cuts would be to win the war against Saddam on their own.'[90] He was concerned that a disproportionate number of British soldiers might pay the ultimate price because of an internal struggle within the US military. This became a factor in the decision to enlarge the British contribution to a division, which would be independent from American tactical control.

Of all the defence reviews since 1945, *Options for Change* had the biggest impact on the Army. The review was undertaken in a piecemeal fashion and was not properly concluded until after the 1992 General Election. The most significant announcements came in July 1991, with the publication of the policy document *Britain's Army for the 90s*.[91] The Army was to be cut by more than a quarter, with manpower reduced from 155,000 to 116,000 soldiers – 4,000 fewer than had been proposed a year earlier. The majority of cuts would be to the British Army of the Rhine, down from more than 50,000 personnel to 23,000, and in Hong Kong, where a Gurkha battalion was to be axed. The number of infantry battalions was to be cut from fifty-five to thirty-eight, with a 35 per cent cut in the frontline teeth arms: the number of armoured or armoured reconnaissance regiments would fall from nineteen to eleven. The insistence by the Defence Secretary that the review was 'strategy-led' rather than 'Treasury-led' was met with a degree of scepticism in the Army, the House of Commons and the Defence Select Committee, which judged that 'Despite repeated denials, there is a pervasive sense throughout the *Options for Change* exercise that financial constraints have overridden purely military considerations.'[92] There was a degree of bafflement about why the figure of 116,000 had been decided upon, rather than the 120,000 that had been proposed a year earlier, especially in the light of the Gulf War. Questions about this, about the overall restructuring of the Army and, in particular, about the rationale behind the amalgamation of regiments, were dodged by ministers. King told the Defence Select Committee 'to embark on a detailed examination of criteria on which judgements about individual regiments had been reached would be divisive, unhelpful for the units concerned, and prolong the sense of uncertainty that changes inevitably cause'.[93] Ministerial buck-passing to the Army Board and its executive – 'it was the Army Board which approved those proposals' – left the Defence Select Committee unimpressed: 'We certainly cannot accept that Parliament should be treated as if it were in the military chain of command, and bidden to shut up and get on with it.'[94] A new dimension to British defence policy appeared with NATO's proposals for the creation of an Allied Command Europe Rapid Reaction Corps (see chapter 7). At home, the visible military presence would diminish, with a cut in the number of training establishments, along with military districts and their headquarters, while the link between civilian and military spheres would be weakened, with a reduction in the number of reservists, down from 75,000 to perhaps 60,000.

Civilian policymakers can forget that when soldiers lose their jobs, they also lose their homes and their regimental family. Soldiers' welfare is one reason why commanding officers fight so hard to resist amalgamation, let alone the abolition of regiments and battalions. Regimental pride and a sense of the responsibility to history also have their place. *Options for Change* led to lobbying and campaigning on regiments' behalf; for example, 100,000 local civilians signed the Save the Staffords campaign petition calling on the government to rethink the Staffordshire Regiment's proposed merger with the Cheshire Regiment, who were considered to be a better fit with the Royal Welch Fusiliers or the King's Regiment – and who placed the Staffords last on a list of preferences for any possible amalgamations.[95] The Colonel of the Cheshires doubted whether, given the Army's existing commitments, thirty-eight battalions would be able to meet the Army target of two years between tours: 'This target has not been met for the last 20 years with 55 battalions.'[96] His counterpart in the Queen's Own Highlanders (Seaforth and Camerons) said the confidence of soldiers and ex-soldiers in the government's defence policy had been severely shaken: 'It seems to us in the Highlands that, to put it bluntly, we have been sold down the river by an uncaring Conservative government.'[97] The Colonel of the Royal Hussars (PWO) considered the cuts arbitrary and unbalanced: 'The overfat bureaucratic tail will not be cut by anything like the same proportion.'[98] The Staffords pointed out that they had been given no chance to make their case against amalgamation and were, in fact, led to believe they would not be merged. There was a suspicion that, because they were not seen to be as prestigious as other regiments and because there were few marginal seats in their recruiting area, their amalgamation could be achieved 'with few military or political repercussions'.[99] Some of the regiment's soldiers, who had just returned from the Gulf, only heard the news from an announcement on the British Forces Broadcasting Service in Germany: 'This should have been avoided and had exacerbated problems of morale among serving officers and soldiers within the regiment.'[100] Given all the controversy, soldiers had little faith in politicians' claims that the Army would be 'smaller but better'.

Northern Ireland

Although the Cold War was ending, Operation Banner in Northern Ireland continued. By the beginning of the 1980s, the conflict had claimed more than 2,000 lives, almost 600 of which were soldiers and police officers.[101] Throughout the decade, soldiers did their duty in the province – and were the target for murderous attacks. The IRA recognised that, to maximise media coverage and minimise the risk of undermining support in Northern Ireland by disrupting daily life there, bombing London was more effective than bombing the province. On 20 July 1982, two remote-controlled bombs killed seven Royal Green Jackets bandsmen giving a lunchtime concert in Regent's Park and four soldiers from the Household Cavalry in Hyde Park, along with seven horses. One horse, Sefton, received thirty-four separate injuries but survived, returning to duty in Knightsbridge within three months. A symbol of resilience and courage, he received fan mail from all over the world.[102]

Prime Minister Margaret Thatcher narrowly escaped assassination in October 1984 when the Grand Hotel in Brighton was bombed by the IRA during the Conservative Party Conference. Two of her close confidants were killed by IRA car bombs: Airey Neave MP in March 1979 and Ian Gow MP in July 1990. Like the Unionist community in the province, Gow had opposed the 1985 Anglo-Irish Agreement which had created a framework to give Dublin a consultative role in the governance of the province. This political concession, London hoped, would boost support for the sort of moderate nationalism espoused by the Socialist Democratic and Labour Party (SDLP), at the expense of the IRA. Since late 1981, the Provisionals had modified their strategy in the Long War and set political goals. In the 1983 General Election, suspected Provisional IRA member Gerry Adams won West Belfast for Sinn Féin.

Despite a small measure of political progress, the violence showed little sign of letting up. The Armalite – among a 136-ton Libyan-supplied arsenal that included Semtex and surface-to-air missiles – continued to predominate over the ballot box. Particularly savage was the February 1985 mortar attack on Newry police station, which killed nine RUC officers, and the bombing of the border town of Enniskillen during a Remembrance Day parade in November 1987, which killed eleven civilians and injured sixty more. The security services managed to avert another attack on a police station at Loughgall in May 1987, when eight IRA men were ambushed and killed. Similarly, an attack in Gibraltar by members of an IRA active service unit was foiled in 1988. In both cases, the European Court of Human Rights ruled that the IRA members' right to life was violated. It can perhaps be pointed out that the right to life of Corporal Derek Wood and Corporal David Howes of the Royal Corps of Signals was violated when they were dragged out of a car near the Milltown cemetery in Belfast during the IRA funeral of one of the Gibraltar three, bundled into a taxi and executed. On 7 February 1991, as the War Cabinet met, a mortar attack was launched on 10 Downing Street. Eleven days later, bombs exploded at Victoria and Paddington stations, which led to all six London mainline stations and some of the tube network being shut – something that had not happened before, even during the Blitz. John Major captured the mood of resignation on the mainland about the Troubles across the Irish Sea: 'It seemed to me that our nation had become so weary of this ever-present scar that people were now willing to accept that nothing could be done.'[103]

The end of the Gulf War brought a humanitarian crisis for Iraq's Kurds and Shi'ite populations who fled the country. At the instigation of Britain and the United States, safe havens were established: more than 8,000 British, American and French troops would deliver food, water, clothing and shelter to them. The humanitarian imperative would be the guiding motive for the deployment of the military for the rest of the decade and into the twenty-first century. Although state-on-state war might prove unlikely, British soldiers found themselves involved in hybrid conflicts where their adversaries were hidden in plain sight among the population the troops were attempting to protect. The Cold War may have ended but war among the people was about to begin.

SEVEN

NEW WORLD DISORDER AND HUMANITARIAN INTERVENTIONISM

Bosnia, the 1998 Defence Review, Kosovo,
East Timor and Sierra Leone

The post-Cold War expansion of democracy across eastern Europe, along with the release of Nelson Mandela in February 1990 and the end of apartheid in South Africa, appeared to herald a new era of freedom and tolerance. The successful UN-mandated Gulf War seemed to fulfil the vision of a new world order of international cooperation, heralded by President George H. W. Bush. The threat of global nuclear confrontation was at an end; in its place was an awareness of global interdependence, reflected best by the Green movement and the first Earth Summit, held in 1992. However, the break-up of the Soviet Union was one indication of possible future instability, which soon came to be realised. So-called 'new wars' broke out in Rwanda, Somalia and the former Yugoslavia, characterised by ethnic cleansing and genocide.[1] Humanitarian crises were integral to such conflicts: a century ago, one in twenty civilians would have been affected by a war in their region, today the figure is nearer nine in ten.[2] Global media coverage has allowed the world to witness the fate of victims of conflict. As a result, the international impulse towards intervention to halt, mitigate or prevent humanitarian catastrophe strengthened throughout the 1990s. Consequently, British soldiers would once again be found on the frontline of trouble spots around the world, deployed as United Nations' peacekeepers rather than as imperial policemen.

This chapter examines the contribution of British soldiers to 'saving strangers' in Bosnia, Sierra Leone, Kosovo and East Timor.[3] Humanitarian intervention is controversial, raising questions about international law and morality. As UN-mandated peacekeepers, symbolised by their blue berets and helmets, soldiers were legally constrained, not least in connection with the use of force. The nature of the mission could change: in Bosnia soldiers were initially peacekeepers, and then peace enforcers after the Dayton Agreement, while Sierra Leone evolved into a combat operation. The 1998 Strategic Defence Review set out the defence policy of the Labour government, elected the previous year. With a belief that Britain should be a 'force for good' in the world and a commitment to an ethical foreign policy, the new government deployed Britain's armed forces to promote its values. Towards the end of the decade, out in the field, soldiers' paths would begin to cross with those of personnel from the newly created Department for International Development (DfID), now in charge of Britain's overseas aid budget.

Bosnia

The Federal Republic of Yugoslavia was said to be made up of six republics, five nations, four languages, three religions, two alphabets and one Tito, president from 1953. After his death in 1980, cracks started to appear within this Communist federation. Following the break-up of the wider Communist bloc in 1989, the Yugoslav federation itself began to fracture. By 1991, war had broken out within, and between, three of its former states: Croatia, Serbia and Bosnia-Herzegovina.[4] This three-way conflict came to be played out in Bosnia. Its capital, Sarajevo, had been the site of the 1984 Winter Olympics and the famous gold-medal-winning ice-dancing performance by Jayne Torvill and Christopher Dean. Beginning in April 1992, Sarajevo suffered the longest siege of any city in modern times. More widely, the four-year war in Bosnia came to be characterised by ethnic cleansing, mass graves and death camps. It highlighted the futility of peacekeeping when there is no peace to keep, but when British soldiers finally exchanged their UN blue berets for NATO's steel helmets, it highlighted the positive impact of a military deployment. This was explored by one senior British commander, General Sir Rupert Smith, in his study about war among the people, *The Utility of Force*.[5]

During the war in Bosnia, neighbour fought neighbour. The country's population was 44 per cent Muslim, 32 per cent Serb and 25 per cent Croat. Before the war they were all jumbled together. Towns, villages and apartment blocks were mixed; about one-third of marriages in Sarajevo cut across ethnic lines. In March 1992, Bosnia's nationalist Serbs formed a breakaway republic, the Republika Srpska. They would be encouraged by Serbia and its leader, Slobodan Milo-sevic, who would arrange for them to take over many of the weapons and much of the equipment from units of the former 2nd Military District of the Yugoslav National Army (JNA), which had been based in Bosnia. In April, Bosnia's predominantly Muslim government in Sarajevo declared independence. Sectarian violence broke out and quickly escalated. By June, the refugee agency UNHCR reported that 1.5 million people had fled their homes in the former Yugoslavia in the previous twelve months; 500,000 from Croatia, the remainder from Bosnia.[6] Others were pinned down, unable to flee the fighting, including many in Sarajevo. The city came to represent the human cost of the conflict. For General Sir Michael Rose, another UN com-mander in Bosnia, Sarajevo was 'a grim symbol of the savagery of man and the fragility of civilisation'.[7]

The conflict in Bosnia awoke the West to the horrors of war among the people. For all its high-tech weaponry that had recently amazed global television audiences, the Gulf War had been an old-fashioned state-on-state conflict, not too dissimilar from the Falk-lands. Both had a clearly identifiable objective and enemy, both were fought by soldiers in uniform, both had seen a decisive battle and even a frontline. The conflict in Bosnia was a three-sided civil war, fought by regular and irregular forces and militias. The Bosnian Serb army, led by Ratko Mladic, was backed by the Serbian army, as well as a multitude of irregular forces. The Serbian Volunteer Guard, known at Arkan's Tigers, was led by the warlord Arkan – Zeljko Raznatovic – a former bank robber and head of the Belgrade Star football team fan club. Bosnian racketeer Jusuf Prazina formed a 3,000-strong private army, Juka's Wolves, to defend Sarajevo during the siege.

Analysts tried to make sense of Bosnia and other conflicts in the post-Cold War world. For Mary Kaldor, Bosnia was an example of a 'new war', in which the distinctions between war, organised crime and violations of human rights become blurred: at root are the politics of identity, 'based on the reconstruction of a heroic past, the memory of injustices real or imagined, and of famous battles, won or lost'.[8] Robert Kaplan predicted that future conflict would emerge when environmental factors such as the scarcity of water fused with existing ethnic disputes, which would be exploited by gangsterism.[9] This was being seen in Somalia, a failing state where drought had exacerbated longstanding clan warfare. In 1993, the American political scientist Samuel Huntington predicted a 'clash of civilisations'. Perhaps most alarmingly for professional soldiers, in 1991 the Israeli military historian and strategist Martin van Creveld suggested that familiar forms of armed conflict were becoming history. Consequently, 'a ghost is stalking the corridors of general staffs and defense departments all over the "developed world" – the fear of military impotence, even irrelevance'.[10] However, in these post-Cold War wars among the people, it is often only soldiers who can provide effective humanitarian relief because it is only they who are trained, equipped and authorised to operate in the hostile environment of conflict.

Columns of refugees, corpses lying in roads, burned-out buildings … The human suffering in Bosnia and the wider former Yugoslavia was happening on the doorstep of the European Union. Known to millions of Europeans as a holiday destination, Croatia had been the first site of unrest: the ancient city of Dubrovnik was shelled in October 1991. The United Nations first took action in connection with the former Yugoslavia in Croatia. An arms embargo imposed in September was followed by the creation of UNPROFOR – the UN Protection Force – in February 1992. It would attempt to uphold a ceasefire between the warring factions in three designated Protected Areas: Krajina, Western Slavonia and Eastern Slavonia. By mid-1992, UNPROFOR comprised 14,000 personnel from thirty-one countries under a Canadian commander. The British component was a field hospital of 300 personnel – a minimal gesture bowing to political and popular pressures.

Western governments were reluctant to get involved in this messy, three-way ethnic conflict, either in the wider former Yugoslavia or in Bosnia. Britain's hands-off approach was shared by the United States: Secretary of State James Baker had declared in June 1991, 'We don't have a dog in this fight.' Despite the humanitarian crisis unfolding a few hours' flight away, in early 1992 the British government was preoccupied by the Maastricht Treaty, which changed Europe from a 'Community' to a political 'Union'. In a foreign policy debate, MPs from all parties ruled out any further military deployment of British forces. Foreign Secretary Douglas Hurd stated: 'When, night after night, people see on television destruction and massacre in a European city, most of them do not expect us to send in troops, but they expect us to take some sensible action, if we can, to bring that suffering to an end.'[11] His Labour shadow maintained that the situation was far too confused for forcible intervention from the outside to do any good.[12]

Ethnic cleansing characterised the conflict in Bosnia. The United Nations describes ethnic cleansing as 'rendering an area ethnically homogenous by using force or intimidation to remove persons of a given group from the area'. Families who had lived in villages and towns for generations were either killed, forcibly expelled or fled in terror for their lives. Making the process even more savage was the obliteration of any evidence of these previous inhabitants: places of worship – whether churches or mosques – homes, crops, livestock, even hayricks were destroyed. As the earth was scorched, rape became a weapon of war. Serb detention centres for skeletal Muslim prisoners were discovered by journalists in July and August 1992, making headlines around the world. The *Daily Mirror* described the camp at Trnopolje as 'Belsen 92' and the accompanying image as 'the picture that shames the world'. Public pressure demanding that governments do something, anything, to put a stop to the conflict-related suffering they saw on TV was first identified in the 1990s as 'the CNN effect'. It was apparent in 2015 in connection with the images of a dead toddler washed up on a beach, who came to represent the migrant crisis that had resulted from the Syrian civil war. The Major government was cautious about gestures to appease the 'something must be done club' in connection with Bosnia. However, John Major sensed the beginning of a new mood concerning foreign policy, with calls for troops to be deployed to ease the plight of civilian populations. 'The old Cold War consistencies of British politics were breaking up.'[13] In early August, the Prime Minister asked military chiefs how many soldiers were needed to keep the warring factions apart. He was told 400,000, nearly three times the size of the

British Army.[14] The CGS at the time, General Sir Peter Inge, whose instinct was also against committing British troops, argued successfully that any soldiers deployed must do so with the best equipment available, including the Warrior infantry fighting vehicles.

British soldiers arrived in Bosnia as part of an expanded UNPROFOR mission in late 1992. UN Resolutions 770 and 776 had established a separate command in the country, where some 7,800 peacekeepers would be based, including soldiers from France, Spain and Canada. The principal elements of Britain's initial contribution to the force were the 1st Battalion Cheshire Regiment, under the command of Lieutenant Colonel Bob Stewart, with detachments from 2nd Battalion Royal Irish Regiment, 9th/12th Royal Lancers, 35 Engineer Regiment and other supporting units. The operation, codenamed Grapple, was to assist the humanitarian aid effort being coordinated by UNHCR. The primary job of the 3,000 soldiers would be escorting aid convoys. Along with their white-painted, UN-emblazoned Warrior APCs and pale blue helmets, the orange card 'Rules of Engagement' issued to soldiers reminded them that they were there as peacekeepers: it spelt out that they could deploy force in self-defence, but that the 'minimum force necessary' must be used.[15] Peacekeeping requires the consent of all the warring factions and is essentially passive: soldiers can react if attacked, but not initiate attacks. It also assumes that there is a peace to keep: in Bosnia, as soon as ceasefires were declared, these assumptions were often swiftly confounded.

Caught up in three-sided ethnic anarchy in Bosnia, Britain's soldiers discovered the frustrating limitations of peacekeeping. Arriving in the Croatian port of Split, they would drive across the rugged, potholed mountain roads to central Bosnia. The frontline would be discovered when 'you were shot at by something that looked Serbian'.[16] The Cheshires' signals officer stayed in a house rented from Muslims: the husband had gone to fight the Serbs, in an area that had been ethnically cleansed by Croats. There was no Geneva Convention in Bosnia; rape, torture and mutilation were rife. With the deliberate targeting of women and children by all three factions, and following the massacre at Ahmici when Cheshires soldiers had to clear charred corpses from a cellar, many concluded that there was no side to take.[17] In Mostar, in the predominantly Croat part of Bosnia, UN personnel intercepted a phone call between the Serb and Muslim commanders haggling over the price in Deutschmarks for shelling the Croats, their common enemy.[18] The Cheshires' second-in-command, Major Bryan Watters, said: 'What was going on was outside the realms of civilized behaviour ... We represented the forces of good and we were surrounded by the forces of evil.'[19]

Peacekeeping is not a soft option. Its dangers were highlighted with the death of Lance Corporal Wayne Edwards of the Royal Welch Fusiliers in January 1993. He was shot by a sniper as he escorted an ambulance evacuating wounded civilians. Aid convoys came under regular attack and roads were littered with mines, which soldiers would move out of the way. The news and images from Bosnia confirmed to many politicians back in London that their caution was justified: how far should British lives be risked to save others in a humanitarian operation? Soldiers themselves were more sanguine. Lieutenant Colonel Stewart declared: '1st Battalion The Cheshire Regiment is in Bosnia to save life.' Whether moving aid to starving villagers, collecting casualties or building roads, soldiers knew that while they were saving lives, there was every reason to be in Bosnia. One said, 'The humanitarian imperative drove you.'[20] Here was the moral motivation of the British soldier in action. Over the winter of 1992/3, British troops escorted 244 convoys, carrying almost 18,500 tons of food, medicine and other supplies to towns such as Tuzla and Gorazde.[21] As the Defence Secretary said: 'There are many people in Bosnia today who owe their very survival to the presence of British and other United Nations forces.'[22] But the humanitarian aid that the soldiers tried to deliver became part of the problem: a good percentage of it was syphoned off by racketeers and sold on the black market, which in turn raised money for warlords and paramilitaries to continue the fighting. The British did what they could but, as one soldier said, it felt like they were 'chasing atrocities'.

Peacekeeping is founded upon consent, impartiality and even-handedness. However, impartiality was perceived as support for the bad guys, usually the Serbs but sometimes the Croats and occasionally the Bosnian Muslims. The restrictions on military action became increasingly galling to soldiers and incomprehensible to many civilians, particularly to the media. In response to the calls for a more robust military response, a defence minister stated: 'Our troops are in Bosnia for a humanitarian purpose and we do not intend to convert them into an Army of occupation or an Army fighting to impose a particular solution on the problem by force.'[23] But by not intervening to stop the bloodshed, UNPROFOR appeared to be colluding in atrocities and war crimes. Despite successive increases in troop numbers and an ever-growing pile of UN resolutions which extended its mandate, UNPROFOR was collectively ineffectual. Force levels eventually reached 38,000 personnel, but they could not change the reality on the ground. The peacekeepers were likened to 'eunuchs at an orgy' – not a great situation for the proud British Army to be in.[24]

Sarajevo symbolised the Bosnian conflict. Like Srebrenica, it was one of six UN-designated safe areas. By early 1994, the Serbs were entrenched in the surrounding mountains and the city was being shelled up to 1,200 times a day. Memorials known as 'Sarajevo roses' were created by filling holes made in the city's streets by mortars with red resin. Some 350,000 people 'lived like rats in cellars only venturing out at night to search for the means of survival'.[25] Parallels with Warsaw in 1944 sprang to mind. Water, electricity, food and fuel were meagre. The Bosnian Deputy Prime Minister, Hajika Turajilic, was shot while under French military escort. Sarajevo was a hub for the international media, who berated UN commanders and were in danger of losing their objectivity. As CNN correspondent Christiane Amanpour later explained: 'This was the era of "never again" and it was happening again. Ethnic cleansing and genocide here in our own backyard, and on our watch.'[26]

Arriving in January 1994, Lieutenant General Sir Michael Rose took over command of UNPROFOR in Bosnia. The former head of the SAS was unimpressed by the regional HQ in Kiseljak: 'It had ceased to resemble a military command and looked more like a holiday camp.'[27] He saw his job as preventing the collapse of the UN mission.[28] Following an attack on the Markale market in Sarajevo on 5 February 1994, when sixty-eight people were killed, Rose ordered the Serbs to withdraw their weapons behind an exclusion zone or face NATO air strikes. The Serbs retreated and some semblance of normal life returned to the city. It underlined to Rose that either the UN should be better supported by the international community in its efforts to negotiate peace or that NATO should replace it and attempt to impose a political solution by force of arms.[29]

Peace would only start coming to Bosnia with deployment of a strong international military force with a robust mandate. For almost three years since the start of conflict in the wider Yugoslavia, NATO had been curiously uninvolved. Given the men and military hardware at its disposal, as it watched from the sidelines, the hierarchy of NATO seemed to acquiesce that, with the Cold War over, it was indeed finished. It was urged to get involved: 'Bosnia alive or NATO dead.'[30] The lack of professionalism of many of UNPROFOR's troops, some of whom had arrived in the Balkans without winter kit, emphasised how much military expertise was going to waste because of the hands-off approach taken by NATO – and its chief paymaster, the United States. Both as a candidate and as a newly elected President, Bill Clinton had called for a policy of 'lift and strike': lift the arms embargo against Bosnia – in order to give the Muslims a chance – and use air strikes in support of UNPROFOR. However, the UN feared air strikes would put peacekeepers at risk: the Serbs might seek reprisals, and the potential for blue-on-blue was considerable. Washington itself had no intention of putting any American boots on the ground. In October 1993, a disastrous reversal during a humanitarian operation in Somalia saw eighteen US Rangers killed in a fire fight in Mogadishu, which would be depicted in the film *Black Hawk Down*. The incident underlined the potential in Bosnia for what Lieutenant General Rose identified as 'crossing the Mogadishu line', when peacekeepers are perceived as belligerents and parties to a conflict.

Eventually, NATO paved the way for peace in Bosnia. The futility of UN peacekeeping was seen in the summer of 1995. For almost two weeks, the Serbs held hostage 250 troops, including thirty soldiers from 1st Battalion Royal Welch Fusiliers. The massacre of 8,000 Muslim men and boys in Srebrenica as Dutch peacekeepers – caught in indecision – stood by, made a mockery of the UN's 'safe havens' policy. On 28 August, Serbs once again mortared a Sarajevo market, killing thirty-eight people. This was an outrage too far. Rose's successor as UNPROFOR commander, Lieutenant General Rupert Smith, in concert with NATO, launched the 3-week-long Operation Deliberate Force, which combined air strikes and ground attacks on Bosnian Serb positions. Concurrently, having attacked Serb positions in Krajina and expelled the Serbs in Operation Storm, Croatian ground forces, in concert with the Bosnian 5th and 7th Corps, entered

Bosnia and made inroads into Serb-held positions there. Successive peace plans – Carrington, Vance–Owen, Owen–Stoltenberg, and the Contact Group – which outsiders had tried to broker had all floundered. The intransigence of all sides was typified by Bosnian President Alija Izetbegovic, who stated that 'he would prefer to let 10,000 Bosnians die rather than accept a single Serb on Bosnian territory'.[31] Military force, international pressure and both manpower and logistic exhaustion finally brought the Bosnian Serbs to Dayton, Ohio, in November 1995 to negotiate peace.

Under the terms of the Dayton Accords, Bosnia would remain a single state but would be divided into two: a Muslim–Croat federation and the Republika Srpska. NATO's multinational Implementation Force (IFOR) had a year-long mandate to monitor security. A British officer attached to IFOR said the symbolism of soldiers removing their blue UN peacekeepers' helmets was not lost on anyone on the ground in Bosnia.[32] However, despite the international criticism of UNPROFOR, in the three years between the start of Operation Grapple and the Dayton Peace Accords, as the British Army itself acknowledges, British troops had stabilised the ground war in their areas of operation and prevented any further extension of the conflict.[33] The British Warrior infantry fighting vehicle was the only vehicle serving with international forces with sufficient mobility, firepower and protection to be able to force aid convoys through the lines of the heavily armed warring factions. Soldiers' ingrained discipline brought about through training at the high end of the warfighting spectrum served them well in the peacekeeping operation.

Martin Bell, the veteran BBC war reporter, had frequently appealed for main battle tanks to be deployed to Bosnia during the UN years. Ironically when the British 4th Armoured Brigade, complete with the Challenger tanks of the Queen's Royal Hussars, deployed as the first wave of the NATO IFOR, local people were heard to remark: 'You have brought us peace, but you have taken away our roads' as the near 70-ton leviathans churned up the thin Bosnian tarmac. Sadly, twenty years on, it has become apparent that, although the Dayton Peace Accords were an excellent ceasefire document, they represented a compromised formula for a prosperous and stable future for Bosnia-Herzegovina. That country remains one of the very poorest in Europe. In 1995, the international community did not realise how strong a position that the negotiating skills of the US diplomat Richard Holbrooke or the military muscle of NATO had placed it in. More could have been demanded in order to establish not just the framework for peace but to provide a more realistic chance of a better and brighter future.

New Labour, the Strategic Defence Review and an Ethical Foreign Policy

'New Labour, New Life for Britain' was promised in the Labour Party's 1997 General Election manifesto. The Blair era appeared to offer a radical departure from the Conservatives, who had been in office since 1979. Never fully recovering their reputation for economic competence after the Black Monday debacle, John Major's government seemed tired, bereft of ideas and was judged – albeit unfairly – to be mired in sleaze. If the Tories seemed to be pining for a mythical golden age, the new government, and Tony Blair especially, appeared completely at home in Cool Britannia. Labour represented a Britain that was socially liberal and increasingly intolerant of sexism, racism and homophobia. In the years leading up to the new century and beyond, the British Army would be forced to change to keep in step with the country that had overwhelmingly endorsed the new government's vision of Britain, although its natural inclination was to remain one step behind, perhaps acting as something of a well-meaning drogue anchor wedded to traditional values.

Throughout the 1990s, the international community gradually came to recognise the principle of military intervention to save life. Former Conservative Foreign Secretary Douglas Hurd observed in 2003: 'What is now settled doctrine was for almost all of us 10 years ago arguable and obscure.'[34] Humanitarian intervention, however, remains a direct challenge to state sovereignty. Since the 1648 Peace of Westphalia, states have been recognised as sovereign, able to act freely within their own borders. The United Nations accepts this, prohibiting any intervention 'in matters which are essentially within the jurisdiction of any state'.[35] Crucially, Chapter VII of the UN Charter also allows action to be taken in the interests of international peace and security. However, such action can easily be blocked by members of the UN Security Council, particularly China and Russia, wary of allowing outside powers to meddle in their internal affairs. Similarly,

Britain would have fought off any attempt by the UN to intervene in Northern Ireland. The UN Charter also recognises human rights, as well as human worth and dignity. In the wake of the first Gulf War in 1991, action taken by British, American and French forces to protect the Kurds in safe areas in northern Iraq had set a precedent. In 1992, the UN Secretary General, Boutros Boutros-Ghali, stated: 'The time of absolute and exclusive sovereignty [however,] has passed.'[36]

The 1994 genocide in Rwanda challenged the sanctity of state sovereignty. In the most shocking crime against humanity since the Second World War, more than 800,000 Tutsis were killed by rival Hutu extremists in the former Belgian colony. Moderate Hutus who tried to halt the violence were also slain. After 1990, some 2,500 peace-keepers had been based in the troubled country as part of the United Nations Assistance Mission to Rwanda (UNAMIR). As they tried to protect Rwanda's prime minister, ten Belgian troops were killed. As the International Criminal Tribunal for Rwanda (ICTR) would later discover, the notorious Interahamwe militia were far from the sole perpetrators of the atrocities: 'The genocide had been planned and implemented with meticulous care. Working from prepared lists, an unknown and unknowable number of people, often armed with machetes, nail-studded clubs or grenades, methodically murdered those named on the lists. Virtually every segment of society partici-pated: doctors, nurses, teachers, priests, nuns, businessmen, govern-ment officials of every rank, even children.'[37] With Rwanda sliding into anarchy, the UN's Canadian commander, Major General Roméo Dallaire, demanded a change to the mission's mandate to allow his troops to attempt to enforce control and halt the killing. It was refused and most of the peacekeepers pulled out. In June, in Operation Tur-quoise, France deployed a force of 2,600 personnel in the south-west of the country that proved to be ineffectual. It was too little, too late. Dallaire observed: 'While most nations agreed that something should be done, they all had an excuse why they should not be the ones to do it. As a result, the UN was denied the political will and material means to prevent tragedy.'[38]

The Rwandan genocide made a powerful case for the interna-tional community to take a different approach. Intervention to save life not only corresponded with the zeitgeist, but also with thinking within the Labour Party. The Blair era saw Britain giving a global lead on military intervention on humanitarian grounds. In April 1999, during the Kosovo air war, the Prime Minister set out the 'Doctrine of the International Community' in Chicago. Written largely by the historian Lawrence Freedman, it set out the basis for military intervention. Five questions would have to be asked before the resort to force: 'Are we sure of our case?' 'Are all diplomatic options exhausted?' 'Can a military operation be sensibly and prudently undertaken?' 'Are we prepared for the long term?' 'Do we have national interests involved?' As Tony Blair explained: 'It was an explicit rejection of the narrow view of national interest, and set a policy of intervention in the context of the impact of globalization.'[39] The Doctrine drew criticism for making foreign policy a 'moral cause'. However, Blair was unrepentant: for him, military intervention should be bound up with defending values such as human rights. 'Intervention to bring down a despotic dictatorial regime could be justified on grounds of the nature of that regime, not merely its immediate threat to our interests.'[40]

With missions in Kosovo and Sierra Leone, British soldiers would be the shock troops of humanitarian intervention. After the 1997 election, the new Foreign Secretary, Robin Cook, vowed 'to make Britain once again a force for good in the world'. He suggested: 'The Labour Government does not accept that political values can be left behind when we check in our passports to travel on diplomatic business. Our foreign policy must have an ethical dimension and must support the demands of other peoples for the democratic rights on which we insist for ourselves.'[41] For Tony Blair, traditional foreign policy, based on an analysis of national interest, was 'flawed and out of date'; it was also 'immoral'.[42]

The Prime Minister conceded that his views were not shared by all international leaders, with President Vladimir Putin in particular considering them 'at best odd, at worst dangerous'. For the Russian leader, 'major powers should work out their interests in a fairly traditional, hard-headed way and implement them. Talking of moral causes was a serious mistake.'[43] Emotionally intelligent and a superb communicator, Blair was able to articulate why Britain's Armed Forces should be deployed to save strangers, who were often the victims of the new wars. He could relate to the television audiences who were moved by the images of suffering far away: he expected people's sympathies and emotions to become involved.

Travel, mass media, the internet and modern communications were pulling the world together: 'We feel at a human level more connected across national boundaries than ever before.'[44] It was only natural to him that the British people were members of the 'something must be done club'; Blair was himself.

A change of emphasis in defence policy was introduced in parallel with the new values-based dimension to foreign policy. Three weeks after Labour's landslide election victory, the government began its defence review. The investigation, which Defence Secretary George Robertson promised would be 'foreign policy led and not Treasury led', resulted in the Strategic Defence Review (SDR), published in July 1998.[45] It was the fifth major White Paper which attempted to reshape the Armed Forces since 1945. *Options for Change*, introduced at the end of the Cold War, had been supplemented in 1994 by *Frontline First*, which more truthfully lived up to its secondary title, *The Defence Costs Study*. In 1997, the reappraisal process took longer than expected, partly because the government had quite bravely stepped outside Westminster and Whitehall, calling for contributions to the debate both from the public and from service personnel. Some 450 people made their views known.[46]

The Strategic Defence Review reoriented Britain's Armed Forces towards expeditionary operations and increased tri-service cooperation. Setting out the thinking behind the new strategy, George Robertson stated: 'In the post-Cold War world, we must be prepared to go to the crisis, rather than have the crisis come to us.'[47] Building on the 'joint' foundations laid down by the previous government, with, for example, the creation of the Joint Rapid Deployment Force and the foundation of the Joint Service Command and Staff College, the SDR created the Joint Rapid Reaction Forces, 'a pool of powerful and versatile units from all three Services'.[48] Integral to this would be the Permanent Joint Headquarters and units such as the Joint Helicopter Command and Joint Force 2000, the latter combining the Harrier jump jet fleets of the RAF and Royal Navy. Support for the Armed Forces would be overhauled, with the creation of the Defence Logistics Organisation which aimed to create greater standardisation. 'Smart procurement' aimed to bring equipment programmes, from the Eurofighter to the long-delayed Bowman radio, under better control. In Opposition, Labour had committed itself to the retention

of the nuclear deterrent, although Trident would have fewer warheads in future – down from 300 to 200. Two aircraft carriers would
be commissioned, to come into service in 2012 and 2014 – dates that,
even at the time, appeared optimistic. Echoing the government's
commitment towards an ethical foreign policy, a values-led approach
had been incorporated into the SDR: 'We do not want to stand idly
by and watch humanitarian disasters or the aggression of dictators go
unchecked. We want to give a lead, we want to be a force for good.'[49]

The Army faced some restructuring under the SDR. Fortunately,
the process was fairly painless compared with the demoralisation and
regimental rivalries provoked by *Options for Change*, which had led
to defence expenditure being cut by 23 per cent in real terms and
personnel numbers by one-third.[50] In 1998/9 defence spending stood
at 2.7 per cent of GDP, down from 5.3 per cent in 1984/5. As the
SDR pointed out, during the preceding eight years, 'more British
troops have been on active operations at any one time than during
the Cold War'.[51] The missions ranged from the Gulf War – 'by far
our biggest operation since Suez' – to the rescue of British citizens
from a series of crises overseas and operations at home in support of
the civil authorities. Reviews usually mean cuts to troop numbers;
instead, the SDR acknowledged the Army's manning problem, which
had led to chronic overstretch. The Army's forty infantry battalions
were below strength by more than 2,000 personnel.[52] Overall, the
review promised to increase Army numbers by 3,300, bringing total
manpower up to 111,300. The reserves would be cut, with the Territorial Army reduced from 57,000 to 40,000 – less than half its 1991
strength of 91,000.[53]

The 1998 Review extended the range of missions in which the
Armed Forces were anticipated to take part. It had considered likely
developments in the international system until 2015, but did not
expect Britain to act unilaterally as in the Falklands: any involvement in a major regional conflict would be 'as part of NATO or a
wider international coalition'.[54] Peacekeeping and humanitarian missions were given a far higher profile: 'As a Permanent Member of the
Security Council, we intend to give a lead by making our national
contribution to UN operations more effective.'[55] Overall, the Review
envisaged that the Armed Forces would be able to sustain one large
operation of a similar scale and duration as the Gulf War or would be

able to undertake a medium-sized enduring overseas operation that lasted longer, such as Bosnia, along with a second campaign, which might involve a combat brigade but only for a six-month period. Crucially, given what the Army would be asked to undertake the following decade: 'We would not, however, expect both deployments to involve warfighting or to maintain them simultaneously for longer than six months.'[56] After 2003, the dual deployments to Iraq and Afghanistan would confound the SDR's planning assumptions.

As in all the previous reviews for almost half a century, NATO lay at the heart of the Strategic Defence Review. Operation Banner in Northern Ireland was hardly mentioned. Commitment to NATO's Allied Rapid Reaction Corps (ARRC) was stressed, reflected by some changes to the overall structure of the Army. *Options for Change* had cut BAOR to one armoured division (1 UK Armoured Division) in Germany. It would be retained, along with another division (3 UK Division) stationed in Britain. Both were part of NATO's ARRC pool of forces. The existing force of five heavy brigades (three armoured and two mechanised) and three light brigades (airborne, airmobile and one attached Royal Marine Commando Brigade) was restructured. The airborne brigade would be replaced by a third mechanised brigade, thus providing three ground manoeuvre brigades to each division, with the parachute role being transferred to the airmobile brigade and becoming 16th Air Assault Brigade.[57] Eight tank regiments would be reorganised into six. Although some 2,500 soldiers would be brought back from Germany, more than 20,000 remained, along with their dependants.

While the presence of British forces in Germany was becoming increasingly anachronistic, it was justified in the context of NATO, rather than on the slightly more honest grounds of its financial benefits to Britain. While spending on defence was expected to rise, up from £22.295 billion in 1999/2000 to £22.987 billion in 2001/2, it was actually projected to be cut in real terms by £915 million, its share of GDP falling from 2.7 per cent to 2.4 per cent. In summary, the policy outcome of the 1997–8 Strategic Defence Review was excellent; but its Achilles heel was funding – especially when the Treasury imposed a 3 per cent efficiency savings target on the Ministry of Defence.

If the government was serious about being a force for good in the world, Britain needed her Armed Forces to be strong. UN Secretary General Kofi Annan observed: 'You can do a lot more with diplomacy backed up by firmness and force.' Quoted in the final Defence Review document, his words would be put to the test in Kosovo, East Timor and Sierra Leone.

Kosovo

A little more than three years after the Dayton Peace Accords had concluded the war in Bosnia, security was rapidly deteriorating in another part of the former Yugoslavia – the autonomous province of Kosovo. Once again, Serbian security forces tried to halt a move to independence; once again, a humanitarian catastrophe was threatened. This time the international community did not sit on the sidelines. Consistent with his views about the moral justification for intervention, Prime Minister Blair argued for decisive military action and British airmen and soldiers found themselves in another part of the Balkans. While questions about the legality of the air war against Serbia were raised, few questioned the moral legitimacy of the action. Once again, however, air power alone did not prove decisive. It was the threat of NATO boots on the ground, allied with actual Kosovar ground forces, which prompted Belgrade's eventual capitulation – a lesson from the end of the twentieth century for the twenty-first, especially in connection with Syria.

Kosovo is about the size of Yorkshire, with a population of some 2 million. Although the vast majority of its population was Muslim Albanian (Kosovar), the province was regarded as quasi-sacred by Serbs, being the site of the 1389 Battle of Kosovo Polje, and numerous historic Orthodox monasteries and churches. Although in a minority, making up just 20 per cent of the population, the Serbs controlled Kosovo. Society was segregated and Kosovar civil rights undermined. Kosovar separatists demanded an independent state, but hopes that their cause might be taken up by the international community at Dayton had come to nothing. In response, radicals set up the Kosovo Liberation Army (KLA) and in February 1996 began a bombing campaign against Serb targets. The Serbs retaliated by deploying air power and heavy weapons. The cycle of violence began. By 1998, the KLA claimed to have 30,000 men under arms.[58] In February, the massacre of KLA leader Adem Jashari in the village of

Prekaz, along with fifty members of his family and clan, alerted the world to the instability in Kosovo.

The action taken by the international community in Kosovo highlights its previous inaction over Bosnia. Both conflicts underline the imperative of a decisive military intervention to halt humanitarian disaster. International agencies, including the UN, NATO and the OSCE (Organization for Security and Co-operation in Europe), along with the EU and the US, sought to find a solution to the Kosovo conflict far earlier than in Bosnia – a reflection of lessons learned or perhaps of collective guilt. Throughout 1998, as security worsened, hundreds of thousands of Kosovars began to flee for the safety of neighbouring states, including the Former Yugoslav Republic of Macedonia (FYROM), Albania and Montenegro. US Secretary of State Madeleine Albright declared: 'We believe that in 1991, the international community stood by and watched ethnic cleansing ... We don't want that to happen again.'[59] Meanwhile, the United Nations passed its usual resolutions, typically condemning Serbia and demanding a ceasefire, Serb withdrawal and refugee return, all of which proved pretty ineffectual. Far more robust was NATO's response. In June, it staged a 'Balkan air show', with eighty-five fast jets flying over Kosovo in a show of force. On 23 September UN Security Council Resolution 1199 declared that the situation in Kosovo was a 'threat to peace and security in the region' and that unspecified measures would be taken in accordance with Chapter VII of the UN Charter. On 13 October NATO's ruling body, the North Atlantic Council, agreed that Resolution 1199 allowed for the deployment of force and authorised a limited bombing campaign against Serb targets. In response in Belgrade, the President of Serbia, Slobodan Milosevic, backed down and agreed to a ceasefire.

As the situation had deteriorated in Kosovo throughout 1998, soldiers from NATO's Allied Rapid Reaction Corps had been gearing up for deployment. Corps commander Lieutenant General Sir Mike Jackson observed there was never a complete ceasefire: 'Within NATO, there was little faith that this deal would outlast the winter.'[60] Troops from Britain, France, Germany and Italy, among others, were integrated into the corps, coming under NATO command, and started arriving in Skopje, the capital of FYROM, towards the end of the year. A former shoe factory was chosen as the ARRC's headquarters.

Meanwhile, across the border in Kosovo, the ceasefire was monitored by the Kosovo Verification Mission, which included British soldiers quietly undertaking reconnaissance.[61]

Evidence of ethnic cleansing was provided in January 1999 with the discovery of a massacre at Racak, in which forty-five Kosovars had been executed in retaliation for the deaths of two Serb policemen. At a meeting with an increasingly dismayed Tony Blair, Kosovar leader Ibrahim Rugova gave him a piece of Kosovo crystal and told him, 'They're killing us.'[62] Talks with President Milosevic in February in Rambouillet, near Paris, had achieved nothing. Convinced that force was the only way to halt Serbian violence, Blair sought to convince his fellow leaders to take military action. France's Jacques Chirac was initially as reluctant as Bill Clinton. Blair knew that the United States would be providing the bulk of any force: 'Even if we took action only by air, 85 per cent of the assets used would be American. In truth, without the US, forget it; nothing would happen. That was the full extent of Europe's impotence.'[63] Although he agreed to NATO airstrikes, President Clinton stated 'unequivocally' that he was not prepared to commit ground troops to any operation in Kosovo. Blair was prepared to take a risk on that basis: 'Without that statement, there would have been no air action, so I thought it worth agreeing to. We could work out how to unravel it later.'[64]

Operation Allied Force began on 24 March, with NATO air strikes attacking Serbian military installations, including an air base. NATO's bombing campaign, however, exacerbated the refugee crisis. An estimated 500,000 Kosovars fled for the safety of neighbouring states, with President Milosevic claiming that it was the air strikes rather than ethnic cleansing that was provoking the mass migration. The campaign seemed a catalyst for an upsurge in the violence it was meant to prevent. In Macedonia (FYROM), aid agencies such as UNHCR were overwhelmed.

Soldiers on the ground had to act fast to avert disaster. Just before Easter 1999, Brigadier Tim Cross, commander of the British 101st Logistic Brigade, found himself near the Kosovo–Macedonia border crossing at Blace, where thousands of refugees were crammed into fields. More were arriving by the hour. 'There was no shelter, food or medical cover and the tired and hungry people were in a bad way, indeed some were beginning to die.'[65] Existing camps were too small or poorly located. Along with UNHCR staff, Cross found a more suitable area close to a river which was both large enough and provided a source of water. Within four hours, a tactical headquarters had been set up and field kitchens began preparing chicken and rice, which would be transported up to the border area, along with supplies of food, blankets and medicine. Only soldiers could help the refugees: 'No other organization was in a position to help and we could not stand idle.' After a night of planning, construction work started on the first of a series of four camps, while men from the Logistic Brigade continued to move supplies to the border. Latrines were dug, Royal Engineers constructed a bridge over a stream with parts of a broken-up Antonov crop-spraying aircraft, the first tents were set up and the medics began to prepare reception centres. Water purification and pumping systems were all established. Cross noted: 'All this was being done in a vacuum as I had received no orders.'[66] But the British Army's ethos of mission command – acting on your own initiative in order to meet your higher commander's intent, whether implied or specified – would pay huge dividends. Three days after work had begun, 'the dam broke' and buses brought in thousands of refugees every hour. 'All through the night soldiers from the brigade put up tents, helped families into them, issued food and blankets and provided medical support ... It was a gruelling night but it was just the first of many.' Less than a week later, the camp was housing 40,000 refugees. In that time, 2,800 tents had been erected, 1,800 yards of pipeline laid, tens of thousands of meals cooked and distributed, along with 103,000 jars of baby food and 264,000 bottles of water. In the medical facility, five people had died, but twenty-four babies had been born, 'our proudest statistic', according to Cross. The military withdrew from the camp after a fortnight, handing over to aid agency staff. It was one of four camps established by NATO forces. In May, Cross moved to Albania, a state riven by gang warfare and corruption; his reports to PJHQ 'read more like a John Le Carré novel than a military update'.[67] Camps for 100,000 people were set up, while NATO personnel also took over humanitarian operations at Tirana airport and at Durres port, as well as improving roads and bridges to facilitate the movement of aid.

Many of the civilian aid agencies were far from happy with the concept of humanitarian intervention by the military. In Macedonia,

Mike Jackson noted that some aid workers 'took a certain exception to the military being involved in the humanitarian effort'. This
was echoed in a report by Parliament's International Development
Select Committee, which also acknowledged that without NATO's
intervention in the aid effort, 'we are convinced that the already
desperate plight of the refugees would have been even more appalling, with more lives tragically lost'.[68] However, ever since the foundation of the Red Cross, humanitarian assistance in conflict zones
has been neutral, and here is a dilemma. Humanitarian aid is vital
and has been effective and, in many cases, permitted by warring
factions, because agencies such as UNHCR or Doctors Without
Borders are perceived as not taking sides. However, allowing the
military into the humanitarian space is thought by some to compromise that neutrality, especially if, as in Kosovo, NATO soldiers were
regarded by some as belligerents. The Select Committee heard that
'the principles of neutrality, impartiality and independence' must be
preserved: the military could offer logistical support to a humanitarian operation, but should not take the lead and coordinate it.[69] This
judgement, though intellectually sound, was a practical nonsense, as
Tim Cross found. Whitehall turf wars between DfID and the MoD
would be played out later between soldiers and DfID staff in Iraq
and Afghanistan.

In Kosovo and Albania, as NATO soldiers on the ground battled
to help refugees, the air war was beset by problems. An operation that
was supposed to last three days dragged on into almost three months:
in all 34,000 sorties were flown.[70] Without UN direct authorisation,
international arguments broke out about its legality, a precursor to
similar rows in 2003 over Iraq. Foreign Secretary Robin Cook told
the House of Commons, 'The consequences of NATO inaction would
be far worse than the result of NATO action.'[71] Up against NATO's
fast jets and smart bombs such as cruise missiles, the Serbs were
expected to crumble. This did not happen. In fact, not only was a spy
suspected of being in the NATO camp who had tipped off the Serbs
in advance about prospective targets, allowing the safe evacuation
of troops and weapons, but a series of decoy tanks and other military equipment had been constructed out of plywood and littered
the countryside. Coated in chemicals that would attract heat-seeking
missiles, these $50 fakes made NATO an expensive laughing stock.[72]

In response, NATO started bombing non-military targets in Serbia. After two bridges were bombed in Belgrade, local people, including children, started camping out on the rest, wearing target cards. The carnival atmosphere was captured by the international media. Protests against the bombing spread across Europe, particularly in Germany, with opponents of the campaign demanding to know why NATO was targeting non-combatants in contravention of the laws of war. Blair observed: 'If you are not careful, the aggressor starts to assume the mantle of victim.' Errors were made, including strikes on a Serb TV station and the Chinese Embassy. A column of refugees outside Djakovica was mistaken for a Serb army convoy: seventy people died. The historian Michael Ignatieff observed that even the campaign's rare mistakes consumed its legitimacy.[73] If many in western Europe were troubled by the ethics of NATO's air campaign to stop ethnic cleansing from 15,000 feet, the Kosovars actually supported it. Local billboards with Nike's trademark slogan 'Just Do It' were changed from Nike to NATO.[74]

The ineffective air war led the British Prime Minister to explore the option of putting ground troops into Kosovo. He suggested: 'Kosovo demonstrates the fundamental, unavoidable and irredeemable limitations of a pure air campaign against a determined opponent who cares little about losing life ... They cannot dislodge a really dogged occupation of land by an enemy willing to sustain losses and wait it out.'[75] He raised the issue of ground forces with an unreceptive President Clinton in late April. In Macedonia, after a hero's welcome from Kosovar refugees, he said: 'This is not a battle for NATO. This is not a battle for territory. This is a battle for humanity. It is a just cause.'[76] The Prime Minister had new resolve: 'However high the cost, my decision was that the price of allowing Milosevic to triumph was so high it couldn't be countenanced. Therefore, if the only way of avoiding the price was a ground campaign, we had to do it.'[77] The price was indeed high. The Chief of the Defence Staff (CDS), General Sir Charles Guthrie, told the Prime Minister that any ground offensive would need hundreds of thousands of troops, with the British supplying 50,000 to the United States' 100–150,000.[78] The staff at the United Kingdom's 3rd Division headquarters began getting out their maps of the Balkans once again. The attack options of either heading through narrow passes, tunnels and across vulnerable road bridges into Kosovo or a flanking attack through Serb territory both looked distinctly problematic.

Although President Clinton was not prepared to make a definite commitment on the issue of ground forces – and was unlikely to have been able to get Congress's backing anyway – on 18 May he stated, 'We have not and will not take any option off the table.'[79] A few days later, NATO announced it would deploy 50,000 troops to the Macedonian border. Meanwhile in Serbia, shortages were taking their toll: NATO strikes had destroyed all oil-refining capability, were hitting transportation arteries and were turning out the lights in most of Belgrade.[80] Anti-war protests had been held by Serbian mothers worried about their sons, while mutiny had struck the Serb army in Kosovo, with 1,000 soldiers hijacking vehicles and weapons and heading for home.[81] In late May, the KLA launched a ground offensive, which forced the Serb forces into the open, making them vulnerable to air attack. Meanwhile, President Yeltsin's envoy, Viktor Chernomyrdin, was making it clear to Milosevic that Serbia should make peace. Facing attack on all fronts – military, economic, diplomatic, domestic – the Serb leader backed down. On 10 June, following a week of talks, the conflict ended. The parallels with the end game in Bosnia are clear. Above all, Kosovo underscored how hard it is to achieve victory with air power alone.

Kosovo became a UN protectorate, with NATO leading a peace support operation. Civil administration was carried out by UNMIK – the UN Interim Administration in Kosovo; under the terms of Resolution 1244, NATO's KFOR (Kosovo Force) was responsible for local security. Europe provided 85 per cent of personnel for the operation, codenamed Joint Guardian, making up for its underwhelming contribution to the air campaign. Britain's contribution was spearheaded by 4th Armoured Brigade and 5th Airborne Brigade. The priority was to get infrastructure working as soon as possible, particularly water and electricity. The Logistic Brigade, now in Pristina, got to work again. Along with providing engineering and medical support to British forces, it repaired and ran large sections of the Kosovo railway, set up a fire-fighting facility and emergency refugee centres.[82] Mike Jackson said: 'To me all this was basic stuff, which was why I was surprised by the failure to address infrastructure issues promptly in Iraq in 2003'[83] (see chapter 8). Once again, aid organisations resented the military. Tim Cross said: 'Tensions between KFOR and UNHCR at the operational level meant that the Brigade's assets were under utilised, particularly our rail capability.'[84] The Kosovars themselves, who began to return as quickly as they had fled, were delighted to see the troops. In Belgrade, Milosevic would be voted out and become the first head of state indicted in an international court for war crimes and genocide. In Kosovo, the Serbs fled, fearing revenge attacks. The bodies of fourteen Serb farmers found lying in fields about twelve miles from Pristina were a sign that the conflict might not be over, merely frozen.

A bizarre postscript to the Kosovo campaign was the unexpected deployment of a convoy of Russian forces from Bosnia and a number of Russian transport aircraft, which were believed by KFOR to be heading for Pristina airport, ahead of further Russian reinforcements brought in to secure their own 'sector' of Kosovo. It was a distant echo of the race across Europe by the Allies in 1945. Shown on CNN, the news caused consternation, with SACEUR General Wesley Clark particularly alarmed. He ordered Jackson to send troops, block the runway and fight for control of the airport if necessary. As Jackson stated, 'The situation might quickly escalate and become extremely dangerous.'[85] The ensuing row between the two generals reached London, with Jackson telling Clark, 'I'm not going to start World War Three for you.' According to CNN, six large Illushyn aircraft were in the air heading for Pristina. After pressure from Washington, existing member Hungary, and future NATO members, Romania and Bulgaria, denied the Russians the use of their airspace. In a characteristic of modern war, Jackson knew that should Clark have ordered him to secure Pristina airfield with British troops, London had already vetoed the move. The commander of the British KFOR contingent had the national Red Card in his pocket. In the end no Russian airborne troops arrived, just a rather bedraggled column of motor rifle troops who soon had to be fed and watered by the British.

The avoidance of a humanitarian catastrophe had provided the moral justification for NATO's actions in Kosovo, even if they were still technically illegal under international law. Mike Jackson observed: 'Britain had played the lead role in KFOR and Tony Blair had played the lead role in mobilizing world opinion to intervene in Kosovo.'[86] Blair surprised himself by advocating a military solution:

'I look back and can see that throughout, to the irritation of many of our allies and the consternation of a large part of our system, I was totally and unyieldingly for resolution, not pacification.'[87] It represented a watershed for the Prime Minister: 'The Kosovo conflict taught me many things, about government, about leadership, about myself ... It also completely changed my own attitude to foreign policy.'[88] That change would become evident in Iraq.

East Timor

Far away across the Indian Ocean, the East Timorese voted for independence from Indonesia in August 1999. The referendum sparked renewed violence between pro-Jakarta militias backed by the Indonesian army and the Falantil freedom fighters. Law and order broke down across the entire territory, with looting and arson attacks that destroyed whole towns. Almost 1,000 people were killed. The Australian city of Darwin is a comparatively close 430 miles from East Timor's capital, Dili, and so it was very much in Australia's back yard. The UN International Force East Timor (INTERFET), under Australian command, led by Major General Peter Cosgrove, was established and mandated to restore security. The country's CDS described the UN operation as his country's most significant military undertaking since the Second World War.[89]

Some 8,000 miles from Britain, East Timor seemed an unlikely operation in which British forces should become involved. However, according to Brigadier David Richards, who was soon to lead the effort in Sierra Leone and who was on the ground in Dili: 'The Australians needed us, politically and militarily, to come in alongside them, in part to ensure that this did not end up looking like an Australian-only intervention.'[90] The 2nd Battalion Royal Gurkha Rifles, based in Brunei towards the western end of the Indonesian archipelago, seemed the ideal force to deploy in support of our Commonwealth partners. Some 240 of them would stand alongside the Australian troops. By October, the presence of the international intervention force had brought the lawlessness under control. The operation in East Timor would thereafter become a relatively low-key peace enforcement task along with the delivery of humanitarian aid. Indeed, although the dialect was different, the Gurkhas were able to communicate with the dwindling remnants of the Indonesian forces in the capital and established a good rapport with local people. The mystique of the immaculately turned out Nepalese, with their trademark smartly sandbagged checkpoints, attracted media attention, to the irritation of their fellow peacekeepers. One Digger said it was 'great to be one of 2,000 Aussies here in support of 200 ******* Gurkhas'.[91] However, this short and successful deployment of British forces to East Timor seemed to illustrate the informal mantra that was gaining political currency since the 1998 Strategic Defence Review: 'Go first, go fast, go home.'

Sierra Leone
The reshaping of Britain's Armed Forces following the 1998 SDR had indeed enhanced Britain's ability to contribute to peacekeeping and humanitarian operations, and to do so quickly. The pool of units within the Joint Rapid Reaction Force (JRRF), together with the promised additional strategic lift and logistic capabilities, were in theory ideally placed to make a contribution to international emergencies. Although Britain declared most of those capabilities as potentially available to the UN in a United Nations–United Kingdom Memorandum on Peacekeeping in June 1999, Britain's forces would, nevertheless, continue to be trained and psychologically prepared for operations at the higher end of the war-fighting spectrum. The utility of this approach was demonstrated in Sierra Leone in May 2000. Operation Palliser began as a humanitarian operation to evacuate British nationals from the war-torn West African country. It escalated. The armed intervention by British personnel changed the course of the decade-long civil war, helping ultimately to end the conflict.

The conflict in Sierra Leone was another new war. It had begun in 1991 with the overthrow of the country's president, Joseph Momoh. Although ceasefires had been declared, security was never properly established. Along with the conventional forces of the Sierra Leone Army (SLA), there were pro-government militias such as the Kamajors as well as drug-fuelled gangs like the West Side Boys, foreign mercenaries, 'sobels' who were part soldier, part rebel, along with brainwashed, desensitised child soldiers, some as young as eight years old, who had usually been kidnapped from their families. The Revolutionary United Front (RUF) was, throughout, the legitimate government's chief opponent, but with coups and counter-coups by the military, along with the government's power-sharing accommodation with the RUF, allegiances continually shifted. With access to crack cocaine and heroin, a belief in voodoo and a conviction that wearing weird garb – including fluorescent wigs, pink sunglasses, shower caps and even wedding dresses – would make them invincible, the rebels appeared mad as well as bad. They enjoyed ritualistic chanting: 'What makes the grass grow? Blood. Blood. Blood.' The extreme savagery of the war, in which non-combatants were deliberately targeted, was typified by sexual violence and the maiming of the civilian population by the RUF rebels. They would use machetes to chop off hands and feet, calling amputations below the elbow 'long-sleeve' and those above the elbow 'short-sleeve'. In some villages, every third or fourth person had part of their arm missing.[92] The conflict in Sierra Leone was not about ideology or an ethnic conflict as in Rwanda, Bosnia or Kosovo. Like many wars old and new, it was a battle for control of resources – in this case, diamonds.

Sierra Leone brought the issue of blood diamonds to global attention. As in Angola and the Democratic Republic of Congo, the gemstones – also known as conflict diamonds – fuelled the civil war. Whoever controlled diamond production, controlled the country. Throughout the conflict in Sierra Leone, the production of alluvial diamonds in the eastern Kone region continued. The country was ranked ninth in the global production of diamonds, but, according to the World Development Report of 2000/2001, which listed 206 countries according to per capita GNP, Sierra Leone was ranked 203.[93] Almost the poorest country in the world, with an adult literacy rate of 7.7 per cent, in 1999 its GNP per capita stood at $130. The export of diamonds through official government channels was worth just $1.2 million, less than 1 per cent of the total exported.[94] With little or no revenue, the government had no money to invest in infrastructure or to pay public servants, including soldiers – adding to their discontent and creating the conditions for *coups d'état* and further anarchy. The civil war would cost 75,000 lives, create half a million refugees and displace half of the country's 4.5 million people.[95] Although Sierra Leone had been granted independence in 1961, Britain retained an interest in her former colony and was the largest donor of humanitarian aid and reconstruction throughout the turmoil of the 1990s.

The father of Prime Minister Tony Blair had been a lecturer at the university in Freetown, the country's capital. JRRF commander Brigadier David Richards was reminded of the historic links between Britain and Sierra Leone when he visited a hospital in Freetown where a veteran of the West African Rifles was proudly wearing his Burma Star medal.[96]

Any stability in Sierra Leone was fragile. Having been overthrown in May 1997, President Ahmad Tejan Kabbah was returned to power with the help of a British security company, Sandline. Under the terms of the Lome Accords signed in the Togolese capital in July 1999, former UN official Kabbah had to make a deal with the opponents who had ousted him, including the RUF and its leader, Foday Sankoh. RUF members received government posts and guarantees they would not be prosecuted for war crimes. Sankoh was made Vice President and Minister for Mineral Resources. He now controlled the country's diamonds. Troops from UNAMSIL, the United Nations Mission in Sierra Leone, a 6,000-strong peacekeeping force, arrived in late 1999 to implement the accords. They joined troops from Nigerian-led ECOMOG, the military arm of the Economic Community of West African States. By the beginning of the new year, the accords were already unravelling as rebel forces advanced on Freetown. After weeks of bitter fighting they were driven out, leaving behind a devastated city and a trail of brutality and butchery. An estimated 5,000 people were dead, some burned alive. Children as young as six were arriving at hospitals with their arms hacked off.[97] Corpses lay on the street, fed on by vultures – the birds that had 'clattered and clanged' on to the city's corrugated iron roofs, described by Graham Greene in his 1948 novel set in Freetown, *The Heart of the Matter*.[98]

The United Nations responded to the deteriorating security situation by revising its mandate for Sierra Leone. By May, the number of UNAMSIL troops was increased to 13,000. Led by India, the almost 30-nation force was given a Chapter VII mandate – the right to take offensive action to secure UN objectives. However, its risk-averse commander, Major General Vijay Jetley, considered its role to be one of neutral peacekeeping.[99] UN forces came under attack in the diamond-producing region to the east of the country that was under the control of the RUF. Almost 500 UN personnel, mainly soldiers from Kenya and Zambia plus one British military observer, were held hostage by rebel forces. By May, the security situation had reached a critical point, with the rebels renouncing the ceasefire, closing in on the capital and on the brink of controlling the ring road surrounding Freetown that linked major towns and the airport – the so-called Horseshoe Road. The British High Commissioner, fearing the worst, called time and the London government decided to send in British forces to evacuate British nationals. Brigadier David Richards, future head of the Army and CDS under David Cameron, was familiar with the situation on the ground in Sierra Leone from previous visits. He believed the SLA could be transformed and that the ill-disciplined if lethal rabble of rebels could be defeated. Despite his orders from London, he admits: 'My objectives were far more ambitious than simply organising an evacuation of British nationals and other "entitled persons".'

Sierra Leone was the first major test of the JRRF concept, even if the operation was not the one signed off by the Army's political masters. The spearhead battalion, 1st Battalion Parachute Regiment, and members of Special Forces arrived in the country via Dakar in early May 2000. They were deployed as a 'precautionary measure', according to the Foreign Secretary. They were followed by 42 Commando, HMS *Ocean* and a number of support vessels – the Amphibious Ready Group.[100] The soldiers and marines set about evacuating about 450 people and securing the airport. The rebels were advancing on the capital: according to Richards, 'There was an air of Saigon 1975 about the place – panic and mental paralysis all at once.'[101] However, he was convinced that British forces could turn around the situation on the ground, with the help of a more resolute effort from UN forces. General Jetley's reluctance to get involved may be explained by his mistrust of some of his allies, who, it emerged, had been keen to sabotage the peace effort for a share of the blood diamond trade.[102] In addition to putting some backbone into the local UN forces, Richards set about putting together his 'Unholy Alliance' of pro-government forces, which included some highly irregular irregulars among them the Kamajors, who believed that wearing woolly coats would protect them from gunfire and 500 former members of the Sierra Leone Army who had backed Johnny Paul Koromo, a renegade officer who had been a leader in the 1997 coup. Richards told an aide: 'I've just volunteered Britain for a war.'[103]

In London, the government was in the dark about what was going on 4,000 miles away in West Africa. Some MPs were decidedly uneasy that British troops were apparently becoming involved in a civil war. However, Defence Secretary Geoff Hoon asserted: 'We are not involved in a civil war; we are not taking sides in a civil war.'[104] Conceding that British troops on the ground had helped stabilise the situation in Sierra Leone and were lending technical advice, he insisted that they would not 'be deployed in a combat role as part of UNAMSIL'.[105] One MP wanted to know what CDS Sir Charles Guthrie was up to on his flying visit to Freetown – it was obviously not to conduct a drill parade or inspect the stores.[106] Politicians, including the Shadow Defence Secretary Iain Duncan-Smith, were relying on the media for their information about what was happening on the ground: 'Reports over the weekend show that British troops are patrolling Freetown and manning road blocks. We hear that special forces are operating in the countryside and that British officers are, to all intents and purposes, running the day-to-day operation of UN forces.'[107] In his memoirs, Richards implies he deliberately briefed the media to pre-empt any attempt by the politicians to stop his unofficial operation. Alan Little of the BBC told the world that it was only British military intervention that was preventing Sierra Leone from sliding back into civil war: 'Britain is running the war now. British officers have taken command, not only of the UN troops but of Sierra Leone's own Army and its pro-government militia groups.'[108] Presented with a fait accompli, especially one welcomed by the democratically elected Kabbah government, ministers were not going to stop Richards. The military action was in line with their objective of Britain being a force for good in the world. According to Richards, 'I more or less ignored my orders from London and committed my soldiers to leading the fight against the rebels, a decision that helped turn the course of the war.'[109]

The JRRF provided a show of military strength to intimidate the rebels while boosting the morale of the civilian population. With her thirteen Harriers, HMS *Illustrious* was stationed just off the Atlantic coast of Freetown ten days into the operation. The planes flew low over the water, careful to avoid overflying any land, but sending an unmistakable message. By early June some 4,000 British service personnel were deployed in Sierra Leone. Chinook helicopters airlifted soldiers and heavy artillery into place. In the form of a scripted conversation between two actors, communications experts arranged daily updates on progress at 5 p.m. for local radio stations, the local population's prime source of news. The situation remained fragile. Unrest broke out as a 10,000 civilian mob tried to storm Foday Sankoh's vice-presidential compound. He managed to flee, but was later arrested and charged with war crimes.

In the heat and humidity of the jungles of Sierra Leone, soldiers on the ground battled rebel forces. The village of Lungi Lol, a collection of about fifty mud huts at a T-junction some thirty-five miles north-east of the airport, was seen as a key strategic goal in the defeat of the RUF. They had codenamed their operation 'Kill British'. Richards said: 'We needed to hit them hard so that they realised in no uncertain terms we meant business, something that might act as a deterrent to them continuing their campaign.'[110] A pathfinder platoon of twenty-six members of 1 Para had dug themselves in, digging trenches and man-traps lined with punji (lethally sharp bamboo spikes), as soldiers had done in Malaya and Borneo. They had waited for the impending attack by the RUF for ten mosquito-ridden nights. The isolated British troops called the operation Alamo because the odds seemed so stacked against them. They would prevail against an estimated force of 2,000 rebels, Sergeant Steve Heaney winning the Military Cross. It was the decisive battle of Operation Palliser, which was more or less over after four weeks. As Richards observed: 'We had gone in hard like we meant it and it had paid dividends.'[111] There were no British losses, democratic government was restored and a country saved from more atrocities. One footnote was Operation Barras in August, a mission undertaken by Special Forces and the Paras to rescue five members of the Royal Irish Rangers and a soldier from the Sierra Leone Army being held hostage by the West Side Boys. One British soldier, Brad Tinnion, was killed in the operation. The West Side Boys were destroyed.

In January 2002, the civil war in Sierra Leone was declared to be over. A few months later Kabbah won a second election victory. The international policy on blood diamonds was tightened up, with stones' provenance now having to be properly authenticated. In 2012, the former president of Liberia, Charles Taylor, was found guilty of war crimes and genocide. Although the majority of British forces' personnel left Sierra Leone in July 2002, strong ties continue to bind the two countries. A military mission continues today with an International Military Assistance Training Team, while in 2014/15 British forces played a leading role in bringing the Ebola emergency under control. Tony Blair would frequently cite Sierra Leone as an example of what a humanitarian military intervention could achieve. In a few years, he would be sending British troops to a very different kind of war on a very different basis.

The developments in international policy concerning humanitarian intervention evolved throughout the 1990s. They chimed with the early aspirations of the New Labour government – especially its leader, Tony Blair. He said that he had learned much from Kosovo, which 'had not diminished my appetite for such intervention where I thought it essential to resolve a problem that needed resolution, and where a strong moral case could be made'.[112] Undoubtedly a strong moral case could be made for the interventions of the 1990s: few would doubt that, while NATO's actions in connection with Kosovo were illegal under international law, they were legitimate. The end – the prevention of genocide – justified the means.

Humanitarian intervention raised accompanying questions about the sovereignty of states. Should state borders be sacrosanct if it means the international community standing by and tolerating crimes against humanity? In 2000, UN Secretary General Kofi Annan summed up the dilemma as one of defending sovereignty and defending humanity: 'If humanitarian intervention is, indeed, an unacceptable assault on sovereignty, how *should* [sic] we respond to a Rwanda, to a Srebrenica, to gross and systematic violation of human rights that offend every precept of our common humanity?'[113] Following a study initiated by the Canadian government – whose forces had been involved in both UNPROFOR and Rwanda – a new doctrine began to emerge: the Responsibility to Protect (R2P). Endorsed by the 2005 UN World Summit, R2P acknowledged that sovereignty entailed a responsibility by states to protect their populations from crimes such as genocide. The concept involved three aspects of responsibility, defined as three 'pillars', the most controversial of which was the third: the international community's responsibility to protect a population when a state manifestly failed to do so, which could involve using coercive force.[114] R2P would be cited in connection with the 2011 Anglo-French intervention in Libya (see chapter 10).

British soldiers were caught between the conflicting demands of peacekeeping and war fighting in the 1990s. General Sir Rupert Smith, who had commanded many of them in the Gulf, Bosnia and as Deputy Supreme Allied Commander, NATO, examined how the conflicts and confrontations in which those soldiers were involved had changed from the industrial wars that their grandfathers and great-grandfathers would have fought. His influential book, *The Utility of Force*, highlighted how war is now among the people. For him, war as so many had understood it no longer existed: the era of war as a massive deciding event in a dispute in international affairs was over.[115]

The 1998 Strategic Defence Review did not expect a strategic attack on NATO or its principal members. It predicted: 'It would, however, be unwise to conclude that one could never reappear, but the conventional forces needed to threaten such an attack would take many years to create.'[116] In the context of traditional thinking about war this statement was reasonable but, as Rupert Smith observed, war was changing. From a clear blue sky – and with no warning – the forces of al-Qaeda would launch a strategic attack against the United States, Britain's principal NATO ally, on 11 September 2001.

EIGHT

'GO FIRST, GO FAST, GO HOME'

Change after the Cold War, Values and Standards, Macedonia,
the Peace Process in Northern Ireland, Afghanistan and Iraq

The dawning of the new century was a time of reflection and anticipation. The information revolution was underway and the dot.com bubble continued to grow, as investors poured money into internet start-ups. Google was taking off, but the world would have to wait a while for Facebook, Twitter and smart phones. For the British Army, network-enabled capability (NEC) would offer the potential for transformation, identified by the military in the United States, which considered that information technology would revolutionise the conduct of warfare once again.[1] A glimpse of its potential had been seen in the Gulf War. Future war in the information age might involve more robots and fewer soldiers. The sort of conflict in which the British Army might be involved had changed. An existential threat that Britain had faced in the twentieth century was almost unimaginable at the start of the twenty-first. It seemed that wars would no longer be fought out of necessity, but out of choice – not least from a humanitarian impulse. The expeditionary focus of the 1998 Strategic Defence Review had tied in with these types of conflicts, raising questions about the sort of army that Britain wanted. Should it be a force trained to the high end of the war-fighting spectrum or a peacekeeping gendarmerie? Academics and historians debated whether the military was becoming 'postmodern', although it has to be said, that this wasn't much of a topic in the officers' mess or the NAAFI of busy frontline units although it was at the Staff College.[2] A parallel debate concerned the Army and the nation: how far should the military keep in step with the country it served? On the cusp of the twenty-first century, social attitudes were changing rapidly. If soldiers considered military effectiveness would be compromised, should the Army keep pace with the civilian world? Did the Army have the 'right' or the 'need' to be different from it?

The new century was a good place to do a stocktake. Army numbers had fallen dramatically with the end of the Cold War, down from 153,000 soldiers in 1990 to just over 100,000 a decade later.[3] Soldiers could be found in the Falklands, in Cyprus, in Sierra Leone and in Northern Ireland, where Operation Banner continued. Troops were also part of the stabilisation forces in Bosnia and Kosovo, and were overseeing demilitarisation in Macedonia. With the formal handover of Hong Kong in 1997, Britain had now fully withdrawn East of Suez: the sun had finally set on the Empire. The continuing British military presence in Germany seemed anachronistic to some observers. Post-Cold War Europe had become increasingly demilitarised as country after country abolished conscription, instead relying on smaller, professional armed forces. Former Warsaw Pact enemies – the Czech Republic, Hungary and Poland – became new allies as they joined NATO. In 1998, the Anglo-French defence agreement signed at Saint-Malo signalled greater military cooperation between the two powers. This was welcomed in Washington: the operations in Bosnia and Kosovo had highlighted that Europe should do more for its own security and defence. Whether this was the first step towards a European army remained to be seen. Such a move was not welcomed by most in the United Kingdom.

So once again the British Army at the start of the new century was at something of a crossroads. Not even ten years earlier, soldiers out in the Gulf had depended on a military post office to send their 'blueys' home; before long, webcams would be attached to helmets. Despite its increasingly hi-tech kit and equipment, the Army became – or was forced to become – more aware of the human factor, as this chapter examines. Recruitment remained below target. The imperative to recruit more women and people from ethnic minority backgrounds challenged many existing attitudes and assumptions within the Army. Outside, developments such as the introduction of human rights legislation hastened more change. In short, the Army had no choice but to become an employer more in step with the civilian world.

Iraq was the most controversial military operation in the seventy years this book covers – perhaps in the Army's history. This chapter looks at the mission in Basra and southern Iraq. A factor was public support, which saw the initial 'rallying round the flag' effect change to disenchantment as it became obvious that the government had taken Britain to war on questionable grounds. The US-led intervention had followed the unrelated attack of 11 September 2001 on the American homeland, the direct response to which was the operation against al-Qaeda and the Taliban in Afghanistan. One of the principal downsides to the operation in Iraq was that it drew focus and effort away from Afghanistan, leaving behind a great deal of unfinished business – for soldiers to resolve in 2006.

The Twenty-First Century Army

'The purpose and measure of the British Army is military effectiveness: success in war and on other operations.'[4] This could be the Army's mission statement. It is, above all, a fighting force. In the post-Cold War 1990s, however, senior commanders became concerned that the Army could be reduced to little more than a gendarmerie, a fate befalling other armed forces across Europe, notably in Holland. Labour's election landslide in 1997 reinforced their concern. Foreign Secretary Robin Cook told the Chief of the General Staff, General Sir Roger Wheeler, that the Army should be trained for peacekeeping rather than war-fighting.[5] The architect of New Labour, Peter Mandelson, was taken to task by the media for dismissing members of the Household Division – somewhat unimaginatively – as 'chinless wonders': his description of Trooping the Colour as 'doing incomprehensible things with flags' indicated a certain lack of empathy with the military. Labour MPs were more likely than their Conservative counterparts to have been supporters of CND, Troops Out or the Greenham women.

As an institution closely associated with traditional values, the Army seemed to many to be increasingly out of step with civilian society. It had always enjoyed a separate system of military justice and exemptions from certain laws: for example, soldiers do not have an employment contract. The Blair government was determined to bring the Army into line with the new civilian legislation relating to human rights, in particular equal opportunities and perhaps even the Working Time Directive. The government and the Army were at odds. The Army believed that the war-fighting ethos of the British military was under threat, along with its in-house disciplinary system, and that military effectiveness – fighting power – could be compromised by this creep of civilian law into its professional space. It sought exemptions from the threatened legislation. A paper endorsed by the Army Board explored *The Extent to Which the Army Has the Right to be Different*. In the CDS's annual lecture at the Royal United Services Institute in 2000, General Sir Charles Guthrie appealed against the Armed Forces being subject to 'inappropriate legislation'.

By the 1990s, to many critical observers the Army's everyday values seemed to include racism, sexism and homophobia. In 1993, the ban on homosexuality was reaffirmed: two years later, the Commission for Racial Equality's formal investigation into the Household Cavalry was described as the 'nadir for race relations in the Armed Forces'. Attempting to secure a Commons debate on the racism issue, Diane Abbott MP cited the difference between the United States, where African-American Colin Powell was Chairman of the Joint Chiefs, and Britain, where, at the start of the decade, a minister had given assurances that all was being done to stamp racism out: 'Tell that to Jacob Malcolm, who in 1991 was barred from the Household Cavalry because of his colour. Tell it to Stephen Anderson, another black man, who in 1991 was awarded damages for years of racial abuse. Tell it to Mark Campbell, who was the first black man in the Guards. In 1994, he was driven out by the taunts of "nigger", the abuse, the violence and the bed soaked in human urine.'[6]

It appeared that an institutional malaise was setting in, with a blind eye being too often turned to poor conduct within the chain of command. With more women becoming soldiers, a spate of liaisons took place between senior male NCOs and junior female officers. Trials and courts martial provided lurid headlines for the press. Stories emerged about initiation ceremonies and bullying in Germany. For many years, the Army had resisted the introduction of compulsory drug testing. It appeared to many that the Army had not woken up to the fact that there might be an issue with the standard of conduct of some of its soldiers. The controversy surrounding Deepcut would reinforce the sense that all was far from well.

The Army was in urgent need of an ethical shake up. It had to improve collective conduct throughout the chain of command, while explaining why it needed to be different from civilian society. Chronically undermanned, the Army needed recruits, but recruits represented the Britain of social change. They appeared to disconcert their senior commanders as much as the malnourished Boer War volunteers had dismayed theirs a century earlier. Potential officers, including women, came from far more socially and educationally diverse backgrounds than previously and were more questioning of authority. One former Commandant of Sandhurst, Major General Andrew Ritchie, said: '"Ours not to reason why" no longer exists.'[7] CGS Wheeler was concerned not only that some recruits had never played team games, did not understand teamwork and lacked physical fitness, but also that they came from a society in which the individual and individual rights were all-important.[8] The Army, however, runs on teamwork and trust: individualism is sacrificed for group cohesion, the bedrock of combat effectiveness.

The result of the Army's self-examination in the late 1990s was a groundbreaking doctrine which tried to convey the unique nature of military service. *Values and Standards of the British Army* was published in 2000. Along with a companion essay, *Soldiering: The Military Covenant* (see chapter 9), it would become the moral component of the Army's fighting power. It set out to explain how being a soldier differed from all other jobs and why, in the interests of military effectiveness, that difference was vital. Mindful of the external civilian audience, the doctrine also tried to justify the seeming irreconcilability of the Army's ethos with the values of modern Britain. It was a difficult balancing act. The initiative for what Ritchie termed this 'ethical up-armouring' of soldiers came from CGS Wheeler: 'He devoted a lot of the Army Board's time to this. It came from the top of the Army. Usually the focus is on the latest tank.'[9]

The moral component provided an enduring guide for soldiers' conduct. The first edition of *Values and Standards* was produced in two formats: a 22-page version for officers and a 4-page leaflet for all ranks. The values that soldiers were expected to sign up to were self-less commitment – deliberately chosen by Wheeler to be at the top of the list – courage, discipline, respect for others, loyalty and integrity. Each value was described not just in the context of the individual soldier, but its importance stressed in relation to being a member of a team. The necessity of mutual trust between comrades in the midst of mortal danger was emphasised: 'They share the closest of quarters with their comrades; in tanks and in trenches they share food, drink and plastic bags for lavatories; they give each other blood and the kiss of life. They must have the profoundest respect for the individual not because of political correctness, but in the service of the greater good, because their cause and their lives depend upon it.'[10] While respect for others goes up and down the command, it extends to all, especially the victims of conflict: the dead, the wounded and refugees. 'Values' concern individual character, while 'standards' set out a code for personal and interpersonal conduct to which soldiers are expected to adhere. The standards section stressed that the Army is different from most other employers, taking a more proscriptive approach to behaviour that others might consider to be 'purely as a matter of individual choice or morality, and of no concern to the wider community'.[11] Conduct proscribed for soldiers included discrimination and harassment, bullying and drug and alcohol misuse. The moral component was designed by a small group of senior officers including Ritchie, Major General Sir Sebastian Roberts, Major General Peter Currie, who wrote the first draft of *Values and Standards*, and TA padre and theologian Iain Torrance. Ritchie explained: 'We had to make clear that it wasn't enough simply to shoot straight and to be fit. We needed to set out for the first time the rules of the road in terms of the personal values and standards of behaviour we required. And that you don't just spout them, you buy into them.'[12]

The late 1990s saw the Army address personnel matters with greater rigour. The 1998 Strategic Defence Review was the first to examine 'people issues': it undertook to 'put our people first'.[13] The previous year, CGS Wheeler publicly committed the Army to equal opportunities and to ending racial discrimination, while Defence Secretary George Robertson announced an increase in the number of regular Army posts open to women. The percentage of women in the Armed Forces went from 8.6 per cent in 1998 to 12.3 per cent in 2003, while those from ethnic minorities rose from 1.2 per cent in 1998 to 6.5 per cent in 2003.[14] The Defence Select Committee observed that equal opportunities policies had facilitated a 'profound' cultural change within the Armed Forces.[15] It did not, however, solve the problem of under-manning, which would be exacerbated by operations in Iraq and Afghanistan. As an attempt to head off the encroachment of civilian law into the Army, the emphasis on the moral component failed. However, that was no bad thing. The European Court of Human Rights and employment tribunals to which, following the Woolf reforms to civil procedures, Armed Forces personnel could appeal in cases of discrimination, ensured the forces' compliance with the Human Rights Act. The Army was forced to adapt to the civilian world and end all forms of discrimination. In doing so, it boosted its legitimacy in the eyes of the society it serves and protects. Meanwhile, events in the world moved on.

Macedonia

Operation Essential Harvest in Macedonia in the summer of 2001 was one of the many unsung missions undertaken by the Army. As its commander, Brigadier Barney White-Spunner, noted, whenever there is a problem overseas, the government's first instinct is to turn to the Armed Forces.[16] Chapter 7 detailed how military intervention on humanitarian grounds became established in the aftermath of the Cold War. Stabilisation missions, for example those undertaken by SFOR in Bosnia and KFOR in Kosovo, ultimately benefited the wider world as much as the nations in which they were conducted. Failing states such as Somalia, Iraq, Syria and Libya are breeding grounds for instability way beyond their borders.

A NATO task force was deployed to Macedonia to oversee the surrender of weapons and the disbandment of the Albanian National Liberation Army (NLA), led by Ali Achmeti. Ethnic Albanians were the minority in the country, making up just under a third of the population, although exact numbers were disputed. Their civil rights were curtailed: their language was not officially recognised and they could not work for the civil service.[17] Given the upheaval across the Balkans, but particularly in Kosovo, which prompted an exodus of Kosovars to Macedonia, it was perhaps inevitable that local Albanians would seek to get a better deal. A short-lived insurgency began against the government in Skopje in February 2001. A Bosnian-style civil war was prevented, thanks to early, resolute action taken by the international community, and a ceasefire was declared in May 2001. In a peace deal signed three months later in the Macedonian city of Ohrid, the government agreed to introduce constitutional reforms, while the NLA would hand over its weapons to a NATO force and subsequently disband.

Taking the lead in Operation Essential Harvest was 16th Air Assault Brigade. The force was actually one week into its summer leave but, following NATO's decision to deploy, its headquarters was established in Skopje within three days. With the brigade having been alerted that it might be deployed some two months earlier, some limited planning and reconnaissance had been undertaken.[18] Soldiers from fourteen nations would join the operation, including Turks and Greeks. Among the British troops taking part were members of 2 Para and a Special Forces Task Group. Explosive ordnance disposal (EOD) would be undertaken by Portuguese forces, members of the Norwegian navy and Royal Engineers. Canadians and troops from the Household Cavalry would carry out further reconnaissance, while the United States provided helicopters. Belgians provided transport and Czech paratroopers were tasked with headquarters protection. 'The weapon destruction task was undertaken with great enthusiasm by a mobile Hungarian team from a company which specialised in destroying ex-Warsaw Pact tanks after the end of the Cold War.'[19] The multinational force was too large, according to White-Spunner, who suggests that the job needed one battalion rather than the four that were deployed. Skopje suspected that it was an invasion force intent on dividing the country in favour of the NLA. 'The most sceptical believed that the operation was some sort of NATO/Albanian plot to create a greater Albania, an option aired regularly by the paranoid Macedonian Slav media.' It reflected the drawbacks of putting together a force package far away from the theatre, 'in the glorious isolation of London or Brussels'.[20]

NATO troops had to tread carefully between the insurgent NLA, Macedonian troops and some local police who, resolutely opposed to any deal with the insurgents, were forming paramilitary groups. Four-man Harvest Liaison Teams acted as pathfinders, going to local areas to parley with the rival factions to arrange weapons collection. The three-phase weapons handovers varied: sometimes they were collected up by a quartermaster and casually dumped; at other times there was a disbandment parade, with the weapons and ammunition borne by horses and mules. The operation was completed in seven weeks, by which time there was an effective ceasefire, the Macedonian army had withdrawn to barracks, some 40,000 refugees had returned, schools had reopened and farmers were working in the fields in Albanian areas.

The presence of NATO forces not only provided the stick for compliance, but held out a tangible carrot to all the factions in Macedonia – future membership of the alliance, which in turn would make membership of the European Union more likely. In Eurosceptic Britain, it is easy to forget that, for those outside, this offered huge benefits, especially in terms of improving the standards of living. According to White-Spunner, 'We succeeded because we were seen as the means to a better way of life and economic opportunity; we should never forget that.' The informal mantra of 'Go First, Go Fast, Go Home' had had another successful outing – in very sharp contrast to the long-running Operation Banner in Northern Ireland, now into its fourth decade.

Northern Ireland

The Good Friday Agreement signed on 10 April 1998 marked the beginning of the peace process in Northern Ireland. Signed by the British and Irish governments and the major local political parties, it provided a political framework for the future government of the province. It had an immediate impact on soldiers on the ground. Captain John Flexman of the Royal Gloucestershire, Berkshire and Wiltshire Regiment (RGBW), whose first tour of the province began after the Agreement, said that his experience was completely different from that of those who came before him: 'They served in an environment where on every patrol there was a high likelihood of contact, I did not.'[21] For Tony Blair, the Agreement marked a beginning not an end: he considered that the process would not be finalised until May 2007, nine years into the future. The Agreement had involved many compromises, fudges and loose ends, but, according to Blair, 'by the squeakiest of squeaks we got it through'.[22]

While the level of terrorism and violence in Northern Ireland had declined steadily throughout the 1980s and 1990s, it had not disappeared. An estimated 5,400 kilograms had been used in bombs in 1990, but this was down to 900 kilograms by 1996. The same year, 1,677 kilograms of explosives had been found, along with 10,000 rounds of ammunition, while 488 people had been charged with terrorism offences.[23] Although 1,000 fewer troops were deployed in 1996 compared with the start of the decade, they were hardly 'out': there were 10,500 on duty in the province.[24] Primarily, their role was to aid the local police. Their presence was necessary, particularly during the summer 'marching season' when the area around Drumcree would be besieged by rival sectarian factions.

Northern Ireland had been one area unaffected by the end of the Cold War. The military commitment to the province had not been reduced under *Options for Change*, whose most notable local development had been the creation of the Royal Irish Regiment out of an amalgamation of the Ulster Defence Regiment and the Royal Irish Rangers. Northern Ireland remained heavily militarised, a place of checkpoints and watchtowers. A recurrent myth is that the Army regarded Northern Ireland as a mere training ground, which offered 'real soldiering' compared with tours of Germany, producing invaluable operational experience, especially at junior levels of command, and was a vital source of group cohesion and morale.[25] The reality was that soldiers were there because there was a job to do. Because of the threat, soldiers still avoided the roads and relied on helicopters: the military heliport at Bessbrook Mill, Armagh, was the busiest heliport in Europe. Just a month before the Good Friday Agreement, a watchtower was bombed and a company base at Forkhill mortared.[26] A new development was the detonation of bombs via mobile phones, something that would be seen in Iraq to deadly effect. Tactics on the ground were constantly evolving.

Operation Banner continued long after Good Friday 1998. While all sides worked towards the best, they were prepared for the worst. The fledgling Agreement could still fracture, not least because it needed to be approved by referenda in North and South, before Northern Ireland's new Assembly and power-sharing Executive could begin to be set up. Three key issues threatened it: the decommissioning of paramilitary weapons; prisoner release; and the reform of the Royal Ulster Constabulary. The hopes of the people of Northern Ireland had been raised too often. On 31 August 1994, the IRA had announced a ceasefire and their lead was followed by the loyalist paramilitaries in October. For the first time in twenty-five years the province was officially at peace: 1995 was the first year when no British soldiers were killed in the province or anywhere else in connection with the Troubles since they had started. The ceasefire unravelled in February 1996, with the detonation of a truck bomb at Canary Wharf. Together with a blast at Bishopsgate in April 1993 and at the Baltic Exchange a year earlier, more than £1.5 billion of damage was caused to the City of London. In June 1996, another truck bomb exploded in Manchester's city centre. In the spring of 1997, the IRA caused chaos on the mainland's motorways and railway stations with a series of bomb hoaxes, and surely committed a major tactical blunder when a bomb threat led to Aintree racecourse being evacuated and the Grand National postponed.

The Good Friday Agreement itself built on foundations laid by John Major. In 1992 Northern Ireland Secretary Peter Brooke had first declared that Britain had no 'selfish strategic or economic' interest in Northern Ireland: if the majority of the province's inhabitants chose to unite with the South, it would not stand in their way. The 1993 Downing Street Declaration, made jointly with Irish Taoiseach Albert Reynolds, had underscored that any united Ireland would only be achieved by consent of the people of Northern Ireland. These simple affirmations of the principle of self-determination – accepted by the international community since the time of President Woodrow Wilson – had taken decades to achieve. However, a hindrance to progress in Northern Ireland was the Major government's small majority, which made him dependent on the Unionist bloc in Parliament: they had enabled him to get the Maastricht Treaty through the Commons in 1993. But Tony Blair, unencumbered by the loyalist link, ever-optimistic and acknowledging a 'Messiah complex' which compelled him to try to succeed where others had failed, was the ideal premier to push for peace.[27] After decades of dissembling by politicians, who made public statements about never speaking to terrorists while, in fact, sanctioning back-channel talks, in October 1997 the new Prime Minister met Sinn Féin leaders Gerry Adams and Martin McGuinness. He also grasped that central to peace in the North was the Republic, where EU membership had triggered the start of its transformation into the 'Celtic tiger': 'The South was sprinting down the track towards the future ... For the Republic this was no longer a dispute to be clung to as a unifying symbol of Irish identity, but a painful and unwelcome reminder of Ireland's past.'[28] Militant emerald nationalists were as out of tune with the day-to-day reality south of the border as the most bigoted of Orangemen to the north. The Blair government's constitutional reforms, which devolved power to assemblies in Scotland and Wales elected on the basis of proportional representation, made the political stalemate in Northern Ireland appear even more anachronistic. In January 1998, in an effort to break the deadlock, Secretary of State Mo Mowlam visited the Maze prison to negotiate with loyalist inmates, urging them to back peace talks, while in the same month Tony Blair announced another inquiry into Bloody Sunday to be led by Lord Saville.

In the aftermath of the Good Friday Agreement, peace seemed as elusive as ever. Paradoxically, Northern Ireland became more dangerous in 1998, with the number of Troubles-connected deaths doubling, up from twenty-two in 1997 to fifty-five.[29] Tensions mounted as the marching season approached: in July, in one of a series of arson attacks on Catholic properties, the firebombing of the Quinn family home in Ballymoney, County Antrim, by the Ulster Volunteer Force killed three young brothers. On 15 August, a bomb at Omagh killed twenty-nine people. It was one of the worst atrocities of the Troubles. A breakaway Republican group, the Real IRA, claimed responsibility.

A tiny measure of political progress was made the following month when Gerry Adams had talks with the First Minister David Trimble at Stormont, the first time Unionist and Sinn Féin leaders had met. It prompted uproar among Unionist hardliners, such as the Reverend Ian Paisley. For both sides of the province's sectarian divide, the issue of disarmament – euphemistically known as 'weapons decommissioning' – remained an obstacle. International mediators and observers, including US Senator George Mitchell, had been drafted in by both John Major and Tony Blair to resolve the long-standing impasse, through the Independent International Commission on Decommissioning. Decommissioning was one of the Good Friday fudges: neither side had immediately to disarm, but would 'use any influence they may have, to achieve the decommissioning of all paramilitary arms within two years following endorsement in referendums North and South of the agreement'.[30] For the IRA, decommissioning had connotations of surrender. On being asked when he might give up his weapons, one IRA commander replied, 'Five million years, in the short term.'[31] Decommissioning was purely symbolic, but it was crucial. After all, existing weapons might be placed beyond use, but they could always be replaced. The international dimension to decommissioning reminded both sides that the world, including Washington, was watching.

The peace process affected the role of the Army and the conduct of soldiers. The commanding officer of 1st Battalion Royal Gloucestershire, Berkshire and Wiltshire Regiment, Lieutenant Colonel Richard Hall, said that to reduce the military profile in the wake of the Good Friday Agreement, patrolling patterns and tactics had to change. Although the Provisionals had not disarmed and hardliners were forming the Real IRA, soldiers 'knowingly reduced their guard and increased their vulnerability'. He said it made for a different sort of tour: 'the Battalion's success can be measured by the failure of the Real IRA to gain popular support or Sinn Féin to make political capital out of the Battalion's operations'. Any failure by soldiers to adapt would have undermined the peace process.[32] According to the Prime Minister, for the IRA, the watchtowers were a constant source of friction, an ever-present reminder of the British Army's presence. 'Our military, of course, regarded the towers as a vital point of surveillance, especially on dissident Republicans coming up from the south to commit acts of terror.'[33] One Northern Ireland senior commander described the towers, which were undoubtedly intimidating and dominating, as a 'political and military millstone'.[34] Symbolic of perceived oppression and of the UK government's resolve to protect Unionist minorities in the 'deep green' areas, they went against the grain for a force committed to manoeuvre, tying troops to fixed positions that could themselves come under attack.

Gradually, operations were scaled back, with Army patrols withdrawn from Belfast and Derry. Lance Bombardier Stephen Restorick, who was shot by a sniper in February 1997, is acknowledged to be the last British soldier to be killed by the IRA. His killer was also found guilty of perpetrating the Canary Wharf explosion. Thanks to the early release of terrorist prisoners agreed on Good Friday, Restorick's killer served just sixteen months in prison.

The new Northern Ireland Executive began its job of governing the province in December 1999, in time for the new century. A fresh start was heralded. Decommissioning – and, in fact, the demise of IRA terrorism – would be hastened not by politicians in Northern Ireland, but by an attack on New York.

Afghanistan

On 11 September 2001, al-Qaeda demonstrated that it fully grasped the value of the modern media. In this, it set an example to its successors such as ISIS – who showed themselves far more adept at getting their message across to the world than those who were trying to combat them, for example by sending out almost hourly updates via Twitter in twenty-three different languages. Al-Qaeda's chosen targets symbolised Western, and specifically American, power: the World Trade Center; the Pentagon; the White House.

The attack on the Twin Towers was especially shocking. Crystalline sharp because of the bright sunlight, the resulting images were unforgettable. The missiles deployed – civilian aircraft – came out of the clear blue sky above New York, both literally and metaphorically. Like other terrorist groups before them, al-Qaeda understood the power of the 'propaganda of the deed'.[35] The strike against the United States that September morning joined the dots of previous terrorist attacks dating back more than a decade, revealing the reality of jihad. This holy war was being fought by fanatical Islamists, willing to sacrifice themselves for their cause. Whether members of al-Qaeda or one of the numerous other radical Islamist groups, jihadist activists could be found across the globe: in the Middle East, Chechnya, Indonesia, Africa and Europe, including Britain. Of the nineteen perpetrators of the attack, fifteen were Saudis, four had lived in Hamburg.

The images of the falling towers induced collective global shellshock. With the attack on the second tower, Tony Blair knew he was witnessing a 'world-changing' event.[36] That evening, President George W. Bush asserted that, while bloodied, the United States was unbowed. He declared that the federal agencies whose offices had been attacked would immediately get back to work and that the American economy remained open for business. The hunt was on for those behind the evil, who would be brought to justice: 'We will make no distinction between the terrorists who committed these acts and those who harbour them.'[37] At NATO HQ, a meeting of the Alliance's ambassadors was convened by the Secretary General, former British Defence Secretary George Robertson: 'We knew that something fundamental had happened and that for the world a new chapter had opened.'[38] Underscoring the collective nature of the Alliance, for the first time in its history, on 12 September, NATO invoked Article 5 of the Washington Treaty: an attack on one ally was regarded as an attack on all allies. Similarly, on the same day UN Security Council Resolution 1368 called on 'all States to work together urgently to bring to justice the perpetrators, organizers and sponsors of these terrorist attacks'.[39] Addressing Congress a little over a week later, President Bush declared a 'war on terror'. He warned that every regime in every region had a choice to make: 'Either you're with us or you're with the terrorists.' He stated that America had no truer friend than Britain: 'Once again, we are joined together in a great cause.'[40]

On 9/11 the West paid a terrible price for meddling in Afghanistan in the 1980s and its subsequent neglect of the country in the 1990s. Its support for the mujahideen, the holy warriors who fought back against the Soviet Union, paid off in February 1989, when the Red Army retreated. A few weeks later, journalist and Afghanistan expert Ahmed Rashid was on the country's border with Pakistan. He saw a truck taking thirty foreign fighters to Peshawar for some weekend leave: swathed in ammunition belts and carrying Kalashnikovs, 'The group was made up of Filipino Moros, Uzbeks from Soviet Central Asia, Arabs from Algeria, Egypt, Saudi Arabia and Kuwait and Uighurs from Xinjiang in China ... They had come to fight the jihad with the mujahideen and to train in weapons, bomb-making and military tactics so they could take the jihad back home.'[41] These so-called Arab Afghans were frequently looked down upon as amateurs by the battle-hardened native warriors, whose war-fighting skills had been the stuff of legend since the time of Alexander the Great.[42] Dilettantes or not, it is estimated that some 35,000 foreign militants joined the battle in Afghanistan.[43] Military training camps and bases sprang up, including *al-Ma'sada* (Lion's Den), built by the wealthy Saudi Osama bin Laden. His elusive, cellular organisation, al-Qaeda (The Base), would surface in the mid-1990s, named, according to him, after a training camp for mujahideen.[44]

Afghanistan was torn apart by civil war following the Soviet withdrawal. The country's rival warlords and their militias battled for control, worsening the plight of one of the world's poorest, least developed countries. The UN Secretary General Boutros Boutros-Ghali described the civil war there as an 'orphaned conflict', ignored by the West in favour of the former Yugoslavia. One faction, the Taliban, took control of Kandahar, the country's second city, in 1994; in September 1996, they finally seized the capital, Kabul. Led by Mullah Mohammed Omar, the Taliban – from student (*talib*) of Islam – immediately imposed Sharia law. Public executions and amputations took place in Kabul's main football ground. The Taliban's uncompromising zealotry was underlined by the destruction of the 1,700-year-old statues of Buddha at Bamiyan in early 2001. It was a foretaste of the attempted obliteration of world heritage by jihadists in Syria and Libya. Intensely tribal, multi-ethnic, home to rival warlords, ideally suited to growing the opium poppy, Afghanistan also became a haven for international terrorists. In 1996 bin Laden was given sanctuary in the country, where he planned the 9/11 attacks.

An outpouring of international sympathy and goodwill was generated towards the United States following 9/11. Terrorism was a new phenomenon for Americans, notwithstanding the regrettable support for, and funding of, the IRA by a tiny minority of them. What 9/11 underlined was that Islamist terrorism could be of a different order of magnitude from anything governments had previously confronted. Its pan-nationalism, its chilling self-sacrifice and its deadly readiness to inflict limitless casualties pointed to a new paradigm of terror. Conversely, the IRA, for example, was comparatively containable. It had a command and control structure and a limited, local political goal, linked to a territorial state. While committed, its activists were not suicide bombers. Likened to a global multinational, al-Qaeda deployed the 'cellular structure of drugs cartels and the flattened networks of virtual business corporations'.[45] It was, principally, the enabler of Islamist terrorism, providing the finance for training camps and operations. Describing it as the 'Holy War Foundation', analyst Jason Burke argued that al-Qaeda's effectiveness lay in its ability to access resources 'of a scale and with an ease that was hitherto unknown in Islamic militancy'.[46] It was only one of many Islamist terrorist groups. However, as the perpetrators of 9/11, al-Qaeda and its leader, bin Laden, provided a focus for Western counter-terrorism efforts in the immediate aftermath of the attack.

The war on terror officially began on 7 October 2001 with air strikes on Afghanistan. Operation Enduring Freedom aimed to capture bin Laden, destroy al-Qaeda and oust the Taliban. Some three weeks earlier, President Bush had approved a campaign plan drawn up by the CIA, which would see Special Forces join with local fighters supported by the deployment of air power. Key to the US effort was the anti-Taliban Northern Alliance, whose charismatic leader Ahmed Shah Massoud had been killed on 9 September in a suicide attack instigated by bin Laden. Heading to the Panjshir valley in north-east Afghanistan, CIA officers paid out millions of dollars to secure the Alliance warlords' loyalty. Having pledged that Britain would stand 'shoulder to shoulder' with the United States, Prime Minister Blair delivered. British forces went into action as part of the US-led coalition: the RAF provided reconnaissance and refuelling for US strike aircraft, while Royal Navy submarines deployed Tomahawk missiles. Several thousand British troops were on 48-hour notice, including elements of 3 Commando Brigade and 16 Air Assault Brigade.[47] Formal permission was given by the British government for the Indian Ocean island of Diego Garcia (already used by the USAF) to be a base for the operation. The initial wave of air strikes against terrorist training camps lasted five days. The city of Mazir-i-Sharif fell on 10 November, thanks to a combination of air strikes and a cavalry charge by Northern Alliance fighters on horseback. The following day Bamiyan fell and, on 13 November, the Taliban abandoned Kabul. Prime Minister Blair announced that the 'Taliban regime is in a state of collapse across Afghanistan'.

The first British boots on the ground in Afghanistan officially arrived when Royal Marines from 40 Commando helped to secure the area around the airfield at Bagram, north of Kabul. Kunduz, a Taliban stronghold in the north, was overrun by the Northern Alliance on 26 November. In the south of the country, a hotchpotch of different factions and militias were rallying against the Taliban. A credible interim leader was also emerging: the urbane Pashtun, Hamid Karzai. On 6 December, Mullah Omar and his lieutenants fled from Kandahar: a key goal of Enduring Freedom had been achieved. The operation's success appeared to vindicate the 'war-lite' approach of autocratic US Defense Secretary Donald Rumsfeld, who was a Darth Vader-like figure in the eyes of many within his own department. His

imperious 'snowflake' memos and complaints that the military represented islands of feather-bedded near-socialism in the shining sea
of American capitalism did not endear him to the top brass; nor did
his habit of calling them in for meetings on Saturdays.[48] The success
of Enduring Freedom, however, appeared to justify his transformation agenda for a leaner, meaner US military, focusing on information technology, air power and Special Forces.

What of bin Laden? From Jalalabad in eastern Afghanistan,
he and his followers headed some thirty miles south-east to Tora
Bora, a mountainous area honeycombed by caves – and vanished.
For President Bush, who declared he wanted him 'dead or alive', and
for those hunting him down, frustration at his evading capture must
surely have intensified on hearing that the Saudi was giving media
interviews. In November, he stated chemical or nuclear weapons
would be deployed in retaliation for any such attack by the US.[49]
In March 2002, in an attempt to track down al-Qaeda forces, Operation Anaconda was launched in Afghanistan's Shah-i-Kot valley.
It was believed hundreds of hardcore jihadists were holding out in
this remote area.

The mission involved the largest deployment of US ground
forces since the Gulf War. More than 2,000 troops, primarily conventional forces from the 10th Mountain and 101st Airborne Divisions, along with coalition troops, including British Special Forces
and 350 local Pashtuns led by Zia Lodin, were deployed. The most
intense fighting was in the first week, with six US troops being killed
in twenty-four hours. A 'nearly perfect guerrilla redoubt', the valley's rocks, crevasses and gulleys provided cover for snipers. Apache
helicopters took so much fire 'it just sounded like someone had lit
off a whole bunch of firecrackers every time they flew over', while
when taking evasive action, their pilots 'felt like a fly getting chased
by a swatter'.[50] A 'mopping-up', expected to last a few days, stretched
into almost three weeks. The al-Qaeda leader probably slipped away
and crossed the border into the remote regions of tribal Pakistan
sometime around mid-December 2001.[51] It is suggested that the fact
that he survived, escaped and was at large for so long, bolstered the
'mythology and attractiveness of the bin Laden and al Qaeda "brand"
around the world'.[52] Like 9/11, his escape would become the stuff of
febrile conspiracy theories. Within months, the rhetoric about his

capture had been scaled back: after March 2002, George Bush never publicly referred to him and, in April, the Chairman of the Joint Chiefs stated that 'the goal had never been to get bin Laden'.[53]

The NATO-led International Security and Assistance Force (ISAF) was deployed to Afghanistan in December 2001. Britain took command of the multinational force, mandated by UNSCR 1386 to assist the Afghan Interim Authority in maintaining security in Kabul and the surrounding area. After a busy six months it would hand over command to Turkey in June 2002. Troops would flit between working for ISAF and for Operation Enduring Freedom, whose headquarters was at Bagram. Under the command of Major General John McColl, originally of the Royal Anglian Regiment, some 1,700 troops were initially deployed, with numbers expected to rise to 4,500–5,000. The British contingent comprised members of 16 Air Assault Brigade, along with 36 Engineer Group, 9 Squadron Royal Engineers and 30 Signals Regiment, while cooks from 3 (UK) Division provided everyone with three meals a day. For Royal Engineer NCO Scott Jinks, Kabul was a fairly benign environment, while ISAF 'was seen as a force for good by pretty much the whole population … Just being there was saying we wanted to help.'[54]

After more than two decades of occupation, civil war and religion-inspired terror, local people needed stability. The war against the Soviet occupation had cost 1.5 million Afghan lives: one in eight families had someone killed or maimed by the mines that littered the Afghan countryside and, even years later, could be found on the outskirts of Kabul. McColl said that if his children asked what he did in Afghanistan, he would answer, 'Drink tea and eat kebabs' with local tribal elders, which he regarded as crucial for any commander. 'A critical element is forging relationships that deliver leverage, at the operational and strategic level.'[55] The ISAF troops were the welcome guests of the fledgling Afghan government, which officially came to power on 22 December. Practical aid was given through funding local contractors to work on projects such as rebuilding schools, which benefited the local economy.[56] On 15 February 2002, ISAF won local hearts and minds with a football match at the main football ground, which had been the site of executions under the Taliban. An estimated 30,000 people turned out to see Kabul United beat the ISAF team 3–1.

Iraq: Phases I–III

Perhaps in the early years Afghanistan was too easy. If the United States had been confronted by a little of the sustained resistance that Soviet troops had faced twenty years earlier, the Bush administration might have paused in its rush to invade Iraq. Hamid Khazai had hardly reached Kabul before the United States' attention turned to Iraq, identified as part of an 'axis of evil'. Months after 9/11, the attack was still fresh in the memory of the American public, whose fears were exploited by the Administration, which began groundlessly to link Saddam and Iraq with al-Qaeda and the Twin Towers attack. Consequently, in an address to the West Point military academy, when the US Commander-in-Chief asserted the right to take preventative military action – action questionable under international law – his public backed him. When, however, Tony Blair declared that Britain would be part of the 30-nation 'Coalition of the Willing' against Iraq, more than a million people marched in protest, considering any military action illegal, illegitimate and contrary to Just War conventions.

Iraq was to become the most controversial issue in British public life since Suez. In the months before the invasion in March 2003, and for years after it, arguments raged. Adept at media management, the Labour government spun Britain into a conflict, reflected not least in its 'dodgy dossier', which exaggerated the threat from the Iraq's weapons of mass destruction (WMD) and its capability to manufacture them. The dossier's flimsy intelligence was key to shoring up the legal case for the intervention via a UN resolution, an effort which was abandoned when President Jacques Chirac made clear that France would use its veto. The 'cheese-eating surrender monkeys', along with Germany, which was equally opposed to the invasion, were dismissed as 'old Europe' by the acerbic Rumsfeld. Further UN resolutions were not needed anyway, ruled the British Attorney General Peter Goldsmith somewhat belatedly: war would be legal under existing UN mandates. Clare Short, Secretary of State at the Department for International Development, the lead government agency for the reconstruction effort, would later allege that Lord Goldsmith had been 'leant on'.[57] Labour was split on Iraq, with former Foreign Secretary Robin Cook resigning ahead of an eve-of-war Commons vote, which saw a rebellion against the government.

The lack of transparency before the invasion had consequences after it. Many suspected what Tony Blair would never admit: that in April 2002, in Crawford, Texas, he had secretly agreed that Britain would join an American campaign against Iraq to effect regime change. If this is the case, all his government's subsequent efforts over the next year to justify the intervention – including parking tanks at Heathrow and making claims about being forty-five minutes from attack – were actually a farcical waste of time. As long as any intervention was conclusively on the right side of international law, military action in Iraq should surely have been presented as Britain standing shoulder to shoulder with her most important ally. They would be there, so we would be there – a practical expression of the so-called 'special relationship'. However, because the government could not come clean, and was anxious publicly to be seen sticking to the diplomatic path, furtiveness surrounded British preparations for war. The US military had begun tentative thinking about possible action in Iraq in late 2001, with plans being sent from the Pentagon to the White House the following May.[58] As US resolve to take military action strengthened over the coming months, so too did the British commitment to take part. Behind the scenes, by the end of July 2002, senior British commanders had discussions at US Central Command, the possibility of a land contribution of 40,000 British personnel had been raised in a ministerial meeting and the Prime Minister had promised the President 'I will be with you, whatever.'[59] However, the issue of Iraq would continue to be played down in public. As Tony Blair later stated, '… We were doing as much as we could under the radar': Defence Secretary Geoff Hoon was made aware of Downing Street's wish to minimise publicity and 'for avoiding the visibility of preparations.'[60]

The government's furtiveness deprived it of the opportunity to make a good case for conflict and delayed the necessary preparations for the military operation. Consequently, shortages of vital equipment ensued, including desert boots and clothing, night-vision goggles and body armours, as well as nuclear, biological and chemical (NBC) detection and protection kits. Given that weaponry featuring NBC agents was a reason for war and therefore the government must have been convinced that Saddam's forces would deploy them, delays in getting the appropriate protection to soldiers were hardly ideal. Any shortage of desert kit was resented, with soldiers telling the Director of the National Audit Office: 'We're out here fighting and you can't be bothered to buy us a proper uniform.'[61] Generally, shortfalls were made good and overall the logistical effort was impressive. More than 9,100 shipping containers were used on seventy-eight ships and 360 aircraft sorties were flown to transport personnel, supplies and equipment.[62] In 2001 an extended military exercise in Oman, Exercise Saif Sareea II, designed to test the effectiveness of the new Joint Rapid Reaction Force, had provided valuable training for desert operations. It meant that some issues, such as the 'desertification' of Challenger 2 tanks, were addressed in advance of deployment to Iraq.

Codenamed Operation Telic by the British and, more grandly, Operation Iraqi Freedom by the United States, the combat phase of the operation, which began on 20 March 2003, was a three-week display of military might and tactical acumen. A week earlier, the thousands of soldiers amassed in their assembly areas in the greyish desert of northern Kuwait were visited by General Sir Mike Jackson. They were eager to get going. One private from the Royal Regiment of Fusiliers told the CGS in characteristically soldier language: 'What we need to do is get across that bloody border, kick that bugger's arse, get home and have a few bloody beers.'[63] British forces had expected to advance through Turkey, as part of a two-front campaign. The plan was redrawn at the eleventh hour when the government in Ankara refused to allow the coalition transit rights. Already sailing for the Middle East, some British ships had no idea whether 'they were going to turn left or right in the Mediterranean'.[64] The British would now attack from Kuwait in the south. At its simplest, the battle plan was for the US forces to make a three-pronged, 300-mile assault on Baghdad, while British forces took care of Basra, Iraq's second city. In a joint action with a US Marine Expeditionary Force unit, the British would also secure southern Iraq's oil fields, known as the 'Crown Jewels'.[65] 'Shock and awe' signalled the start of the campaign, with air strikes on Baghdad: it ended on 9 April, when victorious American troops helped jubilant Iraqi civilians tear down a statue of Saddam in the heart of the city, an act of symbolism broadcast around the world. Some resistance had been encountered by US forces in their blitz on Baghdad, but mainly from *Fedayeen*, or irregular fighters; the fearsome Republican Guard and regulars who made up what had been the world's fifth biggest army had vanished. The advance had been hampered as much by a *shamal*, or dust storm, as it had been by enemy forces. In reality, the Iraqi army of 2003 had never recovered from its pounding in Operation Desert Storm in 1991.

Britain deployed the 1st (UK) Armoured Division. At its core was 7th Armoured Brigade, 3rd Commando Brigade and 16th Air Assault Brigade, comprising 1st and 3rd Battalions Parachute Regiment, 1st Battalion Royal Irish Regiment, 7th Regiment Royal Horse Artillery and elements of the Household Cavalry. Shipped from Germany, the 'Desert Rats' brought together 1st Battalion Black Watch, 1st Battalion Royal Regiment of Fusiliers, 2nd Royal Tank Regiment, the Royal Scots Dragoon Guards and the Queen's Royal Irish Hussars. However, just as in the Gulf War, tanks had once again to be cannibalised. Additional elements from various regiments – including the Queen's Dragoon Guards, the Queen's Royal Lancers and from four infantry battalions, including the Irish Guards and the Duke of Wellington's Regiment – were bolted on to the brigades. Supporting these frontline units were soldiers from the Royal Corps of Signals, Royal Logistic Corps, Royal Electrical and Mechanical Engineers and the Royal Engineers. In all, 46,150 personnel were deployed by Britain.[66] Operation Telic called out more than 8,400 reservists, the largest number since Suez.[67] As a result of a clash of domestic and international issues, overall force numbers were limited by the demands of Operation Fresco, which diverted thousands of personnel into fire-fighting duties because of a firemen's strike. The long-standing penny-pinching policy of the MoD to use military manpower in support of the civil authorities only out of 'spare capacity' began to look a little thin on this occasion when there was a significant war to be fought at the same time.

Brought forward by forty-eight hours by the US commander, General David McKiernan, the land battle for British forces began with a Commando assault on the al-Faw peninsula to secure oil assets and the port of Umm Qasr. By 23 March, 7th Armoured Brigade and 16th Air Assault Brigade had surrounded Basra. In what one analyst described as 'an excellent demonstration in the use of minimum force in a major war environment', divisional commander Major General

Robin Brims avoided a direct attack on the city and halted his forces on its outskirts and bridges.[68] For almost two weeks small armoured columns pulsed in and out, Special Forces personnel gathered intelligence and the British dominated the psychological space. On 6 April, troops finally entered the city unopposed and set up headquarters in Saddam's Basra palace. With a chilling foretaste of what was to come later in both Iraq and Afghanistan, one elderly sheikh greeted the commanding officer of 2nd Royal Tank Regiment, saying: 'You are welcome to my country. This is not the first time I have welcomed British soldiers to Basra, but if you stay too long we will shoot at you.'

Three weeks later, aboard USS *Abraham Lincoln*, President Bush stood in front of a banner that declared 'Mission Accomplished'. However, for coalition troops the mission had hardly begun.

Iraq – Phase IV

Having sent British forces to war, the Blair government was reluctant to commit to the post-conflict stabilisation that is an integral part of any military campaign. With every day that passed without the fabled WMD being found, the government's justification for the invasion weakened and its approval ratings fell. The anger of the war's opponents grew more implacable, stoked by the suicide of UN weapons inspector David Kelly in July 2003. Like 'Calais' being found on Mary Tudor's heart, 'Iraq' would indelibly taint Tony Blair and his government. Successive inquiries – the Foreign Affairs Select Committee, Hutton, Butler and Chilcot – examined issues connected with Iraq. A convincing *casus belli* proved as elusive as those WMD. As Iraq descended into the chaos of insurgency and near civil war, polls in Britain reflected an increasingly hostile public mood: on 12 April 2003, a Populus/Times survey reported 64 per cent in favour of military action; by February 2006, pollsters found 64 per cent were opposed and just 24 per cent in favour.[69] No wonder ministers urged the country to 'move on'.

Thousands of miles away, out in the heat, dust and danger of a shattered country, British soldiers did their best to stabilise southern Iraq. Fortunately, some of the dire predictions about the consequences of combat turned out to be wrong: there was no humanitarian catastrophe; the oil infrastructure had not been destroyed causing an environmental disaster; and neither had US forces been confronted by Stalingrad-on-the-Tigris. Equally, across government there had been no concerted effort to anticipate or plan for Phase IV of Operation Telic or the vacuum created by the ousting of Saddam Hussein. Just who was to succeed him? Iraqi chancers-in-exile? To be fair to Whitehall, Washington had been equally negligent. A chief cheerleader for the invasion, Defense Department official Paul Wolfowitz, predicted US troop numbers would be down to 34,000 by the summer of 2003, in contrast to US Army Chief, General Eric Shinseki, who had studied the Occupation of Germany and believed that almost ten times that number could be needed.[70] Joint Force Logistic Component Commander Major General Tim Cross, who had set up refugee camps in Kosovo, was charged with liaison between London and Washington on the Phase IV effort: he found no focus or enthusiasm in either for it.[71] Indeed, DfID was actively hostile. However, as a joint occupying power, confirmed by UNSCR 1483 in May 2003, Britain had responsibilities towards Iraq under international law. As Blair himself states: 'The military campaign of conquest was a brilliant success. The civilian campaign of reconstruction wasn't.'[72] However, it was soldiers not civilians who would be picking up the pieces.

Oust Saddam, be feted by a grateful flower-throwing population as liberators, hand over to an interim authority and go home, leaving behind a democratic country with some of the world's largest oil reserves ... That was the expectation, but 'stuff happens'. Donald Rumsfeld's memorable phrase hardly did justice to the scale of the looting and lawlessness in the immediate aftermath of the combat operation, when government buildings were ransacked, stripped bare of even their window frames, and man-hole covers ripped from the roads. Although Iraq was a particularly troublesome parcel that Washington and London wanted to pass as quickly as possible, the Iraqi state no longer existed. They were stuck with running the country. 'Go First, Go Fast, Go Home' had run its course.

While the Kurdish north could be left to more or less run itself, the coalition would have to take over the rest. After turf wars in Washington between the Pentagon and the State Department, the Coalition Provisional Authority (CPA) became the new ruling body in Iraq. Ideologically driven, it focused on grandiose projects such as introducing a stock exchange. The disconnect between the CPA's aspirations and the reality of day-to-day life for Iraqis led its Green Zone headquarters to become known as the Emerald City, after the place of illusions in *The Wizard of Oz*.[73] Arriving in Baghdad in June 2003, the CPA chief Paul Bremer immediately disbanded the Iraqi army and police, and sacked any officials who were members of the Ba'ath party, which had controlled Iraq under Saddam. State employees, including teachers, immediately lost their jobs. A security vacuum, on top of the governance vacuum, was created.

With its population of 2 million, the port of Basra was Iraq's second city. Many soldiers could learn from their regimental histories of the 1920s how tough any occupation of Iraq could turn out to be. Informed by such episodes of imperial policing, they adopted a typical softly-softly approach. In May, all coalition forces were restructured. Britain led Multi-National Division South East (MND-SE), which covered four provinces: Basra, Maysan, Muthanna and Dhi Qar. By then, British personnel numbers had fallen to 18,000 and would be down to about 8,000 a year later. Divisional GOC Major General Graeme Lamb was told by coalition commander General Rick Sanchez that his job was to 'keep the south quiet'. With its Shia population rejoicing at the downfall of Saddam, Basra was a more benign environment for the occupying forces than Baghdad. However, its infrastructure was creaking due to decades of underinvestment by the Sunni-dominated government. One of Lamb's first tasks was to obtain 900 tons of plastic to enable tomato farmers to grow their crops.[74] For the first year of the occupation, Iraq was seen as a bit of a sunshine tour. One soldier says: 'Particularly down in Basra, guys had been going down to the market and buying their little furry camels and tourist stuff.'[75] Reconstruction was to remain a muddle. Army reservist Andrew Alderson, a former investment banker, found himself in charge of containers full of millions of CPA dollars that were regularly flown down from Baghdad. Bankrolling Basra, he found the lines of authority between the CPA and CPA-South, let alone the military and civilian officials in Basra, and the British in Basra and various departments back in Whitehall were confused, leading to duplication and wasted effort.[76] Meanwhile, as the months passed, the basics the Americans identified as SWET – sewage, water, electricity, trash – were actually in a worse state in

Basra and Baghdad than under Saddam. In 45 degrees or more of heat in summer, electricity shortages led to rioting. The ticket home for all the coalition powers and their personnel was to hand Iraq back to the Iraqis. This involved elections to restore a sovereign Iraqi government and a policy known as Security Sector Reform – training a new Iraqi army and police force.

Security in Iraq was fragile but, initially at least, Basra was relatively stable. Soldiers elsewhere viewed the city's British bases as oases of relative calm, with the Shaiba logistic base becoming known as Shaibiza.[77] Away from the bases, the picture was different, particularly in Maysan province. In June 2003, on routine visits to local police stations, six members of the Royal Military Police were cornered by a mob at Majar al-Kabir in the south of Maysan province and executed. At the time it was seen as a dreadful one-off incident, rather than a portent. Among the soldiers killed was Tom Keys, aged twenty, whose father Reg campaigned for the full truth about the Iraq War to come out. After the attack, the town of Majar al-Kabir was perceived by British forces to be like Mogadishu in *Black Hawk Down*. Two months later outside the UN HQ in Baghdad, a suicide bomber detonated a truck bomb, killing more than twenty staff, including the Brazilian head of mission, Sérgio Vieira de Mello, well known to British soldiers from Kosovo just four years earlier. Foreign fighters began to enter the country, including Jordanian jihadist Abu Musab al-Zarqawi, head of a new group, the self-styled al-Qaeda in Iraq (AQI).

Insurgency would bring Iraq to the brink of civil war and an unthinkable coalition defeat. In March 2004, a year into the conflict, two images signalled that all was far from well: one showed the torture of Iraqi detainees at Abu Ghraib prison by American soldiers; the other the charred corpses of four Blackwater security contractors hanging from a bridge at Fallujah. The coalition was soon facing trouble on multiple fronts: in the so-called Sunni triangle between Baghdad, Tikrit and Ramadi; and from foreign jihadists and dissident Shia militia groups, some backed by Iran. One, the Jaish al-Mahdi (Mahdi Army), whose stronghold was the Baghdad suburb of Sadr city, would cause the British problems in Basra in the years ahead. It was led by Iraqi nationalist Muqtada al-Sadr, whose rock star-like appeal was based on tribal and religious loyalty: his father had been

17. The Falklands Conflict was a testament to the resilience of the fighting soldier – Marines 'yomped' and Paras 'tabbed' across East Falkland to secure the surrender of the Argentines on 14th June 1982.

18. Two columns of Fox armoured reconnaissance vehicles driving through West Berlin on 17 June 1989 as part of the Allied Forces Day parade in which the Allies demonstrated their commitment to the people of the City.

19. Major General Robert Corbett CB, the last British General Officer Commanding Berlin, briefs the media beside a gap in the Berlin Wall which fell on 9 November 1989, soon to be followed by the disbandment of the Warsaw Pact, the dissolution of the Soviet Union on 25 December 1991 and the end of the Cold War.

20. Private Thomas Gow of 5 Platoon, B Company, 1 Royal Scots throwing hand grenades to destroy an Iraqi vehicle that was holding up the advance to liberate Kuwait in March 1991. Gow was later awarded the Military Medal for his bravery.

21. Warrior Infantry Fighting Vehicles were integral to the success of British forces in Bosnia as part of the United Nations mission 1992–5.

22. Enthusiastic crowds of Kosovar Albanians cheered the advance of British soldiers to Pristina on 12 June 1999.

23. The intervention in Sierra Leone in 2000 began as a Non Combatant Evacuation operation as the rebels threatened the capital, Freetown, but was transformed into a successful stabilisation operation. British forces found themselves in an unholy alliance with many irregular groups of fighters.

24. Preparing for battle – 1st Battalion Irish Guards commemorating St Patrick's Day on 17 March 2003 in Kuwait, prior to the invasion of Iraq which started three days later.

25. The commander of a Royal Scots Dragoon Guards Challenger tank observes the outskirts of Basra on 4 April 2003.

26. Having trained to fight an armoured enemy in Europe for over forty years, British armoured units were outstanding in both Gulf Wars. The foundations for success were laid on the prairie of Western Canada. A battlegroup poses with its armoured vehicles for an end of exercise photograph.

27. The operation to move a new turbine through Helmand Province to the Kajaki Dam was an important statement of NATO's commitment to the future of Afghanistan.

28. In contrast to the desert and the mountains, the lush 'green zone' around the Helmand River became a most testing and dangerous environment in which to fight. A handler and his dog lead a patrol.

29. Silent crowds pay their respects to the fallen of Iraq and Afghanistan passing through Royal Wootton Bassett.

30. Help for Heroes has played a major role in revitalising the Service charity sector and providing support to the wounded, injured and sick of recent campaigns. The H4H Big Battlefield Bike Ride culminated in the Mall in June 2014.

31. Public Duties and State Ceremonial occasions are high profile aspects of the Army's contribution to national life. The Queen's Birthday Parade – Trooping the Colour – is a major event in the annual calendar.

32. *(Above)* The Army is also the nation's reserve of trained manpower available to assist the civil community. Whether fighting fires, dealing with foot and mouth disease, assisting in flood areas, running prisons or underpinning the security and administrative success of the London Olympics in 2012, the Army invariably rises to the challenge.

33. *(Bottom left)* In 2015, the biggest deployment by the British Army in 2015 was to Sierra Leone – to fight Ebola. 34. *(Bottom right)* Warfare and technology are in constant evolution. A Tarantula-Hawk Micro Remote Piloted Air System – a drone – in operation in Afghanistan as part of a counter-IED task force. However, the most sophisticated and valuable resource on the battlefield remains – the British soldier.

a revered cleric, and his brothers had all been assassinated by Saddam. On 6 April 2004 came proof that insurgency had spread to the south. Basra saw thirty-five shooting incidents and attacks before 7.30 a.m. and there were running battles in Amarah in Maysan. MND-SE commander Major General Andrew Stewart likened it to a switch being flicked.[78] The violence escalated across Iraq, spreading to Sadr city, as well as to the holy cities of Najaf and Karbala, which was taken by the Mahdi Army. On 21 April, five suicide bombs were simultaneously detonated outside police stations in Basra and Al Zubeir, killing more than seventy people and injuring 450. In June, Fusilier Gordon Gentle, aged nineteen, was killed by the first of many roadside improvised explosive devices (IEDs). These would become progressively more lethal.

Iraq was sliding out of control. On one day in 2004, 164,000 coalition troops from thirty countries were stationed in Iraq – ranging from nine Norwegians to almost 140,000 Americans.[79] However, the forces were neither structured nor resourced to quell the unrest. Apart from the Americans, British and Australians, many forces had only signed up for peacekeeping duties and were forbidden to do more than that. In April 2004, the CPA centre at al-Kut was nearly overrun, but the Ukrainian troops stationed there were forbidden to take any action unless in self-defence.[80] While the British had considerable counter-insurgency expertise, there were too few British soldiers to make a difference. With its warrior ethos, the United States' military was culturally allergic to any mission other than war-fighting: its forces' heavy-handed tactics, such as searching houses with dogs, alienated Iraqi civilians and played into the hands of its opponents. The full might of the US Marine Corps was apparent during the second battle of Fallujah, which began in early November 2004. The six-week operation to retake the city from insurgents cost almost a hundred American lives. Soldiers from the Black Watch battle group were deployed to the Camp Dogwood base, twenty-five miles southwest of Baghdad, to free up the Americans for Fallujah. They came under attack almost daily. Five men were lost. Arriving back in Basra, the soldiers heard confirmation that the Black Watch would be amalgamated into a new Royal Regiment of Scotland as part of Army restructuring – not what they wanted to hear.

Back in the south, British soldiers in Amarah were bearing the brunt of attack. The capital of Maysan had a population of about 400,000. The city was coated in yellow dust from local brickworks and pervaded by the stench of raw sewage. In 2004, unemployment was running at 85 per cent and annual inflation for goods such as cooking oil was almost 400 per cent. The average salary was $8 a day, but insurgents could earn $50 for every twenty-four hours they were in action or for every bomb a three-man mortar team fired.[81] The primary targets for the majority of attacks were the British base Camp Abu Naji, known as Camp Incoming, and CIMIC House beside the Tigris, the headquarters of the combined civil and military reconstruction effort, which was mortared 600 times in three weeks in August. One indication of possible trouble was whether the $10-a-day locally employed civilians (LECs), such as barbers, would turn up for work in the camp.[82] Convoys resupplying the beleaguered compounds with water, food and ammunition were also targeted. On 1 May 2004, Private Johnson Beharry of 1st Battalion Princess of Wales's Royal Regiment (1PWRR) was driving a Warrior armoured infantry vehicle that was hit by multiple rocket-propelled grenades, injuring the soldiers inside. Beharry was forced to open his hatch to steer his vehicle, putting himself in the line of fire, but drove the crippled Warrior through the ambush. Under relentless fire, he then pulled his wounded comrades from the vehicle to safety. He was seriously wounded in another attack six weeks later when his Warrior came under attack again. His successive acts of valour, saving the lives of perhaps thirty comrades, earned him the Victoria Cross, the first awarded since the Falklands. Beharry has continued to serve in the British Army but has never experienced a day without significant physical pain from his head injuries.

On 14 May 2004, the five-hour Battle of Danny Boy saw soldiers go into action with fixed bayonets for the first time since the Falklands. It started when a patrol from the Argyll and Sutherland Highlanders were ambushed near the Danny Boy checkpoint, coming under fire from members of the insurgent Mahdi Army. Reinforcements from 1 PWRR arrived. Lance Corporal Brian Wood said: 'I just led my boys in and hoped for the best ...'[83] He would win the Military Cross. Despite their courage during Danny Boy, soldiers would later be tainted by false accusations of war crimes (see chapter 10).

While the military battled it out with insurgents, politicians in Britain battled to save face. Labour ministers refused to admit that Iraq was a disaster. The rationale for the invasion looked even flimsier when London was bombed on 7 July 2005. Whether this attack was a direct consequence of the British presence in southern Iraq remains contested. Despite winning the May General Election, the government lost more than a hundred seats, almost certainly as a consequence of the unpopularity of Iraq. Grieving father Reg Keys stood as a candidate in the Prime Minister's Sedgefield constituency. Violence continued to escalate in southern Iraq, but British troop numbers were cut. In contrast, in terms of manpower or money, Washington did not shirk its responsibilities. Three years after the invasion, 120,000 US service personnel remained in Iraq, compared with 7,200 British personnel.[84] General David Petraeus, who arrived in Iraq with 230 helicopters in his division, would remind one British MND commander about his mere fourteen.[85] According to one analysis, the war would end up costing American taxpayers an estimated 3 trillion dollars.[86] The United States would continue to take heavy casualties. Conversely, back in London, instead of focusing on Iraq, the government's attention began to shift towards an expanded NATO mission in Afghanistan, making a drawdown in Basra imperative. The Army was not organised and resourced to fight two significant and extended campaigns simultaneously.

Progress to an Iraq run by Iraqis was far from smooth. The country was sovereign from June 2004, when the shambolic CPA ceded its authority and handed power back to an Iraqi interim government. The date of the handover had to be brought forward because of security concerns. In March 2005, as the first step towards a new constitution, the Transitional National Assembly met and in December a general election was held. The election result, however, was inclusive and a compromise candidate, Nouri al-Maliki, became prime minister in May 2006. At a provincial level, Britain sought to hand power back under the Provincial Iraqi Control (PIC) policy but nevertheless was warned by the US against a 'rush to failure'. Ever-deteriorating security meant that the United States would not give a date for any further withdrawal of forces: without its doing so, Britain could not. In February 2006, following the bombing of the Great Mosque at Samarra, a fresh wave of anarchy broke out in

Iraq. Prime Minister Maliki declared a state of emergency. Despite the less-than-ideal conditions, Britain handed over Muthanna province to Iraqi control, followed by Dhi Qar in September. With one eye firmly on the new operation in Afghanistan, it suited the British government to continue to pursue the original US-driven PIC policy and reduce its footprint in Iraq.

By 2006, all was far from well in Basra, however. Various Shia political groups, backed by their armed militias, were struggling for power and a share of the oil wealth. In a damning report by UNHCR, Basra was described as a 'flashpoint for violence', with clashes between the local security forces and the militias.[87] A dismal picture was painted of a city of criminal gangs, suicide bombers, kidnappings and assassinations, where Islamist zealotry was on the march and women were retreating from the public space. Mahdi Army supporters visited hospitals and told male doctors not to treat female patients.[88] Water and electricity supplies were far from guaranteed. Unemployment stood at 60 per cent. May 2006 was the deadliest month for the British since Operation Telic began. Among the casualties were five service personnel, killed when their Lynx helicopter was shot down, and four soldiers killed by roadside bombs. In June, Prime Minister Maliki imposed a state of emergency in Basra city, introducing curfews. As one British commander later identified, a cycle of insecurity was emerging: 'No security meant no reconstruction and development, it meant a loss of consent, the militia filled the gap and, effectively, the militia controlled the city.'[89]

Security Sector Reform, one half of London's exit strategy, was not going to plan. Local police numbers had risen from 3,500 in 2003 to 14,000 by 2006, but many police personnel were either insurgents themselves or insurgent supporters.[90] In September 2005, two SAS soldiers on a surveillance mission in connection with insurgent infiltration were captured by Iraqi security forces and taken to Basra's Jamiat police station. Pictures of the pair were broadcast, angering local people who surrounded the compound. Concerned that two men might be summarily executed, a British Quick Response Force was dispatched. Outside the police station soldiers came under attack from petrol bombs, while inside senior officers attempted unsuccessfully to negotiate the men's release. When the pair were later taken to a nearby villa, a decoy attack was ordered on the police compound.

As walls and cars were crushed by armoured vehicles, the men were rescued by an SAS team. Reluctant to reveal any problems within the Iraqi police, permission for the rescue attempt was, it is alleged, initially refused by PJHQ in Northwood and the MoD. General Sir Mike Jackson later made clear which side he was on, describing the rescue operation as brave and necessary: 'The British Army looks after its own. Underline that three times.'[91]

Following the incident, Basra's governor and governing council suspended cooperation with the British in February 2006 for three months. Bomb disposal expert Kevin Ivison said the police were 'corrupt, notoriously unreliable and had been accomplices in more than one British fatality'.[92] British soldiers taking part in an operation against a local arms dealer in Amarah in December discovered that it was little more than a stunt to boost the image of the local police – who had tipped him off anyway.[93] Divisional commander Major General Richard Shirreff, who arrived in Basra in July 2006, considered the Iraqi police Serious Crimes Unit little more than a death squad, 'intimidating, murdering, kidnapping ordinary Basrawis', and as bad as the rival militias.[94]

Meanwhile, unsung and unthanked, soldiers got on with the job. The sackfuls of mail that arrived from the public after a 'lonely soldier' ad appeared in *Take a Break* magazine were gratefully received, not least because it showed that they were not entirely forgotten. A visit by members of the House of Commons Defence Select Committee shone a light on the soldiers' plight, including the 60 degree temperatures in the back of Warriors, the inadequacy of pay and allowances, and the frequent breakdown of the air bridge between Iraq and home that ate into their leave. The Committee was obviously sceptical about official briefings: 'The MoD's confidence that the UK Armed Forces are not overstretched contrasts with what we heard from Service personnel on the ground.'[95]

Operation Sinbad attempted to reclaim control of Basra. Shirreff was determined that 'the British Army was not going to lose its name in Iraq',[96] although Afghanistan had already become the British main effort. Beginning in late October 2006, Sinbad involved British and Iraqi security forces delivering consecutive three-day-long security 'pulses' in each of Basra's fifteen districts, with lockdowns, checkpoints and patrols: in parallel, community improvements such as drainage ditch repairs were undertaken. Local leaders were consulted about where $80 million of US – not British – aid money should be spent, underlining the importance of money as an additional 'weapons system' in complex stabilisation operations.[97] On 25 December, a few days before the execution of Saddam Hussein, the Jamiat police station was destroyed. The militiamen hit back, attacking Basra Palace with rockets and mortars. The base came under fire 1,200 times between September 2006 and May 2007, making it one of the most besieged targets in Iraq. Despite Sinbad – dubbed 'Spinbad' by the cynics – and the best efforts of soldiers on the ground – described as the 'Lions of Basra' by one local paper, because of the bravery with which they fought pitched battles against the militias – there were limits to what such a small force could usefully achieve. Sinbad's final pulses were undertaken by Iraqis.

Operation Zenith was drawn up to hand all of the British bases over to the Iraqi security forces. By January 2007, 85–90 per cent of all attacks in Basra were against the British forces rather than against local people.[98] Consequently, it appeared sensible to transfer day-to-day responsibility for security to the Iraqi security forces' 10th Division, although Britain, in its 'overwatch' role, would remain in overall charge. The remaining base, Basra Palace, was ceded in September 2007 and British forces were transferred to the airport. In addition, following talks, a series of agreements – seen by some officers as Faustian – were made with elements within the militias. In December, control of Basra would be handed to the Iraqis under the Provincial Iraqi Control policy. That month, a BBC Newsnight poll found that 86 per cent of local people thought that the British had been a negative influence on Basra since 2003.[99] By May 2008, British troop numbers would fall to 4,100. Coming to power in June 2007, Gordon Brown had little appetite for 'Blair's Wars'.

As the British were switching their attention to Afghanistan in what some perceived as retreat, Washington had announced a surge of 20,000 more troops. It coincided with the adoption of a new COIN (counter-insurgency) doctrine by the US military. The surge allowed the Americans to train significant numbers of Iraqis. In addition, the Sunnis woke up to the danger of foreign jihadists and began to turn their fire on them. This so-called Sunni Awakening helped alter the course of the conflict.

The British withdrawal to Basra airport, while strategically logical, presented tactical problems. With no boots on the ground, intelligence was lost and the militias were given the run of the city, including taking control of the port of Umm Qasr. The estimated $30,000 a day they raised from levies on truck drivers financed the Sadrist insurgency across Iraq, much to the dismay of the Americans. In 2008, Prime Minister Maliki took personal charge to impose order on Basra in Operation Charge of the Knights. Launched unexpectedly on 28 March, for a few days it appeared Maliki and his forces might be defeated, 'in what was the first major Iraqi security initiative since the 2003 invasion'.[100] The arrival of the experienced 1st Iraqi Division with their embedded Military Transition Team (MiTTs) from the US Marine Corps immediately reinforced the military effort and turned the tables. In addition, the coalition's corps forward headquarters switched from Mosul to Basra, bringing with it armed Predator drones and attack helicopters. The unfortunate media portrayal was one of the Americans coming to the aid of the Brits in Basra. One of the British authors of the operational plan, Colonel Richard Iron, argued that this perception is wrong: 'It was always a joint UK–US effort to support the Iraqis who actually did the fighting.'[101] By 2 April, the city was back under Iraqi government control and a cease-fire declared. It bolstered Maliki's position as prime minister and showed that security was back in the hands of the Iraqis.

In 2004, the Defence White Paper *Delivering Security in a Changing World* envisaged that Britain would be regularly engaged in stabilisation and post-conflict efforts for the foreseeable future. As the Defence Select Committee noted: 'Experience has taught us that, if nation-building exercises, such as that in Iraq, are to succeed, they must have a serious commitment of time, energy, financial resources and political resolve.'[102] In the first few years of the twenty-first century, soldiers showed their commitment: 197 died in Iraq and many more suffered life-changing injuries before the last British soldiers withdrew in July 2009. British soldiers would continue to do their duty when they were sent back to southern Afghanistan in 2006.

NINE

SERVICE, SACRIFICE AND PUBLIC SUPPORT

Operation Banner in Northern Ireland Ends,
Afghanistan 2006–10, the Military Covenant

On 14 July 2009, the human cost of the war in Afghanistan was literally and metaphorically brought home. Eight soldiers had been killed in twenty-four hours in Helmand province. They were flown home to RAF Lyneham in Wiltshire and then driven to Oxford, their route taking them through the small market town of Wootton Bassett. There, an informal ceremony had spontaneously grown up, with townsfolk and soldiers' families and friends lining the high street as the flag-draped coffins were driven past on their melancholy journey. The procession of hearses that mid-July afternoon was filmed by news teams; later, their reports led the bulletins. Having slipped from the headlines, Afghanistan once again came to the attention of the British public.

By the summer of 2009, British troops had been in Afghanistan for more than three years, as part of an expanded NATO mission. In Iraq, Operation Telic was drawing to a close. However, the two campaigns had overlapped dangerously, putting the Army and its soldiers under huge pressure. Eleven years earlier, the Strategic Defence Review had envisaged the possibility of two medium-sized campaigns of limited duration and the Armed Forces had been shaped accordingly. The Army was neither structured, manned, equipped nor resourced for two concurrent missions on the scale or duration of Iraq and Afghanistan. Soldiers were paying the price for a government which had endorsed an ambitious defence policy back in 1997/8, but failed to fund that policy fully. Public and parliamentary discussion of the cost pressures on the Army all contributed to the impression that the Labour governments of Tony Blair and Gordon Brown, while prepared to deploy the military on operations, did not understand the importance of providing sufficiently for the equipment and welfare needs of the individual soldiers and their families. The government found itself on the wrong side of public opinion, which demanded soldiers be properly looked after.

Public mood had changed. Previous indifference had given way to unprecedented support. People may have disapproved of the intervention in Iraq more than ever, and be mystified about why soldiers were being sent to Afghanistan, but they appreciated the service and sacrifice of 'our boys' – and our girls. Almost overnight, it seemed, they began spontaneously to demonstrate this support, whether turning out at homecoming parades or raising funds for military charities, including the newly founded Help for Heroes. Opinion polls found that the Armed Forces were among the most respected of all institutions. Such backing meant that the government could no longer ignore the welfare of soldiers – or soldiers' families. From 2007, this support was put in the context of the Military Covenant. At its simplest, the Covenant is an informal understanding: in exchange for their military service, soldiers will be supported by their chain of command and by the nation, in whose name they act. Many considered the Covenant had become dangerously out of balance because of the demands of war-fighting on two fronts.

This chapter looks at the campaign in Afghanistan that brought the Army to the brink, but also sparked an outpouring of goodwill among the general public towards the Armed Forces. In June 2007, Blair's wars became Gordon Brown's responsibility after he became Prime Minister. By then, the surge of US troops in Iraq, along with the US military's formal recognition and adoption of counter-insurgency, was showing the first signs of paying off, with Baghdad and its surrounding provinces gradually becoming more stable. In US military circles, less was heard about the Global War on Terrorism and more about the Long War. It was indeed long to a war-weary British public, which, however, began to show its backing for soldiers. This change in public mood is examined, together with the concept of the Military Covenant. The Army itself was becoming ever smaller following yet another shake-up. In Northern Ireland, a long episode in the Army's history came to an end with the conclusion of Operation Banner.

Policy

The Defence White Papers produced during the Blair government's second term have, with hindsight, an air of unreality about them. *The Strategic Defence Review: A New Chapter*, dated July 2002, does not anticipate any military action on the scale of Iraq, despite the preparations which were already underway behind the scenes. Published in December 2003, *Delivering Security in a Changing World* acknowledges the deployment of 46,000 personnel to the Gulf, but omits any comment or detail about the impact on the Armed Forces of delivering security in the very changed world of Iraq. Neither paper was designed to be the wholesale examination of defence policy achieved by the groundbreaking 1998 Strategic Defence Review. Its emphasis on expeditionary warfare had been vindicated by the operations in Kosovo, Sierra Leone, East Timor, Macedonia and Afghanistan, which had demonstrated the ability of the Armed Forces to be deployed and sustained across the world.

The *New Chapter* followed a re-examination of existing defence strategies in the wake of the 11 September attacks, which had all too graphically highlighted the impact of 'asymmetric action to achieve strategic effect'. Or, in simpler terms, how an act of terrorism can change everything. The government appeared cautious about the Global War on Terrorism, instead referring to 'the overall goal of eliminating terrorism as a force for change in international affairs'.[1] It was prepared to deploy service personnel overseas to achieve this, not least because 'it is much better to engage our enemies in their backyard than in ours, at a time and place of our choosing and not theirs'. Future defence spending seemed slanted towards the more cloak-and-dagger stuff of hunting down terrorists: emphasis was placed on Special Forces' capabilities, drones, intelligence-gathering and night operations, as well as 'improved mobility and fire power'.[2] Ships, submarines and fast jets were hardly mentioned, apart from in the context of home capability. Eight months before the deployment to Iraq, the paper accepted that many service personnel were already working at, near or beyond the boundaries of what had been planned four years earlier in the SDR.[3] Given this, it seems bizarre that a year later the government chose to make further cuts to defence.

The 2003 *Delivering Security in a Changing World* White Paper brought more change for the Army. Its overarching conclusion was that, 'It is highly likely that the Armed Forces will, in future, be more frequently employed on peace support and counter-terrorist operations where the focus will be on conflict prevention and stabilization, rather than the defeat of opposing forces.'[4] Defence was looked at through a counter-terrorism prism: 'There are currently no major conventional military threats to the UK or NATO'; the Armed Forces must be able to 'protect our citizens at home and counter international terrorism across the globe'.[5] Defence policy would be planned to support three concurrent operations, one of which would be a peace support operation. Ambitions, compared to 1998, became relatively modest, with operations on the small and medium scale envisaged, as, for example, in Macedonia (2001) and Afghanistan (2002). 'Intervention against state adversaries' would only be undertaken 'if the US are engaged': retaining influence necessitated interoperability with the American military.[6] Emphasis was placed on technology and network-enabled capability (NEC), but the White Paper was light on detail about funding, force structures and procurement. Former CDS Lord Guthrie said it was full of 'buzzwords and platitudes',[7] but the war-fighting capability of the Army was in effect reduced, with the number of armoured and mechanised brigades being cut from six to five, with the sixth reduced to a light brigade which could not be deployed as a whole. However, details about the changes to the Army were not fully spelt out, which was unsettling for both soldiers and their families.

In July 2004 *Future Capabilities* gave more details about how the Armed Forces were to be restructured. The war-fighting core of the Army of the future would comprise two heavy armoured brigades and three medium-weight brigades centred on medium-weight Future Rapid Effects Systems (FRES) vehicles which were theoretically in the pipeline. The Apache helicopter, Javelin missiles and Watchkeeper drones would be in this new model army's arsenal. With the phasing out of the Infantry Arms Plot – the system which aimed to rotate most battalions' location and role every two to four years

– the Army would become far more static. The number of regular battalions would be reduced from forty to thirty-six, with one of the cuts coming from the six Scottish regiments. Manpower would be cut by 1,500, bringing the Army's strength down to 102,000, a long way from the manning target of 108,500. Details about which battalions were to be disbanded or amalgamated were left to the Army Board. The government's opponents, for whom *Future Capabilities* was nothing more than an opportunity for more cuts to the Armed Forces, accused it of cutting the defence budget in real terms by almost 6.5 per cent, producing an equipment overspend of £1 billion a year and issuing post-dated cheques.[8]

The twenty-first century Army would be completely restructured, organised into new, large multi-battalion regiments such as the Mercian and Yorkshire Regiments and later the Rifles. This subsuming – or, as many saw it, axing – of historic regiments inevitably provoked dismay and anger. One Labour MP pointed out that in their 300-year history, the Staffords had seen off the French, Germans, Americans, Bolsheviks, Burmese, Zulus and assorted African and Indian armies, but might be defeated by his own government.[9] During the months before the Army Board's conclusions were announced in December 2004, the usual lobbying, jostling and jockeying ensued. Across Cumbria, tens of thousands of people signed petitions in support of the King's Own Royal Border Regiment. North of the border, the King's Own Scottish Borderers were to be merged with the oldest British infantry regiment, the Royal Scots, to become part of the new Royal Regiment of Scotland. The loss of the Black Watch, who had just returned from fighting alongside the Americans in Iraq, as an independent regiment was denounced as a 'massive betrayal'.[10] In an attempt to retain what the Army has always regarded as the 'golden thread' of history, a decision was taken that as far as possible historic names would be retained. The Green Howards, for example, who, along with the Duke of Wellington's Regiment and the Prince of Wales's Own Regiment, would form part of the new Yorkshire Regiment, would in future be known as 2nd Battalion The Yorkshire Regiment (Green Howards). Regimental traditions and 'accoutrements' were also to be preserved as best they could. Decisions like this reflected the dilemma that the Army has always faced – to retain the best of the past while embracing the future.

Defence reviews reflect assumptions about future commitments; however, it is only with hindsight that the cuts imposed on the Army seem premature. In June 2004, NATO had committed itself to expanding its mission in Afghanistan, in what was expected to be a medium-scale stabilisation effort. The British government was clearly optimistic about progress in Iraq, which that year had returned to sovereignty. Tony Blair seemed delighted by the news: it can be inferred that he considered the intervention vindicated and that freedom would indeed reign in Iraq, as President Bush exhorted.[11] Another factor influencing the Army's restructuring was the final drawdown in Northern Ireland.

Northern Ireland

On 31 July 2007, after thirty-eight years Operation Banner came to an end. Given the difficulties that soldiers were experiencing in Iraq and Afghanistan at the time, there were many lessons to be learned from what turned out to be a successful counter-insurgency operation. Northern Ireland highlighted that, ultimately, success in such operations is as much a matter of political as of military will. Governments must be prepared to have the 'strategic patience' to stick with a campaign and the ability to do so even if public opinion is against them. In an era of 24-hour news, soundbites and spin, this is far from easy. From 1975 when regular surveys of public opinion began, almost two-thirds of people in mainland Britain were in favour of the withdrawal of British troops from the province; on the twentieth anniversary of the Troubles, 77 per cent of those polled wanted the soldiers to leave.[12] Ministers like the political uplift that goes with a short, sharp, successful military operation, which ideally rights a simple wrong. The 1991 Gulf War was perhaps a politicians' ideal template for a twenty-first century conflict; the Troubles were not. They are, however, far more typical of what soldiers are likely to confront in the future.

Operation Banner was the longest campaign in modern British military history. In all, some 300,000 soldiers took part in it; 763 British servicemen were killed, among them 197 members of the Ulster Defence Regiment, 155 of them off-duty.[13] On the eve of its formal conclusion, the last senior commander, Lieutenant General Sir Nicholas Parker, said: 'What I believe the military have done here is make a significant contribution to security in Northern Ireland that has allowed other people to make the difference through politics, social programmes and economics.'[14] With this emphasis on social development, he was echoing the doyen of counter-insurgency doctrine, General Sir Frank Kitson, who suggested that there is 'no such thing as a purely military solution because insurgency is not primarily a military activity'.[15] The military task is to create the appropriate security conditions for civilian agencies to tackle the political, social and economic causes that fuel the radical discontent. As a result, somewhat paradoxically, military 'victory' is not the ultimate objective. While in the short term insurgents can be defeated militarily, in the long term an insurgency can only be defeated by tackling its root causes. On 31 July, the end of Banner was marked as little more than a bureaucratic formality: the BBC noted that no bugles sounded at the remaining Army bases and there was no symbolic lowering of flags. 'Nothing in short that smacks of withdrawal or departure or redeployment.'[16] Indeed, of a significant military success, patiently achieved over nearly four decades.

Operation Banner highlighted how military operations can evolve and that the Army needs to respond appropriately. It also reflected changes within the Army: as soldiers left for Belfast and Londonderry in 1969, pay and allowances were being revised, with 'comparability' introduced, along with operational pay. Force protection became a priority; body armour was introduced and then modified. Medical care improved, with the vast majority of cases being treated within the crucial 'golden hour' after a soldier was wounded. Troops had been sent to Northern Ireland to provide aid to the civil authorities. From about 1971 they were confronted by an insurgency; by 1976 and the era of police primacy over security, they were conducting an intelligence-led counter-terrorism operation. Above all, their decades-long presence in Northern Ireland symbolised the British government's strategic commitment to the province. Was it really as British as Finchley, as Margaret Thatcher declared? The province was, as has been observed, perhaps the only part of the world riven by decades of violent sectarianism where Marks & Spencer stayed open throughout. However, the death toll provides a grim snapshot of the Troubles. More than 3,300 people were killed: 2,148 at the hands of Republican terrorists; 1,071 by loyalist terrorists. An estimated 131 terrorists were killed, 11 of them loyalists. A further 170 deaths are ascribed to the security forces.[17] It is surely unlikely that Mrs Thatcher would have tolerated this level of violence in her leafy north London constituency or indeed put up with troops on its streets for more than a third of a century.

The formal end of Operation Banner came nine years after the 1998 Good Friday Agreement, reflecting the choppy nature of the peace process. 'In the end, the GFA was an agreement to disagree.'[18] A key player in the negotiations, Prime Minister Blair's Chief of Staff, Jonathan Powell, suggested that the Unionists still wanted to be a part of the United Kingdom while the Republicans still wanted to be part of a united Ireland: 'They just agreed to carry on the conflict by political means rather than armed force.'[19] With almost half of the peace deals that supposedly conclude intra-state conflicts breaking down, the process was not inevitable. The Republicans considered that the Unionists would never share power with the Catholics, while the Unionists were convinced that the Republicans would never give up their weapons.[20] The IRA's prevarication over weapons decommissioning did little to promote trust between the two sides. When it eventually started, decommissioning followed a model developed in the wake of the conflicts in Bosnia and Kosovo. Disagreements about 'On-the-Runs' – the former terrorist suspects who had fled the province – the reform of the RUC and the creation of the Police Service of Northern Ireland, the Northern Bank robbery of December 2004 and the murder in January 2005 of Robert McCartney, allegedly by the Provisional IRA, also threatened the peace process. Despite the setbacks, after the Agreement, troop numbers steadily declined: between 1997 and 2005 they almost halved, coming down from 11,500 to 5,800, which was about the size of the peacetime garrison before 1969. Much of the province's military infrastructure – watchtowers, permanent checkpoints and barracks – was gradually dismantled. Nevertheless, in 2005 Army bomb disposal experts were still clearing about thirty devices a month.

As Operation Banner concluded, an inquiry into one of its most controversial episodes continued: the Saville Inquiry into Bloody Sunday, which would not report until 2010 (see chapter 10). In its official review of the campaign, the Army concedes that internment and the use of deep interrogation techniques was wrong.

Before internment 'there was very little actionable intelligence': it yielded 'valuable intelligence and short-term tactical advantage'. However, 'put simply and with the benefit of hindsight, it was a major mistake'.[21] As he negotiated with both sides to bring about the Good Friday Agreement, Powell observed that the Republicans kept referring back to Bloody Sunday, the Castlereagh detention centre, internment, unemployment, the lack of housing and the civil rights movement, 'a combination of myth and actual realities about contemporary life and the quite recent past'. While both sides wanted to focus on 'past unfairnesses, deaths, murders and mistreatment', Powell saw his job as trying to get them to focus on the future.

Operation Banner began twenty years before the formal introduction of a modern Military Doctrine. The Army now sees it as 'a campaign without a campaign plan' according to *Operation Banner*, the Army's review of the campaign issued in July 2006. In addition, there was little evidence of a strategic vision and no long-term plan – 'muddling through', as more than one junior officer was exhorted to do, was no substitute for a plan. Stormont and the Northern Ireland Office, the MoD and the RUC were 'poorly coordinated' and 'there was no single authority in overall charge of the direction of the campaign'.[22] The UDR was crucial, providing 'a level of continuity and local knowledge not achievable by resident battalions'.[23] For those planning the 2006 deployment to Afghanistan, *Operation Banner* provided some useful insights. Perhaps within the Army more heed should have been paid to the section which talked about the initial period of about three months after the arrival of a military force in a peace support or peace enforcement operation. 'The term "honeymoon period" is a misnomer. *It is not a honeymoon. It is the most important phase of the campaign*' – as British soldiers in Afghanistan were finding out.[24]

Afghanistan (2006–10)

From March 2003, as the British Army was focused on Iraq, the operations in Afghanistan were almost forgotten. After the handover of ISAF command to Turkey in June 2002, a few hundred British soldiers had stayed on, the majority as part of a Provisional Reconstruction Team (PRT), based in the northern city of Mazar-i-Sharif. In addition, a contingent of Americans remained assigned to the counter-terrorism-oriented Operation Enduring Freedom. In August 2003, under a UN mandate, NATO took formal command of ISAF. It could be argued that, with the Cold War long over, the organisation had too much time on its hands and was seeking out 'out-of-area' operations such as Afghanistan to justify its continuing existence.

As Iraq approached near anarchy and became the crucible of jihadist terrorism, Afghanistan turned into yesterday's news. For the leadership in the United States – whose military was averse to nation-building and increasingly facing a quagmire in Iraq – the mission in Afghanistan was more or less accomplished, however imperfectly. The Taliban had been ousted, Hamid Karzai became the first demo-cratically elected leader in October 2004 and Osama bin Laden had vanished – along with the country's former leader, Mullah Omar. While fragile, the security situation appeared stable enough. Questions might remain about how far the government's writ actually extended beyond Kabul, but Afghanistan was no longer a rogue state providing a safe haven to terrorists bent on destroying the West. The country remained one of the poorest and least developed in the world, with a legacy of more than two decades of conflict; however, the Taliban were dormant, with many having gone over the border to Pakistan.

From the spring of 2006, British soldiers found themselves back in Afghanistan. Controversy will continue to dog this mission, code-named Operation Herrick. Various inquiries, including Chilcot and the Defence Select Committee, sought to get definitive answers to questions raised in connection with it. The major puzzle was why, given the deteriorating security situation in Iraq, it was deemed a good idea for British personnel to be sent back to Afghanistan in large numbers. As Lawrence Freedman, one of the Chilcot examiners, observed, surely someone must have said, 'Please wait, we really can't do this until we are absolutely sure that we can get out of Iraq.'[25] One theory – that the Army pressurised the government into signing off on Operation Herrick to make up for a less-than-glorious effort in Iraq – is wrong. As Lieutenant Colonel Stuart Tootal of 3rd Battal-ion Parachute Regiment, part of 16th Air Assault Brigade, observed: 'The military does not decide government policy. You're according the Army a level of influence they haven't had since the Parliament of 1659.'[26]

The most likely explanation is that London wanted to reinforce its credentials with Washington as a dependable ally. In spring 2004, with security deteriorating in Baghdad, and parts of the north and west of Iraq looking increasingly fragile, the US administration had invited Britain to consider taking on responsibility for all nine Shia provinces in the relatively stable south of the country, freeing up US troops to operate further north. Not wanting to get further embroiled in Iraq, London declined. However, at the Istanbul NATO conference, on 29 June – the day after the formal announcement that the occupation of Iraq by coalition forces had ended, Prime Minister Blair pledged that Britain would be taking the lead in a new operation in the south of Afghanistan. The junior partner was standing shoulder to shoulder once again with its senior partner. In between the 2004 commitment to send British forces to Afghanistan and their deployment in 2006, Iraq descended into near civil war. Nevertheless, planning for Afghanistan proceeded on the assumption that by 2006 the Armed Forces would be, as one MP described, 'sweeping up in Iraq with a couple of guys left behind to turn the lights off'.[27]

The Joint UK Plan for Helmand set out the British mission in Afghanistan. Embedded with 16 Air Assault Brigade in 2008, journalist Sam Kiley observed that soldiers like clarity: 'an easily understood mission statement, a clear set of orders and a simple plan'.[28] A cross-government civilian–military effort, involving the MoD, the Foreign Office and DfID, the Plan was overseen by the Cabinet Office and developed in 2005. The expectation was that Helmand, one of thirty-four provinces in Afghanistan, would be transformed by the British mission, expected to last three years. Defence Secretary John Reid told MPs that soldiers were being deployed to 'support the government of Afghanistan, facilitate reconstruction and development, improve security and counter the narcotics trade'.[29] To fulfil this ambitious wish list, they would be concentrated in central Helmand, bolstering security so that civilians, whether from DfID or non-government agencies, could build up local infrastructure. After the first 'lozenge of security' was established in an area that included Camp Bastion, Gereshk and the provincial capital Lashkar Gah and reconstruction was underway, focus would shift to the next area.[30] The plan was not too different from Briggs and Templer's ink-spot strategy in Malaya. On the eve of the troops' departure for Afghanistan,

Reid infamously painted an upbeat picture of the mission. His words that troops would leave without firing a shot were, in fact, misquoted; he actually said that they would be perfectly happy to leave without firing a shot. During its six-month tour of duty from April until October 2006, Stuart Tootal's 3 Para Battlegroup fired more than 479,000 rounds of ammunition.

The Helmand Plan was redundant before all the 3,300-strong task force had even arrived in Afghanistan. In May 2006, the province's governor, Mohammed Daoud, appealed to the commander of 16 Air Assault Brigade, Brigadier Ed Butler, for help to retain control of the north of Helmand. Claiming it was about to be over-run by the Taliban, he warned Butler: 'If the black flag of Mullah Omar flies over any of the district centres, you may as well go home because we'll have lost our authority to govern in Helmand, and if we lose our authority to govern and our ability to govern, then that will threaten the south. Kandahar will be next. We'll lose the south before you've even started. What are you going to do about it?'[31] Pressure to move north also came from the Afghan president, Hamid Karzai. In redeploying his forces, Butler did not act in isolation but was confident that he had cleared the action up his chain of command. Soldiers were sent to the district centres to uphold the authority of the Kabul government. Whether at Sangin, Musa Qala, or Now Zad, they found themselves fighting for their lives in desperate fire fights and beating back wave after wave of attacks from the Taliban.

In August 2006, soldiers' helmet-cam footage began to appear on TV news bulletins in Britain, circumventing a MoD media blackout. Having been sold a stabilisation and reconstruction mission, the public were shocked by the images they saw. John Reid later argued that the move north changed the strategic nature of the mission, while the Defence Committee stated that the Cabinet in London should have authorised the shift. Unjust criticism was meted out to the high-flying Butler, who had already demonstrated the potential to go towards the very top of the Army. However, the brigadier was following the logic of the overarching strategic goal: British forces had been sent to Afghanistan explicitly to extend the Karzai government's authority and to shore up security.

Although the move north tore up the Helmand Plan, it was a flawed document from the outset. It was based on intelligence that had reported a generally benign situation on the ground. Butler had correctly anticipated the hostility the British presence would provoke and, before he had even left for Afghanistan, urged that more resources be assigned to the mission: 'We used to say that there would be a reaction to our size 12 boots going into Helmand province, whether from the Taliban, from the opiate dealers or from the warlords, because we were threatening their very existence.'[32]

With high mountains and deserts, Helmand is roughly the size of Wales. The Helmand river cuts through the middle of the province, providing a verdant belt of land that can be farmed, as well as feeding a network of canals and irrigation ditches that had been dug by the Americans in the 1950s and 1960s. They are not just reminders of more stable and prosperous times but, like the shells of burnt-out Soviet tanks, evidence of the numerous attempts by outsiders, benign or not, to reshape Afghanistan. In a culture where literacy is low, folk memory is powerful. Engrained in local legend are the three Afghan wars that the British had previously fought. The first saw the evacuation of the British garrison at Kabul in 1842: of the 16,000 soldiers and camp followers who left, only one European reached safety; the second saw the Battle of Maiwand (1880) – in what is today's Helmand province – in which the British, despite an heroic last stand by the 66th (Berkshire) Regiment of Foot, were routed; the third recognised Afghanistan's independence and the Durand Line, which theoretically divided the country from the future Pakistan. Although the British were eventually to prevail in all three wars, it was only 'after penalties in extra time' – as Iraq would later be described. The historical resonances of Afghanistan were not lost on some of the British soldiers arriving in twenty-first century Helmand. This was the ground their predecessors may have known:

> When you're wounded and left on Afghanistan's plains,
> And the women come out to cut up what remains,
> Jest roll to your rifle and blow out your brains
> An' go to your Gawd like a soldier.

Kipling would surely have thought it unlikely that British soldiers would ever be in Afghanistan without firing a shot, especially as some locals saw their arrival as a chance to settle old scores.

As British forces began to arrive in the spring of 2006, the military situation on the ground in southern Afghanistan was confused, with the different multinational forces pursuing different objectives. About 20,400 US troops were in the country as part of Operation Enduring Freedom, reflecting the continuation of the Global War on Terrorism.[33] Operating in the east of the country, this mission was oriented towards the war-fighting end of the military spectrum. Separately, as part of the expanded NATO–ISAF mission to extend government control over Afghanistan, different countries had been assigned to lead the effort in different provinces: the British were in Helmand, the Canadians in Kandahar and the Dutch in Uruzgan. Forces in these various provinces were multinational: for example, the British would be working with personnel from Denmark, Estonia and the Czech Republic. Each country's forces had their own Rules of Engagement: Germany remained in the relatively peaceful north of Afghanistan, only undertaking peacekeeping, working at the opposite end of the military spectrum from the United States. While the NATO–ISAF forces were focused, at least in theory, on reconstruction, the US saw their mission as a combat operation. The two approaches would clash. In addition, the command structure was tangled. From May 2006, the NATO–ISAF mission was led from Kabul by the British Headquarters, Allied Rapid Reaction Corps, under the command of Lieutenant General Sir David Richards, formerly commander of the British mission in Sierra Leone. However, it was not until 31 July that the United States transferred formal control of the south to NATO–ISAF. Pursuing their separate objectives and taking different approaches, the two missions in Afghanistan would continue to work in parallel, but sometimes at odds. Richards had to reconcile the Americans' 'instinctively muscular approach with NATO's greater emphasis on reconstruction and development'.[34]

The NATO–ISAF initiative built on international reconstruction efforts that had been underway in Afghanistan since 2002. The 'five pillars' strategy had divided up security and governance tasks between difference nations. The United States oversaw rebuilding the Afghan National Army, while Italy oversaw the judicial system. With Britain taking the lead in combating the drugs trade in Afghanistan, it was logical that British forces should be sent to Helmand to attempt to deal with the problem at source. Helmand's poppy crop not only contributed to more than half the global supply of heroin, including an estimated 90 per cent of the drug sold in Britain, but provided an income for many local people. Soldiers found themselves in the geographic centre of the narcotics trade, with all its endemic corruption, criminality and turf wars, and also on the frontline of the global war on drugs. In early 2006, Governor Daoud's predecessor was sacked, having been caught with 9 tonnes of opium. Eradicating the poppy which, along with marijuana, grew like a weed in Helmand, would destroy local livelihoods. Before he arrived in Helmand, one officer was told to watch *The Sopranos* to get some idea about what to expect.

Camp Bastion symbolised the changing nature of the British mission. Growing from a few tents to an area the size of Reading, it came to be likened to 'Aldershot with Gatwick stuck on the side'.[35] This giant fortress stood in the middle of the Dasht-e Margo or Desert of Death, itself a stark contrast to the verdant land around the Helmand river. There, the irrigation channels allowed crops to be grown, including eight-foot-high maize, pomegranates, tomatoes, limes and the ubiquitous poppy. As Richards described, this was 'perfect defensive country – orchards, irrigation ditches, high walls, small villages'.[36] Local buildings had three-foot-thick walls made of concrete-like compacted mud and stone.[37] Sand as fine as talcum powder coated every surface and the dust thrown up by logistics vehicles was visible twenty-five miles away. Temperatures plummeted to below freezing at night but exceeded 45 degrees during the day; the metal of the armoured vehicles could burn like a hot iron.

The arrival of British forces in Helmand stirred up a hornets' nest of resistance and turned the province into a war zone. In May 2006, General Richards noted: 'Effective enemy attacks, lots of casualties and not much on the upside. We have a war on our hands, whatever our reluctant politicians like to think, and they'd better start giving us the tools, rules and resources required to win it.'[38] Matters were further complicated by a change of Defence Secretary in May 2006, with Des Browne replacing John Reid, as well as a change at the top of the Armed Forces, with former jet pilot Air Chief Marshal Sir Graham 'Jock' Stirrup becoming Chief of the Defence Staff.

Deployed north, British soldiers were soon fighting for their lives in a series of Rorke's Drift-type battles. Isolated enclaves were the sites of ferocious fighting against a determined enemy. For the tiny contingents of Gurkhas and Fusiliers battling to hold off a Taliban onslaught on their compound at Now Zad – renamed Apocalypse Now Zad – the difference between political posturing from the safety of the House of Commons and military reality on the ground was surely stark.[39] Stuck for 107 days, soldiers felt they had been left to rot.[40] In Musa Qala, where 3 Para's Easy Company had relieved a Pathfinder unit and a Danish contingent, Tootal's 'Toms' along with Rangers from the Somme Platoon, 1st Battalion Royal Irish Regiment endured twelve-hour battles defending the District Centre compound, which included a sangar on top of the jail known as the Alamo.[41] The eighty-eight men came under ferocious fire for fifty-six days. In Sangin, soldiers from the Household Cavalry, the Royal Irish and the Paras came close to running out of food. A Canadian supply team forced to stay the night was attacked three times with small arms, rocket-propelled grenades and mortars.[42] On 6 September, some soldiers were trapped in an old Russian minefield near Kajaki: Corporal Mark Wright, who was awarded a posthumous George Cross, asked the men stranded with him to tell his uncle that he had been 'a good soldier'.[43] Three men would be killed in action that day, along with eighteen wounded, six of them losing limbs. A few days later, twelve Armed Forces personnel were killed when their Nimrod XV230 crashed near Kandahar, following a fire on board. In 2006, thirty-nine servicemen would lose their lives in Afghanistan. Subsequent inquests and public inquiries would find that some of these deaths were avoidable. Military personnel on the ground were paying a heavy price for those who were only too eager to put troops in harm's way, but who had consistently refused properly to invest in defence.

With all the controversy that has surrounded Operation Herrick, the professionalism of British soldiers has too often been overlooked. A general public which is also becoming increasingly risk averse, sedentary and protected by health and safety legislation will find it hard to understand the sheer exhilaration of combat. Some civilians are prone to see the military as victims. They are wrong. Soldiers are men and women who have chosen a career which they find enormously fulfilling; they are trained for a role, they know the risks and they want to be tested in the most demanding of circumstances. Firing a £70,000 Javelin missile – known to soldiers as a Porsche – beats working in an office, yet it is an expensive way to knock a Taliban fighter off his motorcycle. Patrick Hennessey, a junior officer in the Grenadier Guards who was in the thick of fighting around Patrol Base Inkerman, describes how 'I would probably rather be anywhere else in the world right now than here, but if I was anywhere else in the world I would just want to be back here.'[44] The danger and cama-raderie of war came to be captured by the award-winning 2008–9 documentary series *Ross Kemp in Afghanistan*, which highlighted the tiny details of military life that soldiers take for granted, such as marking their uniforms with their blood group. When the going got tough for 3 Para at Sangin and their supplies ran low, they were reminded that Paras had held the bridge at Arnhem for nine days, having only planned for two.[45] Later in the campaign, a memorial in the town inspired other soldiers. Major Graeme Wearmouth of B Company of the newly formed Royal Scots Borderer battalion observed: 'The daily reminder to do our duty is the cross bearing the names of those who have fallen here before.'[46] Royal Irish Ranger Phil Gillespie, aged nineteen when he returned to Helmand, observed that if he weren't there, 'Who will my mates have on either side of them?'[47]

In a tribal, war-torn region like Afghanistan, the state did not have the monopoly of violence: indeed, beyond Kabul, there was little official state of which to speak. Along with the Afghan National Army were irregular fighters, allied to one of the numerous war-lords, tribal chiefs or local strongmen, such as former Helmand governor Sher Mohammed Akhundzada. Deposed at the insistence of the British, this tribal elder and former mujahideen ended up serving in the Afghan senate. Unable to pay his followers, he encouraged 3,000 of them to join the Taliban.[48] With the ousting of their government in November 2001, the Taliban fighters had simply melted back into their civilian lives, many crossing the porous border into Pakistan. The arrival of the British in Helmand was a call to return to arms. However, although it was a convenient shorthand to call all the enemy as Taliban – or 'Terry', as the soldiers called them – the situation was more nuanced. The British would be confronted by fanati-cal holy warriors as well as local farmers keen to earn $10 a day, and those loyal to rival tribal leaders and drugs lords. Even if Helmand had remained relatively stable, the initial British force of 3,300 personnel was too small to make more than a token contribution to reconstruction. Given that the ratio of troops to population should be about 1:20 for a post-conflict mission on the lines of Kosovo, what Helmand required was a minimum force of 30,000.

Sangin, Marjah, Nad-e Ali … Dusty, sun-bleached towns and villages across Helmand became emblematic of a mission that had spiralled from reconstruction to war-fighting. Too few in number, soldiers became pinned down in these remote compounds and forward operating bases which were uncomfortable anathema to an army whose doctrine favours manoeuvre. Soldiers sometimes found the Afghans, whose security and quality of life they had been deployed to improve, were not to be trusted: in Sangin in September 2006, one interpreter wanted to abandon his unit having overheard the local police chief talking on the telephone about the number of British troops, reaction times and how long it would take for helicopters to arrive.[49] The shortage of helicopters, especially to airlift the wounded, became apparent. All commanders on the ground feared the loss of one of the few available Chinooks. Towards the end of October 2006, when Musa Qala was handed back to the Afghans following a controversial agreement with the local elders, the soldiers present had to leave in unprotected 'jingly trucks'. Four months later, the town was once again under the control of the Taliban. It was then retaken by British forces, acting with soldiers from the Afghan National Army, in December 2007.

The steady increase in force numbers reflected the deteriorating security situation in Helmand. Just days after the original 16th Air Assault Brigade's full force complement for Operation Herrick 4 had arrived in mid-2006, the new Defence Secretary announced that reinforcements would be sent to the province, raising force numbers by a thousand to 4,500. They rose again, up to 6,500 during Herrick 6 led by 12th Mechanised Brigade (2007), then to 7,700 for Herrick 7 during 52nd Infantry Brigade's tour. By the time 16th Air Assault Brigade returned to Helmand in 2008, it numbered some 8,500 British personnel, creeping towards three times the strength of the original force. Even then, with numbers constrained because of Iraq, there were too few soldiers for the task in hand. Brigadier Gordon Messenger of 3rd Commando Brigade, back for Herrick 9

(October 2008–April 2009), later told the Defence Select Committee that 'insufficient resources were being allocated to the challenge in southern Afghanistan'.[50]

To the surprise of many, particularly the Afghans, the numbers of personnel present bore little relation to the numbers actually available on the ground. The British Army's logistic 'tail' has grown successively longer, as its 'teeth' have become relatively fewer. Of Op Herrick 4's 3,300 soldiers, only about 600 could be assigned to combat, such were the manpower demands of supply, transport and medical support. As the mission unfolded, many began to question the wisdom of the six-month rotation. There was a view that there was pressure on commanders to make their mark on the campaign in a very short space of time – to do something 'appropriately military', as one analyst suggested – which might not necessarily accord with the overall objective of bringing security to the province to allow reconstruction and development.[51] However, the objective of winning local hearts and minds became more remote as soldiers increasingly had to call in destructive heavy fire support from the air to resolve tactical problems on the ground. Paradoxically, questions were being asked about whether the war-fighting culture within the British Army was actually counter-productive. The pressure was on to find a more nuanced way forward. The counterpoint view on the length of tours had more to do with the long-term health of the Army. Longer deployed tours might have brought more operational continuity on the ground, but this had to be balanced with the retention of expensively trained manpower, often and unsurprisingly driven by the attitude of the families at home in the garrisons.

In February 2007, during Herrick 5, British forces' fighting spirit was demonstrated. Apache helicopters were central to a perilous mission, when a team of four – three Royal Marines and a Royal Engineer – rescued a fallen comrade. Lance Corporal Matthew Ford had been shot during a raid on Fort Jugroom, a Taliban headquarters near Garmsir. In the mêlée of battle, a miscommunication between the Viking armoured vehicles extracting the men and a mix-up over names led to Corporal Ford being left behind. All British air intelligence was scrambled to find him, including an MR2 Nimrod which reported Taliban reinforcements were swarming up from the Pakistan border. An RAF Desert Hawk drone pilot spotted Ford's figure lying outside the fort's walls. An immediate rescue was imperative, but anyone attempting it would be coming under enemy fire and the only available helicopters were the fearsome gunships – which had no room for passengers. A possible solution was offered by Warrant Officer One Mike Rutherford, a pilot with 9 Regiment Army Air Corps. Taking their positions as best they could on the fuel tanks and Hellfire missiles, four volunteers strapped themselves to the fuse-lages of two Apaches and clung on as the helicopters flew the four miles back towards Jugroom in the dawn light. Under covering fire, the men managed to retrieve Corporal Ford, who had been fatally wounded.[52] A subsequent Board of Inquiry revealed that he had been shot accidentally by one of his own colleagues in the confusion of the battle – a reminder of the pervasive fog of war.

As soldiers battled the Taliban, efforts were also made to progress with reconstruction in Helmand. Rural Afghanistan was socially conservative, a place where few women would be seen outside their homes and those who were, were shrouded by burkhas. A senator in the Afghan Parliament, Heela Achekzai, described how she put herself in voluntary purdah and remained at home and out of sight while living in her husband's village in Uruzgan during the Taliban era, not least because other women judged women harshly for break-ing the engrained social code.[53] If offered by a Western man, medical treatment would often be refused. When asked how many children he had, one elder gave the number of sons: his daughters literally did not count. The burden of cultural awareness expected of soldiers was immense.

Operation Herrick was a nation-building mission. In Kipling's day, the British Army officer corps would have been expected to speak the language of the nation it was trying to build. Few soldiers knew more than a couple of phrases of Pashtu or Dari. Some of the local people spoke Russian, a legacy of the Soviet occupation, like the tens of thousands of mines that had been laid. Indeed, in the early days of Herrick, some Afghans thought the British were Russian. Just as one writer described how the Afghans marvelled at hearing Mozart on his Sony Walkman during the Soviet era, thirty years on local people were intrigued by one officer's iPod with its Girls Aloud video.[54] Soldiers tried to reach out to local people, whether by shopping in the bazaars, setting up walk-in clinics or giving books to a mosque. Carpets, glasses and teapots were bought for *shuras* (consultations) with local elders. Such friendly interaction assumed security existed; in many parts of Helmand, it did not. In the early days, there were instances of well-meaning female DfID staff struggling to make progress with local tribal leaders. Dressed in jeans and T-shirts that hardly met in the middle, it was unsurprising that they found agreements hard to reach – the cultures grated awkwardly. The soldier sahibs of the Raj would have turned in their graves.

Operation Oqab Tsuka, or 'Eagle's Summit', reflected all the demands that can confront the twenty-first-century army. At Kajaki, in northern Helmand, a dam and hydroelectric plant supplied southern Afghanistan with electricity, although the power supply in Helmand itself was sporadic. A new turbine was needed at the power station there to protect the electricity supply. Somehow, British forces had to deliver the giant machine, worth £3.4 million, from Kandahar airfield to the dam, 115 miles away in the heart of Taliban-infested territory. This was perhaps the ultimate 'hearts and minds' mission: if successful, it would be tangible proof to local people going about their daily lives that the Kabul government was committed to improving the country. However, in order to deliver the turbine, not only did the route have to be secured, it turned out that part of it had to be built. Helmand has very few roads. Bisected east–west by Highway 1, which is effectively Afghanistan's ringroad, Helmand's other major road is the north–south 611, along which the turbine might have been expected to be carried. In the stretch north of FOB Robinson towards the Upper Sangin valley lay 'the greatest density of IEDs anywhere in Afghanistan': the painstaking and time-consuming work of trying to clear them would leave soldiers open to attack.[55] Brigadier Mark Carleton-Smith was, however, mindful that if the British did not deliver, their credibility would be undermined. He told his men he did not want to hear that the mission was not possible, not least because of pressure from the Americans. The embedded journalist Sam Kiley noted: 'Many American officers continued to admire the fighting energies of the ordinary, and badly equipped, British soldier. But they questioned the commitment of the British government.'[56]

The mission seemed impossible. Just in time, a new route was discovered by a Pathfinder team, racing across the desert in their

MWMIK Jackals – typically starring in their own *Mad Max*-style adventures, according to their envious detractors. It was a back road between Kandahar and Kajaki. A few days later, in late August 2008, a 20-vehicle decoy convoy began to trundle along the 611, while to the east, near Maiwand, a 100-vehicle convoy of Vikings, Mastiffs, Vectors, Land Rovers and Heavy Equipment Transporters (HET) had gathered to transport the turbine. Simultaneously, up at Kajaki, members of the Afghan National Army, their mentors from 1 Royal Irish and paratroopers from 3 Para began to surround the dam but came under attack from the Taliban. Shortly before the convoy reached its destination, the road – 'Route Harriet' – ran out, vanishing into a goat track in a deep wadi. But within eight hours a team of Royal Engineers carved a new road out of the surrounding hillsides. Five hours later, the turbine was safely delivered. Commanded by Lieutenant Colonel Rufus McNeil of the Royal Logistic Corps, the six-day operation, involving a multinational force of 4,000 troops, was the biggest military convoy assembled by the British Armed Forces since 1945.

As war-weary as their electorate, the Blair/Brown governments had little appetite to commit whole-heartedly to Afghanistan. Members of the public would begin to show their support for soldiers, even if they were less than convinced that the mission was worthwhile (see next section). There was little evidence that Britain was actually rebuilding much in Helmand; energies were focused on trying to establish security. Brigadier John Lorimer had likened the process to 'mowing the grass': no sooner had the enemy been cut down, it would – Whac-a-Mole-like – return. His successor, Brigadier Andrew Mackay, made it clear that 'body counts are a particularly corrupt measure of success' and tried to refocus efforts towards the classic counter-insurgency goal of winning hearts and minds: 'the people are the prize'.[57] Mackay's brigade in Afghanistan was an interesting comment on the state of the Army at the time. His headquarters, 52 Infantry Brigade, was based in Edinburgh Castle at the time of his appointment, with a very limited role for home defence in Scotland. But the Army needed to grow two more deployable brigade headquarters to meet the overlapping demands of Iraq and Afghanistan. Headquarters 11 and 52 Brigades were formed – both did one operational deployment and then disbanded again. However, there were no new units – just the existing pool of battalions and regiments working that little bit harder. Such pressure lent weight to retaining the six months' length of deployed tours of duty, unlike the Americans, who extended some units' tours from twelve to fifteen months – and paid a huge price in fatigue, stress and premature resignations.

A key goal throughout remained improving the Afghan National Army through Operational Mentoring and Liaison Teams (OMLTs, inevitably known as Omelettes), based at Camp Shorabak next to Bastion. It was an uphill task, as Patrick Hennessey described: 'They couldn't shape their berets. They didn't get up early and they stopped everything for meals, for prayer, for a snooze. They had no discipline. They smoked strong hashish and mild opium. They couldn't map-read ... They wore what they wanted, when they wanted and walked around holding hands.'[58] However, having been involved in irregular fighting, some had seen more action than their mentors.

The tours of duty established their own rhythm. Taking over from the Mercians, Lieutenant Daniel MacMahon of 3 Company, 1st Battalion Coldstream Guards, said: 'There were us junior officers turning up with no operational experience at all. And there were all these strong, tanned guys talking as if it was the most normal thing in the world to have fire fights, to have rocket-propelled grenades going round, and mortars landing.'[59] Rookies became veterans very quickly, but no one could afford to become complacent. Soldiers never knew what the day was going to bring. Trooper Pete Sheppard observed: 'You can prepare yourself for a big engagement – and we all convince ourselves it's going to happen – and the day goes off without a whisper. And other days, routine days when it should be quiet – all hell breaks loose.'[60]

With the focus on Helmand, it was easy to overlook the larger strategic picture in Afghanistan. British forces were part of a 36-nation coalition. Throughout Herrick, the British relied heavily upon US air power and American helicopters. However, the relationship between the two forces could be scratchy, with US General Dan McNeill, who succeeded David Richards as ISAF commander, being particularly critical when Musa Qala fell back under Taliban control in early 2007. As far as he was concerned, the British 'had made a mess of things in Helmand'. Conversely, British commanders, including Carleton-Smith, had reservations about the heavy US use of firepower, particularly by their Special Forces, who were outside his chain of command: too many civilians were getting caught up in fire fights and bombing raids. During Herrick 8, the US 24 Marine Expeditionary Unit began to arrive in Helmand. While the quality of British equipment had begun to improve, there continued to be a lack of quantity. The US Marine Corps' 2,200-man unit in Helmand were estimated to have the same amount of firepower as the entire British contingent of over 9,000 men.

The US Marine Corps set up its base, Camp Leatherneck, adjacent to Camp Bastion. Like its British counterpart, it was to expand and expand again. Unsurprisingly, the USMC presence created wariness among some of the British. With the unfortunate perception having taken hold of a defeat in Basra after the British withdrawal from the main city to the airport, both the US government and its army were concerned that the US deployment in Helmand would be portrayed as 'bailing out the Brits – yet again'. For those, however, who understood the overall concept of operations, the US deployment was a necessary numerical boost in the number of boots on the ground in order to clear areas of Taliban, then hold those areas securely in order to begin to build a better future. The strategy of 'Clear, hold and build' required sufficient boots on the ground to stand a chance; it did not matter whose feet were in those boots – British, American or Afghan – but sufficient numbers were essential.

Aiming to secure key river and canal crossings in Helmand, Operation Panther's Claw was launched on 19 June 2009. This would involve some 3,000 British soldiers, as well as members of the ANA and troops from Estonia and Denmark. It began with an air assault on Taliban positions near Babaji, north-west of Lashkar Gah, by soldiers from the Black Watch battalion of the newly formed Royal Regiment of Scotland. From 25 June, the Welsh Guards secured crossing points on the Shamalan canal. Their mission could have faltered following the death of their commanding officer, Lieutenant Colonel Rupert Thorneloe, who was killed along with Trooper Joshua Hammond on 1 July when an IED exploded beneath their Viking. Rupert Thorneloe had been doing what came naturally to good British commanders – leading by example – 'barma-ing' (checking for IEDs) and riding top cover, watching out for the safety of his soldiers. He was the highest ranking Army officer to be killed since Lieutenant Colonel H. Jones in the Falklands: in a poignant twist, H's son, Lieutenant Colonel Rupert Jones, would temporarily take over Thorneloe's command. July 2009 turned out to be a grim milestone for the Army; the month with the highest number of deaths and serious injuries among soldiers in the whole campaign. It provoked a crescendo of criticism among the British press and public about the lack of appropriately armoured vehicles and a perceived shortage of helicopters – a fact reported from the ground by Sarah Montague of BBC Radio 4's *Today* programme, who was visiting Afghanistan a few days later.

Like Iraq, Afghanistan underscored the necessity of having sufficient manpower in a counter-insurgency situation. Both campaigns would be transformed by a surge – a massive influx of American personnel. Ironically, it was an opponent of the US intervention in Iraq, the newly elected President Barack Obama, who would follow his predecessor's lead and pour troops into Afghanistan from late 2009 (see chapter 10). With British soldiers deployed on two fronts, Herrick put the Army under huge pressure. On the positive side, it was the catalyst for the British public to start showing unprecedented support for their soldiers.

The Military Covenant

Many myths surround the Military Covenant. One newspaper described it as an 'ancient pledge', another said it was 'historic', while the *Daily Mail* stated that it was drafted in the days of Wellington.[61] The term 'covenant' itself is fairly archaic and it is therefore unsurprising that the Military Covenant was assumed to be drawn up on parchment or vellum and signed with a quill pen, its exact origins and meaning lost in history. When it started to be talked about in late 2006, most soldiers had never heard of it and of those that had, very few knew exactly what it was. However, in interviews with the media, those at the top of the Army, including the then CGS, Adjutant General Sir Freddie Viggers and the former commander in Bosnia, General Sir Michael Rose, began putting the welfare of soldiers in the context of the Covenant. In a speech in January 2007, Prime Minister Tony Blair gave an undertaking that the Military Covenant would be 'renewed'; later that year the Royal British Legion launched its 'Honour the Covenant' campaign.[62] The perception began to emerge among the general public that a centuries-old agreement between the Army and its soldiers on one side and the government on the other was being broken.

Far from dating back to the English Civil War, the Military Covenant can be described as an 'invented tradition', that is, a concept or idea, such as Highland tartan, which is assumed to be ancient but which is, in fact, of more recent provenance.[63] Conjured up by the Army in the late 1990s, the Covenant was the brainchild of a handful of officers who were involved in updating Army doctrine and examining the so-called 'moral component' of fighting power. They sought to codify what would sustain morale and combat effectiveness, including the will to fight and to win. As one soldier in Afghanistan observed, admitting to fear is not a sign of weakness; 'being able to admit to it and carry on regardless is a sign of strength'.[64] This grit and determination is down partly to training but also to something more intangible, which the Army as an institution recognised and wanted to foster with a formal emphasis on the moral component, or put more simply, on its people. One result of this, as chapter 8 details, was *Values and Standards of the British Army*, published in early 2000. In addition, the Army had to make its case that it was different from civilian society and therefore that different rules should apply to it. *Soldiering: The Military Covenant*, a short background essay to *Values and Standards*, tried to explain and justify the Army's uniqueness. Published as a pamphlet, it was sent out to civilian policymakers and almost immediately forgotten, abandoned to box files in archives and left quietly to gather dust on library shelves. All doctrine is regularly updated: when the moral component was reviewed in 2005, *Soldiering* was institutionally sidelined. It was no longer a separate publication: sections of it were rewritten and incorporated into the revised version of doctrine – and that should have been that. However, six years later the Military Covenant, a concept first set out in *Soldiering*, became public policy and recognised in law in the Armed Forces Act 2011. It is an astonishing trajectory for an idea buried away in an obscure Army doctrine publication which most soldiers had never read.

What is the Military Covenant all about? At its most fundamental level, it concerns the nation's support for soldiers' military service. The Covenant seeks to convey that soldiers are prepared to make

312 BOOTS ON THE GROUND

the ultimate sacrifice and that they are entitled to expect support from the nation in return for their readiness to lay down their lives. Like the ancient Biblical covenants, the Military Covenant is a non-enforceable agreement based on trust and the principle of reciprocity. Crucially, it is not a contract, there is nothing transactional about the Covenant: even if the nation fails to uphold its part of the bargain with soldiers, soldiers will carry on doing their duty to the nation. Those who codified the concept of the Military Covenant sought to convey that military service – not least because of its potential for self-sacrifice – was unique. Soldiering and being a soldier, with the possibility of taking life or being killed, is unlike any job in the civilian sphere. Soldiers don't have an employment contract and can't go on strike. The job of trying to put all this across was devolved to the then Brigadier (later Major General Sir) Sebastian Roberts of the Irish Guards, who wrote *Soldiering* with a copy of the *Rule of Saint Benedict* and the 'Declaration of Independence' to hand.[65] He has been described as 'the most cerebral soldier of his generation'. One paragraph of *Soldiering*, 103, encapsulates the Covenant:

> Soldiers will be called upon to make personal sacrifices – including the ultimate sacrifice – in the service of the Nation. In putting the needs of the Nation and the Army before their own, they forgo some of the rights enjoyed by those outside the Armed Forces. In return, British soldiers must always be able to expect fair treatment, to be valued and respected as individuals, and that they (and their families) will be sustained and rewarded by commensurate terms and conditions of service. In the same way, the unique nature of military land operations means that the Army differs from all other institutions, and must be sustained and provided for accordingly by the Nation. This mutual obligation forms the Military Covenant between the Nation, the Army and each individual soldier, an unbreakable common bond of identity, loyalty and responsibility which has sustained the Army throughout its history. It has perhaps its greatest manifestation in the annual commemoration of Armistice Day, when the Nation keeps covenant with those who have made the ultimate sacrifice, giving their lives in action.[66]

Stirring stuff. However, not only was it open to challenge – had the bond between Army, nation and individual soldier really been so unbreakable since the 1660s? – but there was little evidence around 2000, when *Soldiering* was published, of personal sacrifice by soldiers. They were certainly serving the nation during the foot and mouth crisis, the firemen's strike and the fuel protests, but that was hardly what many had signed up for and failed to test whether the nation was keeping its side of the Covenant bargain.

Without the concurrent campaigns in Iraq and Afghanistan, it is unlikely that the Military Covenant would have left the confines of military doctrine and become established in public policy. By the summer of 2006, pressure on the Army and its soldiers was mounting. The government was determined to press on into Afghanistan, despite the ongoing mission in Iraq. It seemed unconcerned that the double deployment would breach the Harmony Guidelines – the length of time soldiers can expect between tours, which is ideally two years. Despite good initiatives during the Blair government's early years in the 1998 Strategic Defence Review towards improving soldiers' welfare and conditions of service, after 2003 Iraq came to subsume everything else. However, neither the Cabinet nor the government departments were on a war footing, and nor did they exhibit the strategic patience to see the job through.

Paradoxically, the defence budget does not cover the extra costs of operations such as Herrick or Telic, which are funded separately by the Treasury through emergency supplements and the Urgent Operational Requirement process. Although this is somewhat hand-to-mouth, and worked reasonably well in connection with Iraq and Afghanistan, it did little for forward planning or the truly cost-effective procurement of equipment. A short-term sticking plaster solution could not make up for the chronic under-investment in defence since the end of the Cold War. The Conservative government of John Major had taken too large a peace dividend under *Options for Change*, but, after the Labour Strategic Defence Review of 1997–8, Blair's wars were being fought on Brown's very tight defence budgets.[67] The perception grew that soldiers were being short-changed, whether on the frontline or back in Britain. Particularly controversial were the issues of force protection such as the supply of body armour and, with the closure of dedicated military hospitals, the medical treatment for the wounded on civilian wards in NHS hospitals. In addition, in both Iraq and Afghanistan a shortage of helicopters and the use of lightly armoured vehicles came to symbolise cut-price conflict. The successful prosecution of both campaigns was being hampered because the Army was not being 'sustained and provided for' as the Military Covenant demands. Although the government was only too happy to deploy the Armed Forces as an instrument to implement its global ambitions, it appeared unwilling properly to fund them.

With a second front opening in Afghanistan, soldiers' sacrifice became only too apparent, but this was not matched by corresponding support for them. The government was failing to give proper material backing, but the wider nation seemed to be withholding moral support as well. In a front page story in November 2005, the *Sunday Times* reported that soldiers believed 'that the MoD is not supporting them and nobody in the UK cares about what is happening in Iraq'.[68] Indeed, a series of press articles indicated active hostility towards soldiers. Reports about the wounded being jeered at in Birmingham's Selly Oak hospital, or soldiers being told not to wear their uniforms either off-base or travelling through airports on their way back from tour, gained currency, along with tales about how they were being barred from pubs and clubs and thrown off trains. The most controversial stories centred on the rehabilitation centre at Headley Court in Surrey, where local people were alarmed at the sight of wounded service personnel using the public swimming baths and objected to the conversion of a nearby house into accommodation for family visitors. While much of this can be ascribed to nimbyism, soldiers themselves perceived that the prevailing national mood was anti-military, according to one government-commissioned report.[69] The enthusiastic support enjoyed by service personnel in the United States was nowhere to be seen. However, contrary to media reports, the majority of the British public were not hostile to soldiers but indifferent. Returning from Iraq, troops marched through empty streets. They had become the scapegoats for the Blair government's intervention in Iraq, the dissembling surrounding the decision-making process and the disastrous consequences that had ensued from it.

The Military Covenant was deployed by the Army to bolster material and moral support for soldiers. In the second half of 2006, copies of *Soldiering* were tracked down, the dust blown off them and Paragraph 103 duly appeared on the Army's website. Unexpectedly, the Covenant turned out to be an extremely powerful weapon. In the early years of the Iraq and Afghan campaigns, General Sir Mike Jackson, CGS from 2003 to 2006, began to get a lot of unfair stick from soldiers who perceived that not enough was being done to improve their lot. The facts were that some soldiers were paid less than traffic wardens; if wounded their compensation was pitiful; in some cases, their housing was awful, worse than accommodation in Afghanistan, as the *Sun* memorably described in an article headlined 'From Helmand to Hellhole'.[70] However, the Army is not only subordinate to the civil power, but should stay well out of politics. Convention requires that serving soldiers should never go public with their concerns. Sir Mike followed longstanding British civil–military conventions and lobbied ministers behind firmly closed doors.[71] He did his best, followed the rules, but could not get far enough. He saved his major broadside for the BBC 'Dimbleby Lecture', which he gave some three months after his retirement in 2006. But time was pressing and manpower levels were dropping in the Army just as operational demands were increasing further. A different approach was needed. In a major – and what proved to be hugely controversial – interview with the *Daily Mail*, the new CGS – this book's author – spoke openly about the Army's difficulties, albeit some six weeks after he had set them out in a lengthy letter to the Secretary of State for Defence. Nevertheless, one defence minister later said that the CGS should have been sacked.[72] In the wide-ranging article that was published, the criticisms were placed in the context of the Military Covenant. A few months later, the Prime Minister unwittingly legitimised the concept of the Covenant, despite its somewhat shaky historical credentials. Perhaps, like many others, Tony Blair – or his advisors – assumed that the Military Covenant was indeed some sort of antique compact. By stating that it should be 'renewed', he implied that the Military Covenant was a matter of historical fact. Its migration from Army doctrine to the civilian sphere was beginning.[73]

Central to waking up the public's latent support for soldiers were the military charities and the media. After visiting the wounded at Selly Oak hospital, former soldier Bryn Parry and his wife Emma began fundraising. Out of that came the fastest growing charity in British history – Help for Heroes. Founded on 1 October 2007,

H4H offered a fresh approach and turned the rather staid military charity sector upside down. In doing so, it unleashed the public's latent support and goodwill for soldiers, sailors, airmen and marines. The *Sun* urged its readers to buy the charity's wristband, making the crucial point that wearing it showed 'not that you support the war in Iraq. Just those having to fight it.' The tabloid understood wider public sentiment: the controversy and division over Iraq would not go away, but it could be put to one side in order to support the troops who were putting their lives on the line for the country. Soon, Prime Minister Gordon Brown wore a wristband. Help for Heroes tapped into popular culture, getting the backing of Princes William and Harry as well as sports stars and members of the music business. A charity rugby match at Twickenham in September 2008 attracted a crowd of 52,000 people, while in 2010 a cover of the David Bowie song 'Heroes' by *X Factor* finalists – very different from the sainted Dame Vera Lynn – went straight to Number 1.

As they came back from Afghanistan, soldiers began to notice a change in public mood. In late 2007, both the *Daily Telegraph* and the *Sun* actively promoted homecoming parades, while the Local Government Minister wrote to councils urging them to do more to support the Armed Forces. The parades idea gained traction, culminating in 20,000 people turning out in Leicester to welcome home the 9th/12th Lancers, while two days later 10,000 watched a parade in Northampton. In late 2008, the *Sun* organised its first annual military awards, or Millies, with the enthusiastic support of the Prince of Wales, and the paper's then editor, Rebekah Wade. Successive public opinion polls began putting the Armed Forces among the most respected of all organisations – despite support plummeting for the interventions in Iraq and Afghanistan. After 2007, thanks to the lead given by Help for Heroes, the military charity sector was re-energised. Donations to the major charities are a good barometer of public support: between 2006 and 2010, donations surged. Combat Stress saw its income almost double from £6.73 million in 2006 to £12.55 million in 2010. The Army Benevolent Fund rebranded itself, becoming the less workhouse-era sounding ABF The Soldier's Charity, and donations rose from £5.7 million in 2006 to £12.1 million in 2010.[74] The Royal British Legion broke its own Poppy Appeal records in successive years. Most people wanting to show their appreciation for the forces, whether through military charities or turning out at parades, had probably never heard of the Military Covenant. However, unknown to them, through their support they were upholding it.

The Royal British Legion's 'Honour the Covenant' campaign ensured that politicians could no longer ignore soldiers' welfare. Launched in late August 2007, it enlisted the help of the Legion's members, 22,000 of whom lobbied their MPs via postcards. The charity had a list of welfare concerns it wanted the government to tackle, including better compensation for the wounded and a more streamlined inquest system. As organiser of the annual commemoration of Remembrance, the Legion has enormous moral authority. Politicians ignore this particular charity at their peril: Defence Secretary Des Browne told its annual conference in 2008, 'When the Legion speaks, governments listen.'[75] As the *Guardian* noted, in offending the Legion, the government could be judged to be 'trampling on the memory of the 20th century's war dead'.[76] In the first defence debate after the launch of Honour the Covenant, the campaign's impact was obvious: Opposition MPs – many of whom had never taken any interest in defence – invoked the Military Covenant, which they claimed was 'broken'. The Covenant was a gift to the Conservatives, allowing them to get back on the right side of public opinion: they had initially given the government a very easy ride over Iraq, only to get into a mess in the 2005 General Election campaign when they tried to distance themselves from the decision. From late 2007, the government's opponents consistently put any welfare matters affecting the Armed Forces in the Covenant context. The Covenant, and the military welfare issues it symbolised, became politicised whether or not this was what the Army intended or wanted.

In formalising the nation's obligations to soldiers, the Military Covenant helped to engender practical and moral support for Armed Forces personnel. Stung into action, the government's Service Personnel Command Paper of 2008, *The Nation's Commitment: Cross-Government Support to Our Armed Forces, Their Families and Veterans*, reflected the public pressure on ministers to address welfare issues. The Command Paper broke new ground and the Armed Forces Minister, Bob Ainsworth, who championed it in Whitehall, deserves more credit than he received at the time.

However, the Blair/Brown governments were often their own worst enemy in any matter connected with the Army and its soldiers. An attempt to gag Assistant Oxfordshire Coroner Andrew Walker, who was unafraid to criticise both the MoD and the Army for any short-comings that could have contributed to the deaths of servicemen and women in Iraq, was clumsy and counter-productive. It should be acknowledged that Brown's government suffered the fall-out from Blair's wars: the delay in hearing inquests meant that inquiries in connection with deaths in Iraq were sometimes held, quite coinci-dentally, when there was bad news from Afghanistan. The problems of one campaign being mirrored in the other reinforced the public's growing sense that the government simply did not care. Any sym-pathy for Prime Minister Gordon Brown is, however, tempered by his view that, notwithstanding British soldiers being in combat on two fronts, being Defence Secretary was nevertheless regarded as a part-time job – an appointment to be shared with being Secretary of State for Scotland. The decision to double-hat Des Browne was seen as a major political blunder.

By 2010, the Army had lost control of the Military Covenant. In civilian hands, its scope was extended and its reach extended to the frontline of Afghanistan. It became a weapon used by the govern-ment's opponents to attack it: one future Defence Secretary, Liam Fox, described the Covenant as being 'shattered by New Labour'.[77] A think-tank paper described it as being 'almost beyond repair'.[78] In 2008, the Covenant was central to a High Court judgment about immigration rights for Gurkha veterans, when Mr Justice Blake quoted Paragraph 103.[79] In October 2009, the concept was integral to recommendations of the Haddon-Cave Inquiry into the crash of Nimrod XV230 in Afghanistan in 2006. Complications arose when the coalition government of David Cameron and Nick Clegg, elected to power in 2010, attempted to put this moral obligation on a legal basis (see chapter 10).

Throughout history, societies have sporadically recognised the debt that is owed to their soldiers. Regrettably, what is apparent in war can be forgotten in peace, as Kipling's Tommy Atkins could testify. In 1593, Elizabeth I's parliament passed an 'Act for Necessary Relief of Soldiers (and Mariners)'. The Act's enforcement was dependent on local authorities whose efforts were, at best, half-hearted, and in many places non-existent. In 1601 her Secretary of State, Robert Cecil, observed: 'War is a curse to all people, and especially the poor creatures that come from the wars poor, friendless and unhappy.'[80] In the late 1620s, after attacks on Cadiz and La Rochelle, MPs were shocked to see soldiers and sailors dying on the streets of West Country ports. In 1681 Charles II authorised work to begin on a Royal Hospital at Chelsea to take care of veterans 'broken by age or war'. In a twist that reinforced the Military Covenant's legitimacy, in 2009 the magnificent Christopher Wren-designed Hospital declared it was 'Keeping the Nation's Covenant with Our Old Soldiers'. Today, the Royal Hospital and its red-coated pensioners are said to be evidence of how the nation has looked after its veterans. However, throughout the Army's history, soldiers could testify that the nation has not honoured the debt it owes to them. Peninsular War veteran George Baller of the 95th Rifles was not atypical; in 1819 he was living in 'grinding poverty and great physical pain' on a pension too small to provide for his children.[81] An estimated one-quarter of Edwardian Army veterans were unemployed or vagrants.[82] Far from the nation supporting the Royal Hospital, for more than 200 years it was private soldiers themselves who financed the institution out of deductions from their meagre pay packets and the 'prize' money that should rightfully have been theirs.

During the first decade of the twentieth century, the British Army learned some painful lessons from the Boer War. A century later, while a successful conclusion was arrived at in Northern Ireland, there were plenty of lessons to be learned from the campaigns in Iraq and Afghanistan, not just by the Army but across government. For soldiers themselves, many of whom had felt forgotten in Afghanistan and blamed for the misadventure in Iraq, the sudden change in public mood back home was startling. Even if they were reluctant to be labelled 'heroes', the gratitude and respect they enjoyed was appreciated – and justified. During one of the Chilcot public hearings, one commander in Iraq who was asked what worked in that campaign replied, 'The soldiers were brilliant.'[83]

TEN

INTERVENTION: PART OF THE PROBLEM OR PART OF THE SOLUTION?

*Withdrawal from Afghanistan, the
Arab Spring – Libya and Syria*

Following the inconclusive General Election of May 2010, Britain had its first coalition government since the Second World War. While political pundits are always quick to point out that there are no votes in defence, both the Labour and Conservative parties had played the khaki card. In the first line of Labour's manifesto, Gordon Brown had stated: 'This General Election is fought as our troops are bravely fighting to defend the safety of the British people and the security of the world in Afghanistan. They bring great pride and credit to our country: we honour and will always support them.'[1] Not to be outdone, under the banner of 'a stronger Britain in a safer world', the Conservatives had promised to defend national security and 'support our brave Armed Forces in everything they do'.[2] The party issued a separate 27-page Armed Forces manifesto.[3] When the coalition finally announced its *Programme for Government*, it pledged to 'support our troops in Afghanistan'.[4] If they read any of this, soldiers probably did so with a degree of scepticism. With a global financial crisis after 2008 having a massive impact on the public finances, and consequently on public services, in the battle for resources between warfare and welfare, civilian interests inevitably trumped military matters.

Even if money was very tight, the coalition inherited a number of expensive defence-related issues from the Brown government, above all Afghanistan. Moreover, although he had been largely forgotten, Osama bin Laden remained at large. The Saville Inquiry into Bloody Sunday continued. Having promised to retain the nuclear deterrent and to cut Ministry of Defence running costs by a quarter, the coalition's next priority was to 'rebuild the Military Covenant'. One other promising new initiative was the National Security Council, which was all the more necessary following the Commons Select Committee conclusion that Britain had lost the ability for strategic thought.[5] The most unexpected international development that the coalition government would have to confront from early 2011 was the pro-democracy movement across the Middle East. The Arab Spring was welcomed by many; its potential to destabilise an already fragile region was anticipated by few. The primary focus of the coalition would be trying to put right Britain's finances, primarily dealing with the national deficit. Austerity would have a huge impact on defence, reflected in two key policy documents that would define the government's approach.

The *National Security Strategy* and the *Strategic Defence and Security Review*

On its very first day of government, the coalition established a National Security Council (NSC). Essentially it was a Cabinet committee which met to discuss security, intelligence and defence issues. The CDS, General Sir David Richards, who would be the only council member from the Armed Forces, suggested it was set up partly as a return to collective responsibility after the 'sofa government' of New Labour.[6] A cross-departmental forum to look in depth at matters which are acknowledged by every government to be its primary responsibility seems, with hindsight, to have been long overdue. However, like all Whitehall initiatives, its success was dependent upon the commitment of those at the top. According to Prime Minister David Cameron, in 2011 he chaired some thirty-six NSC meetings, which covered fifty foreign policy topics and nine domestic policy issues, as well as fourteen security-related issues, such as counter-terrorism.[7] The CDS, who supported the Council in principle, sometimes became frustrated that it would focus on the near-term and the tactical, rather than on broader foreign policy and grand strategic issues. Some of its secretariat were tempted to meddle in military campaigns, such as the conduct of the war in Libya, for which they had neither the experience nor the skill.[8] A lack of understanding at the top of Whitehall about what was fully meant by 'strategy' always presented the risk that the NSC would be tempted to dip down into the 'operational' and 'tactical levels' – the first was the proper preserve of the Chiefs of Staff Committee, which already met weekly with wide cross-Whitehall participation; and the second, of those actually fighting on the ground.

The National Security Council's initial deliberations resulted in the National Security Strategy, set out in the policy document *A Strong Britain in an Age of Uncertainty*. It was launched in October 2010, the day before the Defence White Paper, the *Strategic Defence and Security Review*. Indeed, these two documents should be considered together. The National Security Strategy had given some thought to Britain's place in the world and the role it should play: 'We are a country whose political, economic and cultural authority far exceeds our size' and 'We must project our influence abroad.' However, a slide down the world rankings was implied by the observation that 'As the global balance of power shifts, it will become harder for us to do.' Britain, declared the Strategy, 'is both more secure and more vulnerable than in most of her long history'. Conventional military threats such as existed during the Cold War had disappeared but, as an open society, the country remained at risk in a more networked world. 'Terrorism, cyber-attack, unconventional attacks using chemical, nuclear or biological weapons, as well as large scale accidents or natural hazards – anyone could do grave damage to our country.' The threats could come from states and non-state actors, whether terrorists, insurgents or criminals. 'The security of our energy supplies increasingly depends on fossil fuels located in some of the most unstable parts of the planet. Nuclear proliferation is a growing danger. Our security is vulnerable to the effects of climate change and its impact on food and water supply.' Such threats demanded a 'radical transformation in the way we think about national security and organise ourselves to protect it'.[9] The following day, the *Strategic Defence and Strategy Review* revealed the extent of the transformation.

The 2010 *Strategic Defence and Security Review* (SDSR) was bitter reading for all members of Britain's Armed Forces. Although there had been a minor recalibration of the country's defence capability following the White Papers of 2002 and 2003, a wholesale examination of policy was long overdue. Since the 1998 Review, twelve frenetic years had passed and British forces had been heavily committed to operations from Kosovo in 1999 to southern Afghanistan in 2006 and elsewhere, as chapters 8 and 9 have described. Like its twin policy document, the SDSR tried to balance the impossible: national strength and near national bankruptcy. The coalition government had inherited a Treasury with no money – according to the departing Labour Chief Secretary Liam Byrne – and a defence budget with a £35 billion black hole in it. The Chancellor, George Osborne, was quite clear that the country was entering an age of austerity, yet the Foreign Secretary, William Hague, was on record as saying that he sensed no appetite in the country for 'strategic shrinkage'. Indeed, the foreword to the 2010 SDSR, *Securing Britain in an Age of Uncertainty*, began: 'Our country has always had global responsibilities and global ambitions. We have a proud history of standing up for the values we believe in and we should have no less ambition for our country in the decades to come.'[10] It continued: 'The difficult legacy we have inherited has necessitated tough decisions to get our economy back on track. Our national security depends on our economic security and vice versa.'[11]

From these opening comments, the die was cast. Notwithstanding the two decades of intense operational commitment since the end of the Cold War, the lack of resources following the financial crash of 2008 would result in yet another major reduction in defence spending, with the British Army – still doing the fighting and dying in Afghanistan – destined to suffer the lion's share of the cuts in manpower. The 2010 Review will be remembered for its axing of the Harrier force, the scrapping of HMS *Ark Royal* and the decision to continue with the building of two new aircraft carriers – without an agreed plan to provide the aircraft to fly off them. Also for the scrapheap were many of the C-130 Hercules transport aircraft as well as the Sentinel and Nimrod surveillance capabilities. The number of new heavy-lift Chinook helicopters was halved to twelve, while Challenger 2 main battle tanks were being cut by 40 per cent and heavy artillery by 35 per cent. The Army was to undergo more restructuring, with the number of deployable ground manoeuvre brigades set at five. The global financial crisis had hit most of the West's defence budgets: defence spending among NATO members fell by £45 billion between 2009 and 2011, leading US Defense Secretary Robert Gates to warn about 'Europe's demilitarisation'.[12] Washington was becoming increasingly exasperated by its NATO allies' reliance on the American taxpayer to pick up the tab for Europe's security. However, government spending is a matter of choice and the coalition chose, for example, to increase its spending on overseas aid through the Department for International Development rather than on defence.

The British Army, with 102,000 regular soldiers, would inevitably be the target of the Treasury's axe. After all, it was larger in manpower terms than the two other services put together. Initially under Defence Secretary Dr Liam Fox, the cut was to be down to 95,000 soldiers. This was bad enough. However, when his cost-conscious successor, Philip Hammond, looked at the books again a year later, he decided to cut it further. The Army's strength would be reduced to 82,000 – the UK's smallest regular Army for a century. The compensation – to make up the Army with 30,000 trained reservists – was seen as a political compromise and a near-impossible target to achieve. The architect of the review of reserves which offered the recommendation – but offered to defence ministers merely as an option to be considered among several others – was General Sir Nick Houghton. Having succeeded David Richards as CDS, he would have to witness the final hurrah of his old regiment, the Green Howards, as the further reorganisation of the regular Army's order of battle saw the loss of more units, including the Green Howards battalion of the newly formed Yorkshire Regiment. Field Marshal Sir Nigel Bagnall had predeceased, albeit prematurely, the demise of his original regiment. Against the realities of cash there is no room for sentiment, but even the late Company Sergeant Major, Stan Hollis, who won the only Victoria Cross on D Day in June 1944, would have looked pensively into his beer in the pub that he ran on Teesside called – The Green Howard.

Afghanistan

In November 2009, NATO formally adopted a new counter-insurgency strategy for Afghanistan that had been proposed a few months earlier by the US commander, General Stanley McChrystal.

A gaunt, ascetic athlete who ran eight miles a day, the fabled general had commanded Special Forces in Iraq and was at the forefront of implementing the successful troop surge there. In December at West Point military academy, President Barack Obama announced that an additional 30,000 troops would also be committed to the mission in Afghanistan. It was a victory for the military, who had been pressing their Commander-in-Chief for additional forces almost from the moment of his inauguration at the beginning of the year. An opponent of the intervention in Iraq, the President might have considered Afghanistan the 'good war', but was wary of being drawn into a Vietnam-style quagmire.[13] Consequently, while a surge was announced, 'after 18 months our troops will begin to come home'.[14] The President's detractors would criticise this as 'surge and retreat'. Almost as significantly, his speech re-emphasised how the White House was now viewing Afghanistan in the context of Pakistan, described as 'the epicentre of violent extremism practiced by Al Qaeda'. The United States stepped up its drone strikes against targets on both sides of the Durand Line, the border between Afghanistan and the tribal areas of Pakistan, coming to view the region as 'Af-Pak', and conjoined in terror.

The British military effort remained almost exclusively focused on Helmand province, which had experienced its own mini-surge of American troops. The US Marine Corps had first arrived in 2008, reinforced by 10,000 personnel in 2009. The corps prides itself on having its own airlift and supply chains, a legacy said to date from the Second World War when it considered itself short-changed by the US Navy in the Pacific. The US ambassador said that such was the Marine Corps' independence, it was the 42nd element in the existing 41-nation coalition in Afghanistan.[15] Envious British soldiers could only marvel at their kit and their tactical methods. In Marjah, within days of arrival, the marines had flattened buildings either side of the main road, which they resurfaced with tarmac to stop the Taliban laying IEDs. The British attitude towards their American comrades-in-arms was ambivalent: they were welcome, they were necessary, but their warrior posture might well prove counter-productive. The US Army's adoption of counter-insurgency was now formally enshrined in a military doctrine manual, FM3–24. Senior American commanders such as McChrystal recognised that the people are indeed the prize. There was a danger, however, that the US marines' methods, kinetic by doctrine and default, which had been used to such good effect in Fallujah in Iraq, might well mean that there were no people left whose hearts and minds could be won.

The new American strategy in Helmand was a continuation of the existing British strategy – only with more boots on the ground. Without that surge in manpower, however, it has to be asked how much difference it would have made. By the end of 2010, ISAF forces would number 150,000, of whom 30,000 were in Helmand.[16] Overall, 2009 can be seen as the year that the United States assumed far greater control of the mission in Afghanistan. One analyst observed that it was becoming less of a NATO out-of-area mission and more of an American mission with British forces in a strong supporting role.[17] The introduction of ISAF Joint Command gave it greater clarity. There had been a tendency for national forces to focus on their individual missions rather than on the bigger, national picture, which General McChrystal assessed in the summer of 2009. He elected to undermine the insurgency in the south of the country, particularly in Helmand and around Kandahar.

As the influx of American forces got underway in Helmand, British force numbers increased by 500, thereby rising to more than 10,000, just as their mission was being recast thanks to the increased US presence. The revised effort was not too different from the original pre-deployment Helmand Plan drawn up in 2005, which had focused on creating a lozenge of security around Lashkar Gah. The British withdrew from northern outposts such as Now Zad and Musa Qala. Along with putting local people at the core of the mission, ISAF was committed to handing over security to the Afghans themselves. Training members of the Afghan National Army and the Afghan National Police was accelerated through the NATO Training Mission. However, the results were patchy. Operation Moshtarak (Together), underway since February 2009, was a joint effort by British personnel and US marines, along with local soldiers. It was estimated that, despite years of training and there being 200,000 soldiers under arms, only one battalion of about 1,000 Afghans could carry out independent counter-insurgency operations.[18] As worrying were the small number of 'green-on-blue' incidents, when Afghan personnel turned on their mentors. In November 2009, five British soldiers

– three from the Grenadier Guards and two from the Royal Military Police – were killed by a rogue member of the Afghan police at a checkpoint in Nad-e Ali. Every such incident caused huge distress. In 2012, one senior commander reminded newspaper readers that there were 337,000 Afghan security personnel working alongside coalition forces and asked them to keep a sense of perspective.[19]

British soldiers were locked in a war of attrition with the enemy, whose tactics had inevitably evolved. There were fewer direct fire attacks on British compounds and more IEDs. Of the 9,304 attacks on NATO/ISAF troops in 2009, three-quarters of the casualties resulted from IEDs.[20] By 2010, one-third of the casualties in Afghanistan were British soldiers, although they comprised just one-tenth of coalition troops.[21] It took enormous courage to continue to go out on patrol. Lieutenant Charles Fraser Sampson, who would 'barma' the route ahead of his patrol with a metal detector, said: 'It is just the most awful feeling in the world thinking that every step you take could be your last, or you might miss the device and someone will be killed.'[22] Detection became harder when the enemy switched to using graphite rather than metal. However, improvements to medical care meant that more soldiers were surviving life-changing injuries.

At his first Prime Minister's Question Time, David Cameron backed the counter-insurgency strategy, but made clear he wanted Britain out of Afghanistan. On 2 June 2010, he told the House of Commons, 'What is in our national interest – that is what we should focus on – is an Afghanistan stable and secure enough to bring our troops home.'[23] He reconfirmed the direction of government policy less than a fortnight later: 'Our forces will not remain in Afghanistan a day longer than necessary.'[24] Two days earlier, Royal Marine Richard Hollington, aged twenty-three, had been injured in a blast in Sangin that would prove fatal. He would be the 300th member of the Armed Forces to be killed in Afghanistan. Later that month, the Prime Minister announced an extra £67 million for measures to counter the IED threat, including better equipment for bomb disposal teams and more Mastiff armoured patrol vehicles.

The issue of force protection had become perhaps the most politicised in relation to any aspect of defence. However, no matter how much money was invested, the country had had enough of what were perceived as New Labour's wars. The general public had grown weary of ministers giving them upbeat, confusing statistics about progress in Helmand, while all they saw were Union Jack-draped coffins being driven through Wootton Bassett. Although they over-whelmingly supported the Armed Forces, half of them had no idea why Britain was in Afghanistan, according to polls. Like marine Hol-lington's father, they wanted the government to explain and justify the mission.[25] Public confidence in Britain had been further dented by the 2009 General Election in Afghanistan, which was character-ised by fraud and corruption. In addition, by the time the coalition came to power, Operation Herrick was estimated to have cost the country somewhere in the region of £10 billion. At a time of the worst global financial crisis since the 1930s depression, nation-build-ing – to paraphrase Barack Obama's later observation – was badly needed at home.

A deadline was set for British combat forces to leave Afghani-stan by the end of 2014. Endorsed at the NATO summit in Lisbon in November 2010, the Prime Minister declared it was 'a firm deadline that we will meet'.[26] The withdrawal was linked to the phased hand-over of control of the country's security from ISAF to local Afghan forces. However, although the training of Afghans was stepped up, question marks remained about their competence and integrity, par-ticularly the members of the police force. In addition, giving any date for withdrawal is militarily unwise. Knowing they would lose the protection of foreign soldiers and be left high and dry after their withdrawal, local people were unlikely to align themselves too closely to the security forces. Similarly, the enemy could just quietly bide his time and wait for the foreigners to leave. Conversely, there was always the temptation to let the mission drag on inconclusively; a deadline, however, concentrates the minds of military planners. In touch with the national mood, David Cameron told the Defence Select Commit-tee: 'I believe the British public deserve to know there is an end point to this.'[27] The announcement had been anticipated by the handover of Sangin on 19 September to the US Marine Corps, part of a wider 'tactical realignment and rebalancing' of ISAF.[28] However, the Prime Minister said he was 'absolutely clear we had to come out of Sangin'. The town that seemed little more than a giant unmarked minefield ultimately claimed 106 British lives: the US marines lost 26 men in the first four months of being there, while 140 more were seriously injured. In all, 496 US personnel would be killed in Afghanistan in 2010.[29] A possible crisis with ISAF had been averted in the summer with the appointment of Iraq supremo General David Petraeus as successor to Stanley McChrystal, who had been sacked by President Obama after his disrespectful observations about the Commander-in-Chief had been published in *Rolling Stone* magazine.

Although the British soldiers and US marines were meant to be moving from a combat to a training and mentoring role, the enemy had different ideas. Patrols continued, with soldiers 'watching them, watching us'. Surreally, as locals went about their day-to-day business, tending their crops or heading to market, fire fights could open up. Interaction with Helmandis, key to a counter-insurgency operation, could mean delivering books to mosques, buying potatoes at the market to make home-made chips, tearing down Taliban flags or having the binoculars shot from your hands.[30] ISAF had a list of metrics that indicated progress, such as rising school attendance, but the number of attacks showed little sign of any significant drop-off. While Royal Engineers literally built bridges with, and for, the local community, for example at Singhazi on Highway 1, stretches of which the 2nd Battalion Royal Welsh cleared of numerous wrecks in March 2011, violence continued. Whether setting up a boxing club in Noorzai or giving children in Sayedabad winter coats, hats and yellow wellies, or holding a veterinary clinic, soldiers sought to build trust with local people.[31] Soldiers observed that the local people wanted security, irrigation, electricity, roads and jobs, while well-meaning Western aid workers seemed fixated on elections and women's rights. While coordination between the British military and civilian officials continued to improve, the cultural divide between the two groups remained. With soldiers on frequent operational deployments, many were less than impressed by the box-ticking bureaucracy that characterised the civilian deployment. As British civil servants insisted that they knew what was best for Afghanistan, wider questions about neo-colonialism were rarely raised, let alone honestly addressed. Did the projects dreamt up by the West work with the grain of local society? How far was the local economy being distorted by billions of dollars of aid?

The death of Osama bin Laden on 2 May 2011 was proof that al-Qaeda was being neutralised. The hunt for the terrorist leader had been going on for years, with Pakistan continuing to deny any knowledge of his whereabouts. There was acute embarrassment in Islamabad that he was found to have been living in Abbottabad, a military garrison and home to the Pakistan Military Academy. The denouement shone an unwelcome spotlight on Pakistan's often less-than-straightforward relationship with the enemies of the West, particularly the Taliban. In 2009, the International Institute of Strategic Studies had described Pakistan as the official epicentre of global jihadism. Its border region with Afghanistan, the Federally Administered Tribal Areas (FATA) which included the Khyber Pass, and the North-west Frontier Province, location of the notorious Swat valley, had come under growing Taliban influence. Women were retreating from the public space and girls being prevented from going to school, reflected by the shooting of 14-year-old Malala Yousafzai in October 2012. A first drone strike was launched on the FATA territories in 2004. By 2010, some 100 strikes had taken place.[32]

Further impetus for the withdrawal of Western forces from Afghanistan came with the NATO summit in Chicago in May 2012. Confirming that the ISAF mission would end on 31 December 2014, it determined that Afghan forces would be taking the lead for the whole country's security by mid-2013. Many parts of the country had seen the handover from ISAF to local forces, including Lashkar Gah, where Afghans had been in charge since July 2011. However, doubts remained about their effectiveness. The integrity of the local police had been called into question with the break-out from Kandahar's Sarposa prison in April 2011, when more than 470 inmates escaped, many of them Taliban insurgents. The fragility of security had been highlighted by the siege of the American Embassy in Kabul in September 2011. For the British, a grim milestone was reach in March 2012 when the 400th British soldier was killed. The number of deaths had doubled after 2009 compared with the previous years, reflecting the intensity of the fighting and the threat from IEDs. On 8 March the MoD announced the deaths of six British soldiers, killed when their Warrior armoured vehicle was hit. Corporal Jake Hartley, 20, and Privates Anthony Frampton, 20, Christopher Kershaw, 19, Daniel Wade, 20, and Daniel Wilford, 21, were from 3rd Battalion Yorkshire Regiment. Sergeant Nigel Coupe, 33, was on secondment from 1st Battalion Duke of Lancaster's Regiment. Their commanding officer, Lieutenant Colonel Zac Stenning, acknowledged their loss: 'As their brothers-in-arms, we remain committed in our duty to continue with our mission. They would want nothing less.'[33] The six dead were from the battalion's advance party; the rest of the unit, including the CO, were still in Warminster awaiting their turn to deploy. If ever there was a leadership and morale challenge, Zac Stenning had no option but to rise to it, something he did with great skill.

If soldiers' commitment did not falter, political will was less steady. CDS David Richards had sensed that there was no real affection for Afghanistan. 'People wanted out but didn't have the guts to say so.'[34] There was a similar reserve within the British Cabinet, not least because Helmand had become 'toxic politically'.[35] The rapid closure of British bases was indicative of the winding-down of the British effort in the province. Of the eighty bases in April 2012 only thirty-two remained active by the end of October, the rest having been either closed or handed over to the Afghans. In September 2012, a Taliban attack on the Camp Bastion complex, which included Camp Leatherneck, resulted in the deaths of two US marines and the wounding of eight US and eight British personnel. The destruction of six American Harrier jets and a C-130 transport aircraft worth $200 million was described as 'the worst day for American air power since the Tet Offensive'.[36] Guarding the camp had been a British responsibility. Apache pilot Captain Harry Wales, HRH Prince Harry, was one of the thousands of soldiers stationed at Bastion at the time. Inquiries on both sides of the Atlantic determined the obvious: arrangements for manning the perimeter towers were inadequate. Only one of the fifteen Taliban attackers, some of whom had crossed the border from Pakistan, survived. The complexities of the situation on the ground in Helmand were symbolised by the opium poppies growing within sight of the camp's 30-foot-high perimeter fence. In December 2012, the Defence Secretary announced that by the end of the following year British forces numbers would be cut to 5,200.

To those thousands of miles away back home in Britain, progress in Afghanistan often appeared glacial and events contradictory. However, soldiers returning for their second or even third tour noticed the difference on the ground. From 2012 women sat on the district community council in Gereshk and half of Helmand's schools were open, teaching 30,000 girls. All over Helmand, projects were up and running to help women get an education, acquire skills and find work: according to one reservist, 'as with so much in Afghanistan, progress is made in small quiet steps. Often the outside world doesn't even notice.'[37] ISAF's deputy commander, Lieutenant General Nick Carter, reported in April 2013 that twenty out of twenty-five Afghan brigades were capable of acting independently or were effective with advisers, up from just one the year before. However, in June, to huge consternation in Kabul, the Taliban opened an office in Qatar, proof that they were still a viable political force. On 16 December 2013, the Prime Minister visited Helmand and, in reply to a journalist's question, agreed that the mission had been accomplished. Although there was some quibbling that the announcement was premature, the UN-mandated objectives had been more or less met. Since 9/11 not one international terrorist incident had been planned in, or exported from, Afghanistan – the original reason for deploying to Afghanistan had been achieved. However, while al-Qaeda had been marginalised, the Taliban remained undefeated.

The last UK combat troops left Afghanistan on 26 October 2014 as the Union Jack was lowered in Camp Bastion. The Stars and Stripes also came down in the handover ceremony. Since 2001, 453 British personnel had been killed in Afghanistan and more than 2,600 wounded, 247 of them with severe life-changing injuries. Double and triple amputee survivors were among their number. As in Iraq, the British soldiers had done everything asked of them, and more – much more.

The Covenant in Action
The townsfolk of Wootton Bassett came to represent the wider nation showing its respect and appreciation for servicemen and women who had made the ultimate sacrifice on behalf of Britain. Like many of the rituals surrounding Remembrance and the commemoration of the country's war dead, including the Two Minute Silence marking Armistice Day, the town's ceremony had evolved quite spontaneously. Unlike the sombre rituals at the Cenotaph every November led by the Sovereign and attended by representatives of Church, State and the Armed Forces, Wootton Bassett was remarkable for its lack of official pomp and circumstance. Politicians kept well away: if any senior member of the Royal Family or the military attended, they did so in a private capacity. Wootton Bassett gave the bereaved families,

friends and comrades of the dead men and women the opportunity to acknowledge their return. The ceremony, such as it was, was simple, dignified and profoundly moving. There were no military bands or military escorts for the funeral cortèges. The closest they came to any military ritual were the lowering of flags by members of the Royal British Legion. They could be described as the people's processions.[38]

Wootton Bassett resulted from chance. In 2007, repatriation flights had been switched from RAF Brize Norton to RAF Lyneham: the route from the base took the cortèges through the town. In August 2011, they returned to RAF Brize Norton and the ceremonials stopped. A few months later, Wootton Bassett was awarded Royal letters patent in recognition of its support and adopted a new motto: 'We honour those who serve'. Although the ceremonials have concluded, what remains relatively unexplored is what might be called the Wootton Bassett effect: whether the televised ritual of repatriation had an impact on the future of the Armed Forces and the job they do, particularly their combat role. As much as the Army, in particular, was grateful to Wootton Bassett for showing its appreciation for soldiers' sacrifice, there was an accompanying risk that all soldiers would be seen as victims. The pictures of grieving families and flag-draped coffins being driven through a quintessentially English market town could not help but stir the emotions. Soldiers want support, not pity. The MoD provided biographies and photographs of the fallen, many of them in their early twenties, some still teenagers, underlining that they were sons or daughters, perhaps brothers or sisters – the First World War concept of the unknown warrior had vanished. But the more that was known about the dead soldier, the more likely the public was to question whether their sacrifice and the mission were worthwhile. When the curtain came down on Wootton Bassett after 167 repatriation ceremonies, the government determined the new repatriation route. It avoided any town centres. It could yet turn out that the repatriation of the fallen, with the accompanying inquests, has profound long-term consequences for the Armed Forces.

Military doctrine states that the Military Covenant is best expressed at Armistice, 'when the Nation keeps Covenant with those who have made the ultimate sacrifice, giving their lives in action'. Since 1919 and the first national ceremonies centred around a cenotaph, the country has chosen to remember those who gave their lives in its service. As the previous chapter has outlined, from late 2007, many policymakers and commentators began putting the material and moral support for soldiers in the context of Military Covenant, which was frequently described as 'broken'. Although they would not have thought about it in these terms, the general public who turned out to line Wootton Bassett's streets to show their respect to the fallen were, in fact, keeping the Covenant with the nation's soldiers. With the advent of the coalition government in 2010, the Covenant became the subject of political wrangling as the government attempted to square an impossible ethical circle: how to put a trust-based Military Covenant into law. After much delay, rows, threatened U-turns and doubtless all-important scrutiny by government lawyers, the result was the Armed Forces Covenant, which became part of the 2011 Armed Forces Act.

The Armed Forces Covenant put the government's practical support for the entire Armed Forces community – service personnel, their families and veterans – on a formal, accountable basis. Every year, an Armed Forces Covenant report is now signed off by the Defence Secretary following the agreement of other key ministers. It tracks progress relating to welfare matters, including healthcare, the education of service children, housing and the operation of inquests. This annual report provides a cross-departmental audit trail. The areas being monitored are not set in stone and are expected to evolve, as different demands are placed on the Armed Forces. At the top of the list will probably remain medical treatment for the wounded; for example, the provision of prosthetics. In addition, in the context of the Armed Forces Covenant in Action, the Defence Select Committee now continually monitors welfare matters such as military casualties.

The Armed Forces Covenant was the culmination of a series of initiatives underway since 2008 to improve the welfare of the Forces community. In July 2010 for example, Prime Minister Cameron convened a task force under the chairmanship of historian Sir Hew Strachan to rebuild the Covenant. Among the measures it proposed was the Armed Forces Community Covenant, which aimed to forge better links between local authorities and the Armed Forces. By the end of 2015 every local authority in mainland Britain and two in Northern Ireland had signed a commitment to support the Armed

Forces community, while more than 800 companies signed the Corporate Covenant. Dozens of policies were introduced under the Armed Force Covenant umbrella to improve the lives of service personnel and their families. The Schools Admission Code in England was amended to prioritise service children: almost 25,000 of them benefited from grants to schools to mitigate the effects of the pupils moving so often, not least those whose families have moved from Germany. Since 2011, almost £150 million in Libor fines were given to help deliver Covenant commitments. For veterans, a new Career Transition Partnership supported service leavers. Reservists were now eligible for the Armed Forces Pension Scheme. By 2015, more than £85 million had helped 5,600 personnel to buy or improve their homes through the Forces Help to Buy Scheme.[39]

The principle of support to those who have served their country was given statutory recognition by the Armed Forces Covenant. This sense of commitment has been around for as long as there have been soldiers, but throughout history it has been imperfectly upheld. After the First World War, the British Legion was set up to fight for a better deal for veterans. George Bernard Shaw pointed out: 'The duty of the country is perfectly clear. These men were disabled in its service and should be supported by it unconditionally.'[40] The Coalition's Armed Forces Covenant built on welfare foundations laid down by the previous Labour government, particularly its 2008 Service Personnel Command Paper, which was a cross-Whitehall delivery plan. Often the problem has not been a lack of policies to improve the welfare of the forces community but policy implementation. For the most part, this was beyond ministerial control, but was devolved to local health services and town halls. For example, few knew that from 2008, priority access to NHS treatment was available to service personnel ahead of civilians with identical needs. Improving the quality of life for members of the forces community was always perhaps less about shiny new initiatives and more about the small day-to-day stuff of ensuring that everyone knew what services were available, as well as better coordination between all the existing providers. The focus on the Covenant opened up other lines of inquiry. Were Armed Forces personnel 'citizens-plus', deserving special treatment because of their service? Eventually the principle of 'no disadvantage' was settled upon; that is, that members of the forces community should not suffer any penalty because of military service. Who was a veteran? The definition – someone who had done one day's training – surprised many civilians who had assumed 'veteran' status related to combat. That definition is probably worthy of further debate.

The military charity sector represents the Armed Forces Covenant in action. The leading charities all act as agents to deliver practical welfare to serving personnel and veterans on behalf of the government. Chevasse VC House is one of a number of Personnel Recovery Centres, part of the government's Defence Recovery Capability to help the wounded. Located just 'outside the wire' of the military garrison in Colchester, it is run by Help for Heroes and supported by the Royal British Legion. Newly-built and light-filled, it provides twenty-seven en-suite bedrooms, as well as family units. Offering a gym and therapy rooms, along with other facilities such as IT, the centre aims to foster physical, mental and emotional wellbeing. A tranquil garden has been designed to represent the sometimes arduous personal journey back to recovery. Financed by money raised by the public, the centres, like the military charity sector itself, embody Britain's current support and pride in her Armed Forces.

Upholding the Covenant is primarily about ensuring that those soldiers and families who need support are not forgotten. With the end of combat operations, Iraq and Afghanistan will become the stuff of history. However, for the soldiers who were there, especially the wounded, the experience will stay with them. Back in the civilian world, some struggled to make sense of what they have been through. Bomb disposal officer Kevin Ivison describes returning to Hanover airport after a tour of Iraq: 'As the baggage carousel jolted loudly into action I hit the deck. I had spent four months learning that loud noises were lethal and it would take some time to adapt to real life.' He later realised that, like many other soldiers, he was suffering from Post Traumatic Stress Disorder. 'We had changed but the world had stayed the same.'[41] One of the most profound recent changes within the Armed Forces is the recognition given to mental health issues. Although not as bad as is often reported – for example, a misperception of the high rate of suicide among Falklands veterans has gained currency – mental illness is an issue, particularly for reservists who, in the past, have lacked the strong post-combat support network that regular soldiers enjoy. There is a danger that in wanting to maintain support, some military charities over-emphasise the negative: myths are sometimes perpetuated by the media, with the impression being given that military service leads to nothing but the misery of mental illness, sleeping rough or prison. Nothing could be more wrong. It should be remembered that about 10,000 soldiers leave the Army every year. The overwhelming majority look back on their time as soldiers as positive and simply get on with their civilian lives.

The original Military Covenant was part of the moral component of fighting power – part of the Army's doctrine. The Armed Forces Covenant that was recognised in the 2011 Armed Forces Act bore little relation to it. There was certainly no mention of the Military Covenant's 'commensurate terms and conditions of service' or similar open-ended commitments. The difficulties the government encountered in giving statutory, legal recognition to this trust-based compact highlighted the wisdom of the small team of senior commanders who, in the late 1990s, had quite deliberately ensured that the Military Covenant was not a legally enforceable contract. However, the combat operations in Iraq and Afghanistan showed how far the civilian 'legal component' was advancing into the Army's professional space.[42]

Lawfare

Caught up in military action, the first instinct of civilians is usually to flee. As weapons-bearers sanctioned by the state to deploy lethal force whenever the circumstances demand, soldiers have potentially enormous powers of coercion. As much as it can reassure, their very presence can intimidate and instil fear. Wherever state institutions and/or democracy are fragile, military *coups d'état* are a possibility. Given soldiers' latent or actual coercive power, as well as the huge moral responsibility they have in deploying that power, the state has always sought to constrain soldiers. Their actions have been governed and limited by laws, conventions and regulations. For centuries, soldiers have been subject to civilian law, international law and a separate body of military law, which includes the court martial process.

In recent years, civilian law has made its presence felt as never before, challenging the Army's ethos and threatening combat effectiveness. In 2005, the former CDS, Admiral of the Fleet Lord Boyce,

described the Armed Forces as being under 'legal siege'.[43] The operations in Iraq and Afghanistan, which introduced a body of case law
in connection with overseas combat, continually reshaped the legal
terrain in which soldiers manoeuvre. Along with the International
Humanitarian Law and the Law of Armed Conflict, which include the
Geneva and Hague Conventions, soldiers' actions can be governed by
the terms of a UN mandate, a Status of Forces Agreement between
the sovereign host nation and the United Kingdom, Rules of Engagement, British domestic legislation and the law of the land where they
are deployed. In addition, soldiers have to abide by Queen's Regulations and, less formally, be mindful of the Army's *Values and Standards*. The International Criminal Court Act covers war crimes. This
body of legal regulation was balanced by the concept of combat immunity, which traditionally exempted the MoD and service personnel
from legal action in connection with conflict. In Afghanistan, some
Taliban nicknamed British troops 'donkeys' because of the enormous
amount of kit they carried, weighing on average 110 pounds. An
invisible but necessary additional load has been the legal constraints
on every soldier, whose training is as much about inculcating the
rules as it is about learning to fire a weapon. The 1998 Human Rights
Act, encroaching on the battlespace, challenged the concept of combat
immunity and has added to the legal burden to such an extent that
military effectiveness could be undermined. A report for the Policy
Exchange think-tank warned: 'None has succeeded in defeating the
Armed Forces of the United Kingdom. Napoleon, Falkenhayn and
Hitler could not. But where these enemies failed, our own legal institutions threaten to succeed.'[44] Criticising 'legal mission creep' and the
'judicialisation of war', a subsequent report concluded: 'The result
will be an excessive degree of caution which is antithetical to the war-
fighting ethos that is vital for success on the battlefield.'[45]

Following the intervention in Iraq in 2003, a handful of long-
running and high-profile legal cases connected to that deployment
made their way up through the British courts. Testing how far the
Human Rights Act should apply to overseas military operations,
they forced a consideration of the MoD's duty of care to soldiers,
as well as the rights of foreign nationals while in British military
detention or employed by the British. The families of Private Phillip
Hewitt, Private Lee Ellis and Lance Corporal Kirk Redpath clearly

considered that the men had been failed by the Army and the Ministry of Defence following their deaths in separate incidents in Iraq. In June 2013, the Supreme Court ruled that the soldiers, although in Iraq, were within the jurisdiction of the United Kingdom, were therefore subject to Human Rights legislation and that their families could claim compensation for negligence. The case of *Al-Skeini* v. *UK* involved the deaths of five Iraqi civilians shot by soldiers on patrol and of Baha Mousa, who had been detained at a British Army base. In July 2011, the European Court of Human Rights ruled that because Britain had assumed security of south Iraq and was exercising 'control and authority' over Iraqis, it had a duty under the European Convention to conduct an effective investigation into the circumstances surrounding the deaths. In July 2015, the Court of Appeal ruled that British forces personnel in Afghanistan had unlawfully detained Serdar Mohammed, an insurgent believed to be a Taliban commander involved in the large-scale production of IEDs.[46] The cumulative impact of these and other cases was to bring the law – and lawyers – into the military's area of operations. From the comfort of the Appeal Court, judges seemed not to have considered that it might be critical to the mission to remove an enemy bomb-maker from circulation for a few months. As one retired senior commander stated to the Defence Select Committee: 'The need to arrest and detain enemy combatants and insurgents in a conflict zone should not be expected to comply with peacetime standards such as those exercised by a civilian police force in Tunbridge Wells on a Saturday night.'[47]

In parallel with the rise of lawfare were public inquiries into military operations. Whether their establishment was politically motivated or to ensure compliance with the human rights legislation, they opened up the Army to an alternative form of scrutiny and accountability. Hutton, Butler, Chilcot, Gage and Al-Sweady examined issues relating to Iraq, Haddon-Cave to Afghanistan, while twelve years after being set up, in 2010, Saville finally reported on Bloody Sunday. The 5,000-page report of what happened on 30 January 1972 in Londonderry concluded that soldiers of 1 Para 'caused the deaths of 13 people and the injury to a similar number, none of whom were posing a threat of causing death or serious injury'.[48] In the House of Commons, Prime Minister David Cameron said he was 'deeply sorry' and cited the rest of Saville's conclusion: 'What happened on Bloody Sunday strengthened the Provisional IRA, increased nationalist resentment and hostility towards the Army and exacerbated the violent conflict of the years that followed. Bloody Sunday was a tragedy for the bereaved and the wounded, and a catastrophe for the people of Northern Ireland.' Stating that Bloody Sunday should not be the defining story of Operation Banner, the Prime Minister observed, 'You do not defend the British Army by defending the indefensible.'[49]

Another breach of military discipline was revealed by the inquiry led by Sir William Gage which reported in 2011. In September 2003, soldiers from the 1st Battalion Queen's Lancashire Regiment arrested 26-year-old hotel worker Baha Mousa in Basra. Along with nine other Iraqis, he was detained at a British base, where two days later he died. He had ninety-three injuries to his body. A court martial into the incident held in 2007 found one corporal, who had previously confessed, guilty of war crimes – the first such conviction in Britain – but acquitted six others, including the commanding officer. The inquiry found that the 'five techniques' of interrogation, outlawed in 1972 after their use in Northern Ireland, had been deployed. Soldiers on one online military forum registered their dismay about the case: 'This sorry episode has cast the entire British Army into disrepute'; 'It makes all soldiers, and ex-soldiers appear dishonest'; 'This incident was a shameful abuse of power and has tainted the whole of the British Army.'[50] Posts on the same forum expressed robust support for seven soldiers from 3 Para whose trial in 2005 for the murder of Iraqi teenager Nadhem Abdullah collapsed.[51] In that case, Iraqi witnesses, who had been paid, were found to have lied. Similarly, the Al-Sweady inquiry led by Sir Thayne Forbes into the 2004 Battle of Danny Boy and its aftermath established that the most serious allegations of murder and mutilation made against British soldiers were wholly without foundation and were the product of 'deliberate lies, reckless speculation and engrained hostility' from Iraqi witnesses.[52]

In recent years the Army has found itself increasingly in the dock – occasionally justifiably, usually not. Human rights legislation, suitable for the peaceful, prosperous first world, has at its heart the right to life. This has been somewhat at odds with the primary tasks set for the Army by the government in 2003 and 2006 – the deployments to Iraq and Afghanistan. The death, destruction and brutality of war cannot be mitigated by the insistence on the human rights of Iraqis and Afghans, who, if consulted, probably would have preferred their countries not to have been invaded and occupied by foreign troops. While British courts determined the extent of the reach of the Human Rights Act and lawyers earned a lucrative living out of taxpayer-funded legal aid that funded baseless Iraqi claims against the British military, thousands of miles away soldiers continued to put their lives on the line. Atrocities allegedly committed by British personnel against the Mau Mau and Greek-Cypriot EOKA insurgents half a century ago became the subject of inquiry and financial claim. According to Defence Secretary Michael Fallon in 2015, the cost of legal proceedings in connection with Iraq and Afghanistan stood at some £87 million, the majority of which has gone to lawyers: the Al-Sweady inquiry cost £30 million of taxpayers' money 'to expose what appear to have been barefaced lies'.[53]

The Army needs constantly to strive to adapt to new legislation, which is after all a reflection of the civilian society it serves. Those who are worried about the impact on combat effectiveness of the Human Rights Act should perhaps reflect on a development it influenced, which at the time was hugely controversial but rapidly became unremarkable. In 2000, two cases brought under Article 8 of the European Convention on Human Rights led to the lifting of the ban on homosexuals serving in the Armed Forces. The Army was forced to adapt. In 2008, the Army began working with the charity Stonewall to recognise gay rights within the institution. In 2015, it was recognised in Stonewall's Top 50 Employers list – a listing that may have made some traditionalists choke on their evening glasses of whisky! Society at large may move on in its opinions, and the Army needs to keep a careful watch on developments in order to preserve operational effectiveness. The Army may wish to have a right to be different but it cannot march out of step indefinitely from the society from which its soldiers are drawn. Civilian policymakers must, however, be aware that the Army's priority has always been, and will remain, operational effectiveness, the bedrock of the Army's contribution to the defence of the realm.

The Arab Spring and Libya

In December 2010, in a small town in the heart of Tunisia, fruit seller Mohamed Bouazizi set fire to himself in protest against the local government corruption which was hurting his chances of earning even a meagre living. This act of desperation by someone who symbolised the disenfranchised and dispossessed set off a chain reaction across the Middle East, its impact anticipated to be as far-reaching as the fall of the Berlin Wall. With the help of social media, populist uprisings spread through the region in early 2011. The Arab Spring saw the overthrow of long-entrenched tyrannies, one after the other, beginning in Tunisia and Egypt. In Bahrain, the government was shaken but did not fall. The international community watched and waited on the sidelines as history was being made. However, the transition from despotism was far from easy. In Syria and Libya, unrest and revolt escalated into civil war.

Libya's Colonel Muammar Gaddafi – 'a striking combination of menace and eccentricity' – was determined to retain his grip on power.[54] The initial challenge to his regime came in February 2011, with an uprising in Benghazi, a city with a population of 700,000 in the Cyrenaica region, close to the border with Egypt and the site of the 1942 Battle of El Alamein.[55] From sponsoring the IRA, to the killing of police officer Yvonne Fletcher outside its London embassy in 1984, to orchestrating the bombing of Pan Am Flight 103 which exploded over Lockerbie in December 1988, Gaddafi's Libya remained a rogue state, hostile to British interests. However, a thaw in relations that had been underway since 9/11 was hastened by the 2004 'Deal in the Desert' between Tony Blair and the Libyan leader. The unrest first seen in Benghazi spread, with violence between government forces and rebels escalating throughout the east of the country. As with many of the region's dictatorships, government was viewed as a family business. The Gaddafi regime dug in, with the dictator's son Saif pledging to fight the rebels 'to the very last bullet'. This was in marked contrast with neighbouring Egypt. There, the regime of Hosni Mubarak had capitulated relatively peacefully in February 2011 following mass demonstrations in Cairo and other major cities, where the protestors were helped by the passive support of the Army. By the second week in March, Gaddafi's fightback looked as if it might be successful: regime forces sweeping east from the capital

Tripoli took Zawiya, and the rebel stronghold of Benghazi seemed about to fall.

The Anglo-French orchestrated intervention in Libya reflected the hard lessons learned from Iraq. The campaign was legally water-tight, it had the backing of Arab nations and some thought was given to its aftermath. In addition, no action by Western powers would be taken that hinted at invasion or occupation of another Muslim country: there would, officially, be no British boots on the ground. Although President Nicolas Sarkozy of France had envisaged a joint Anglo-French operation, CDS Richards insisted on NATO involve-ment: 'We needed the Americans alongside us.'[56] On 17 March 2011, United Nations Security Council Resolution 1973 judged that the widespread attacks against Libyan civilians may constitute 'a crime against humanity' and represented a Chapter VII threat to interna-tional peace and security. The UN mandated that 'all necessary meas-ures' – which would include enforcing a no-fly zone and an arms embargo – should be taken to protect civilians and civilian-populated areas under threat of attack, including Benghazi. Crucially, members of the League of Arab States were called upon to cooperate, while all necessary measures specifically excluded 'a foreign occupation force of any form on any part of Libyan territory'.[57] A clear message was being sent: Libya was not going to be another Iraq. Two days later air strikes were launched, including cruise missiles fired from HMS *Triumph*, while RAF Tornado GR4s were deployed from the United Kingdom and RAF Typhoons sent to a base in southern Italy. On 27 March, NATO took command of the military operation in Libya. Within weeks, the Gaddafi advance east was reversed.

For many politicians and commentators, the Libyan interven-tion resembled the Kosovo campaign. It was similarly, and repeatedly, justified on the grounds of averting humanitarian catastrophe: Sreb-renica was invoked. The fall of Benghazi, being run by the oppos-ition National Transitional Council, could have led to a massacre that would have 'stained the conscience of the world', according to US President Barack Obama. However, after some initial cruise missile strikes, the United States was decidedly reluctant to stay involved, although it continued to play a behind-the-scenes role through its logistical and intelligence assets.[58] The day after the handover to NATO, the President told the American people, 'I said that America's role would be limited; that we would not put ground troops into Libya; that we would focus our unique capabilities on the front end of the operation and that we would transfer responsibility to our allies and partners.'[59]

Although the campaign was focused on air power, the Prime Minister had seemingly questioned its utility a month earlier during a visit to post-Mubarak Egypt: 'I am not a naïve neo-Con who thinks you can drop democracy out of an aeroplane at 40,000 feet.'[60] However, there was no intention of committing British troops to Libya, although perhaps significantly David Cameron did not specifically rule out any military presence on the ground during a Commons debate on 21 March, following the first air strikes. Throughout, he stressed the humanitarian nature of the mission and that, although he was in favour of regime change, this was to be a matter for the Libyan people. 'I have been clear. I think Libya needs to get rid of Gaddafi. But in the end we are responsible for trying to enforce that Security Council Resolution; the Libyans must choose their own future.'[61]

Just as in Kosovo, a campaign which had been expected to be short and sharp dragged on for months. The RAF was to fly more than 1,000 sorties. By May, Western leaders were acknowledging deadlock. Essentially, Libya was divided into the rebel-held east and the government-held west, centring on Tripoli and Misrata. The CDS was looking for some means of influencing events on the ground: any sizeable British presence was ruled out, especially given the demands in Afghanistan. Instead, Arab forces, particularly from Qatar, acted as proxies, helped by British and French 'advisers'. According to the CDS, 'We deployed some liaison officers of our own. They played a limited but useful role. Later there was also a small number of advisers deployed in an ad hoc headquarters in Benghazi and then in Misrata'[62] The role of British Special Forces in the campaign to overthrow the regime has never been officially acknowledged; however, journalist Mark Urban asserted that it 'tipped the balance in favour of the revolutionaries'.[63] The stalemate was ended by the switch of military focus from the east to the west of the country, with an advance on Sirte and Tripoli via the Nafusa mountains in the south of the country. In August, opposition forces took Tripoli, bringing to an end to Gaddafi's regime after forty-two years. The dictator was captured and executed in October in fairly inglorious circumstances.

NATO action in Libya highlighted the shortcomings of the 2010 Strategic Defence and Security Review. Many of the capabilities used in the campaign were to have been scrapped, including HMS *Cumberland*, one of three frigates destined for the breaker's yard. Sentinel surveillance aircraft were given a brief reprieve, while the deployment of Tornados called into question the wisdom of cutting the number of their squadrons from seven to five. One Tornado flying from Britain needed more than six air-to-air refuelling operations to complete the mission; the CDS noted that an aircraft carrier – scrapped under the SDSR – 'would have made life a lot easier'.[64] As one analyst argued, if the Libyan uprising had broken out just a few months later, most of the 'decommissionings, disbandments and retirements' would have already taken place, making it impossible for Britain to play any meaningful role in the campaign.[65]

The intervention in Libya was a tactical success, but its long-term strategic effect was hard to determine. There had been a convergence of interest between the country's anti-government forces and the West, particularly Britain and France, who did not want a failed state on Europe's southern border. However, five years on, Libya had yet to recover its equilibrium and security. The overthrow of the Gaddaffi regime fractured the country and unleashed rival militia groups whose battle for dominance spread to the capital. The unforeseen consequences of violent regime change in a tribal nation, no matter how unpalatable that regime is to the West, were graphically shown in a video released on social media in February 2015. It showed the beheading of twenty-one Coptic Christians on a Libyan beach by members of ISIS – the jihadist group spawned by the continuing instability in northern Iraq and civil war in Syria.

Syria and the Rise of ISIS

Syria's President Bashar al-Assad, like Colonel Gaddafi, was another leader determined to resist any challenge to his authority. In March 2011, the Arab Spring that had spread through the Middle East, bringing with it violent upheaval from Morocco across to the Yemen, arrived in Daraa, a small city south of the Syrian capital Damascus. Mass protests were sparked by the arrest of school students who had written anti-government graffiti. Their detention appeared to be yet further confirmation of the repression within the country, a police state ever since Assad's father, Hafez, had seized the presidency in 1970. YouTube and other social media fomented further unrest: within weeks, anti-government demonstrations had spread to provincial cities including Homs, Hama and Aleppo. Revolution seemed about to claim another authoritarian Arab government.

Two years on, Assad's Ba'athist regime clung on as civil war ravaged the country. The United Nations estimated that by June 2013 as many as 92,000 Syrians had been killed, almost 2 million had fled to neighbouring countries and a further 4 million were internally displaced.[66] Unlike in Libya, where their intervention was mainly from the air, Britain and the United States refrained from action in Syria, their governments scarred by more than a decade of conflict in Iraq and Afghanistan. However, with the Assad government's use of chemical weapons in the suburbs of Damascus on 21 August, which resulted in 350 deaths and ten times the number of injuries, this seemed about to change.

To some, the House of Commons' defeat of the British government's proposal to take military action in Syria against the Assad government was unexpected, while to others it was inevitable, given the mood in the country in the days just before the debate. Nevertheless, the decision was condemned as 'shocking and shaming' and a 'catastrophe' by one commentator, although most agreed that the proposed air strike would have been both too little and too late to have been anything other than a fairly meaningless gesture.[67] The Assad regime's violation of the 1925 convention outlawing the use of chemical weapons would, however, have provided a legal pretext for a limited raid. Had parliamentary approval been secured on 29 August, as many of the Prime Minister's supporters expected, Britain would have helped the Obama administration make the case to a sceptical American Congress and public about the need for military action in Syria. It was generally accepted that the President was apparently only envisaging 'a shot across the bow'. Notwithstanding 100,000 already dead in Syria, the British government's humanitarian justification for an intervention cut little ice with its electorate, just 11 per cent of whom were said to favour military action.

With UN weapons inspectors already in Damascus and doubt

about getting a Security Council approval for any attack on Syria, it is unsurprising that the spectre of Iraq hung over the debate. One MP reminded the House that intelligence in connection with another chemical arsenal which had been described by an earlier prime minister as extensive, detailed and authoritative, in fact, turned out to be limited, sporadic and patchy.[68] There was also confusion about the exact objective of any military action. Punishment? Regime change? Losing the vote was humiliating for the government, which had insisted that Parliament be recalled from its summer recess, stoking suspicions that yet another apparently ill-thought-out military attack on yet another Arab country was imminent. Less than two weeks later, having his own difficulties in getting approval from Congress, President Obama announced that strikes against Syria were shelved. Undoubtedly this was the right decision on this specific issue, but the reluctance of the West to become involved gave Russia's president, Vladimir Putin, the chance to take a risk and assert his authority. He took the lead over the dismantling of Assad's chemical weapons arsenal. Russia's pariah status over the invasion of eastern Ukraine and the annexation of Crimea in early 2014 would be redeemed by its decisive military intervention in Syria. Moscow's actions would ultimately influence the situation on the ground.

Russian involvement in Syria was only one aspect of the international dimension of a civil war that could well reshape the Middle East. With the city of Tartous providing Moscow with its only port on the Mediterranean, Syria can be considered Russia's back yard. During the Soviet era, it gave huge military aid to President Hafez. The Assads and their government supporters were from the minority Shi'ite Alawite sect, friendly to Iran. Their opponents were for the most part Sunnis, backed by Saudi Arabia and other Gulf players. However, these opponents were not a unified force, but instead split into about ten major factions. Among them were many unlikely allies – the jihadist al-Nusra front and the moderate Syrian Free Army, which included many former members of the regular army. As well as fighting Assad's forces, the opposition also fought among themselves. From 2011, the civil war gave Syria's Kurds the opportunity to try to establish their own separate state, carved out of their autonomous enclave in the north-east of the country. Kurdish separatism had, however, long been resisted by Syria's neighbour Turkey, where Kurds account for one-fifth of the population. In 2014 a new player, ISIS – soon to declare its own so-called Islamic State – was added to the splintering confusion of rival groups and their international backers, which were all struggling either for the control of Syria or independence from it.

With the world's attention focused on Syria and the resulting humanitarian crisis, little heed had been given to neighbouring Iraq. Thousands of fighters, many of them foreign, had joined ISIS, a radical jihadist movement that had evolved out of al-Qaeda in Iraq. Also known as Islamic State, so-called Islamic State, Daesh and ISIL, ISIS – the Islamic State of Iraq and the Levant/Al Sham – had been steadily gaining ground across Iraq, including around Fallujah, as well as in Syria, where its efforts centred on Raqqa. To global shock, it seized control of Iraq's second city, Mosul, in the country's north on 10 June 2014. Confronted by the ISIS advance, the Iraqi army simply ran away. Training that had cost an estimated $25 billion turned out to be a poor investment, while a supposed strength of 400,000 was made up of tens of thousands of ghost soldiers. One Kurdish official later observed: 'The Iraqi Army took ten years to build and ten hours to collapse.'[69]

On 30 June ISIS declared a caliphate and extended its control southwards towards Baghdad and westwards into Syria, filling the vacuum created by the civil war. Suddenly the world was alive to the reality of the ever-expanding territory under ISIS control, soon to cover an area greater in size than Britain. Their regime of terror was characterised by beheadings, crucifixions and burnings alive, which were quite deliberately publicised via social media. The mass killings and rape of the Yazidi people living near the Turkish border was particularly barbaric. With its savvy use of social media, ISIS was adept at getting its message across, garnering a never-ending supply of young and impressionable recruits from overseas, including Britain. Many would be sacrificed as cannon fodder and suicide bombers. However, radicalised and battle-hardened, some would inevitably make their way back home, jeopardising the nation's security. Other subversives could simply stay in the United Kingdom, being radicalised via their electronic screens. In October 2015, the Head of MI5 said that intelligence agencies had disrupted six plots over the previous year and that Britain was facing an unprecedented threat.[70]

A year after Parliament rejected any intervention in Syria, it did approve limited military action in Iraq. Although the vote in the House of Commons on 26 September 2014 was overwhelmingly in favour by 524 votes to 43, the motion specifically stated that 'it does not endorse UK air strikes in Syria as part of this campaign' and spelt out that 'Her Majesty's Government will not deploy UK troops in ground combat operations'.[71] This echoed a commitment made by the Prime Minister the previous month: 'Britain is not going to get involved in another war in Iraq. We are not going to be putting boots on the ground. We are not going to be sending in the British Army.'[72] Four days after the debate, Britain joined Operation Inherent Resolve, an air campaign being carried out by an American-led multinational coalition. A year later, more than 10,600 separate targets had been hit and an estimated 10–15,000 ISIS fighters killed.[73] Between October 2014 and the end of July 2015, RAF Tornados conducted more than 200 air strikes, while Reaper drones launched 132 strikes. The legitimacy of drones has been questioned by groups such as Human Rights Watch, not least because their deployment is likened to playing a computer game – 'a PlayStation mentality to killing'.[74] New defence technology always brings with it new ethical dilemmas. The successful targeting of British radical Mohammed Emwazi, known as Jihadi John, by the Americans in Raqqa in November 2015 caused some unease, with the Leader of the Opposition suggesting that Emwazi should have been brought to court. The RAF drone strike against another British jihadist, Reyaad Khan, earlier in August that year in Syria provoked comment about military action taken specifically against the wishes of Parliament, which had permitted British action only in Iraq. It illustrated the paradox of the British conducting an operation only on one side of a border, while the enemy not only operated on both sides but did not actually recognise the border.

Drawn by Britain and France almost a century ago in the wake of global war, the borders of Syria and Iraq became almost meaningless, at least in practice if not in law. Internal conflict caused a humanitarian catastrophe, with millions trying to escape and flee to Europe. The migration crisis of 2015 and beyond produced almost Biblical scenes of exodus, as hundreds of thousands of people crossed the continent. Meanwhile, soldiers from 2nd Battalion, Princess of Wales's Royal Regiment were in northern Iraq training the Kurdish

Peshmerga in their fight against ISIS. Special Forces were deployed, along with some 3,500 US troops. Elite Iraqi units were too thinly spread, described by one journalist on the ground as being 'rushed like a fire brigade from crisis to crisis'.[75] In May 2015, ISIS captured Ramadi, the capital of Iraq's Anbar province, and a few days later took the ancient Syrian provincial capital of Palmyra. In September, US General Martin Dempsey, Chairman of the Joint Chiefs, suggested that the fight against ISIS was 'tactically stalemated', however ground started to be recovered. The ISIS-inspired terrorist attacks on Paris that killed 130 people on 13 November were described as an 'act of war' by France's President François Hollande. One result of the attacks was that on 2 December the Westminster Parliament finally approved air strikes against Syria.

The resolute determination not to commit ground troops in Syria earlier in the year was followed by the welcome news of the containment of Ebola, which had broken out in Sierra Leone like a twenty-first century plague. A British hospital ship and more than 300 service personnel had helped combat the epidemic by building treatment centres and helping disseminate the public health message, vital to changing local cultural practices and preventing the further spread of the virus. Since 1945, after seventy years of conducting military campaigns around the world, in 2015 the British Army's largest deployment of forces was not to fight terrorism or insurgency, but disease – such is modern soldiering.

Following the surprise Conservative victory in the May 2015 General Election, the 2015 *Strategic Defence and Security Review* renewed Britain's commitment to defence, atoning in part for the damage of the 2010 SDSR. Along with a doubling of investment in Special Forces' equipment, the organisation of the Army would be reconfigured to include two new strike brigades of 5,000 personnel each. The government expects to have a highly capable expeditionary force of around 50,000, formed around a single Army division by 2025.[76] While brigades are capable of conducting tactical engagements, there is a recognition that the divisional level is the lowest level at which all aspects of modern war-fighting can be properly orchestrated. The retention of this single division is the bottom line of credibility below which the British Army would become nothing more than a gendarmerie with a famous history. From almost 3 million men under arms in 1945, at the end of the Cold War the British Army could still field four fighting divisions to face Warsaw Pact forces on the North German Plain as part of NATO's Central Region force structure. To be struggling in 2015 to hold on to a single deployable division was a telling comment about a globally reduced Britain. Given current international uncertainties, no further reduction in the size of the Army could keep the Army as a serious professional asset for the nation, and the United Kingdom as a meaningful player on the world stage.

Since 1945, British boots have been on the ground across the world; in the years to come they will undoubtedly be needed again. While the softer gloves of diplomacy and development aid are powerful instruments of policy, they are only really effective if those gloves are filled by the mailed fists of meaningful military capability. The temptation to cut defence spending in times of economic pressure has been a recurrent theme since 1945, but if Britain is to retain any influence and standing in the international community then it is key to ensure that her Armed Forces, and the boots on the ground that are the enduring symbol of her influence, are sustained as a credible fighting force. Future generations would not thank the present one, if that were not to be so.

A LOOK BACK, A LOOK FORWARD

Almost seventy years after Field Marshal Montgomery took the surrender of German forces at Timeloberg on Lüneburg Heath, the 7th Armoured Brigade said a formal farewell to Germany. The direct descendants of Monty's legendary Desert Rats were leaving their headquarters at Campbell Barracks, Hohne Garrison. The Brigade's flag with its famous red jerboa emblem was lowered, to be raised again on 14 November 2014 at Chetwynd Barracks, Chilwell, Nottinghamshire. The British Army was coming home.

Like the country it serves, today's Army is almost unrecognisable compared with the force of 1945. That Army's strength stood at more than 2.9 million soldiers, the vast majority of them conscripts – and men. On the home front, most of the Army's drivers, as well its clerks, telephonists, translators and vehicle mechanics, were the women of the Auxiliary Territorial Service, among them the future Queen Elizabeth II. ATS anti-aircraft crews could train their guns on enemy planes flying over Britain but were forbidden to open fire – only their male colleagues were permitted to do this. In 2016, the government gave the green light for women soldiers to serve in close combat roles on the frontline. The decision sparked controversy: some serving women soldiers expressed their doubts about it. What perhaps should be remembered is that many men are ruled out of a frontline infantry role because they are unable to meet the gruelling physical standards demanded. Tests assessing physical capability should be gender-blind, but with no allowances made. The frontline of combat is no place for passengers or for the 'weaker sex' – of any gender.

Often unexamined in the debate about frontline service is the frontline itself. Where is it in today's wars? The Desert Rats in North Africa in 1942 would have recognised it, so would their successors fighting in the first Gulf War in 1991, but would the British soldiers serving in Palestine in 1947 or in Sierra Leone in 2000? The conscripts on the frontline in Korea in 1950 fought a very different type of conflict from the men and women who served in Iraq from 2003. In examining the British Army since 1945, state-on-state conflict, featuring regular forces and decisive battles are rare: British soldiers are usually in uniform, but their enemies often are not. This book has touched on the so-called 'new wars' of the post-Cold War era, making the point that in the long history of the British Army, there is nothing particularly new about them. If not quite Kipling's 'savage wars of peace', they would be recognisable to Colonel C. E. Callwell, the author of *Small Wars: Their Principles and Practice*. First published in 1896, this can be described as a late Victorian era counter-insurgency manual, which has lessons for today and for future conflict. Small wars are not going away. For some of its many critics, Iraq was 'all about oil': the conflicts of the future could be all about water or other scarce resources, as rising numbers of the world's people battle for control of limited supplies, or even just battle for somewhere safe to live.

A subtitle for any history of the British Army since 1945 could be 'tales of the unexpected'. Defence policy tries to anticipate the future threats which might alter the national and international security landscape, but is often confounded. The attacks of 9/11, civil war in the heart of Europe in the former Yugoslavia, the end of the Cold War, the Falklands campaign, military intervention in Northern Ireland, the withdrawal from East of Suez … all had a profound impact on the Army, none had been specifically planned for. Britain's politicians, particularly eager since 1990 to take the peace dividend, apparently assume that what is almost unimaginable will never happen. History suggests they are wrong. The fourth-century writer Vegetius said they are wrong: *Si vis pacem, para bellum*; 'If you want peace, prepare for war.' At the time of writing, a militarily resurgent Russia has been making her presence felt in the Crimea, Ukraine, Syria and the flanks of NATO: she remains a significant threat to our security. What if she overstepped the mark in the Baltic States who are amongst our NATO allies which Britain is committed to defend? What will be the Chinese military posture be like in 2030? In 2050? What of self-styled Islamic State (ISIS) – or its successors – who are making it impossible to draw a double line concluding the 2003 intervention in Iraq? Future conflicts will inevitably occur as unidentified and unquantified threats emerge to challenge the security of the British people.

Following its creation in 1949, NATO has been at the heart of Britain's defence and security policy. The original 12-state alliance has expanded to 28 members. In 2006, they committed to spend at least 2 per cent of GDP on defence, a target which many have rarely met. Although Britain has seemingly honoured her commitment, in recent years this has only been achieved by a financial sleight of hand: for example, by including spending on items that were previously not part of the official defence budget, such as pensions for retired civilian MoD personnel. In the context of national security, political chicanery like this is unfortunate. It also sends a poor signal to Britain's greatest post-1945 ally, the United States, particularly at a time when taxpayers on the other side of the Atlantic are becoming increasingly restive at having to pick up the tab for Europe's defence, reflected by the issue being raised during the 2016 presidential election campaign. For Britain, a country whose Armed Forces are so integral to national identity and a country that has often taken the lead in matters of defence, the 2 per cent target should be a minimum: a floor and not a ceiling.

As a former Chief of the General Staff, I am troubled that the planned strength of the Army was set by Prime Minister Cameron's coalition government at just 82,000 regular soldiers. This means that the Army could simply be too small to do everything that might be asked of it, whether at home, helping the civilian authorities, or overseas, performing tasks ranging from high-intensity combat operations to peacekeeping in all its various forms. Since the end of the Cold War, British soldiers have increasingly been involved in humanitarian missions, often putting themselves at risk to save the lives of others across the world, including in the Balkans and Sierra Leone. In the early 1990s, the Cheshires summed up their mission in Bosnia: 'to save life'. When the 1994 genocide in Rwanda is remembered, many civilians across the world ask why there was no effective military intervention by the United Nations to halt the killing. An ineffective military is also seen as complicit in the 1995 massacre at Srebrenica. Similarly, governments in the West are now berated by the media for not taking military action in the Syrian civil war. Britain cannot have it all ways. Either we resign ourselves to having less global influence or we make the necessary investment to ensure we remain a force for good in the world. With the Army's institutional memory and hard-won experience fading by the day thanks to the post-2010 cuts in personnel, that decision has to be made quickly.

Since 1945, Britain had to adapt from being a global superpower, but has retained a global outlook. Britain remains one of the permanent members of the United Nations Security Council, a member of the G7/G8, the G20 and at the heart of the Commonwealth. As a practical proponent of globalisation, long before the word came into use, it is perhaps not unexpected that Britain found it hard to adapt to being just another European nation. In June 2016, the British people voted unexpectedly in favour of Brexit. Field Marshal Lord Bramall, who took part in the Normandy landings, argued that the EU had helped save the continent from the destructive wars of the past. Conversely, concerned about the impact of a future European Army on the British military, Field Marshal Lord Guthrie ultimately came down on the side of leave. As the wars in Bosnia and Kosovo demonstrated, NATO has always been more relevant to the security of Europe than the European Union – a factor that successive leaders in Moscow, including President Putin, have long recognised. Britain's nuclear deterrent – which Parliament voted to renew in July 2016 – helped keep the peace in Europe throughout decades of Cold War tension and remains the bedrock of the nation's security.

Security Council membership brings with it responsibilities, including the willingness to deploy military force. Founded at the end of the Second World War, the United Nations started life with just fifty-one members: today there are 193, reflecting not least the end of empires. Since 1945, British soldiers have been deployed primarily to uphold Security Council resolutions, sometimes as peacekeepers, and often in response to humanitarian crises engendered by conflict. Any military action should be undertaken with the objective of promoting a better peace, but as Prime Minister Tony Blair observed in his 1999 doctrine for the international community speech, war is an imperfect instrument for righting humanitarian distress, but might be the only option available. As this book relates, it was only the deployment of external military force that halted further bloodshed in Bosnia, Kosovo and Sierra Leone. However, unless such life-saving operations are undertaken by soldiers, such as the British, who are trained to the highest end of the war-fighting spectrum, peacekeeping has too often been ineffective. On occasions, peacekeeping operations have lacked not only a robust international mandate but also have been undertaken by inexperienced soldiers who are without the necessary training which itself engenders confidence and competence, or worse still, the necessary discipline to remain part of the solution rather than add to the problem.

Deployed to zones of conflict, British soldiers know that what local people want above all else is security; everything follows on from that. In hostile situations where government officials and aid workers fear to tread, it is often only the Army that can deliver defence, diplomacy and development in an effective and integrated way, especially in the initial weeks or months of a campaign. Since the establishment of the Department for International Development in 1997, the development cart has too often been put before the stabilisation horse. There have been many instances in recent years – Bosnia, Kosovo and Iraq are stark examples – when stabilisation and the delivery of humanitarian aid, or the beginning of the reconstruction of a country emerging from conflict, has been inhibited by the absence of security. Such security can only be provided by soldiers on the ground. The logic behind the concept of more closely aligning diplomacy, defence and development capability seems inescapable to those soldiers, at the sharp end of trying to deliver policy and ensure its success. The government could also do worse than reappraise the debate that has gone on since the 1960s, in the context about how best to deliver UK aid in a post-colonial era, than to decide to break up the current Department for International Development, and reassign its work and budget to the Foreign and Commonwealth Office and the Ministry of Defence. At the very least there would only be two, rather than three, points of decision-making within Whitehall. The alternative is that the occupant of No 10 imposes her or his will, very firmly, on their three Secretaries of State to ensure that there is but one British foreign policy and one British voice being heard, and enacted, on the world stage. The current status quo is not satisfactory. Experience has also shown that the policy of spending 0.7 per cent of GDP on foreign aid has led to some poor spending decisions, local corruption and waste. These funds would be far better spent on cash-starved defence, in the interests of collective security. If the defence budget was to be increased by £3–5bn, provided at least in part with funds diverted from the foreign aid budget, not only would many of the MoD's budgetary problems be solved, but a powerful message would be sent to Washington and Europe that the post-Brexit United Kingdom takes its responsibilities to European security and to NATO very seriously.

Since 1945, Britain's relationship with the United States has been central to our foreign and defence policy. In future, we are still likely to take our cue from Washington, but Washington's continuing commitment to the security of Europe cannot be taken for granted. There are signs, just as in 1945, that her worldwide priorities are a matter for discussion. Whether criticism about Europe's lack of financial commitment to NATO membership, to a less than whole-hearted involvement in Libya in 2011 and hesitancy over intervention in the civil war in Syria, US disenchantment seems palpable. During the Obama years, the weakness of US world leadership was a worrying consequence. However, one of the lessons learned from the West's twenty-first-century discretionary wars is that the removal of strong, albeit dictatorial, leaders and their regimes by external intervention demands robust post-conflict commitment to ensure stabilisation and prevent a vacuum in governance. Such plans were absent in both Iraq in 2003 and Libya in 2010, leading to political chaos and the breakdown of security, which ultimately affected the wider region and was a major factor in the spawning of the self-styled Islamic State.

Any recent history of the British Army inevitably focuses on the campaigns in Iraq and Afghanistan. The bitter controversy surrounding the circumstances of Britain going to war in Iraq in March 2003 for a long time got in the way of any honest assessment of

British military performance. To some extent, this was remedied by the Chilcot Inquiry. Published in July 2016, its report made for occasionally uncomfortable reading for many senior commanders. One factor that was identified lies in the ethos of the Armed Forces, whose engrained can-do attitude and determination to get on with the job, however difficult the circumstances, can hinder the reporting up the chain of command of adverse conditions on the ground or the sheer magnitude of the task in hand. Lessons must be learned from Operations Telic and Herrick by both military commanders and civilian leaders, not least that Britain's Armed Forces must never again be taken to war deliberately without the approval of Parliament, the support of the British people, a fully thought-out strategy, an operational plan that provides a reasonable prospect of success in the campaign and sufficient resources to win the tactical battles at sea, on land or in the air. And all politicians should remember Churchill's words: 'The statesman who yields to war fever must realise that once the signal is given, he is no longer the master of policy but the slave of unforeseeable and uncontrollable events.'

Following the campaigns in Iraq and Afghanistan, the Army has adopted a policy of regional engagement whereby brigades and units are allocated potential trouble spots around the world to study and understand. The soldier sahibs of the Raj knew their India well, but soldiers entering Bosnia in 1992, Kosovo in 1999, Iraq in 2003 and southern Afghanistan in 2006 knew little about the culture, customs, language and history of the countries within which they were operating. Just as the Army now realises that it has much to learn, it must always remember it has much to teach. The Royal Military Academy Sandhurst enables Britain to wield a great deal of 'soft power': many global leaders, particularly in the Middle East, have been officer cadets. Others have attended the Royal College of Defence Studies in London at a later stage of their career and the majority have benefitted hugely from the international and strategic perspective gained from a year's interaction with a diverse peer group.

Since 1945, the nation has regularly turned to the Army as the manpower resource of last resort in civil and community matters. Whether it was to help keeping trade moving through the docks, providing fire and ambulance cover, running prisons, moving fuel, alleviating flood damage, taking over the control of a foot-and-mouth epidemic or securing the success of the Olympic Games, the Army has always turned its hand to whatever was required – out of its spare capacity. The size of the Army has never been predicated on the capability to intervene at home. It has achieved everything that it has from within the overall resources provided, principally, for overseas operations. At the end of the Cold War, when the Regular Army's strength was around 155,000, meeting demands at home from spare capacity, while never easy, was more possible to do. With a Regular Army not even at its planned strength of 82,000 regular soldiers, this becomes a much greater challenge.

The size of the Regular Army has been a recurrent theme in this book. However, part of the hedge against the unknown or unexpected has always been the pool of trained reservists, known as the Territorial Army until 2014 and now as the Army Reserve. Although the Army Reserve aims for a strength of 30,000 trained soldiers, significant hurdles have to be overcome. Amongst these is the not unreasonable attitude of some civilian employers who can be less than happy when their employees receive the call to mobilise, which can involve a year-long absence. This is a particular challenge for small- and medium-size businesses. While there is no doubting the commitment of reservists, doubt must remain as to whether the overall capability and quality of the Army can be maintained with such a large reliance on part-time soldiers, despite their enthusiasm. However, with fewer and fewer people in the civilian population today ever meeting soldiers, the Army Reserve also serves as an important link connecting the military and civilian worlds. A positive relationship between these two worlds is vital as the Army can only operate to its maximum potential with the consent and support of the nation it serves. While soldiers appreciate support during the operations they undertake on behalf of the nation, they do not want pity. They are not automatically either heroes or victims, they are professionals getting on with a job, assigned to them by the democratically elected government of the day. That job can be difficult and dangerous, and made harder if the nation does not offer sufficient material or moral support, something that was felt particularly in Iraq and Afghanistan at the start of those operations. One message that struggled to get through was the rationale behind the costly British military presence in Helmand – a presence that was crucial to the wider stabilisation of

Afghanistan and the region, and not just combatting Taliban influence in the south of that very volatile country.

As the make-up of the British population becomes more diverse, so too should that diversity be reflected within the overall ranks of the Army. Just as the civilian world has become more tolerant of minorities and less tolerant of conduct such as bullying, so too increasingly must the Army. Controversies such as Deepcut should be dealt with transparently and swiftly. The unprecedented public support that the Army enjoys today must be nurtured and never taken for granted.

The Army remains one of Britain's greatest assets. With 350 years of history behind it, it continues to allow Britain a global role. A source of national pride, it is undermined at the country's peril, not just in the context of security, but of international standing. Ever since the early 1970s, spending on education and health began to overtake spending on defence, an area which has often been the first for any cuts. Politicians seem convinced that there are 'no votes in defence', but this is perhaps open to inquiry. The Falklands campaign and the nuclear deterrent were key factors in the 1983 general election, Iraq in 2005 and issues regarding the welfare of soldiers and other service personnel featured in the 2010 campaign. Royal Wootton Bassett and contributions to military charities such as Help for Heroes reflect the country's huge regard and respect for her Armed Forces personnel.

The recent history of the units that have worn the Desert Rat insignia encapsulates the headlines of the story of the British Army from 1945 to 2015 – extensive service in Germany and Northern Ireland, fighting in the first Gulf War, in Bosnia, Kosovo, in Iraq and in Afghanistan, followed by a return home to England. An increasingly home-based army will undoubtedly experience greater stability for its soldiers and their families – the days of cantonments in faraway places are largely over – but the challenge now is to be ready for whatever the unstable world of the twenty-first century demands. If Berlin agrees, there are political and financial arguments in favour of postponing, if not cancelling, the last phase of the withdrawal of the British Army from Germany. The continued presence in Germany of a modest contingent and forward-based equipment – or better still, one of the three remaining armoured infantry brigades – would send a powerful message from Brexit Britain to friends and potential foes alike. The Desert Rats themselves are now to be known as 7th Infantry Brigade, one of seven lower readiness Adaptable Force brigades made up of both regular and reserve units. The Brigade has no main battle tanks but, in a symbolic link with the past, it retains the red jerboa Desert Rat insignia and the motto – 'All of one company'.

Since Iraq and Afghanistan, the British government has been cautious about deploying boots on the ground, particularly in Muslim countries. There will be circumstances in the future when the government must show the moral and political courage to deploy British troops in an overseas intervention, provided such a deployment is unambiguously within international law. For example, should diplomacy produce a settlement in Syria then an international implementation force, such as in Bosnia in 1995/1996, might well be required to enforce the terms of that settlement on the ground and protect the international reconstruction and development programme that will undoubtedly be needed. Ideally Muslim or non-aligned troops would provide that force but in their absence, in whole or in part, British soldiers, among others, might well be required; however the Russian support for the Assad regime probably makes that particular scenario less likely.

The days of the British Empire and colonial possessions are long gone, but nevertheless there remains a significant historical and moral obligation to those independent countries which were once British colonies. The response to the Ebola crisis in Sierra Leone was a recognition of historic ties. Other crises – of security, or concerning the environment or an epidemic – will inevitably occur elsewhere. Challenges such as the aggressive expansion of Islamist influence or the fierce competition for control of scarce natural resources could all generate circumstances when states with longstanding links to Britain might call for assistance. Britain might respond unilaterally, or through the United Nations or in concert with other NATO members or, indeed, as part of a coalition of the willing. The only certainty is that such unexpected crises will arise. The British people and the British Army have always risen to those responsibilities in the past and will undoubtedly do so again.

***

The future is uncertain, but there is always the legacy of the past to be remembered. Inscribed on the Armed Forces Memorial at the National Memorial Arboretum in Staffordshire are the names of over 16,000 servicemen and women – the majority from the Army – who have lost their lives on operations during the period of British history covered by this book. At the heart of the Armed Forces Memorial is a wreath. In years when the sun is shining at 11am on 11 November, Armistice Day, a ray of sunshine falls exactly on the centre of that wreath – a visible link between those individual men and women who served and fell on operations, and the glory of the wider world of creation in which they lived and died.

For every serviceman or woman who gives their life on operations there is a grieving family left behind. In 2008, Her Majesty the Queen authorised the issuing of an emblem to the next of kin of all those who have died on active service since the qualifying date shortly after the end of the Second World War. The emblem is a silver cross to be known, at Her Majesty's request, as the Elizabeth Cross. By awarding a symbol of sacrifice, the Nation is honouring its debt of gratitude to its soldiers who have given their all – for Britain and her Army since 1945.

NOTES

Introduction

1. Bernard Law Montgomery, *The Memoirs of Field-Marshal Montgomery of Alamein KG* (1958; new edition, Barnsley: Pen & Sword Military, 2005) pp.338–9

2. John Saville, *The Politics of Continuity: British Foreign Policy and the Labour Government 1945–6* (London: Verso, 1993), p. 22.

3. Ibid, p. 20.

4. Benjamin Grob-Fitzgibbon, *Imperial Endgame: Britain's Dirty Wars and the End of Empire* (Basingstoke: Palgrave Macmillan, 2011).

5. Ministry of Defence, Defence Analytical Services Agency, *UK Defence Statistics 2000* (London: National Statistics Publication, The Stationery Office, 2000), p. 68.

6. Ibid, p. 68.

7. Ibid, p. 68.

8. Ibid, p. 68.

9. Ibid, p. 39.

10. YouGov–*Sunday Times*, 'Public: Commit to NATO 2% Spending Target' (15 March 2015) https://yougov.co.uk/news/2015/03/15/uk-should-commit-nato-2-defence-spending-target-pu

11. Chatham House–YouGov Survey 'Internationalism or Isolationism?' (30 January 2015) https://www.chathamhouse.org/publication/internationalism-or-isolationism-chatham-house-yougov-survey

1 The Legacy of War

1. Bernard Law Montgomery, *The Memoirs of Field-Marshal Montgomery of Alamein KG* (1958; new edition, Barnsley: Pen & Sword Military, 2005), pp. 378–9.

2. Berlin Declaration, cited in F. S. V. Donnison, *Civil Affairs and Military Government in North-West Europe 1944–1946* (London: Her Majesty's Stationery Office, 1961), appendix VI.

3. Chapter title of Montgomery, *Memoirs*.

4. Ministry of Defence and Defence Analytical Services Agency, *UK Defence Statistics 2000* (London: National Statistics Publication, The Stationery Office, 2000) p. 68.

5. Paul Addison, *Now the War is Over: A Social History of Britain 1945–51* (London: Jonathan Cape/BBC, 1985), p. 9.
6. Giles Radice, *The Tortoise and the Hares: Attlee, Bevin, Cripps, Dalton, Morrison* (London: Politicos, 2008), p. 120.
7. Addison, *Now the War is Over*, p. 7.
8. June MacDonald, later to campaign against food rationing. Addison, *Now the War is Over*, p. 9.
9. Alan Bullock, *Ernest Bevin, Foreign Secretary 1945–51* (London: William Heinemann, 1983), p. 121, cited in Peter Hennessy, *Never Again: Britain 1945–1951* (London: Jonathan Cape, 1992), p. 95.
10. 'The Effect of Our External Financial Position on Our Foreign Policy, FO 371/45694, cited in Anthony Applethwaite, 'Britain and the World 1945–49: The View from the Foreign Office', *International Affairs*, vol. 61, no. 2 (Spring 1985).
11. Montgomery, *Memoirs*, p. 335.
12. Frank Roberts, FO/371/56763/N4065, cited in John Saville, *The Politics of Continuity: British Foreign Policy and the Labour Government 1945–6* (London: Verso, 1993), p. 49.
13. Winston S. Churchill, 'The Sinews of Peace' speech (5 March 1946), Fulton, National Churchill Museum, Westminster College, Missouri. https://www.nationalchurchillmuseum.org/sinews-of-peace-iron-curtain-speech.html
14. Roger Broad, *Conscription in Britain 1939–1964: The Militarisation of a Generation* (Abingdon: Routledge, 2006).
15. Alan Allport, *Demobbed: Coming Home after the Second World War* (New Haven and London: Yale University Press, 2009), p. 24, and see chapter 1.
16. Ernest Gates MP, HC Deb Mar 1947 c. 637.
17. Laurence Stone, *Road to Divorce: England, 1530–1987* (Oxford: Oxford University Press, 1990), cited in Allport, *Demobbed*, p. 87.
18. Montgomery, *Memoirs*, p. 417.
19. David French, *Army, Empire and Cold War: The British Army and Military Policy 1945–1971* (Oxford: Oxford University Press, 2012), p. 13.
20. Ministry of Defence, Defence Analytical Services Agency, *UK Defence Statistics 2000* (London: National Statistics Publication, The Stationery Office (2000), p. 68.
21. TNA CAB 131/4/DO (47) 44 Report by the Chiefs of Staff, *Future Defence Policy* (May 1947), in Julian Lewis, *Changing Direction: British Military Planning for Post-War Strategic Defence 1942–1947* (London: The Sherwood Press, 1988), appendix 7.
22. A. V. Alexander MP HC Deb 20 Mar 1947 c. 606–609.
23. Peter Chambers and Amy Landreth, *Called Up: The Personal Experiences of Sixteen National Servicemen, Told by Themselves* (London: Allan Wingate, 1955), foreword.
24. A. H. Head, 'European Defence', *International Affairs*, vol. 27, no. 1 (1951), pp. 1–9.
25. Chambers and Landreth, *Called Up*, p. 14.
26. Ibid, p. 15.
27. Ibid, p. 16.
28. Ibid, p. 25.
29. Trevor Royle, *National Service: The Best Years of Their Lives* (London: Andre Deutsch, 2002), p. 30.
30. Christopher Knowles, 'Germany 1945–49: A Case Study in Post-Conflict Reconstruction', *RUSI Journal*, vol. 158, no. 6 (2013), pp. 84–91.
31. Patricia Meehan, *A Strange Enemy People: Germans under the British 1945–50* (London and Chester Springs: Peter Owen, 2001), p. 13.

32. Noel Annan, 'How Dr Adenauer Rose Resilient from the Ruins of Germany', 1982 Bithell Memorial Lecture (London: Institute of Germanic Studies, University of London, 1983), p. 33.

33. Julian Lewis, *Changing Direction: British Military Planning for Post-War Strategic Defence.*

34. Cited by Michael Portillo in *The Things We Forget to Remember*, BBC Radio 4 series (2012).

35. Ian D. Turner, *Reconstruction in Post-War Germany: British Occupation Policy and the Western Zones 1945–55* (Oxford, New York, Munich: Berg, 1989), p. 21.

36. Meehan, *A Strange Enemy People*, p. 13.

37. David Williamson, *A Most Diplomatic General: The Life of Lord Robertson of Oakridge Bt 1896–1974* (London and Washington: Brassey's, 1996), p. 85.

38. Lucius D. Clay, *Decision in Germany* (Westport: Greenwood Press, 1950), p. 32.

39. Annan, 'How Dr Adenauer Rose Resilient from the Ruins of Germany'.

40. John Cloake, *Templer, Tiger of Malaya* (London: Harrap, 1985), p. 150.

41. Donnison, *Civil Affairs and Military Government in North-West Europe 1944–1946*, p. 276.

42. Knowles, 'Germany 1944–49'.

43. Donnison, *Civil Affairs and Military Government in North-West Europe 1944–1946*, p. 207.

44. Knowles, 'Germany 1944–49'.

45. Winston Churchill MP, HC Deb, 22 October 1945 c.1693.

46. Tom Bower, *Blind Eye to Murder: Britain, America and the Purging of Nazi Germany – A Pledge Betrayed* (London: Little Brown, 1995), p. 151.

47. Obituary, 'Trooper Fred Smith: The Soldier Who Helped Liberate Bergen-Belsen', *Independent* (1 July 2011) http://www.independent.co.uk/news/obituaries/trooper-fred-smith-soldier-who-helped-liberate-belsenbergen-2305042.html

48. Williamson, *A Most Diplomatic General*, p. 87.

49. Colonel C. R. W. Norman, Letters to his mother (September 1945–January 1946), IWM Private Papers, Documents 87/52/7.

50. Horst Mendershausen, 'Prices, Money and the Distribution of Goods in Post-War Germany', *American Economic Review*, vol. 39, no. 3 (1949), pp. 646–72.

51. Ibid.

52. Annan, 'How Dr Adenauer Rose Resilient from the Ruins of Germany', p. 5.

53. Meehan, *A Strange Enemy People*, p. 240.

54. Addison, *Now the War is Over*, p. 40.

55. H. J. D. L. McGregor, Menu Card, IWM Private Papers, Documents 89/13/1 Crown Copyright.

56. Private information.

57. Allport, *Demobbed*, pp. 126–31.

58. J. R. Yorke, IWM Private Papers, Documents 86/74/1.

59. Ian Harris, IWM 13389, cited in Allport, *Demobbed*, p. 128.

60. George C. Marshall, speech, Harvard (4 June 1947) http://marshallfoundation.org/marshall/the-marshall-plan/marshall-plan-speech/

61. Ernest Bevin, HC Deb 22 Jan 1948.

62. Anne Deighton, cited in Turner, *Reconstruction in Post-War Germany*, p. 18.

63. Williamson, *A Most Diplomatic General*, p. 139, citing Fo371/70603.

64. Meehan, *A Strange Enemy People*, p. 147.

65. PREM 240/46, cited in Meehan, *A Strange Enemy People*, p. 134.

66. Williamson, *A Most Diplomatic General*, p. 105.

67. Bruce Hoffman, *Inside Terrorism* (London: Victor Gollancz, 1998), p. 50.

68. Menachem Begin, *The Revolt*, translated by Samuel Katz, English version edited with notes by Ivan M. Greenberg (London: W. H. Allen, 1979), p. 52.

69.   E. J. Rooke-Matthews, IWM Private Papers, Documents 2029, p. 364.

70.   Sir Peter Macdonald MP, HC Deb 31 Jan 1947 c.1321.

71.   Martin Gilbert, *Israel: A History* (London: Black Swan, 1998), p. 113.

72.   Begin, *The Revolt*, p. 3.

73.   Gilbert, *Israel*, pp. 47 and 97.

74.   David A. Charters, *The British Army and the Jewish Insurgency in Palestine* (Basingstoke: Macmillan Press, in association with King's College London, 1989), p. 20.

75.   'Report of the Palestine Committee' CP (45) 156 (8 September 1945), cited in Alan Bullock, *Ernest Bevin: A Biography*, Brian Brivati (ed.) (London: Politicos, 2002) p. 432.

76.   Charters, *The British Army and the Jewish Insurgency in Palestine*, p. 22.

77.   Ibid, p. 24.

78.   'Report of the Palestine Committee', cited in Bullock, *Ernest Bevin*, p. 432.

79.   Ibid.

80.   Begin, *The Revolt*, p. 26.

81.   Arthur Koestler, 'Letter to a Parent of a British Soldier in Palestine', *New Statesman* (16 August 1948).

82.   'Jewish Illegal Organisations' (23 June 1947), in Norman, IWM Private Papers 87/57/2.

83.   E. J. Rooke-Matthews, IWM Private Papers, Documents 2029.

84.   Arnold Jordan, British Forces in Palestine (Veterans' website, see www. britishforcesinpalestine.org)

85.   Ibid.

86.   Rooke-Matthews, IWM 2029.

87.   Colonel K. C. F. Chevasse, IWM Private Papers, Documents 98/23/1.

88.   Ministry of Information, *Portrait of Palestine* (1947), IWM COI 171.

89.   Hoffman, *Inside Terrorism*, p. 51.

90.   Oliver Stanley MP, HC Deb 31 Jan 1947 c. 1301.

91.   *Army Quarterly*, vol. 55, no. 1 (October 1947), p. 7.

92.   Arthur Creech Jones MP, HC Deb 22 July 1947 c. 1046.

93.   'Jewish Illegal Organisations' in Colonel C. R. W. Norman, IWM Private Papers.

94.   Begin, *The Revolt*, p. 52.

95.   Ibid, p. 55.

96.   Ritchie Ovendale, 'The Palestine Policy of the British Labour Government 1947: The Decision to Withdraw', *International Affairs*, vol. 55, no. 3 (July 1979), pp. 409–31.

97.   Montgomery, *Memoirs*, p. 469.

98.   Koestler, 'Letter to a Parent of a British Soldier in Palestine' (16 August 1947).

99.   Richard Crossman MP, HC Deb 31 Jan 1947 c. 1325.

100. Gilbert, *Israel*, p. 146.

101. Charles Allen, *Plain Tales from the Raj: Images of British India in the Twentieth Century* (London: Andre Deutsch/BBC, 1975).

102. Daniel Marston, *The Indian Army and the End of the Raj* (Cambridge: Cambridge University Press, 2014), p. 10.

103. Ibid, p. 13.

104. Ibid, p. 19.

105. T. A. Heathcote in David Chandler (General Editor) and Ian Beckett (Associate Editor), *The Oxford Illustrated History of the British Army* (Oxford: Oxford University Press, 1994), p. 38.

106. Philip Warner, *Auchinleck: The Lonely Soldier* (London: Cassell & Co., 1981), p. 193.

107. Ibid, p. 195.

108. Ibid, p. 193.

109. Press Release 8 April 1946 L/WS/1/742 OIOC BL, cited in Marston, *The Indian Army and the End of the Raj*, p. 249.
110. Ibid, p. 246.
111. Ibid, p. 248.
112. M. M. Kaye, *The Far Pavilions* (London: Penguin, 1979).
113. Robin Jeffrey, 'The Punjab Boundary Force and the Problem of Order, 1947', *Modern Asian Studies*, vol. 8, no. 4 (1974), pp. 491–520.
114. Marston, *The Indian Army and the End of the Raj*, p. 34.
115. Byron Farwell, *The Armies of the Raj: From Mutiny to Independence* (London: Viking, 1990), p. 359.
116. Warner, *Auchinleck*, p. 203.
117. Marston, *The Indian Army and the End of the Raj*, p. 261.
118. Ibid, p. 264.
119. Farwell, *The Armies of the Raj*, p. 359.
120. Ibid, p. 358.
121. Ibid, p. 360.
122. Ibid, p. 357.
123. Warner, *Auchinleck*, p. 210.
124. Louis Mosley, *The Last Days of the British Raj* (London: Weidenfeld & Nicolson, 1961), p. 36.
125. Ibid, pp. 193–200.
126. Ibid, p. 194.
127. Jeffrey, 'The Punjab Boundary Force and the Problem of Order 1947'.
128. Mosley, *The Last Days of the British Raj*, p. 207.
129. Jeffrey, 'The Punjab Boundary Force and the Problem of Order 1947'.
130. Farwell, *The Armies of the Raj*, p. 365.
131. David Gilmartin, 'Partition, Pakistan and South Asian History: In Search of a Narrative', *Journal of South Asian Studies*, vol. 57, no. 4 (1998), cited by Copland, 'The Master and the Maharajas', below.
132. Jeffrey, 'The Punjab Boundary Force and the Problem of Order 1947'.
133. Ian Copland, 'The Master and the Maharajas: The Sikh Princes and the East Punjab Massacres of 1947', *Modern Asian Studies*, vol. 36, no. 3 (2002), pp. 657–704.
134. Jeffrey, 'The Punjab Boundary Force and the Problem of Order 1947'.
135. In conversation with Brigadier Ayub Khan and Brigadier K. S. Thimayya. See Mosley, *The Last Days of the British Raj*, p. 234.
136. Ibid.
137. Kirpal Singh (ed.), *The Partition of Punjab* (Patiala: Punjabi University Press, 1972), pp. 99–100, cited in Marston, *The Indian Army and the End of the Raj*, p. 5.
138. Warner, *Auchinleck*, p. 223.
139. Marston, *The Indian Army and the End of the Raj*, p. 2.
140. Farwell, *The Armies of the Raj*, p. 356.
141. Churchill, 'The Sinews of Peace' speech.
142. Note by Joint Secretaries of the Defence Committee, circulating 'Size and Shape of the Armed Forces: Report of the Harwood Working Party' CAB 131/7, DO(49)47 (21 June 1949); 'Report of the Inter-Service Committee Working Party on Size and Shape of the Armed Forces' Misc/P.(49)6, i (28 February 1949).

2 Strategic Shifts

1. Major J. B. Oldfield, *The Green Howards in Malaya (1949–1952): The Story of a Post-War Tour of Duty by a Battalion of the Line* (Aldershot: Gale and Polden Ltd, 1953), pp. 128–34.

2. Thomas R. Mockaitis, 'A New Era of Counterinsurgency', *RUSI Journal*, vol. 136, no. 1 (1991), pp. 73–8.

3. British Pathé, May Day report (1 May 1949) http://www.britishpathe. com/video/police-stop-communist-may-day-march/query/ TRAFALGAR+SQUARE+LONDON+VIEWS

4. Phillip Deery, 'The Secret Battalion: Communism in Britain during the Cold War', *Contemporary British History*, vol. 13, no. 4 (1999), pp. 1–28.

5. DEFE 15/5 memo CIC (FE) (49) 2 (P) (12 August 1949), cited in Deery, 'The Secret Battalion'.

6. *Daily Telegraph* obituary, Chin Peng, 16 September 2013.

7. Han Suyin, *And the Rain My Drink* (London: Jonathan Cape, 1956), p. 259.

8. Sir Michael Burton, 'The Malayan Emergency: A Subaltern's View', *Asian Affairs*, vol. 44, issue 2 (2011), pp. 251–60.

9. Bill Greer, Letters to the Editor, *Asian Affairs*, vol. 3, no. 1 (2012), pp. 106–11.

10. BBC Radio 4, *Last Tales from the South China Seas*, Episode 5 – *Bandits: The Anti-Terrorist War in the Malayan Jungle 1948–56* (1984).

11. Burton, 'The Malayan Emergency'.

12. Richard Clutterbuck, *The Long, Long War: The British Army in Malaya 1948–1960* (London: Cassell, 1967), p. 55.

13. Dick Craig, *A Short Account of the Malayan Emergency* (n.p. 1964).

14. BBC Radio 4, *Last Tales from the South China Seas*.

15. John A. Nagl, *Learning to Eat Soup with a Knife* (Chicago: University of Chicago Press, revised edition, 2005), p. 73.

16. Ibid, p. 70.

17. Ibid, p. 69.

18. BBC Radio 4, *Last Tales from the South China Seas*.

19. J. C. A. Green, IWM 86/47/1.

20. Bill Greer, letter, *Asian Affairs*.

21. BBC Radio 4, *Last Tales from the South China Seas*.

22. Burton, 'The Malayan Emergency'.

23. Huw Thomas, *Fighting the Mau Mau: The British Army and Counter-Insurgency in Kenya* (Cambridge: Cambridge University Press, 2012), p. 83.

24. Harold Briggs, *Early History of Emergency: Report on the Emergency in Malaya from April 1950 to November 1951* (1951), pp. 17–18, cited in Nagl, *Learning to Eat Soup with a Knife*, p. 75.

25. Bill Greer, letter, *Asian Affairs*.

26. John Loch, My First Alphabet, IWM 95/19/1.

27. Nagl, *Learning to Eat Soup with a Knife*, p. 95.

28. J. C. A. Green, IWM 86/47/1.

29. Nagl, *Learning to Eat Soup with a Knife*, p. 98.

30. National Army Museum 'The Malayan Emergency'. Online exhibition, see www.nam.ac.uk/ exhibitions/online-exhibitions/malayan-emergency.

31. Nagl, *Learning to Eat Soup with a Knife*, p. 105.

32. Green, IWM 86/47/1.

33. UN Charter http://www.un.org/en/documents/charter/preamble.shtml

34. UN Doc S/1511 and 1509, cited in Anthony Farrar-Hockley, *The British Part in the Korean War* (London: HMSO Official History, 1990), vol. 1, appendix A.

35. Ibid, p. 33.

36. Address by President Truman about Policy in the Far East, PBS (11 April 1951) http://www. pbs.org/wgbh/amex/macarthur/filmmore/reference/primary/officialdocs03.html

37. Clement Attlee MP, HC Deb 12 Sep 1950 c. 951–955.
38. Cited in Farrar-Hockley, *The British Part in the Korean War*, p. 85.
39. BJSM, Washington AWT 12 to MOD of 301912Z June 1950, cited in Farrar-Hockley, *The British Part in the Korean War*, p. 54.
40. Cab 131/8 DO (50) 15th meeting of 24 July 1950, cited in Farrar-Hockley, *The British Part in the Korean War*, p. 104.
41. Farrar-Hockley, *The British Part in the Korean War*, p. 113.
42. Ministry of Defence, *UK Defence Statistics 2000* (2000).
43. Clement Attlee, MP HC Deb 12 Sep 1950 c. 957.
44. Ministry of Defence, Defence Analytical Services Agency, *UK Defence Statistics 2000*, p. 68.
45. Peter Lowe, 'An Ally and a Recalcitrant General: Great Britain, Douglas MacArthur and the Korean War 1950–51', *English Historical Review*, vol. 105, no. 416 (1990), pp. 624–53.
46. Colonel D. E. Whatmore, IWM Sound Recording 12663.
47. David French, *Army, Empire and Cold War: The British Army and Military Policy 1945–1971* (Oxford: Oxford University Press, 2012), p. 73.
48. A. J. Barker, *Fortune Favours the Brave: The Battle of Hook, Korea 1953* (London: Leo Cooper, 1974), p. 148.
49. David Green, *Captured at Imjin River: The War Memoirs of a Korean Gloster* (Barnsley: Pen & Sword, 2011).
50. Lowe, 'An Ally and a Recalcitrant General'.
51. Sir Pierson Dixon, *Korea: Britain and the Korean War, 1950–51* (London: Foreign and Commonwealth Office Library and Records Department, Historical Branch; second edition, revised 1995), p. 9.
52. Hansard 30 Nov 1950, cited in Farrar-Hockley, *The British Part in the Korean War*, p. 357.
53. United States Army: Center for Military History, *US Army Campaigns: Korean War* (2016) http://www.history.army.mil/html/reference/army_flag/kw.html
54. R. W. Maguire, IWM Private Papers, Documents 12388.
55. Lowe, 'An Ally and a Recalcitrant General'.
56. Colonel D. E. Whatmore, IWM Private Papers, Documents 2530, *War Story*.
57. Tom Driberg MP, HC Deb 2 Aug 1951 c. 1650.
58. Whatmore, *War Story*.
59. WO 32/14248 no. 1B (8 May 1951).
60. Max Hastings, *The Korean War* (London: Michael Joseph, 1987), p. 261.
61. Ibid, p. 262.
62. National Army Museum, *Britain's Greatest Battles* (online exhibition) http://www.nam.ac.uk/exhibitions/online-exhibitions/britains-greatest-battles/imjin-river
63. Barker, *Fortune Favours the Brave*, p. 7.
64. Anthony Head MP, HC Deb 21 Oct 1952 99W.
65. Frederick Peart MP, HC Deb 13 May 1952 c. 1108.
66. J. W. Shaw, IWM Private Papers, Documents 7803.
67. D. G. Kaye, IWM Private Papers, Documents 6809.
68. British Korean War Veterans Association figure. The number of fallen is officially 1,078.
69. Labour Party, *Forward with Labour* (1955) http://www.politicsresources.net/area/uk/man/lab55.htm
70. Conservative Party, *United for Peace and Progress* (1955) http://www.conservativemanifesto.com/1955/1955-conservative-manifesto.shtml
71. Dixon, *Korea: Britain and the Korean War, 1950–51*, p. 9.
72. Selwyn Lloyd MP, HC Deb 2 Nov 1955 c. 1030.
73. G. W. Stuchbery IWM Private Papers, Documents 23409.
74. Lieutenant Colonel P. C. M Buckle, IWM Private Papers, Documents 15688.

75. Daniel Yergin, *The Prize: The Epic Quest for Oil, Money and Power* (New York: Free Press, 1991), p. 461.

76. Julian Amery MP, HC Deb 27 Jul 1956 c. 779.

77. Anthony Eden, HC Deb 2 Aug 1956 c. 1603.

78. Ibid.

79. Professor Pat McKeown OBE FREng FCIRP FEMechE, IWM Private Papers, Documents 19793.

80. Buckle, IWM Private Papers.

81. Frank Bowles MP, HC Deb 23 Oct 1956 c. 491.

82. Peter Hennessy, *The Prime Minister: The Office and Its Holders* (London: Penguin, 2000), p. 233.

83. Cloake, *Templer, Tiger of Malaya*, p. 348.

84. McKeown, IWM Private Papers.

85. Buckle, IWM Private Papers.

86. John Hare MP, HC Deb 23 Oct 1956 17W.

87. Avi Shlaim, 'The Protocol of Sèvres, 1956: Anatomy of a War Plot', *International Affairs*, vol. 73, no. 3 (1997), pp. 509–30.

88. Hennessy, *The Prime Minister*, p. 215.

89. Michael H. Coles, 'Suez: A Successful Naval Operation Compromised by Inept Political Leadership', *Naval War College Review*, vol. 59, no. 4 (Autumn 2006), pp. 100–18.

90. Ibid.

91. Anthony Farrar-Hockley, 'The Post-War Army 1945–1963', in David Chandler (General Editor) and Ian Beckett (Associate Editor), *The Oxford Illustrated History of the British Army* (Oxford: Oxford University Press, 1994).

92. United Nations, *Resolutions Adopted by the General Assembly During Its First Emergency Special Session*, 1–10 November 1956 (New York, 1956) supplement no. 1 (A3354). http://www.un.org/ga/search/view_doc.asp?symbol=A/3354&Lang=E

93. Margaret Thatcher, *The Downing Street Years* (London: HarperCollins, 1993), p. 188.

94. McKeown, IWM Private Papers.

95. Denis Healey, *The Time of My Life* (London: Michael Joseph, 1989), p. 170.

96. Louise Richardson, 'Avoiding and Incurring Losses: Decision-making in the Suez Crisis, *International Journal*, vol. 47, no. 2 (Spring 1992), pp. 370–401.

97. Cloake, *Templer, Tiger of Malaya*, pp. 354–5.

98. Stuchbery, IWM Private Papers.

99. Yergin, *The Prize*, p. 494.

100. Churchill Archives Centre, Churchill College, Cambridge CHUR 2/143, letter (6 December 1956), cited in Benjamin Grob-Fitzgibbon, *Imperial Endgame: Britain's Dirty Wars and the End of Empire* (Basingstoke: Palgrave Macmillan, 2011), p. 350.

101. Michael Howard, 'Strategy in the Nuclear Age', *RUSI Journal*, vol. 102, no. 4 (August 1957).

102. George Brown MP, HC Deb 13 February 1957 c.1283.

103. HMSO, *Defence: Outline of Future Defence Policy* CAB 129/86 (1957), p. 3.

104. French, *Army, Empire and Cold War*, p. 150.

105. George Brown MP, HC Deb 13 Feb 1957 c. 1298.

106. John Smyth MP, HC Deb 13 Feb 1957 c. 1339.

107. CAB 134/1315 PR (56)3, 'The Future of the United Kingdom in World Affairs', cited in Matthew Grant, 'Home Defence and the Sandys White Paper', *Journal of Strategic Studies*, vol. 31, no. 6 (2008), pp. 925–49.

108. French, *Army, Empire and Cold War*, p. 163, and Anthony Head MP, HC Deb 24 Jul 1956 c. 180.

109. Ibid, p. 157.

110. Ibid, p. 158.

111. HC Deb 19 Feb 1957 c. 177–191.

112. Granada TV, *The Army Game: The New Officer* (1957) https://archive.org/details/armygame-newofficer

113. George Craddock MP, HC Deb 14 Dec 1960 c. 383–5.

114. Sir Walter Monckton, draft letter to Anthony Eden (24 September 1956), Bodleian Library, University of Oxford, Dep. Monckton, 7 fols. 210–11 http://www.bodley.ox.ac.uk/dept/scwmss/projects/suez/monckton-resign.html

115. Wyn Rees, 'The 1957 Sandys White Paper: New Priorities in British Defence Policy?' *Journal of Strategic Studies*, vol. 12, no. 2 (1989).

116. Unpublished memoirs of Edwin Duncan Sandys 17/A/1 (private copy of Lady Duncan-Sandys), cited in Martin S. Navias, *The Sandys White Paper and the Move to the British New Look: An Analysis of Nuclear Weapons, Conventional Forces and Strategic Planning* (PhD, War Studies Department, King's College London, 1989), p. 219.

117. Navias, *The Sandys White Paper and the Move to the British New Look*, p. 220.

118. French, *Army, Empire and Cold War*, p. 159.

119. Navias, *The Sandys White Paper and the Move to the British New Look*, pp. 221–2.

120. Ibid.

121. HMSO, *Defence: Outline of Future Policy* CAB 129/86 (1957), p. 3.

122. Ibid.

123. Ibid, p. 4.

124. French, *Army, Empire and Cold War*, p. 156.

125. HMSO, *Defence: Outline of Future Policy* CAB 129/86, p. 4.

126. Ibid, p. 9.

127. Ibid.

128. Ibid, p. 6.

129. Grant, 'Home Defence and the Sandys Defence White Paper, 1957'.

130. Bill Jackson and Dwin Bramall, *The Chiefs: The Story of the United Kingdom Chiefs of Staff* (London: Brassey's, 1992), p. 306.

131. Julian Amery, cited in French, *Army, Empire and Cold War*, p. 161.

3   Emergencies and Insurgencies: Fighting Small Colonial Wars

1. B. H. Liddell Hart, foreword to *Mao Tse Tung and Che Guevara: Guerilla Warfare* (Cassell, 1962) p. xi. Cited by Frank Kitson, 'Low Intensity Operations: Subversion, Insurgency, Peacekeeping' (London: Faber and Faber © HMSO 1971 and preface to 1991 edition © Frank Kitson).

2. Robert Thompson, *Defeating Communist Insurgency: The Lessons of Malaya and Vietnam* (New York: F. A. Praeger, 1966); Richard Clutterbuck, *The Long, Long War: The British Army in Malaya 1948–1960* (London: Cassell, 1967); John A. Nagl, *Learning to Eat Soup with a Knife* (Chicago: University of Chicago Press, revised edition, 2005).

3. Frank Kitson, *Gangs and Counter-Gangs* (London: Barrie and Rockliff, 1960), p. 28.

4. David French, *Army, Empire and Cold War: The British Army and Military Policy 1945–71* (Oxford: Oxford University Press, 2012), p. 211.

5. Hew Strachan, 'British Counter-insurgency from Malaya to Iraq' *RUSI Journal*, vol. 156, no. 6 (2007), pp. 8–11

6. Gaumont British Newsreel (Reuters), 'Princess Elizabeth and the Duke of Edinburgh Visit Kenya' (7 February 1952). http://www.itnsource.com/es/specials/prince-philip/shotlist//BHC_RTV/1952/02/07/BGU412170002/

7. Brigadier G. A. Rimbault, CBE DSO MC, IWM Private Papers, Documents 1780, Kenya and the Mau Mau p.4 Crown Copyright.

8.   John Newsinger, *British Counter-insurgency: From Palestine to Northern Ireland* (Basingstoke: Palgrave, 2002), p. 61.

9.   John Lonsdale, 'Mau Maus of the Mind: Making Mau Mau and Remaking Kenya', *The Journal of African History*, vol. 31, no. 3 (1990), pp. 393–421.

10.   David Anderson, *Histories of the Hanged: Britain's Dirty War in Kenya and the End of Empire: Testimonies from the Mau Mau Rebellion in Kenya* (London: Weidenfeld & Nicolson, 2006), p. 36.

11.   Rimbault, 'Kenya and the Mau Mau', p. 4.

12.   Graham Greene, *Ways of Escape* (London: The Bodley Head, 1980), p. 188.

13.   Caroline Elkins, 'The Struggle for Mau Mau Rehabilitation in Late Colonial Africa', *The International Journal of African Historical Studies*, vol 33, no. 1 (2000), pp. 25–57.

14.   W. H. Thompson, 'Only the Foothills', IWM 89/13/1.

15.   GHQ East Africa, *The Kenya Picture* (1954) (In Private Papers of G.A. Rimbault, Crown Copyright).

16.   Greene, *Ways of Escape*, pp. 188–9.

17.   Thompson, 'Only the Foothills', p. 70.

18.   HC Deb 31 Mar 1953 c. 1037.

19.   Hector Hughes MP, HC Deb 13 May 1953 c. 1243.

20.   Kitson, *Gangs and Counter-Gangs*, p. 28.

21.   Ibid.

22.   Letter from General Sir George Erskine to Lord Killearn (15 June 1953) in Huw Bennett and David French (eds.), *The Kenya Papers of General Sir George Erskine, 1953–1955* (Stroud: The History Press, 2013), p.35.

23.   Letter from General Sir George Erskine to Lieutenant General Sir Harold Redman (29 June 1953), ibid, p. 37.

24.   Thompson, 'Only the Foothills', p. 79.

25.   Rimbault, 'Kenya and the Mau Mau', p. 5.

26.   Thompson, 'Only the Foothills', pp. 66–70.

27.   Bennett and French (eds.), *The Kenya Papers of General Sir George Erskine, 1953–1955*, p. 49.

28.   Caroline Elkins, witness statement, Ndiku Mutua and 4 Others and Foreign and Commonwealth Office, High Court of Justice claim no. HQ09X02666 (2011) p. 18 https://www.leighday.co.uk/LeighDay/media/LeighDay/documents/Mau%20Mau/Historian%20witness%20statements/Statement-of-Prof-Elkins-Final.pdf?ext=.pdf

29.   Kitson, *Gangs and Counter-Gangs*, p. 190.

30.   Colonel Iain Alexander Ferguson, IWM Sound Recording 10064.

31.   Henry Hopkinson MP, HC Deb 28 July 1954 c. 486.

32.   William Hague MP, HC Deb 6 June 2013 c. 1692.

33.   Kitson, *Gangs and Counter-gangs*, p. 46.

34.   Ibid, p. 46.

35.   Huw Bennett, witness statement to High Court, claim no. HQ09X02666, para. 44, p. 17.

36.   WO 216/851, Blundell to Harding, 18 April 1953, cited by Caroline Elkins, witness statement to High Court, claim no. HQ09X02666, p. 9.

37.   Huw Bennett, *Fighting the Mau Mau: The British Army and Counter-Insurgency in the Kenya Emergency* (Cambridge: Cambridge University Press, 2012), p. 264.

38.   David French, *Fighting EOKA: The British Counter-Insurgency Campaign in Cyprus* (Oxford: Oxford University Press, 2015) p. 44.

39.   Henry Hopkinson MP, HC Deb 28 July 1954 c. 508.

40.   TNA DEFE 11/266 Dickson to Sandys (20 September 1958), cited in French, *Army, Empire and Cold War*, p. 299.

41. Anthony Eden MP, HC Deb 28 July 1954 c. 496.
42. W. Byford-Jones, *Grivas and the Story of EOKA* (London: Robert Hale, 1959), p. 88.
43. Ibid.
44. David French, *Fighting EOKA*, p. 291.
45. Byford-Jones, *Grivas and the Story of EOKA*, p. 56.
46. Ibid, p. 134.
47. Sandy Cavenagh, *Airborne to Suez* (London: William Kimber, 1965), cited in Simon Robbins, 'The British Counter-Insurgency in Cyprus', in Matthew Hughes (ed.), *British Ways of Counter-Insurgency: A Historical Perspective* (Basingstoke: Routledge, 2013).
48. Michael Harbottle, IWM Sound Recording, 10145.
49. Ibid.
50. John Reddaway, IWM Sound Recording, 9173.
51. Charles Foley (ed.), *The Memoirs of General Grivas* (London: Longmans, 1964), p. 204, cited in French, *Army, Empire and Cold War*, p. 48.
52. Byford-Jones, *Grivas and the Story of EOKA*.
53. Ibid, p. 2.
54. John Harding, IWM Sound Recording, 8736, Reel 39.
55. French, *Fighting EOKA*, p. 291.
56. John Harding, IWM 8736, Reel 41.
57. Ibid, reels 47 and 43.
58. Ibid, reel 44.
59. Ibid.
60. Ibid, reel 46.
61. Robbins, 'The British Counter-Insurgency in Cyprus', in Hughes (ed.), *British Ways of Counter-Insurgency*.
62. Reddaway, IWM 9173.
63. Booklet, TNA CO 926/1056, p. 13, cited in French, *Army, Empire and Cold War*, p. 203.
64. Martin Bell, IWM Sound Recording, 22155.
65. Geoffrey Saunders in Adrian Walker, *Six Campaigns: National Servicemen at War 1948–1960* (Barnsley: Leo Cooper, 1993), p. 140.
66. Jack Parker, 'Danger – Boredom at Work', *South Wales Echo* (7 April 1958).
67. Barney Taylor, IWM Sound Recording, 24192.
68. Ronald Russell MP, HC Deb 21 Dec 1956 c. 1621.
69. Richard Norton-Taylor, 'Files Reveal Brutal Treatment Meted Out by British Forces in 1950s Cyprus', *Guardian* (27 July 2012) http://www.theguardian.com/uk/2012/jul/27/brutality-british-forces-1950s-cyprus
70. French, *Fighting EOKA*, p. 291.
71. Ibid, p. 235.
72. Reddaway, IWM 9173.
73. Byford-Jones, *Grivas and the Story of EOKA*, p. 147.
74. David Easter, *Britain and the Confrontation with Indonesia 1960–66* (London: I. B. Tauris, 2004), p. 7.
75. Ibid, p. 36.
76. Harold Macmillan, speech to House of Commons, Cape Town, South Africa (3 February 1960).
77. Cited in Easter, *Britain and the Confrontation with Indonesia 1960–66*, p. 28.
78. Robin Evelegh, IWM Sound Recording, 11148.
79. Pamela Sodhy, 'Malaysian-American Relations during Indonesia's Confrontation against Malaysia, 1963–66', *Journal of Southeast Asian Studies*, vol. 19, no. 1 (1988), pp. 111–36.
80. Easter, *Britain and the Confrontation with Indonesia 1960–66*, p. 30.

81. Tom Pocock, *Fighting General: The Public & Private Campaigns of General Sir Walter Walker* (London: William Collins, 1973), p. 106.

82. Justus van der Kroef, 'Chinese Minority Aspirations and Problems in Sarawak', *Pacific Affairs*, vol. 39, nos. 1 and 2 (Spring–Summer 1966), pp. 64–82.

83. Ibid.

84. Pocock, *Fighting General*, p. 160.

85. BBC 2, *Jungle Green: Borneo* (24 December 1964) http://www.bbc.co.uk/iplayer/episode/poohhrf6/jungle-green-borneo

86. Pocock, *Fighting General*.

87. Harold James and Denis Sheil-Small, *The Undeclared War: The Story of the Indonesian Confrontation* (London: Leo Cooper, 1971), p. 75.

88. Ron Cassidy, IWM Sound Recording, 11138.

89. David Eric Henderson, IWM Sound Recording, 14053.

90. Easter, *Britain and the Confrontation with Indonesia 1960–66*.

91. Toh Boon Kwan, 'Brinkmanship and Deterrence Success During the Anglo-Indonesian Sunda Straits Crisis, 1964–1966', *Journal of Southeast Asian Studies*, vol. 36, no. 3 (October 2005), pp. 399–417.

92. Pocock, *Fighting General*, p. 121.

93. Ian Ward, 'The SAS: The World's Toughest Soldiers?', *Daily Telegraph* (22 July 1966).

94. Pocock, *Fighting General*, p. 215.

95. Denis Healey, *The Time of My Life* (London: Michael Joseph, 1989), p. 289.

96. Ibid, p. 287.

97. BBC 1, *Soldier in the Sun* (7 October 1964) http://www.bbc.co.uk/iplayer/episode/poojrj2t/soldier-in-the-sun

98. Kennedy Trevaskis, *Shades of Amber: A South Arabian Episode* (London: Hutchinson, 1968), p. 206.

99. David Ledger, IWM Sound Recording, 10207.

100. S. R. Ashton and William Roger Louis (eds.), *East of Suez and the Commonwealth 1964–1971* (London: HMSO, 2004), p. 152.

101. Adam Curtis, *The Mayfair Set* (1999) in http://adamcurtisfilms.blogspot.co.uk/2007/09/trap-2007.html

102. Leonard George Drew, IWM Sound Recording, 28546.

103. BBC 1, *Soldier in the Sun*.

104. Alec Douglas-Home MP, HC Deb 4 May 1964 c. 909.

105. Peter Thorneycroft MP, HC Deb 11 May 1964 c. 35.

106. Jonathan Walker, 'Aden Insurgency 1962–67'. Lecture to War Studies Society, King's College London (28 October 2011).https://www.youtube.com/watch?v=7KfFs-FCcOg

107. Trevaskis, *Shades of Amber*, p. 208.

108. Karl Pieragostini, *Britain, Aden and South Arabia: Abandoning Ship* (Basingstoke: Palgrave Macmillan, 1991), p. 75.

109. Ibid, p. 102.

110. Michael Gray, IWM Sound Recording, 28362.

111. Edward Heath MP, HC Deb 19 June 1967 c. 1147.

112. Stephen Peter Day, IWM Sound Recording, 20815, reel 3.

113. George De Carvalho, 'A Case History of Terror', *Life* (8 December 1967).

114. Day, IWM 20815 Reel 3.

115. John Jago, IWM Sound Recording, 20133 Reel 3.

116. Ibid, reel 2.

117. Obituary of Lieutenant Colonel C. C. 'Mad Mitch' Mitchell, *Daily Telegraph* (24 July 1996). Also BBC Radio 4, *From Our Own Correspondent: Return to Aden, without Mad Mitch* (1 December 2007).

4   Conventional Sword and Nuclear Shield

1. *The Army Role* (British Defence Film Library, Chalfont St Peter, Crown Copyright, 1976).
2. Lawrence Freedman, *Britain and Nuclear Weapons* (Basingstoke: Palgrave Macmillan for Royal Institute of International Affairs, 1980), p. 2.
3. Ministry of Defence, Defence Analytical Services Agency *UK Defence Statistics 2000* (London: National Statistics Publication, The Stationery Office, 2000) p. 68.
4. William Warbey MP, HC Deb 12 May 1949 c. 2539.
5. David French, *Army, Empire and Cold War: The British Army and Military Policy 1945–1971* (Oxford: Oxford University Press, 2012).
6. Bernard Law Montgomery, *The Memoirs of Field-Marshal Montgomery of Alamein KG* (1958; new edition, Barnsley: Pen & Sword Military, 2005), pp. 506–29.
7. 'A Report to the National Security Council – NSC-68' (12 April 1950), p. 20.
8. Montgomery, *Memoirs*, p. 514.
9. Ibid, p. 515.
10. Denis Healey, *The Time of My Life* (London: Michael Joseph, 1989). p. 165.
11. Letter from Gladwyn Jebb to Hoyer Millar (29 May 1959) in *Britain in NATO: The First Six Decades* (London: Foreign and Commonwealth Office, 2009).
12. Lawrence Freedman, 'British Foreign Policy to 1985. II: Britain's Contribution to NATO', *International Affairs*, vol. 54, no. 1 (January 1978), pp. 30–47.
13. BBC4 Timeshift, *The British Army of the Rhine* (producer-director, Francis Welsh), 2012.
14. Anthony Kershaw MP, HC Deb 5 July 1962 vol. 662 c. 728.
15. Julian Critchley MP, HC Deb 5 July 1962 vol. 662 c. 744
16. Freedman, 'British Foreign Policy to 1985'.
17. Ibid.
18. John Garnett, 'BAOR and NATO', *International Affairs*, vol. 46, no. 4 (October 1970), pp. 670–81.
19. Cited in John Baylis and Kristan Stoddart, *The British Nuclear Experience: The Roles of Beliefs, Culture and Identity* (Oxford: Oxford University Press, 2014), p. 28.
20. Margaret Gowing, *Reflections on Atomic Energy History: The Rede Lecture 1978* (Cambridge: Cambridge University Press, 1978).
21. Margaret Gowing, *Independence and Deterrence: Britain and Atomic Energy 1945–52* (Basingstoke: Palgrave Macmillan, 1974), p. 51.
22. Andrew J. Pierre, *Nuclear Politics: The British Experience with an Independent Strategic Force* (Oxford: Oxford University Press, 1972), p. 87, cited in Ian Clark and Nicholas J. Wheeler, *The British Origins of Nuclear Strategy 1945–1955* (Oxford: Oxford University Press, 1989), p. 13.
23. Montgomery, *Memoirs*, p. 517.
24. Gowing, 1974, p. 2.
25. Richard Moore, *Nuclear Illusion, Nuclear Reality: Britain, the United States and Nuclear Weapons 1958–64* (Basingstoke: Palgrave Macmillan, 2010), p. 240.
26. Frank Barnaby and Douglas Holdstock (eds.), *The British Nuclear Weapons Programme 1952–2002* (London: Routledge, 2003).
27. Healey, *The Time of My Life*, p. 162.
28. Michael Quinlan, *Thinking About Nuclear Weapons: Principles, Problems, Prospects* (Oxford: Oxford University Press, 2009), p. 118.

29. MoD and FCO, *The Future of the United Kingdom's Nuclear Deterrent*, Factsheet No. 5, 'The History of the UK's Weapons Programme' (2014) https://www.gov.uk/government/uploads/system/uploads/attachment_data/file/27383/Cm6994_Factsheet5.pdf

30. Harold Macmillan, *Pointing the Way, 1959–1961* (London: Macmillan, 1972), p. 323.

31. Ibid, p. 335.

32. Ibid.

33. Nigel John Ashton, 'Harold Macmillan and the "Golden Days" of Anglo-American Relations Revisited', *Diplomatic History*, vol. 29, no. 4 (2005), pp. 691–723.

34. Ibid.

35. Robert Self, *British Foreign and Defence Policy Since 1945: Challenges and Dilemmas in a Changing World* (Basingstoke: Palgrave Macmillan, 2010), p. 192.

36. IWM collections MOD488 http://www.iwm.org.uk/collections/item/object/30018268

37. Moore, *Nuclear Illusion, Nuclear Reality*, p. 242.

38. Hugh Beach, 'The Nuclear Battlefield', in Barnaby and Holdstock (eds.), *The British Nuclear Weapons Programme 1952–2002*, p. 32.

39. Ibid, p. 36.

40. Ibid.

41. Defence Open Government Document 80/23, July 1980, cited in Quinlan, *Thinking about Nuclear Weapons*, p. 125.

42. French, *Army, Empire and Cold War*, p. 24.

43. Canon L. John Collins in *The Nuclear Dilemma: Letters to the Editor, Reprinted from The Times with a Leading Article* (London: Times Publishing Company, 1958).

44. Lord Halifax, ibid.

45. Margaret Thatcher, *The Downing Street Years* (London: HarperCollins, 1993), p. 236.

46. Cited in Bill Jackson and Dwin Bramall, *The Chiefs: The Story of the United Kingdom Chiefs of Staff* (London: Brassey's, 1992), p. 342.

47. Healey, *The Time of My Life*, p. 255.

48. Harold Wilson MP HC Deb 16 Dec 1964 c. 424

49. Robert Self, *British Foreign and Defence Policy since 1945* (Basingstoke: Palgrave Macmillan, 2010) p. 166

50. William Roger Louis, 'The Dissolution of the British Empire in the Era of Vietnam', *American Historical Review*, vol. 7, no. 2 (February 2002), pp. 1–25.

51. Jeremy Fielding, 'Coping with Decline: US Policy Towards British Defense', *Diplomatic History*, vol. 23, no. 4 (September 1999), pp. 633–56.

52. Memo from McGeorge Bundy to Johnson, cited in John Dumbrell, 'The Johnson Administration and the British Labour Government: Vietnam, the Pound and East of Suez', *Journal of American Studies*, vol. 30, no. 2, Part 2 (August 1996), pp. 211–31.

53. Cited in William Roger Louis, *Ends of British Imperialism: The Scramble for Europe, Suez, and Decolonization* (London: I. B. Tauris, 2007), p. 559.

54. Memo from Francis M. Bator to Lyndon B. Johnson (28 July 1966), NSF Memos to the President, box 9 Rostow, vol. 9, cited in Fielding, above.

55. Denis Healey, HC Deb 22 Feb 1966, c.240.

56. Ibid c.239.

57. Basil Liddell Hart *Deterrent or Defence?* (New York: Praeger, 1960) cited in Jeffrey Pickering, *Britain's Withdrawal from East of Suez: The Politics of Retrenchment* (New York: St Martin's Press, 1998) p.133

58. Tony Benn, *Out of the Wilderness: Diaries 1963–67* (London: Hutchinson, 1987), p. 496, cited in Ibid p. 154.

59. Ibid p. 154, above.

60. Rudyard Kipling, 'Mandalay' from *Barrack-Room Ballads, and Other* Verses (1892) http://www.kiplingsociety.co.uk/poems_mandalay.htm

61. James Callaghan MP, HC Deb 13 Oct 1969 c. 48 and Desmond Hamill, *Pig in the Middle: The Army in Northern Ireland 1969–1984* (London: Methuen, 1985), p. 14.

62. Robert J. Savage, *The BBC's 'Irish Troubles': Television, Conflict and Northern Ireland,* (Manchester: Manchester University Press, 2005), p. 52.

63. Christopher Hitchens, 'The Perils of Partition', *The Atlantic* (March 2003) http://www.theatlantic.com/magazine/archive/2003/03/the-perils-of-partition/302686/

64. Peter Taylor, *Brits: The War against the IRA* (London, Bloomsbury, 2001) p. 13.

65. Ibid, p. 18.

66. Andrew Wilson, *Irish America and the Ulster Conflict 1968–1995* (Washington DC: Catholic University Press, 1995), cited in Savage, *The BBC's 'Irish Troubles'*.

67. Defence Select Committee, *Armed Forces Bill* HC 747 (2005), p. 3.

68. Hamill, *Pig in the Middle*, p. 19.

69. Taylor, *Brits*, p. 29.

70. Ken Wharton, *A Long, Long War: Voices from the British Army in Northern Ireland 1969–1998* (Solihull: Helion, 2008), p. 51.

71. Ibid, p. 55.

72. Ibid, p. 56.

73. Hamill, *Pig in the Middle*, p. 7.

74. Rod Thornton, 'Getting it Wrong: The Crucial Mistakes Made in the Early Stages of the British Army's Deployment to Northern Ireland (August 1969 to March 1972)', *Journal of Strategic Studies*, vol. 30, no. 1 (2007) pp. 73–107.

75. Colin McInnes and Caroline Kennedy-Pipe, 'The Dog That Did Not Bark: The British Army in Northern Ireland 1990–1994', *Irish Studies in International Affairs*, vol. 8 (1997), pp. 137–53.

76. Aaron Edwards, '"A Whipping Boy If Ever There Was One"? The British Army and the Politics of Civil–Military Relations in Northern Ireland 1967–79', *Contemporary British History*, vol. 28, no. 2 (2014), pp. 166–89.

77. McInnes and Kennedy-Pipe, 'The Dog That Did Not Bark'.

78. Edwards, '"A Whipping Boy If Ever There Was One"?'.

79. Taylor, *Brits*, p. 16.

80. Savage, *The BBC's 'Irish Troubles'*, p. 44.

81. BBC 1, *As Others See Us: Martin Bell on the Battle of the Shankill* (4 February 2011) http://www.bbc.co.uk/programmes/p00f14vk

82. Peter Mahon MP, HC Deb 13 Oct 1969 c. 63.

83. Bernadette Devlin MP, HC Deb 13 Oct 1969 c. 125.

84. HC Deb 13 Oct 1969 c. 126.

85. Taylor, *Brits*, p. 46.

86. McInnes and Kennedy-Pipe, 'The Dog That Did Not Bark'.

87. Hamill, *Pig in the Middle*, p. 84.

88. Wharton, *A Long, Long War*, p. 100.

89. Denis Healey MP, HC Deb 13 Oct 1969 c. 164.

90. Michael Carver, *Out of Step: The Memoirs of Field Marshal Lord Carver* (London: Hutchinson, 1989), cited in Thornton, 'Getting It Wrong'.

91. Ulster University, Conflict Archive on the Internet (CAIN webservice – Conflict and Politics in Northern Ireland, see http://cain.ulst.ac.uk).

92. Major O. J. M. Lindsay, 'Do Not Pass "Go": Ulster 69', *British Army Review*, vol. 34 (April 1970), cited in Thornton, 'Getting It Wrong'.

93. Savage, *The BBC's 'Irish Troubles'*, p. 81.

94. General Sir Frank Kitson, statement to Saville Inquiry (24 September 2002).

95. Ian Gardiner, *In the Service of the Sultan: A First Hand Account of the Dhofar Insurgency* (Barnsley: Pen and Sword, 2006).

96. Tony Jeapes, *SAS: Operation Oman* (London: William Kimber, 1980), p. 18.

97. Ibid, p. 20.

98. Gardiner, *In the Service of the Sultan*, p. ix.

99. John Akehurst, *We Won a War: The Campaign in Oman, 1965–1975* (Salisbury: Michael Russell, 1982).

100. Walter C. Ladwig III, 'Supporting Allies in Counterinsurgency: Britain and Dhofar Rebellion', *Small Wars and Insurgencies*, vol. 19, no. 1 (2008), pp. 62–88.

101. Ibid.

102. Ibid.

103. Ibid.

104. Gardiner, *In the Service of the Sultan*, p. 55.

105. Jeapes, *SAS: Operation Oman*, p. 31.

106. Tony Geraghty, *Who Dares Wins: The Story of the Special Air Service 1950–1980* (London and Melbourne: Arms and Armour Press, 1980), p. 123, and Jeapes, *SAS: Operation Oman*, p. 37.

107. Jeapes, *SAS: Operation Oman*, p. 59.

108. Akehurst, *We Won a War*, p. 96.

109. Gardiner, *In the Service of the Sultan*, pp. 157–9.

110. Jeapes, *SAS: Operation Oman*, p. 152.

111. Ibid, p. 158.

112. Gardiner, *In the Service of the Sultan*, p. 73.

113. Jeapes, *SAS: Operation Oman*, p. 161.

114. Ladwig, 'Supporting Allies in Counterinsurgency'.

115. Cited in Akehurst, *We Won a War*, p. xiii.

116. Ladwig, 'Supporting Allies in Counterinsurgency'.

117. Michael Carver, Foreword in Akehurst, *We Won a War*, p. xi.

118. French, *Army, Empire and the Cold War*, p. 305.

5   An Army for All Seasons

1.   *The Army Role* (Crown Copyright, 1976) British Defence Film Library, Chalfont St Peter.

2.   Lieutenant Colonel J. F. Stone, 'Trends in Modern Society', *British Army Review*, no. 49 (April 1975), p. 11.

3.   Ibid.

4.   Richard Clutterbuck, *Britain in Agony* (London: Faber & Faber, 1978), p. 19.

5.   W. M. E. Hicks OBE, 'The Maintenance of Operational Standards' *British Army Review* No. 56, August 1977, pp.6–15.

6.   Ibid.

7.   Denis Healey, *The Time of My Life* (London: Michael Joseph, 1989), p. 412.

8.   Roy Mason, *Paying the Price* (London: Robert Hale, 1999) p. 123.

9.   Ibid, p. 127.

10. Ibid, p. 124.

11. Ministry of Defence, Defence Analytical Services Agency *UK Defence Statistics 2000* (London: National Statistics Publication, The Stationery Office, 2000) p. 68.

12. Roy Mason MP, HC Deb 3 Dec 1974 c. 1353.

13. Ken Wharton, *A Long, Long War: Voices from the British Army in Northern Ireland 1969–1998* (Solihull: Helion, 2008), p. 108.

14. Edward Heath, *The Course of My Life: The Autobiography of Edward Heath* (London: Hodder & Stoughton, 1998), p. 421.

15. Peter R. Smith and M. L. R. Neumann, *The Strategy of Terrorism: How It Works, and Why It Fails* (London: Routledge, 2007).

16. Heath, *The Course of My Life*, p. 434.

17. Wharton, *A Long, Long War*, p. 125.

18. Colonel Michael Dewar, *The British Army in Northern Ireland* (London: Arms and Armour, revised edition, 1996).

19. Willie Whitelaw, HC Deb 28 Mar 1972 c. 240.

20. Smith and Neumann, *The Strategy of Terrorism*.

21. Desmond Hamill, *Pig in the Middle: The Army in Northern Ireland 1969–1984* (London: Methuen, 1985), p. 117.

22. Smith and Neumann, *The Strategy of Terrorism*.

23. Hamill, *Pig in the Middle*, p. 115.

24. Dewar, *The British Army in Northern Ireland*, p. 186.

25. Hamill, *Pig in the Middle*, p. 119.

26. Peter Taylor, *Brits: The War against the IRA* (London: Bloomsbury, 2002), p. 139.

27. Marcus Lapsa, in Wharton, *A Long, Long War*, p. 220.

28. Taylor, *Brits*, p. 139.

29. Hamill, *Pig in the Middle*, p. 139.

30. Taylor, *Brits*, p. 133.

31. Peter Taylor, *The Provos: The IRA and Sinn Féin* (London: Bloomsbury, 1997).

32. Ministry of Defence, *Land Operations Volume III – Counter-Revolutionary Operations*. Army Code: 70516 (1969 and 1970).

33. Mark Urban, *Big Boys' Rules: The Secret Struggle against the IRA* (London: Faber & Faber, 1992), p. 19.

34. *Ministry of Defence, Land Operations. Volume III: Counter Revolutionary Operations. Part 2. Internal Security (1969). Army Code: 70516.*

35. Urban, *Big Boys' Rules*, p. 71.

36. Heath, *The Course of My Life*, p. 439.

37. Edward Burke, 'Counterinsurgency against Kith and Kin', *The Journal of Imperial and Commonwealth History*, vol. 43, no. 4 (2015).

38. Frank McManus MP c. 747 and Peter Tapsell MP c. 748, HC Deb 2 Mar 1972.

39. Huw Bennett, '"Smoke Without Fire?": Allegations against the British Army in Northern Ireland 1972–75', *20th Century British History* (February 2012) http://tcbh.oxfordjournals.org/content/early/2012/02/29/tcbh.hws006

40. Ibid.

41. Ibid.

42. Taylor, *Brits*, p. 130.

43. Burke, 'Counterinsurgency against Kith and Kin'.

44. Urban, *Big Boys' Rules*, p. 33.

45. Ministry of Defence, *Land Operations Vol. III, Part 3* (1970), p. 2.

46. Taylor, *Brits*, p. 160.

47. Ibid, p. 168.

48. Dewar, *The British Army in Northern Ireland*, p. 242.

49. Les Robertson and Alan Hill in BBC News 'IRA Birmingham Pub Bombings Remembered Forty Years On' (12 November 2014) http://www.bbc.co.uk/news/uk-england-birmingham-29936619

50. Taylor, *Brits*, p. 183.

51. Hamill, *Pig in the Middle*, p. 245.

52. Dewar, *The British Army in Northern Ireland*, p. 147.

53. Cited in Peter Taylor, *The Provos: The IRA and Sinn Féin* (London: Bloomsbury, 1997).

54. Hamill, *Pig in the Middle*, p. 208.

55. Mason, *Paying the Price*, p. 166.

56. Dewar, *The British Army in Northern Ireland*, p. 118.

57. Mason, *Paying the Price*, p. 218.

58. Ibid, p. 203.

59. Ibid, p. 220.

60. Andrew Dorman, *Introductory Paper*, The Nott Review, Seminar held on 20 June 2001 (Institute of Contemporary British History, 2002) p. 28. https://www.kcl.ac.uk/sspp/departments/icbh/witness/PDFfiles/NottReview.pdf.

61. Cited in Bill Jackson and Dwin Bramall, *The Chiefs: The Story of the United Kingdom Chiefs of Staff* (London: Brassey's, 1992), p. 390.

62. House of Commons Information Office, *Sittings of the House* (2010).

63. HC Deb 3 Apr 1982 c. 633.

64. HC Deb 3 Apr 1982 c. 638.

65. Peter J. Beck, 'The Conflict Potential of the "Dots on the Map"', *International History Review*, vol. 13, no. 1 (February 1991), pp. 124–33.

66. Max Hastings, 'Fortune and the Warrior Spirit: The British Victory in the Falklands', *RUSI Journal*, vol. 152, no. 2 (April 2007).

67. Anthony Parsons, 'The Falklands Crisis in the United Nations, 31 March–14 June 1982', *International Affairs*, vol. 59, no. 2 (Spring 1983), pp. 169–78.

68. Ken Weetch MP, HC Deb 20 May 1982 c. 500.

69. Beck, 'The Conflict Potential of the "Dots on the Map"' and Julian Amery MP, HC Deb 2 Dec 1980 c. 129.

70. John Fowler, cited in Hugh McManners, *Forgotten Voices of the Falklands: The Real Story of the Falklands War* (London: Ebury Press, 2007), p. 13.

71. Alan Clark MP, HC Deb 3 Apr 1982 c. 654.

72. For example, David Owen MP, HC Deb 3 April 1982.

73. Margaret Thatcher, testimony to the Franks Report (18 January 1983), p. 35.

74. Ibid, p. 31.

75. Ibid, p. 16.

76. Ibid, p. 17.

77. Margaret Thatcher, *The Downing Street Years* (London: HarperCollins, 1993), p. 179.

78. Julian Amery MP, HC Deb 3 April 1982 c. 647.

79. Andrew Dorman, 'John Nott and the Royal Navy: The 1981 Defence Review Revisited', *Contemporary British History*, vol. 15, no. 2 (Summer 2001), pp. 98–120.

80. Claire Taylor, *A Brief Guide to Previous Defence Reviews*, House of Commons Library Note SN/IA/5714 (2010), p. 8.

81. See Jackson and Bramall, *The Chiefs*, p. 396.

82. Admiral Sir John (Sandy) Woodward, in The Nott Review, Seminar held on 20 June 2001 (Institute of Contemporary British History, 2002) p. 71.

83. HC Deb 29 Mar 1982 c. 27.

84. Lawrence Freedman, *The Politics of British Defence, 1979–1998* (London: Macmillan, 1999), p. 83.

85. Kenneth L. Privratsky, *Logistics in the Falklands War* (Barnsley: Pen and Sword, 2014).

86. Ibid, p. 13.

87. McManners, *Forgotten Voices of the Falklands*, p. 40.

88. Ibid, p. 56.

89. Ibid, p. 59.

90. Lawrence Freedman, *The Official History of the Falklands Campaign: Vol. 2 War and Diplomacy*, Government Official History Series (Abingdon: Routledge, 2005), p. 726.

91. Stuart Holland MP, HC Deb 20 May 1982 c. 531.

92. Secretary of State for Defence, *The Falklands Campaign: The Lessons* Cmnd 8758 (London: HMSO, December 1982), p. 6.

93. McManners, *Forgotten Voices of the Falklands*, p. 92.

94. Ibid, p. 94.

95. Freedman, *The Official History of the Falklands Campaign: Vol. 2*, p. 726.

96. Ibid.

97. Army Management Service, Report No. 392, p. 24, cited in Privratsky, *Logistics in the Falklands War*, p. 155.

98. Anthony Parsons, 'The Falklands Crisis in the United Nations, 31 March–14 June 1982', *International Affairs*, vol. 59, no. 2 (Spring 1982), pp. 169–78.

99. Margaret Thatcher, HC Deb 20 May 1982 c. 481.

100. Thatcher, *The Downing Street Years*, p. 230.

101. James Callaghan, HC Deb 20 May 1982 c. 518.

102. Freedman, *The Official History of the Falklands Campaign: Vol. 2*, p. 597.

103. McManners, *Forgotten Voices of the Falklands*, p. 50.

104. Freedman, *The Official History of the Falklands Campaign: Vol. 2*, p. 33.

105. McManners, *Forgotten Voices of the Falklands*, p. 52.

106. Ibid, p. 57.

107. Secretary of State for Defence, *The Falklands Campaign*, p. 19.

108. Privratsky, *Logistics in the Falklands War*, p. 71.

109. Thatcher, *The Downing Street Years*, p. 205.

110. Freedman, *The Official History of the Falklands Campaign: Vol. 2*, p. 248.

111. RAF, *The Falkland Islands Campaign* http://www.raf.mod.uk/history/OperationBlackBuck.cfm

112. Lieutenant Commander Graham Edmonds, in McManners, *Forgotten Voices of the Falklands*, p. 148.

113. Commander Ian Inskip, in ibid, p. 149.

114. Thatcher, *The Downing Street Years*, p. 215.

115. Freedman, *The Official History of the Falklands Campaign: Vol. 2*, p. 429.

116. Ibid, p. 464.

117. Jackson and Bramall, *The Chiefs*, p. 414.

118. Company Sergeant Major Peter Richens in McManners, *Forgotten Voices of the Falklands*, p. 194.

119. Ibid, p. 218.

120. Thatcher, *The Downing Street Years*, p. 228.

121. McManners, *Forgotten Voices of the Falklands*, p. 236.

122. Jackson and Bramall, *The Chiefs*, p. 416.

123. Freedman, *Official History of the Falklands Campaign: Vol. 2*, p. 548.

124. McManners, *Forgotten Voices of the Falklands*, p. 259.

125. Freedman, *Official History of the Falklands Campaign: Vol. 2*, p. 561.

126. McManners, *Forgotten Voices of the Falklands*, p. 254.

127. Privratsky, *Logistics in the Falklands War*, p. 173.

128. Freedman, *Official History of the Falklands Campaign: Vol. 2*, p. 592.

129. Secretary of State for Defence, *The Falklands Campaign*, p. 10.

130. Thatcher, *The Downing Street Years*, p. 235.

131. McManners, *Forgotten Voices of the Falklands*, p. 424.

132. Freedman, *Official History of the Falklands Campaign: Vol 2* p. 727.

133. Julian Thompson, foreword to Privratksy, *Logistics in the Falklands War*, p. vii.

134. Freedman, *Official History of the Falklands Campaign: Vol. 2*, p. 729.

135. Jackson and Bramall, *The Chiefs*, p. 418.

136. Colonel G. Read, 'Fings Ain't Wot They Used to Be', *British Army Review*, no. 54 (December 1976), p. 12.

137. Ibid.

138. Rt. Hon. Sir John Nott, in The Nott Review, Seminar held on 20 June 2001 (Institute of Contemporary British History, 2002) p. 50.

139. Gary Sheffield, 'Doctrine and Command in the British Army: A Historical Overview', appendix to Army Doctrine Publication *Land Operations* AC71819 (2010).

140. Sarah Ingham, *The Military Covenant: Its Impact on Civil–Military Relations* (Farnham: Ashgate, 2014), p. 42.

141. Thatcher, *The Downing Street Years*, p. 235.

6   From Cold War to New World Order?

1. Margaret Thatcher, *The Downing Street Years* (London: HarperCollins, 1993), p. 768.

2. Benjamin B. Fischer (ed.) *At Cold War's End: US Intelligence on the Soviet Union and Eastern Europe, 1984–1991* (Central Intelligence Agency: Center for the Study of Intelligence, 1999).

3. Francis Fukuyama, *The End of History and the Last Man* (1992: London, Penguin).

4. John Lewis Gaddis, *The Cold War: A New History* (London: Allen Lane, 2006), p. 196.

5. Remarks made by Ronald Reagan on announcing his candidacy for the Republican presidential nomination, 1979. See Luis da Vinha, 'Ronald Reagan' in Steven Casey and Jonathan Wright (eds.), *Mental Maps in the Era of Detente and the End of the Cold War 1968–91* (New York: Palgrave Macmillan, 2015), p. 199.

6. Thatcher, *The Downing Street Years*, p. 157.

7. Da Vinha, 'Ronald Reagan', p. 201.

8. David Holloway, 'State, Society and the Military under Gorbachev', *International Security*, vol. 14, no. 3 (1989), pp. 5–24.

9. General D. T. Yazov, 'On Soviet Military Doctrine', *RUSI Journal*, vol. 134, no. 4 (Winter 1989).

10. British Commanders-in-Chief Mission to the Soviet Forces in Germany, see http://www.brixmis.co.uk/later-years.html

11. William E. Odom, 'Soviet Military Doctrine', *Foreign Affairs*, vol. 67, no. 2 (1988), pp. 114–34.

12. Michael Heseltine, *Life in the Jungle: My Autobiography* (London: Hodder & Stoughton, 2000), p. 243.

13. Vladislav Zubok, '"Do Not Think I am Soft ..." Leonid Brezhnev' in Casey and Wright (eds.), *Mental Maps in the Era of Detente and the End of the Cold War*, pp. 6–23.

14. Holloway, 'State, Society and the Military under Gorbachev'.

15. Mikhail Gorbachev, *Perestroika: New Thinking for Our Country and the World* (London: HarperCollins, 1987), p. 219.

16. Ibid, p. 221.

17. Ibid, p. 196.

18. Rodric Braithwaite, *Afgantsy: The Russians in Afghanistan, 1979–89* (Profile Books, 2011), p. 8.

19. Archie Brown, 'Mikhail Gorbachev' in Casey and Wright (eds.), *Mental Maps in the Era of Detente and the End of the Cold War*, p. 225.

20. General Sergey Akhromeyev. See Braithwaite, *Afgantsy*, p. 276.

21. Ibid, p. 330.

22. Ibid, p. 263.
23. Gorbachev, *Perestroika*, p. 24.
24. Braithwaite, *Afgantsy*, p. 308.
25. R. J. S. Corbett, *Berlin and the British Ally 1945–1990* (1997), p. 98.
26. Jamie Shea, '1989 – The Berlin Wall Comes Down and the Soldiers Go Home' (Jamie's History Class, NATOChannel.TV, 2013), https://www.youtube.com/watch?v=zoIy10GcXZ8
27. Thatcher, *The Downing Street Years*, p. 814.
28. Corbett, *Berlin and the British Ally*, p. 120.
29. Braithwaite, *Afgantsy*, p. 315.
30. Christopher Bellamy, 'A Prussian Surrender for Action-Ready Armed Forces', *Independent* (8 October 1990).
31. Christopher Fathers, IWM Sound Recording, 12182, Reel 1.
32. Margaret Thatcher at joint press conference with George Bush (2 August 1990) http://www.margaretthatcher.org/document/108170
33. Peter Sluglett, 'The Resilience of a Frontier: Ottoman and Iraqi Claims to Kuwait', *International History Review*, vol. 24, no. 4 (2002), pp. 783–816.
34. Ibid.
35. David Hirst, 'Obituary: Saddam Hussein', *Guardian* (30 December 2006).
36. Sluglett, 'The Resilience of a Frontier'.
37. Peter de la Billière, *Storm Command: A Personal Account of the Gulf War* (London: HarperCollins, 2012), p. 25.
38. Patrick Cordingley, *In the Eye of the Storm: Commanding the Desert Rats in the Gulf War* (London: Hodder & Stoughton, 1996), p. 4.
39. Ibid, p. 4.
40. de la Billière, *Storm Command*, p. 26.
41. Cordingley, *In the Eye of the Storm*, p. 33.
42. de la Billière, *Storm Command*, p. 17.
43. Cordingley, *In the Eye of the Storm*, p. 42.
44. de la Billière, *Storm Command*, p. 63.
45. Ibid, p. 60.
46. Ibid, p. 42.
47. David H. Petraeus, 'Lessons of History and Lessons of Vietnam', *Parameters*, vol. 20, no. 4 (Winter 2010–11), pp. 48–61.
48. de la Billière, *Storm Command*, p. 124.
49. Ibid, p. 78.
50. Ibid, p. 99.
51. Cordingley, *In the Eye of the Storm*, p. 82.
52. de la Billière, *Storm Command*, p. 95.
53. Ibid, p. 53.
54. Ibid, p. 80.
55. Ibid, p. 71.
56. Craig George James Comber, IWM Sound Recording, 27081.
57. Cordingley, *In the Eye of the Storm*, p. 136.
58. Comber, IWM 27081.
59. de la Billière, *Storm Command*, p. 148.
60. Lieutenant Colonel Mike Vickery in Hugh McManners, *Gulf War One: Real Voices from the Frontline* (London: Random House, 2010), p. 122.
61. Colin McInnes, 'The Gulf War, 1990–91', in Hew Strachan (ed) *Big Wars and Small Wars: The British Army and the Lessons of War in the Twentieth Century* (Abingdon: Routledge, 2006), p. 162–79.

62. Ibid.

63. William Hale, 'Turkey, the Middle East and the Gulf Crisis' , *International Affairs*, vol. 68, no. 4 (1992), pp. 679–92.

64. John Major, *The Autobiography* (London: HarperCollins, 1999), p. 235.

65. Ibid, p. 234.

66. Group Captain Andrew Vallance, 'Air Power in the Gulf: The RAF Contribution' http://www.raf.mod.uk/history/AirPowerintheGulfWar.cfm

67. George H. W. Bush Announces War against Iraq (16 January 1991) https://www.youtube.com/watch?v=IFrnQHaQWoA

68. de la Billière, *Storm Command*, p. 224.

69. Cordingley, *In the Eye of the Storm*, p. 165.

70. Cordingley, *In the Eye of the Storm*, p. 240.

71. Major, *The Autobiography*, p. 251.

72. de la Billière, *Storm Command*, p. 65.

73. Martin Shaw and Roy Carr-Hill, 'Public Opinion, Media and Violence: Attitudes to the Gulf War in a Local Population' (Hull: University of Hull, 1991), pp. 9–10, cited in Martin Shaw, *Post-Military Society: Militarism, Demilitarization and War at the End of the Twentieth Century* (Cambridge: Polity, 1991), p. 199.

74. Jean Baudrillard, *The Gulf War Did Not Take Place*, translated by Paul Patten (Sydney: Power Publications, 1995).

75. Defence Select Committee, *Defence Implications of Recent Events*, HC 320, 1989, para. 1.

76. Tom King MP, HC Deb 25 July 1990 c. 468.

77. Tony Banks MP, HC Deb 25 July 1990 c. 485.

78. Tom King MP, HC Deb 25 July 1990 c. 471.

79. Jeremy Black, 'The Revolution in Military Affairs: The Historian's Perspective', *Journal of Military and Strategic Studies*, vol. 9, no. 2 (Winter 2006–7).

80. de la Billière, *Storm Command*, p. 184.

81. Jackson and Bramall, *The Chiefs*, p. 446.

82. Alan Clark, *Diaries* (London, Weidenfeld & Nicolson, 1993) Entry for 14 May 1990 p. 280.

83. Ibid. Entry for 17 May 1990, p. 291.

84. Ibid. Entry for 1 January 1990, p. 272.

85. Colonel David Boyle, cited in Hew Strachan, *The Politics of the British Army* (Oxford: Oxford University Press, 2005; paperback edition, 2008), p. 222.

86. *The Times* (28 November 1956), cited in David French, *Military Identities: The Regimental System, the British Army and the British People c. 1870–2000* (Oxford: Oxford University Press, Paperback Edition, 2012), p. 2.

87. *The Times* (1 December 1854), cited in French, ibid, p. 14.

88. Strachan, *The Politics of the British Army*, p. 197.

89. Ibid, p. 226.

90. de la Billière, pp. 93–4.

91. Ministry of Defence, *Britain's Army for the 90s* Cm1595 (1991).

92. Tom King MP, 24 July 1991 evidence c. 1088, Defence Select Committee, *Options for Change: Army*. Review of the White Paper, *Britain's Army for the 1990s* Cm1595 and ibid, para. 29.

93. Letter from Secretary of State for Defence to the Chairman of the Committee (6 December 1991), appendix.

94. Defence Select Committee, *Options for Change*, para. 84.

95. Memorandum submitted by the Save the Staffords campaign on behalf of the Staffordshire Regiment (1991), ibid, p. 80.

96. Excerpt from a memorandum submitted by the Colonel of the Cheshire Regiment, ibid, p. 86.
97. Extract from a letter from the Colonel of the Queen's Own Highlanders (Seaforth and Camerons), ibid, p. 94.
98. Extracts from a letter from the Colonel of the Royal Hussars (PWO), ibid, p. 95.
99. Memorandum submitted by the Save the Staffords campaign, ibid, p. 81.
100. Ibid, p. 81.
101. Peter Taylor, *Brits: The War against the IRA* (London: Bloomsbury, 2002), p. 260.
102. British Army, *Statue of Sefton, Hyde Park Hero, Unveiled* 18 October 2013 (British Army website, www.army.mod.uk/news/25838).
103. Major, *The Autobiography*, p. 203.

7 New World Disorder and Humanitarian Interventionism

1. Mary Kaldor, *New and Old Wars: Organized Violence in a Global Era* (Stanford: Stanford University Press, second edition, 2007).
2. Tim Cross, *Comfortable with Chaos: Working with UNHCR and the NGOs; Reflections from the 1999 Kosovo Refugee Crisis*, UNHCR working paper no. 42 (April 2001).
3. Nicholas J. Wheeler, *Saving Strangers: Humanitarian Intervention in International Society* (Oxford: Oxford University Press, 2000).
4. Throughout, the Republic of Bosnia-Herzegovina will be referred to as Bosnia.
5. Rupert Smith, *The Utility of Force: The Art of War in the Modern World* (London: Allen Lane, 2005).
6. Lord Hylton HL Deb 1 Jul 1990 c. 852.
7. Michael Rose, *Fighting for Peace: Bosnia 1994* (London: The Harvill Press, 1998), p. 1.
8. Kaldor, *New and Old Wars*, p. 81.
9. Robert D. Kaplan, *The Coming Anarchy: Shattering the Dreams of the Post Cold War* (New York: Vintage 2001).
10. Martin van Creveld, *The Transformation of War: The Most Radical Reinterpretation of Armed Conflict since Clausewitz* (New York: The Free Press, 1991), p. 1.
11. Douglas Hurd MP, HC Deb 2 Jun 1992 c. 718.
12. Gerald Kaufman MP, HC Deb 2 Jun 1992 c. 716.
13. John Major, *The Autobiography* (London: HarperCollins, 1999), p. 535.
14. Ibid.
15. 'Orange Card', Simon Ellis, IWM collection BOS 122.
16. Bryan Watters, IWM Sound Recording 33556.
17. Richard Forde-Johnston, IWM Sound Recording, 14610.
18. Kaldor, *New and Old Wars*, p. 53.
19. Watters, IWM 33556.
20. Ibid.
21. Douglas Hurd MP, HC Deb 10 Feb 1993 c. 969.
22. Malcolm Rifkind MP, HC Deb 14 Jan 1993 c. 1057.
23. Douglas Hogg MP, HC Deb 2 Apr 1993 c. 1168.
24. Kaldor, *New and Old Wars*, p. 62.
25. Rose, *Fighting for Peace*, p. 1.
26. Christiane Amanpour, *Opinion: Bosnia's Lesson for Syrian Slaughter* (CNN, 5 April 2012) http://edition.cnn.com/2012/04/05/world/europe/bosnia-amanpour/
27. Rose, *Fighting for Peace*, p. 14.
28. Ibid, p. 77.
29. Ibid, p. 52.

30. Jamie Shea, 'Nato as a Peacekeeper' (Jamie's History Class, NATOChannel.TV, 2003) http://www.nato.int/docu/speech/2003/s031215a.htm

31. Rose, *Fighting for Peace*, p. 32.

32. IFOR Officer, private information.

33. British Army, *Wider Peacekeeping* (1994), British Army Field Manuals and Doctrine Publications Collection, Liddell Hart Military Archives, King's College London.

34. Douglas Hurd, *Memoirs* (London: Little, Brown, 2003), p. 446.

35. United Nations, UN Charter Article 2 (7), UN Charter, http://un.org/eN/sections/uncharter/un-charter-full-text/index.html

36. Boutros Boutros-Ghali, *Report of the UN Secretary-General: 'Agenda for Peace'* (17 June 1992).

37. Lawyers' Committee Report for Human Rights, *Prosecuting Genocide in Rwanda: The ICTR and National Trials* (Washington DC, 1997), p. 4.

38. See Roméo Dallaire's website, http://www.romeodallaire.com/index.php/rwanda-genocide/

39. Tony Blair, *A Journey* (London: Hutchinson, 2010), p. 248.

40. Ibid.

41. Robin Cook MP, speech, cited in the *Guardian* (12 May 1997) http://www.theguardian.com/world/1997/may/12/indonesia.ethicalforeignpolicy

42. Blair, *A Journey*, p. 225.

43. Ibid, p. 246.

44. Ibid, p. 224.

45. MoD, *Strategic Defence Review* Cmd 3999 (1998).

46. Tom Dodd, 'The Strategic Defence Review White Paper', House of Commons Library Research Paper (Foreign Affairs and Defence Section) 97/106 (1997).

47. MoD, *Strategic Defence Review* Cm 3999, introduction, para. 6.

48. Ibid, chapter 6, para. 92.

49. Ibid, introduction, para. 19.

50. Ibid, chapter 1, para. 11.

51. Ibid, chapter 2, 28.

52. Cited in HC Deb 18/7/97 c. 354w.

53. MoD, *Strategic Defence Review*, chapter 6, para. 109.

54. Ibid, chapter 3, para. 45.

55. Ibid, chapter 3, para. 53.

56. Ibid, chapter 5, para. 89.

57. Ibid, chapter 5, para. 112 and para. 113.

58. General Sir Mike Jackson, *Soldier: The Autobiography* (London: Bantam Press, 2007), p. 281.

59. Wheeler, *Saving Strangers*, p. 258.

60. Jackson, *Soldier*, p. 283.

61. Ibid.

62. Blair, *A Journey*, p. 235.

63. Ibid.

64. Ibid, p. 231.

65. Cross, *Comfortable with Chaos*, p. 4.

66. Ibid, p. 5.

67. Ibid, p. 7.

68. International Development Select Committee, *Kosovo: The Humanitarian Crisis* (HC 422, 1999), para. 25.

69. Mike Aaronson, evidence to International Development Select Committee, ibid, para. 27.

70. Michael Ignatieff, *Virtual War: Kosovo and Beyond* (New York: Metropolitan Books, 2000), p. 94, and Blair, *A Journey*, p. 236.

71. Robin Cook MP, HC Deb 25 Mar 1999.
72. Brook Lapping/BBC *The Fall of Milosevic*, Episode 2 'War' (2002). Produced by Alex Holmes, Brian Lapping and Norma Percy.
73. Ignatieff, *Virtual War*, p. 107.
74. Radio Free Europe, 'NATO commando visits Kosovo, urges "Healing Process",' 15 May 2004.
75. Blair, *A Journey*, p. 236
76. John Kampfner, *Blair's Wars* (London: Free Press, 2003), p. 54.
77. Blair, *A Journey*, p. 236.
78. Ibid, p. 238.
79. Ivo H. Daadler and Michael E. O'Hanlon, 'Unlearning the Lessons of Kosovo', *Foreign Policy*, no. 116 (Autumn 1990), pp. 128–40.
80. Ibid.
81. Brook Lapping/BBC, *The Fall of Milosevic*.
82. Cross, *Comfortable with Chaos*, p. 7.
83. Jackson, *Soldier*, p. 346.
84. Cross, *Comfortable with Chaos*, p. 7.
85. Jackson, *Soldier*, p. 319.
86. Ibid, p. 361.
87. Blair, *A Journey*, p. 227.
88. Ibid.
89. General Sir David Richards, *Taking Command: The Autobiography* (London: Headline, 2014), p. 100.
90. Ibid, p. 99.
91. Ibid, p. 107.
92. Blair, *A Journey*, p. 246.
93. Louis Goreux, *Conflict Diamonds*, World Bank: Africa Series Working Paper Series No. 13 (March 2001), p. 2.
94. Ibid, p. 21, citing figures from *Mining Journal* (16 June 2000) and A. Coxon, 'Recommendations for Sierra Leone and Estimates of Conflict Diamonds' (2000) for De Beers, Kimberley.
95. United Nations, Sierra Leone: A Success Story in Peacekeeping (2005) www.un.org/en/peacekeeping/missions/past/unamsil/background.html.
96. Richards, *Taking Command*, p. 122.
97. Robin Cook MP, HC Deb 2 Mar 1999 c. 894.
98. Graham Greene, *The Heart of the Matter* (London: Vintage Classics, 2004), p. 3.
99. Richards, *Taking Command*, p. 126.
100. Robin Cook MP, HC Deb 8 May 2000 c. 518.
101. Richards, *Taking Command*, p. 134.
102. Chris McGreal, 'Sierra Leone Peace Force Accused of Sabotage', *Guardian* (9 September 2000). http://www.theguardian.com/world/2000/sep/09/sierraleone.unitednations
103. Richards, *Taking Command*, p.135.
104. Geoff Hoon MP, HC Deb 15 May 2000 c. 35.
105. Ibid, HC Deb 15 May 2000 c. 23.
106. Keith Simpson MP, HC Deb 15 May 2000 c. 36.
107. Iain Duncan-Smith MP, HC Deb 15 May 2000 c. 25.
108. Cited in Richards, *Taking Command*, p. 150.
109. Richards, *Taking Command*, p. 2.
110. Ibid, p. 154.
111. Ibid, p. 160.
112. Blair, *A Journey*, p. 246.

113. Kofi Annan, Report of the Secretary General, 'We the Peoples: The Role of the United Nations in the Twenty-first Century' (2000), p. 34, para. 217 http://www.un.org/en/ga/search/view_doc.asp?symbol=A/54/2000

114. United Nations, Office of the Special Adviser on the Prevention of Genocide, 'The Responsibility to Protect', see http://www.un.org/en/preventgenocide/adviser/responsibility.shtml

115. Smith, *The Utility of Force*, p. 404.

116. MoD, *Strategic Defence Review*, para. 56.

8   'Go First, Go Fast, Go Home'

1. Theo Farrell, 'The Dynamics of British Military Transformation', *International Affairs*, vol. 84, no. 4 (July 2008), pp. 777–807.

2. Richard Holmes touches on this in *Dusty Warriors: Modern Soldiers at War* (London: HarperPress, 2006); also Charles C. Moskos, John Allen Williams and David R. Segal (eds.), *The Post Modern Military: Armed Forces after the Cold War* (Oxford: Oxford University Press, 2000).

3. Ministry of Defence, Defence Analytical Services Agency, *UK Defence Statistics 2000* (2000), p. 68.

4. Ministry of Defence, Army Doctrine Publication Vol. 5 *Soldiering: The Military Covenant* (AC71642, 2000) Crown Copyright.

5. Cited in Sarah Ingham, *The Military Covenant: Its Impact on Civil–Military Relations in Britain* (Farnham: Ashgate, 2014), p. 48.

6. Diane Abbott MP, HC Deb 22 Jan 1998 c. 1247.

7. Ingham, *The Military Covenant*, p. 52.

8. Ibid.

9. Ibid, p. 53.

10. Ministry of Defence, Army Doctrine Publication *Values and Standards of the British Army* (Commanders' Edition) (AC63813, 2000) Crown Copyright.

11. Ibid, para. 20.

12. Ingham, *The Military Covenant*, p. 53.

13. MoD, *Strategic Defence Review 1998*, para. 127.

14. See Ingham, *The Military Covenant*, p. 112; MoD 2003 Supporting Essay 5 para 5.15.

15. Defence Select Committee, 'The Strategy Defence Review', HC 29–1 2000–01 para. 7.

16. Barney White-Spunner in Jonathan Bailey, Richard Iron, Hew Strachan (eds.), *British Generals in Blair's Wars* (Farnham: Ashgate, 2013), p. 90.

17. Ibid, p. 91.

18. Ibid.

19. Ibid, p. 92.

20. Ibid.

21. Ken Wharton, *A Long, Long War: Voices from the British Army in Northern Ireland 1969–1998* (Solihull: Helion, 2008), p. 484.

22. Tony Blair, *A Journey* (London: Hutchinson, 2010), p. 166.

23. Ministry of Defence, *UK Defence Statistics 1997* (Defence Analytical Services Agency, 1997) p. 143.

24. Ibid, p. 28.

25. Colin McInnes and Caroline Kennedy-Pipe, 'The Dog That Did Not Bark: The British Army in Northern Ireland, 1990–1994', *Irish Studies in International Affairs*, vol. 8 (1997), pp. 137–53.

26. Wharton, *A Long, Long War*, p. 488.

27. Blair, *A Journey*, p. 157.

28. Ibid, p. 18.

29. Ulster University, Conflict Archive on the Internet Project (CAIN project) http://cain.ulst.ac.uk/sutton/book/#append

30. Good Friday Agreement, section 7, para. 3, https://www.gov.uk/government/uploads/system/uploads/attachment_data/file/136652/agreement.pdf

31. Peter Taylor, *Brits: The War against the IRA* (London: Bloomsbury, 2002), p. 341.

32. Wharton, *A Long, Long War*, p. 488.

33. Blair, *A Journey*, p. 185.

34. General Alastair Irwin in Bailey, Iron, Strachan (eds.), *British Generals in Blair's Wars*, p. 37.

35. Bruce Hoffman, *Inside Terrorism* (New York: Columbia University Press, 2006).

36. Blair, *A Journey*, p. 345.

37. George W. Bush, address to the nation (11 September 2001).

38. George Robertson, 'Being NATO's Secretary General on 9/11', *NATO Review* http://www.nato.int/docu/Review/2011/11-september/Lord_Robertson/EN/index.htm

39. United Nations, UN Security Council Resolution 1368 (2001) http://www.un.org/Docs/scres/2001/sc2001.htm

40. George W. Bush, address to Congress (20 September 2001).

41. Ahmed Rashid, *Taliban: The Power of Militant Islam in Afghanistan and Beyond* (London: Pan Books, 2001), p. 123.

42. Lawrence Wright, *The Looming Tower: Al-Qaeda's Road to 9/11* (London: Penguin, 2007), pp. 99–120.

43. Rashid, *Taliban*, p. 130.

44. Osama bin Laden interview with Tayseer Allouni (October 2001). Available from CNN http://edition.cnn.com/2002/WORLD/asiapcf/south/02/05/binladen.transcript/

45. John Gray, *Al-Qaeda and What It Means to be Modern* (London: Faber & Faber, 2003), p. 76.

46. Jason Burke, *Al-Qaeda: The True Story of Radical Islam* (London: Penguin, 2007), p. 232.

47. Tony Blair, HC Deb 14 Nov 2001 c. 861.

48. Bob Woodward, *State of Denial: Bush at War Part III* (New York: Simon & Schuster, 2007), p. 22–7.

49. Osama Bin Laden interview with Hamid Mir, 'Muslims Have the Right to Attack America', *Guardian* (11 November 2001) http://www.theguardian.com/world/2001/nov/11/terrorism.afghanistan1

50. Philip Smucker, *Al Qaeda's Great Escape* (Dulles: Potomac Books, 2004).

51. Tim Bird and Alex Marshall, *Afghanistan: How the West Lost Its Way* (New Haven and London: Yale University Press, 2011), p. 92.

52. Ibid, p. 93.

53. CNN interview with General Richard Myers (6 April 2002) http://transcripts.cnn.com/TRANSCRIPTS/0204/06/en.00.html

54. Scott Jinks, IWM Sound Recording, 33842.

55. John McColl in Bailey, Iron, Strachan (eds.), *British Generals in Blair's Wars*, p. 110.

56. Jinks, IWM 33842.

57. Clare Short, Chilcot Inquiry (2 February 2010).

58. Thomas E. Ricks, *Fiasco: The American Military Adventure in Iraq* (London: Allen Lane, 2006), p. 37.

59. Report of a Committee of Privy Councillors, The Report of the Iraq Inquiry *Development of the Military Options for an Invasion of Iraq* (London, 2016) Vol. 5 Section 6.1, paragraphs 314–19, 439, 448, http://www.iraqinquiry.org.uk/the-report/

60. Tony Blair, Chilcot Inquiry (29 Jan 2010), p. 167, and Geoff Hoon, Chilcot Inquiry (19 Jan 2010), p. 136.

61. Defence Select Committee, 'Lessons of Iraq' HC 57–1 Session 2003–4, para. 256.

62. National Audit Office/MoD Report by the Comptroller and Auditor General, *Operation TELIC: United Kingdom Military Operations in Iraq*, executive summary, HC 60 session 2003–4, para. 9.

63. General Sir Mike Jackson, *Soldier: The Autobiography* (London: Bantam Press, 2007), p. 408.

64. Admiral Lord (Michael) Boyce, Chilcot Inquiry (3 December 2009), p. 50.

65. John Keegan, *The Iraq War* (London: Ted Smart, 2004), p. 146.

66. Ibid, p. 167.

67. Defence Select Committee, 'Lessons of Iraq' HC57–1 para. 112, p. 67.

68. Frank Ledwidge, *Losing Small Wars: British Military Failure in Iraq and Afghanistan* (London and New Haven: Yale University Press, 2011).

69. Anthony Wells, UK Polling Report, see http://ukpollingreport.co.uk/iraq

70. Ricks, *Fiasco*, p. 97.

71. Major General Tim Cross, Chilcot Inquiry (7 December 2007), pp. 31–2.

72. Blair, *A Journey*, p. 441.

73. Rajiv Chandrasekaran, *Imperial Life in the Emerald City: Inside Baghdad's Green Zone* (London: Bloomsbury, 2007).

74. Major General Graeme Lamb, Chilcot Inquiry (9 December 2009), pp. 6, 16–17.

75. Sergeant Christopher Broome CGC in Dan Collins, *In Foreign Fields: Heroes of Iraq and Afghanistan, in Their Own Words* (Cheltenham: Monday Books, 2007), p. 196.

76. Andrew Alderson, *Bankrolling Basra* (London: Robinson Books, 2007).

77. Holmes, *Dusty Warriors*, p. 128.

78. Major General Andrew Stewart, Chilcot Inquiry (December 2009), p. 68.

79. Andrew Graham, 'Iraq 2004: The View from Baghdad', in Bailey, Iron, Strachan (eds.), *British Generals in Blair's Wars*, p. 103.

80. Ibid, p. 104.

81. Major Justin Featherstone MC in Collins, *In Foreign Fields*, p. 85.

82. Kevin Ivison, *Red One: A Bomb Disposal Expert on the Front Line* (London: Weidenfeld & Nicolson, 2010), p. 55.

83. BBC News, 'UK Combat Operations End in Iraq' (30 April 2009) http://news.bbc.co.uk/1/hi/uk/8026136.stm

84. Defence Select Committee, *UK Operations in Iraq* HC 1241 (2006), p. 6.

85. Lieutenant General William Rollo, Chilcot Inquiry (15 December 2009), p. 15.

86. Joseph Stiglitz and Linda Bilmes, *The Three Trillion Dollar War: The True Cost of the Iraq Conflict* (London: Allen Lane, 2008).

87. UNHCR, *Basrah Governorate Assessment Report* (August 2006), p. 7 http://www.unhcr.org/459ba6462.pdf

88. Ibid, p. 9.

89. General Sir Richard Shirreff, Chilcot Inquiry (11 January 2010), p. 4.

90. UNHCR, *Basrah Governorate Assessment Report*, p. 7.

91. Tim Shipman, 'SAS Defied MoD to Rescue Two of Its Men Held Hostage in Iraq as Top Commanders "Prepared to Quit" over Ban on Mission', *Daily Mail* (6 May 2010).

92. Ivison, *Red One*, p. 10.

93. Ibid, pp. 64–77.

94. Shirreff, Chilcot Inquiry, p. 28.

95. Defence Select Committee, *UK Operations in Iraq*, HC 1241 (2006) p. 3.

96. Justin Maciejewski, in Bailey, Iron, Strachan (eds.), *British Generals in Blair's Wars*, p. 162.

97. Ibid, p. 169.

98. Major General Jonathan Shaw, Chilcot Inquiry (12 January 2010), p. 5.
99. BBC Newsnight-Opinion Research Business poll conducted 3–8 December 2007, cited in BBC News, 'Basra Residents Blame UK Troops' (14 December 2007)
100. Richard Iron, 'Basra 2008: Operation Charge of the Knights' in Bailey, Iron and Strachan (eds.), *British Generals in Blair's Wars*, p. 190.
101. Ibid, p. 191.
102. Defence Select Committee, *Iraq: An Initial Assessment of Post-Conflict Operations*, HC 65-1 (2005), para 255.

9   Service, Sacrifice and Public Support

1. Ministry of Defence, *The Strategic Defence Review: A New Chapter* Cm.5566 (2002) para 5.
2. Ibid, para. 96.
3. Ibid, para. 61.
4. Ministry of Defence, *Delivering Security in a Changing World* (December 2003) Cm6141–1, para. 4.8.
5. Ibid, para. 3.1.
6. Ibid, para. 3.5.
7. Cited in Defence Select Committee, *Future Capabilities* (HC45–1 March 2005), para. 2.
8. Nicholas Soames MP, HC Deb 21 July 2004 c. 350.
9. Bruce George MP, HC Deb 21 July 2004 c. 356.
10. Annabelle Ewing MP, HC Deb 16 Dec 2004 c. 1806.
11. Jack Fairweather, *The Good War: Why We Couldn't Win the War or the Peace in Afghanistan* (London: Jonathan Cape, 2014).
12. Adrian Guelke and Frank Wright, 'The Option of a "British Withdrawal" from Northern Ireland: An Exploration of its Meaning, Influence and Feasibility', *Conflict Quarterly* (Fall 1990), pp. 51–71.
13. Ministry of Defence, *Operation Banner: An Analysis of Military Operations in Northern Ireland*, AC 71842 (July 2006), 2–12.
14. BBC News, 'Army Ending Its Operation in NI' (31 July 2007).
15. Frank Kitson, *Bunch of Five* (London: Faber & Faber, 1977), p. 283.
16. BBC News, 'No Fanfare for Operation Banner' (31 July 2007).
17. *Operation Banner*, 2–12, citing David McKittrick *et al.*, *Lost Lives: The Stories of the Men, Women and Children Who Died as a Result of the Northern Ireland Troubles* (Edinburgh: Mainstream, 1999; revised 2001).
18. Jonathan Powell, 'Managing the Tensions of Difference' interview, in Graham Spencer, *The British and Peace in Northern Ireland* (Cambridge: Cambridge University Press, 2015), p. 322.
19. Spencer, *The British and Peace in Northern Ireland*, p. 310.
20. Ibid, p. 304.
21. *Operation Banner*, para. 220.
22. Ibid, para. 409.
23. Ibid, 3–6.
24. Ministry of Defence: *Operation Banner*, para 807.
25. Lawrence Freedman to Robert Fry, Chilcot Inquiry (16 December 2009), p. 96.
26. Sarah Ingham, *The Military Covenant: Its Impact on Civil–Military Relations* (Farnham: Ashgate, 2014), p. 226.
27. Richard Bacon MP Q113, uncorrected evidence, HC43, 2006–07, cited in Ingham, *The Military Covenant*, p. 153.
28. Sam Kiley, *Desperate Glory: At War in Helmand with Britain's 16 Air Assault Brigade* (London: Bloomsbury, 2009), p. 2.

29. Dr John Reid MP, HC Deb 23 Jan 2006 c. 1158.

30. Defence Select Committee, *Operations in Afghanistan* (HC554, 2011), para. 29.

31. Ed Butler DSO CBE, ibid, para. 46 and Q497.

32. Ibid, para. 35 and Q481.

33. Amy Belasco, *Troop Levels in the Afghan and Iraq Wars FY 2001 – FY2012: Cost and Other Potential Issues*, Congressional Research Service (July 2009) https://www.fas.org/sgp/crs/natsec/R40682.pdf

34. General Sir David Richards, *Taking Command: The Autobiography* (London: Headline, 2014), p. 197.

35. Ministry of Defence, 'Bye-Bye Bastion' (27 October 2014) https://www.gov.uk/government/news/bye-bye-bastion

36. Richards, *Taking Command*, p. 234.

37. Hugo Farmer in Dan Collins, *In Foreign Fields: Heroes of Iraq and Afghanistan, in Their Own Words* (Cheltenham: Monday Books, 2007), p. 262.

38. Richards, *Taking Command*, p. 201.

39. James Fergusson, *A Million Bullets: The Real Story of the British Army in Afghanistan* (London: Bantam Press, 2008).

40. Ibid, p. 157.

41. Tootal, *Danger Close: Commanding 3 Para in Afghanistan* (London: John Murray, 2009), p. 207–23.

42. Fergusson, *A Million Bullets*, p. 344.

43. Tootal, *Danger Close*, p. 251.

44. Patrick Hennessey, *The Junior Officers' Reading Club: Killing Time and Fighting Wars* (London: Allen Lane, 2009), p. 276.

45. Tootal, *Danger Close*, p. 155.

46. Paul Smyth, *Blogging from the Battlefield: The View from the Front Line in Afghanistan* (Stroud: History Press, 2011), p. 84.

47. Kiley, *Desperate Glory*, p. xiii.

48. Damien McElroy, 'Afghan Governor Turned 3,000 men over to the Taliban', *Daily Telegraph* (20 November 2009).

49. Lieutenant Timothy Illingworth CGC, in Collins, *In Foreign Fields*, p. 299.

50. Defence Select Committee, *Operations in Afghanistan* (2011), HC 554 para. 66.

51. Patrick Porter, 'Last Charge of the Knights? Iraq, Afghanistan and the Special Relationship', *International Affairs*, vol. 86, no. 2 (March 2010), pp. 355–75.

52. Ewen Southby-Tailyour, *3 Commando Brigade: Sometimes the Best Form of Defence is Attack* (London: Ebury Press, 2008), pp. 1–30.

53. Anand Gopal, *No Good Men Among the Living: American, the Taliban and the War through Afghan Eyes* (New York: Metropolitan Books, 2014), pp. 73–98.

54. Peregrine Hodson, *Under a Sickle Moon: Journey Through Afghanistan* (London: Hutchinson, 1986) and Smyth, *Blogging from the Battlefield*, p. 117.

55. Kiley, *Desperate Glory*, p. 182.

56. Ibid, p. 183.

57. Stephen Grey, *Operation Snakebite: The Explosive True Story of an Afghan Desert Siege* (London: Viking, 2009), pp. 67–8.

58. Hennessey, *The Junior Officers' Reading Club*, p. 18.

59. Grey, *Operation Snakebite*, p. 62.

60. Smyth, *Blogging from the Battlefield*, p. 169.

61. John Kay, *Sun* (17 September 2007); Audrey Gillan, *Guardian* (15 August 2007); comment, 'Our Boys Betrayed', *Daily Mail* (14 September 2007).

62. Rt. Hon. Tony Blair MP, speech at Portsmouth (15 January 2007).

63. Eric Hobsbawm and Terence Ranger (eds.), *The Invention of Tradition* (Cambridge: Cambridge University Press, 1983).

64. Lieutenant Hugo Farmer in Collins, *In Foreign Fields*, p. 262.

65. Ingham, *The Military Covenant*, p. 53.

66. Ministry of Defence, Army Doctrine Publication Vol. 5 *Soldiering: The Military Covenant* (AC 71642, 2000) Crown Copyright.

67. Paul Cornish and Andrew Dorman, 'Blair's War's and Brown's Budgets: From Strategic Defence Review to Strategic Decay in Less than a Decade', *International Affairs*, vol. 85, no. 2 (2009), pp. 247–61.

68. Michael Smith, 'Iraq Battle Stress Worse than WWII', *Sunday Times* (6 November 2005), p. 1.

69. Quentin Davies MP, Bill Clark OBE, Air Commodore Martin Sharp OBE, MA, RAF and Ministry of Defence, 'The Nation's Commitment: Cross-government Support for our Armed Forces, their Families and Veterans', Cm 1424 (2008).

70. Tom Newton Dunn, 'From Helmand to Hellhole', *Sun* (26 October 2007).

71. Ingham, *The Military Covenant*, p. 143.

72. Kevan Jones MP, interview in Ingham, *The Military Covenant*, p. 130.

73. The term 'migration' in this context was coined by Christopher Dandeker, Emeritus Professor, Department of War Studies, King's College London.

74. Ingham, *The Military Covenant*, p. 102.

75. Ibid, p. 126.

76. Comment, 'Military Covenant: Poppy Politics', *Guardian* (2 November 2007).

77. Liam Fox speech, 'Labour's Economic Policies were a National Security Liability' (6 October 2010).

78. Timothy Edmunds and Anthony Forster, *Out of Step: The Case for Change in the British Armed Forces* (London: Demos, 2007).

79. *R (Limbu)* v. *Secretary of State for the Home Department* (2008).

80. Ian Roy, 'Towards the Standing Army, 1485–1660', in David Chandler (General Editor) and Ian Beckett (Associate Editor), *The Oxford Illustrated History of the British Army* (Oxford: Oxford University Press, 1994), p. 40.

81. Mark Urban, *Rifles: Six Years with Wellington's Legendary Sharpshooters* (London: Faber & Faber, 2003), p. 206.

82. E. M. Spiers, *The Army and Society 1815–1914* (London: Longman, 1980), p. 193.

83. Jonathan Shaw, Chilcot Inquiry (11 January 2010), p. 38.

10   Intervention: Part of the Problem or Part of the Solution?

1. Labour Party, *A Fair Future for All* (2010).

2. Conservative Party, *Invitation to Join the Government of Britain* (2010).

3. Conservative Party, *A New Covenant for Our Armed Forces and Their Families* (2010).

4. HM Government, *The Coalition: Our Programme for Government* (2010), p. 7.

5. HMSO, Public Administration Select Committee, 'Who Does UK National Strategy?' HC435 Session 2010–2011 (2011), p. 3.

6. General Sir David Richards, *Taking Command: The Autobiography* (London: Headline, 2014), p. 307.

7. David Cameron, evidence to the Joint Committee on National Security Strategy (30 January 2014). See Joe Devanny, 'Coordinating UK Foreign and Security Policy: The National Security Council', *RUSI Journal*, vol. 160, no. 6 (December 2015), pp. 20–26.

8. Richards, *Taking Command*, pp. 308–9.

9. HM Government, *A Strong Britain in an Age of Uncertainty: The National Security Strategy* Cm 7953 (Crown copyright, 2010), pp. 3–5.

10. HM Government, *Securing Britain in an Age of Uncertainty: The Strategic Defence and Security Review* Cm 7948 (Crown copyright, 2010).

11. Ibid.

12. Benoit Gomis, 'NATO: Lessons from Libya', *The World Today*, no. 2 (May 2011).

13. Jack Fairweather, *The Good War: Why We Couldn't Win the War or the Peace in Afghanistan* (London: Jonathan Cape, 2014).

14. Barack Obama, 'Remarks by the President in Address to the Nation on the Way Forward in Afghanistan and Pakistan' (1 December 2009).

15. Fairweather, *The Good War*, p. 302.

16. Defence Select Committee, *Operations in Afghanistan* HC554 (2011), para. 69.

17. Michael Codner, 'UK Defence Reform: Watch Assessment from Michael Codner', RUSI commentary (18 August 2010).

18. Fairweather, *The Good War*, p. 369.

19. Lieutenant Colonel Charlie Maconochie, '"Green on Blue" Attacks Must Not Deter Us in Afghanistan', *Daily Telegraph* (18 September 2012).

20. Fairweather, *The Good War*, p. 308.

21. Ibid, p. 356.

22. Ibid, p. 311.

23. HC Deb 2 Jun 2010 c. 434.

24. HC Deb 14 Jun 2010 c. 604.

25. Laura Roberts, 'Afghanistan: Father of 300th Soldier Killed Attacks Britain's Continuing Presence', *Daily Telegraph* (23 June 2010).

26. Ministry of Defence press release (22 November 2010).

27. David Cameron MP, Uncorrected evidence to Defence Select Committee 22 Nov 2010, Answer to Q.127 p.60, Defence Select Committee, Operations in Afghanistan HC 554 (2010).

28. NATO–ISAF press release, 'Rebalancing of Forces in Helmand' (September 2010).

29. Fairweather, *The Good War*, p. 384.

30. Paul Smyth, *Blogging from the Battlefield: The View from the Front Line in Afghanistan* (Stroud: History Press, 2011), pp. 160–89.

31. Ministry of Defence, 'Soldiers Deliver Winter Clothes to Afghan Village' (15 December 2010).

32. *Economist*, 'Drone Strikes: Cause or Effect' (23 September 2015).

33. BBC News, 'Afghanistan Deaths: Six Dead UK Soldiers Named by MoD' (8 March 2012) http://www.bbc.co.uk/news/uk-17295858

34. Richards, *Taking Command*, p. 329.

35. Ibid, p. 330.

36. Matthieu Aikins, 'Enemy Inside the Wire: The Untold Story of the Battle of Bastion', *GQ* (3 September 2013).

37. Charlotte Cross, 'Afghan Heartland', *Index on Censorship*, vol. 42, no. 3 (September 2013), pp. 72–8.

38. Sarah Ingham, *The Military Covenant: Its Impact on Civil–Military Relations* (London: Routledge, 2014), pp. 105–9.

39. Ministry of Defence,*The Armed Forces Covenant Annual Report 2015: Key Facts* (2015).

40. Cited in Ingham, *The Military Covenant*, p.36

41. Kevin Ivison, *Red One: A Bomb Disposal Expert on the Front Line* (London: Weidenfeld & Nicolson, 2010), p. 197.

42. Ingham, *The Military Covenant*, p. 123.

43. Admiral Lord Boyce, HL Deb 17 Jul 2005 c. 1236.

44. Rt. Hon. Lord Justice Moses, introduction, in Thomas Tugendhat and Laura Croft, *The Fog of Law: An Introduction to the Legal Erosion of British Fighting Power* (London: Policy Exchange, 2013), p. 7.

45. Richard Ekins, Jonathan Morgan, Thomas Tugendhat, *Clearing the Fog of Law: Saving Our Armed Forces from Defeat by Judicial Diktat* (London: Policy Exchange, 2015), p. 7.

46. Ministry of Defence blog, 'MoD Responds to Court of Appeal Verdict' (30 July 2015) https://modmedia.blog.gov.uk/2015/07/30/breaking-news-mod-response-to-court-of-appeal-judgement/

47. Brigadier (Rtd) Anthony Paphiti, written evidence to Defence Select Committee (2013–14), *UK Armed Forces Personnel and the Legal Framework for Future Operations*, HC 931, 2013.

48. The Rt Hon The Lord Saville of Newdigate, The Hon William Hoyt OC, The Hon John Toohey AC, 'Principal Conclusions and Overall Assessment of the Bloody Sunday Inquiry' (London: The Stationery Office, 2010), para. 5–5.

49. BBC News, 'Bloody Sunday: PM David Cameron's Full Statement' (15 June 2010).

50. Army Rumour Service, 'Baha Mousa – The Official Verdict' (28 August 2011) http://www.arrse.co.uk/community/threads/baha-mousa-the-official-verdict.168465/

51. Army Rumour Service, 'UK Soldiers Have Murder Charges Dropped' (3 November 2005) http://www.arrse.co.uk/community/threads/uk-soldiers-have-murder-charges-dropped.21799/

52. Tim Ross, 'Al-Sweady File Exposes the Smearing of British Soldiers' (*Daily Telegraph*, 1 March 2015).

53. Michael Fallon, 'Clearing the Fog of Law', speech to Policy Exchange seminar (9 December 2014) https://www.gov.uk/government/speeches/clearing-the-fog-of-law-policy-exchange-seminar

54. Paul Cornish, 'UK Defence: A Test Case', *The World Today*, no. 1 (May 2011).

55. Yehudit Ronen, 'Britain's Return to Libya: From the Battle of El Alamein in the Western Desert to the Military Intervention in the Arab Spring Upheaval', *Middle East Studies*, vol. 49, no. 5 (May 2013), pp. 675–95.

56. Richards, *Taking Command*, p. 313.

57. UN Security Council Resolution 1973 (2011) http://www.nato.int/nato_static/assets/pdf/pdf_2011_03/20110927_110311-UNSCR-1973.pdf

58. Richards, *Taking Command*, p. 314.

59. White House, 'Remarks by the President in Address to the Nation on Libya' (28 March 2011) https://www.whitehouse.gov/the-press-office/2011/03/28/remarks-president-address-nation-libya

60. See John Rentoul, 'David Cameron's 40,000-foot Drop', *Independent* (3 February 2013).

61. BBC News, 'Libya: Key Quotes on Targeting Gaddafi' (22 March 2011) http://www.bbc.co.uk/news/uk-politics-12818062

62. Richards, *Taking Command*, p. 316.

63. BBC 2 *Newsnight*, Mark Urban, 'SAS on the Ground During Libya Crisis' (19 January 2012) http://www.bbc.co.uk/news/world-africa-16624401

64. Richards, *Taking Command*, p. 315.

65. Cornish, 'UK Defence'.

66. United Nations, News Centre, 'Nearly 93,000 People Killed in "Vicious" Syrian Conflict – UN Human Rights Chief' (June 2013) http://www.un.org/apps/news/story.asp?NewsID=45162#.V4obb1c-Ci4

67. *The Economist*, Blighty Britain blog, 'Britain and Syria: The Vote of Shame' (30 August 2013) http://www.economist.com/blogs/blighty/2013/08/britain-and-syria

68. Richard Bacon MP, HC 29 Aug 2013 c. 1451.

69. Falah Mustafa Bakir, address to RUSI 10 Dec 2014, cited by Peter Quentin in Elizabeth Quintana and Jonathan Eyal (eds.), 'Inherently Unresolved: The Military Operation against ISIS', Royal United Services Institute Occasional Paper (2015), p. 18.

70. Andrew Parker, 'A Modern MI5' Lord Mayor's Defence and Security Lecture (28 October 2015) https://www.mi5.gov.uk/news/a-modern-mi5

71. Motion for Debate: House of Commons, 26 September 2014.

72. *Sunday Telegraph*, cited in Eyal and Quintana (eds.), 'Inherently Unresolved'.

73. Justin Bronk, in Eyal and Quintana (eds.), 'Inherently Unresolved', p. 12.

74. Philip Alston, 'UN Report on Targeted Killings', cited in Thomas Nagel, 'Really Good at Killing', *London Review of Books*, vol. 38, no. 3 (3 March 2016).

75. Patrick Cockburn, 'Why Join Islamic State?', *London Review of Books*, vol. 37, no. 13 (2 July 2015).

76. HM Government, *National Security Strategy and Strategic Defence Review and Security Review 2015: A Secure and Prosperous United Kingdom* Cm 9161 (2015).

Epilogue

1. Report of a Committee of Privy Councillors, The Report of the Iraq Inquiry: Executive Summary (London: 2016) HC 262 p. 139 para 836 http://www.iraqinquiry.org.uk/media/246416/the-report-of-the-iraq-inquiry_executive-summary.pdf.

SUGGESTED READING

As the Army has grown smaller and fewer people experience military service, the appetite for military history appears to grow. Britain's twenty-first-century campaigns in Iraq and Afghanistan have created whole new sections in libraries and bookshops to suit every reader. Stirring stories from the battlefields and eyewitness accounts can be found alongside more academic work, often providing an in-depth look at perhaps just one aspect of an operation. And if more is required, there are films and documentaries, journals and many online sources. The most significant ones used in the compilation of this book are recorded below.

It is hoped that *Boots on the Ground* has told the story of the Army since 1945 in a way that has done justice to the soldiers involved. The priority has been to get their voices heard, so that they can convey something of what it was like to serve, whether as a war-fighter on the frontline of combat, a peacekeeper or a National Serviceman doing his time. Soldiers' private papers and recorded interviews, found at London's Imperial War Museum Documents and Sounds Section, have been invaluable. In addition, anthologies of eyewitnesses' stories help build a picture of military life, even if it can, at times, be quite an ugly one. Ken Wharton's *A Long, Long War: Voices from the British Army in Northern Ireland 1969–1998* (Solihull: Helion, 2008), Hugh McManners' *Forgotten Voices of the Falklands* (London: Imperial War Museum) and Dan Collins's *In Foreign Fields: Heroes of Iraq and Afghanistan in their Own Words* (Cheltenham: Monday Books, 2007) are all recommended. *Six Campaigns: National Servicemen at War 1948–60* (London, Leo Cooper, 1993) by Adrian Walker highlights the bolshy attitude of some conscripts, as well as the huge responsibilities thrust on young men, some still in their teens. Like many books on the military it provides a glimpse into prevailing civilian attitudes: during the Emergency in Kenya, some settlers were troubled that the colony's social ecology would be threatened by the arrival of National Service 'other ranks', which for the first time drew attention to the fact that not all whites were of the ruling, officer class.

For those interested in high level policy, the government-commissioned official history of any military campaign demands to be read. Outstanding is Sir Lawrence Freedman's *The Official History of the Falklands Campaign*, especially the second volume *War and Diplomacy* (Abingdon: Routledge, Government Official History Series, 2005). Also recommended are Anthony Farrar-Hockley's *The British Part in the Korean War* (London: HMSO Official History, 1990), F. S. V.

398 BOOTS ON THE GROUND

Donnison's, *Civil Affairs and Military Government in North-West Europe 1944–1946* (London: Her Majesty's Stationery Office, 1961) and Margaret Gowing's accounts of the development of the British nuclear deterrent, particularly *Independence and Deterrence: Britain and Atomic Energy 1945–52* (Basingstoke: Palgrave Macmillan, 1974). As yet, there is no official history of Operation Telic (Iraq) or Operation Herrick (Afghanistan), but perhaps after the Chilcot Inquiry reported this is not so urgent. Anyone who predicted that Sir John and his team would provide an establishment whitewash, or who criticised them for their softly-softly approach to witnesses, has not read the evidence they elicited – much of which was available online long before the official report was published and will be an invaluable research resource for years to come. As much as many soldiers themselves might disagree with it, Frank Ledwidge's *Losing Small Wars* (New Haven and London: Yale University Press, 2013) is perhaps the most compelling of works critical of recent British military performance, however without criticism there cannot be learning. Crucial to an earlier, unequivocal military victory was logistics, as highlighted by Kenneth L. Privratsky's fascinating *Logistics in the Falklands War* (Barnsley: Pen and Sword, 2014).

Britain has many world-class academic military historians, the doyen of whom is Sir Michael Howard. Among his many achievements is helping to found the War Studies Department and the Liddell Hart Centre for Military Archives at King's College London, which holds many of the Army doctrine publications that have been referenced. Among other leading historians whose work has been included are Professors Sir Hew Strachan, Jeremy Black and David French. The latter's *Army, Empire and Cold War: The British Army and Military Policy 1945–1971* (Oxford: Oxford University Press, 2012) is an invaluable guide to the Army from victory in Europe until the end of the British presence East of Suez. For anyone interested in the big picture of British defence policy, the House of Commons Defence Select Committee reports and papers by the Royal United Services Institute (RUSI) are essential reading. A must-watch for those wanting the story of NATO, that cornerstone of British defence strategy since the 1950s, is *Jamie's History Class* a series of entertaining and informative lectures by alliance official and spokesman Dr Jamie P. Shea (http://www.nato.int/history/jamie-history-class.html).

Despite sending troops into action, the memoirs of politicians generally make scant mention of the Armed Forces. At times other than conflict, defence is pretty much off their radar, which is telling. However, both Margaret Thatcher's *Downing Street Years* (London: HarperCollins, 1993) and John Major's *The Autobiography* (London: HarperCollins 1999) give some idea of the burden of political leadership at a time of conflict. Harold Macmillan's *Pointing the Way, 1959–1961* (London: Macmillan, 1972) highlights how maintaining Britain's special relationship with the United States is far from easy. Tony Blair's chatty *A Journey* (London: Hutchinson, 2010) is a breezy read, which provides a useful reminder to his successors that war can rarely be won by airpower alone. For a glimpse into the role of a Defence Secretary, Denis Healey's *The Time of My Life* (London: Michael Joseph, 1989) will surely not be bettered.

As much as it tries to examine Britain's place in the world and the Army's place in Britain, *Boots on the Ground* comes back to soldiers, and their story. *Taking Command: The Autobiography* (London: Headline, 2014) by former Chief of the Defence Staff General Sir David (now Lord) Richards and *Soldier: The Autobiography* (London: Bantam Press, 2007) by General Sir Mike Jackson paint a picture of senior command, while also providing first-hand accounts of British operations from Northern Ireland to Afghanistan, via Bosnia, Kosovo and Sierra Leone. Similarly, other senior commanders have contributed essays about recent conflict in *British Generals in Blair's Wars* (London: Routledge, 2013), a collection edited by Major General Jonathan Bailey, Richard Iron and Hew Strachan. Works by General Sir Frank Kitson, including *Bunch of Five* (London: Faber and Faber, 1977) and *Gangs and Counter-gangs* (London: Barrie and Rockliff, 1960) give an insight into fighting Britain's small wars of the second half of the twentieth century, while General Sir Rupert Smith looks at war among the people in his *Utility of Force: The Art of War in the Modern World* (London: Allen Lane 2005). *Danger Close: Commanding 3 Para in Afghanistan* (London: John

Murray, 2009) by Colonel Stuart Tootal gives a first-class, first-hand account of Herrick 4, when it became obvious that all would not go to plan in Afghanistan. Any reader interested in soldiers' points of view should look online at the Army Rumour Service, a recommendation which comes with a health warning for all those of delicate disposition. Most individual regiments also have a lively, but useful, online presence. Above all, whether East of Suez or closer to home, probably the first place to look for British military history are the websites of veterans' associations. It is these former soldiers who knew exactly what it is like to have their boots on the ground.

LIST OF ILLUSTRATIONS

INDEX